B&T
$12.95

*Cultural Regions of the United States*

# Cultural Regions

# of the United States

*Raymond D. Gastil*

FOREWORD BY NATHAN GLAZER

University of Washington Press

*Seattle and London*

**Library of Congress Cataloging in Publication Data**

Gastil, Raymond D
 Cultural regions of the United States.

 Bibliography: p.
 Includes index.
 1. United States—Description and travel—
1960–    2. Anthropo-geography—United States.
3. Regionalism—United States. I. Title.
E169.02.G32      309.1′73      75-8933
ISBN 0–295–95426–4         3-3-76

*To the family that joined Indiana and Texas*
*in California, and the family that joined*
*California and Tennessee in the new Northwest*

# Foreword

AMERICAN regionalism, it seems, is not much studied these days, or if studied is not much in the public eye or the consciousness of opinion-makers. One contrasts the present situation sadly with the 1930s, when there was a remarkably urgent and rewarding concern with the variations and rich detail of American culture. Thus, one looks back with awe at the great series of WPA guidebooks which covered every state in the Union, and many of the cities. We are now a nation without guidebooks, or at least without guidebooks of the scope and interest that were evident in the WPA series. It was a time when American folksong and folklore were explored and recorded with a gusto not seen before or since, and when a National Resources Planning Board served to draw national attention to each of the major distinct areas of the country. Walker Evans and other great photographers recorded the distinctive lives of different regions and cities, and painters worked in—or maybe invented—regional modes to cover the walls of public buildings. Perhaps one must accept the judgment of current critics that American art reached greater heights when it abandoned storytelling picturesqueness in the style of Grant Wood and Thomas Hart Benton and Ben Shahn to take up abstract expressionism, "action" painting, and their varied spawn, so that American painting and sculpture from San Francisco to New York, and all the places in between, could be devoid of any regional accent, original or acquired as a sign of respect to place. Perhaps. But one doubts it.

Of course, regional studies did not completely disappear: technical econometric analyses of regional flows and economic bases have flourished in recent decades as never before, using ever more elegant technical methods. What has been comparatively ignored, however, are the cultural aspects of regionalism, the variations in life styles, values, outlooks. It is on this aspect of regionalism that Raymond Gastil concentrates. *Cultural Regions of the United States* is, as anyone who gets into it will see, a remarkably wise as well as a broad and interesting book. Drawing on a wealth of studies of dialect, house styles and architecture, settlement patterns, regional history, and many other matters, and combining them with statistical analyses of violence, education, health, and other elements of social life, Gastil demonstrates that there is still much more life in American regionalism than many of us believed. He points out that some of our analytical approaches to studying American society are not well suited to displaying significant regional differentiation. Thus, we are heavily dependent on public opinion polls and relatively small national samples for insight into many questions of opinion, political attitude, and cultural behavior. Inevitably, owing to the size of the samples, our analyses run to differences in education, occupation, age, sex, race, and ethnicity; we often cannot disaggregate the data to the level of significant regions. Indeed, even the census will give its most detailed breakdowns of information on many questions on a national level.

Undoubtedly, regional history, geography, culture are interesting: every secondhand bookstore in the country generally has a section up front devoted to books on the region, and for many these provide the modest difference between failure and survival. But Gastil argues—and persuasively, I believe—that regionalism should be a matter for more than those proud about local distinctions and curious about them. "In studying regional cultures," he writes, "I hope to give these cultures and the regions associated with them new meaning and respectability. This is important, because the lives of people and their surroundings need to be given more subjective experience. The effort may help self-confidence and loyalty to grow, and great communal achievements can often be traced to loyalty and self-confidence."

Gastil places himself directly in the line of Tocqueville, who saw that democracy needed the help of social institutions mediating between central government and the individual. These institutions served to limit governmental power and to reduce the loneliness that could follow the leveling of traditional social forms and connections. Region has undoubtedly played such a role in American life.

Yet in the past two decades we have thought less and less of region as serving this, or any other, role. The egalitarian and leveling tendencies of democratic (and all modern) societies seems in many people's minds to reduce regional differences so radically that it can only be a set of oddities of no significance and no possible value. Gastil argues that we exaggerate the disappearance of regionalism. Even the nationwide media, since the 1950s more overwhelming than ever before because of national television, do not all work in the same direction: Gastil points to the phenomenon of "message rejection" stemming from the simultaneous beaming of the same message by the national media. This strengthens differences of opinion—and conceivably regional differences. He points out, too, that the enormous mobility of American life, with one-fifth of the population moving annually, does not totally *reduce* regional differences: owing to the differential attractions of different areas and types of living, it also serves to *re-create* and *maintain* regional difference.

The issue is not only the maintenance of the storehouse of cultural difference that our marvelously rich human experience has created, even in a new nation such as ours, though that would be reason enough for concern for regionalism. There are more pragmatic reasons for maintaining a living regionalism. It has been pointed out that as new and more efficient seeds are produced, the endless variety of food grains available after millions of years of development and thousands of cultivation is being radically reduced, as the new seeds developed in laboratories rapidly replace indigenous seeds all over the world. Valuable and irreplaceable genetic material created by millions of years of evolution is being irreparably lost; and if one of the new and

efficient seeds succumbs to a new disease, the disaster will be all
the greater than when each region and country and district used
its own variants.

One may tell a similar story for regionalism (as one may for
ethnic difference). Gastil does not want to maintain people
museums against the will of the people living in them; neither
would I. At the same time, he would want us to study and pay
attention to the wonderful array of differences created by land,
culture, and people. One should be as undesirous of having the
distinctive Mormon region, for example, disappear into a homogeneous American mass, and lose its remarkable combination of
high fertility, low infant mortality, high education, and highly
developed nongovernmental self-help institutions, as of seeing a
variant of some food disappear because it was being replaced by
something similar but hardier and better adapted to long-distance
transportation and lengthy storage.

Unhappily, both the regional differences and the natural
differences are under pressure today. One way of helping them to
survive under pressure is simply to pay attention. Gastil points out
sadly "how small a constructive role academics play in the regions
in which they reside." He ascribes this charitably to their mobility.
One may also point to features of their disciplines and recruitment
patterns which set the eyes of academics on distant and abstract
topics rather than the vivid reality around them. There is no
program here: there is only the record of a painstaking search for
still rich, living regional cultures. One hopes others will now pay
attention.

NATHAN GLAZER

*Harvard University*
*Cambridge, Massachusetts*

# Acknowledgments

This book represents a collection and sifting of information from a wide variety of sources. Although its preparation required the support and aid of many more persons and organizations than I can mention here, certain debts cannot be ignored. First, of course, is Battelle Memorial Institute, which gave me the time for the study at its Battelle Seattle Research Center, as well as the assistance of its excellent support staff. I would also like to mention my research assistant Rob Coppock, who helped especially with the material in Chapter III. The persons who first guided me to the geographical and historical literature that forms the core of the theoretical background were Gene Martin, Earl Pomeroy, and Peter Simpson of the University of Oregon. Although the footnotes already attest to the fact, I would like to emphasize the debt of the text to the published works of the geographers Donald Meinig and Wilbur Zelinsky, and the historian T. J. Wertenbaker.

# Contents

# Illustrations

*Cultural Regions of the United States*

# CHAPTER I

# Introduction

## *Why a Book on Cultural Regions?*

THE most elementary reason for studying the cultural regions of the United States is to learn more about the country. Regional analysis integrates, in a way that has never been seriously attempted, the scattered information that is available on variations in our society. Seeing our society from a new point of view may generate new approaches that will lead to improved understanding of ourselves, and in some areas to new social and economic policies.

This is an age of re-evaluation, of testing, of trying to get a feel for the balance of good and evil in our society. Everyone agrees that there are problems to be solved. Although there have always been problems, we wonder why the wealthiest and most powerful nation in the world still has the injustice, poverty, violence, and ugliness that it does. Why, for example, do a number of indices of social health suggest that nations such as England or Sweden have achieved more with slighter resources?

If one wishes to improve his understanding of the country, he will find many descriptions already available. Yet these books generally offer us both too much and too little. There are many scholarly treatments of the country as a whole in terms of its family system, its religious beliefs, its political system, even its values.[1] Less sociologically, we can develop descriptions of American culture ranging from an analysis of personal habits to a monograph on the fine arts.[2] Attempts to grasp the essence or spirit of America have been around since before de Tocqueville, and they are often highly valuable and insightful. But they are not too useful to anyone who actually looks about him: the variation he sees is too great; the differences often swamp the similarities.

Variations in American society are generally understood in terms of standard sociological categories. The population is divided either mechanically into W. Lloyd Warner's five or six classes from upper-upper to lower-lower, or more intuitively into high-brow, middle-brow, and low-brow.[3] Significantly, "upper middle class" is often used to designate a cultural or professional type rather than strictly a class position in a hierarchy. Many analyses use economic categories as a basis for looking for more general differentiations. Workers are seen as farmers, white-collar, blue-collar, or professional. The reader will find studies that describe in detail the life styles of groups such as Negroes, Indians, or Spanish-Americans, or of smaller, highly variant white groups such as the Hutterites. Each of these breakdowns adds to our understanding. In recent years a number of studies have pointed out that the American melting pot that was supposed to merge all racial, religious, and ethnic groups into one homogeneous society has been only partially successful.[4]

However, most American scholars and intellectuals continue to see the country in terms of (1) their own personal backgrounds; (2) the highly cosmopolitan stratum to which they belong, which constitutes a small minority of the population; and (3) a great, undifferentiated mass beyond. It is popularly recognized that New York City is not the United States, but concern of those in the mass with further differentiations is generally viewed as whimsy or prejudice.

I hope that this book can demonstrate that the mass "out there" is differentiated into a wide variety of cultural groups, and is often quite conscious of this fact. Not only are WASPs distinguishable from other peoples in America, but WASPs are themselves differentiated into a number of quite different groups. Their differences are often related to differing regional backgrounds. For example, in a series of comparative studies centering around Ramah, New Mexico, the two "Anglo" cultures—Texan and Mormon—were found to be significantly different.[5] Such differences exist on a number of levels of generality. On the one hand, Texan culture is a variety of Southern culture; but on the other, an examination of Ramah "Texan culture" in terms of my own background suggested that Farmer Texan culture from the Panhandle and Rancher Texan culture from southwest Texas should have been distinguished. The former has roots going back through Arkansas to Tennessee, while the latter has a more cosmopolitan past and quite different standards of behavior. Incidentally, this example suggests that in terms of his own background the alert reader will easily go beyond the generalizations and categories he will encounter in this book. In spite of a few beginnings, there has been remarkably little serious attempt to describe, trace, and compare regional differences in American society and culture, or to analyze how these variations affect or delimit variations in quality of life.

Many academics, including some students of regional differentiation, believe that regional differentiation is largely a reflection of regional differences in degrees of progress or "modernity." For example, Charles Lerche writes: "The norm of the idealized 'Southern way of life' is rural or small town in orientation, while Anglo-Saxon Protestant (WASP) in culture, individualistic in philosophy and pragmatic in point of view: in no important way different in fundamentals, in other words, from the broader American viewpoint. [However,] the myth remained active in the South long after it had been sharply modified . . . elsewhere." [6] The student finds frequent discussions of the nature of WASP society, or of contrasts between ethnics and WASPs, or blacks and WASPs. Yet the story of the country lies to a large extent in the struggle of two quite different WASP cultures, that of New England and that of the South. Calling Southern and Northern Protestant whites "WASPs" is little more enlightening than calling East European Jews and Irish "ethnics." Because of long-term birth differentials there are more WASPs of Southern background today than of New England and Mid-Atlantic. The noted individualism and anti-intellectualism that characterizes so much of "middle America" (especially as defined geographically) was noted very early as characteristic of the South. One result of the Southern expansion was recently remarked by Samuel Lubell: "Always in the past the assumption has been that the South, as it changed, would come to resemble the North. Wallace raised the prospect that the North, as it changes, may become southernized." [7] He goes on to point particularly to the interplay of race and economics that has always characterized Southern politics.

The desire to change the course of American society has developed a natural desire to know more, to collect useful information. We need to know where we are, and we need to have yardsticks by which we can measure what has evidently worked in the past and what is likely to work in the future. It will be a mistake if citizens or their leaders believe they are dealing with one, homogeneous American people. We know that Jews, Chinese, and Japanese have made rapid economic and social progress in the last fifty years in this country. This rise has *not* been attributable to the special benevolence of the majority population in providing good housing, schools, or friendly law enforcement. Since the progress of these groups was due to their own traditions, if the percentage of people of these groups in a city increases, the quality of life in that city will tend to improve. And to a greater or lesser extent changes of this type are, and will continue to be, critical for the local contexts in which we all live.

Recently a great deal of controversy has centered around the question of whether there is a national subculture that can be meaningfully referred to as the "culture of poverty." To what extent does poverty make poor people behave in ways that keep them poor? How fast would having more money affect this behavior? Is it more significant to look at the behavior first or the poverty first? Another way to approach the question is to ask how fast people of different cultures or subcultures change in their deeper behavioral tendencies—unless, of course, they can be torn from family and community and brought up in government-authorized total environment such as has been proposed by some overenthusiastic behavioral scientists.

We need, then, a comparative study of the people who make up the country, the characteristics of their subcultures, and their persistence. It is hoped that in these pages the reader will come to know more of the country, and through this knowledge become more able to contribute to a reasoned evolution of his community and society.

In order to involve the reader immediately in the subject, this introduction will summarize the course of settlement, the evolution of regional economic patterns, and the outline of the cultural regions with which the rest of the book is concerned. In addition, it will expose the reader to the theoretical considerations on which the regional analysis is based.

# The Course of Settlement[8]

In some cases the patterns that we find today antedate the original settlement of Englishmen in America. However, many of the differences in the character of the settlers along the Atlantic seaboard, which we can still see in their descendants, emerged in the colonies in the first half of the seventeenth century. These differences were, of course, modified by later experiences of living in the New World, as well as subsequent technological and social change.

The original settlers of New England frequently came in community groups and nearly always lived in villages within organized "towns." Houses were situated side by side and civic participation was high. Although not democratic communities by later standards, they were democratic for their time. And the society of their day was the prototype of the later democracy. Interest in religion was intense, as was the religious intolerance that almost always accompanies strong belief. In New England interest in education, in each man understanding religion himself, was also high, and the inevitable result was repeated fission and eventual evolution away from the traditional dogma.

The people of Massachusetts came as families to settle and stay. Companies were involved in underwriting some ventures, and financial sponsors had to be paid off; but the original goals of the New England colonists were not economic. Large grants of land were not made to individuals; plots at first were generally small. The land was divided among the settlers by their leaders, and a good deal of land was held in common, although this did not constitute primitive communism (see Chapter II, "Housing and Settlement Styles"). These original tendencies were re-enforced by the absence of any important cash crop that would lend itself to large field exploitation.

Settlement from Virginia south was almost the antithesis. It fit the pattern of settlement found in the rest of the New World. In fact, if later historians had had only early Virginia settlement to judge by, they would have found little difference between French, English, and Spanish colonies in the New World. Grants in Virginia were for economic exploitation; the original men came to get wealthy and get out. The objective of many of those who first came was to find gold in the Spanish pattern. These settlers came without families, working for the companies that brought them, almost as slaves. While the indentured servant came to all of the colonies, he was especially common in the seventeenth-century South. Moreover, as the Southern colonies grew slowly, the increasing demand for more people led to the sending of criminals as indentured servants. After a few years the indentured servant earned his freedom and was given a piece of land on the plantation or, if he so chose, one farther afield. The result was that by the middle of the seventeenth century the South consisted of modest plantations (eighteenth-century plantations were to be much larger), with a large proportion of the population at least temporarily enslaved, and many isolated, poor, individual farms. What civilization and culture there were centered on the plantations. There were few towns or churches and little civic participation. Economically, the system was fostered by the development of cash crops, such as tobacco, which formed a basis for plantation wealth and a society tied to the land investor's desire to get a return on his money.

The Middle colonies presented a mixed picture. At first, New York was Dutch, New Jersey and Delaware were Swedish, and Pennsylvania and Maryland were English. In general these colonies began as company efforts founded on the basis of large land or trading grants, and were autocratically ruled or managed. Indentured labor played a less important role in peopling the Middle colonies than in the South, but was more important than in New England.

Differences among the Middle colonies were more important than their similarities. Pennsylvania was especially attractive to Quakers, Germans, and Scotch-Irish. It was a colony of families. In behavior and thought, German separatists and Quakers had much in common with the settlers of New England. Because William Penn was more interested in establishing a better world than in making money, Philadelphia became the center of tolerance and advanced ideals in the early colonies. Colonial Maryland attracted many of the same people as Pennsylvania. However, its rulers were different; Catholics took the place of the Quakers; and agriculture was more plantation-Southern. In the middle of the seventeenth century, New York and northern New Jersey were still primarily trading colonies with only a small number of settlers. Colonists had few democratic rights here, although the people were primarily from Great Britain, and from Holland, which was also relatively democratic in this period. Along the Hudson the land was divided into great estates ruled by owners who exercised feudal rights over their tenants. Speculative holdings of this kind reduced the attractiveness of New York for a century.

With the growth of population and the passage of time the original centers of population on the Atlantic coast grew and expanded. New England was largely populated from Massachusetts, although some people of differing creeds came directly to Rhode Island because of its more tolerant attitude. Since the population of New England grew faster than in neighboring areas, New Englanders spread onto Long Island and into upper New York State and eventually into parts of northern Pennsylvania and New Jersey. Even in New York City Englishmen were as common as Dutchmen before the colony was acquired by England, and many of the "Englishmen" were natives of New England.

Generally the South grew slowly. Cities were already flourishing in Northern and Middle colonies when serious colonization began in the Carolinas and Georgia. After 1650 Negro slaves became the primary solution to the Southern labor problem, thus further segmenting Southern society. Negroes came to be seen as property without the right of eventual freedom that was open to white indentured servants. Many of the latter moved up out of the lowlands to establish themselves in scattered areas as subsistence farmers in intimate contact with Indians. As plantation agriculture developed, more and more whites were driven west.

The influence of Philadelphia rapidly spread into Delaware and southern New Jersey. Added to the natural increase in the settled parts of Pennsylvania, New Jersey, and Maryland, there was a new influx of Germans and Scotch-Irish after 1700 that caused land prices to rise steeply. Further movement west was inhibited by mountains, border disputes between Maryland and Pennsylvania, and the relative unwillingness of Philadelphia's Quaker government to further dispossess the Indians (or to protect the frontier adequately). Therefore, both old and new immigrants were diverted south to the Cumberland and Shenandoah valleys and North Carolina. This movement down the eastern side of the Appalachian Mountains eventually reached into Georgia. While this group included most of the nationalities and sects of Pennsylvania, the Scotch-Irish were predominant.

After mingling with independent farmers from the coastal South, the next generation crossed over the Appalachians into what became Kentucky and Tennessee. The colonial governors opposed this movement in the eighteenth century, just as William Penn had opposed the Western expansion of the same people in the seventeenth century; both wanted to preserve friendly relations with the Indians. In addition, the British did not like the increase in people settling well beyond their control and influence; in the Revolutionary period they were, of course, even more opposed to the expanding frontier. The nature of the frontiersmen made settlement possible beyond British outposts. Given insufficient protection on the Appalachian frontier by regular forces, the pioneers had learned to rely on their own society. The relative weakness of the Indian tribes on the Kentucky frontier was also a factor, for north and south of the Kentucky-Tennessee frontier stronger and better organized Indian tribes were able to contain white advance until after the Revolutionary War.

The result was that the South played a major part in the West in 1850 (see Map 1). Along the frontier of North and South, the westward salient in Kentucky and Tennessee continued for many years to exert a dominating influence. The first people into Ohio, Indiana, and Illinois were from the South—even the first extensive settlements in Wisconsin were of Southern miners. Following the pattern of parallel western movement, Missouri was largely settled from this salient, as was much of Kansas and Colorado. Alabama, Mississippi, and northern Louisiana were first penetrated from Tennessee. In Texas the people of Kentucky-Tennessee were

MAP 1. Population by Origins, 1850. Source: modified from appended map in Frederick Jackson Turner, *The United States: 1830–1850* (New York: Holt, Rinehart & Winston, 1935)

preceded by special colonies, such as that of Stephen Austin; but here, too, Southerners quickly became the dominant element. Texas is heavily impressed with their conquest and special brand of Americanization. The same people played a large part in the population of Oklahoma, New Mexico, and Arizona, and later of California. To the north the original society of Kentucky and Tennessee expanded into Missouri and Iowa and thence throughout the West. Relatively they were probably more numerous in the first migrations to the Oregon country than to California. However, the total impact of their westward movement was often insubstantial. Never much at serious farming or the founding of towns, the Kentucky frontiersman was continually on the move. He made a better mountain man, trail blazer, or Indian fighter than settler.

The progress westward of New Englanders through New York State and the Upper Middle West was slower but often more lasting and visible. They founded towns as well as homesteads; and when they came, the land quickly filled, the Indians and the animals retired. (The Indians sometimes had already been decimated by the more aggressive Upland Southerners.) Even when numerically greatly outnumbered, the New Englanders played an important role in education and business throughout the West. The influence of New England culture in the farther West was transmitted through its Midwest colonies as well as directly.

The special contribution of the Middle Atlantic societies is harder to find in the West. Pennsylvania finally expanded into the Ohio basin, and its colonists were able to take part in the movement into Ohio before 1800. Evidence of the further movement of this cultural stream can be found throughout the Central Midwest, particularly in the spread of standard American religious denominations and dialect, and perhaps the Midwest family farm and grid-pattern towns. Scattered German and Quaker communities are found throughout the Midwest. Almost as important a part of Pennsylvania's contribution was the indirect movement south through the mountains and Piedmont, and then west, which is not reflected in Map 1.

Since both tobacco and cotton culture rapidly exhaust soil, Southern plantation agriculture demanded new territory before it was able to support a high population density by contemporary Northern standards. In the early nineteenth century the Indian barrier to the westward expansion of Southern plantation society was overwhelmed, and cotton culture swept west through Mississippi into Texas. It also swung north along the Mississippi as far as Missouri and southern Illinois, bringing with it both the best and the worst of Southern life.

West of the Plains the three currents of Atlantic seaboard culture are more mixed, but there is still parallel westward motion. Utah forms the most distinct exception to this pattern. Mormon society was a direct outgrowth of the New England tradition of upstate New York, with its leaders originally from Vermont. It was the most successful of the many religious movements generated by the revivalist spirit in upstate New York in the early nineteenth century. In Utah the Mormons laid out towns in the New England style rather than in the isolated homestead patterns that characterized most of the West. Outside of the Northeast, Mormonism did not recruit many in this country. Many of the Mormons brought to Utah came directly from northern Europe, especially England.

Immigration considerably altered the composition of the American population in the nineteenth and early twentieth centuries.[9] However, except where immigration was concentrated, there was little change in the basic patterns established by the earlier American migration. One reason for this may have been the domination of the education of the immigrant young by native American teachers. Among specific groups of immigrants, the English and English-speaking Canadians came steadily into the country in large numbers, but in most places their quick assimilation makes their influence hard to trace. German-speaking people played an important part in many states, North and South (see Map 1). Their most decisive influence was in Pennsylvania, Ohio, and Wisconsin, but was significant in Iowa (after 1850), northern Illinois, and other parts of the Middle West—especially in cities such as Saint Louis. While a German intellectual and business elite helped form the civilization of the larger Midwest cities, prosperous German farmers dominated many rural areas. The fact, however, that German speakers were both Catholic and Protestant and originally represented different German states diluted their impact on previous American patterns even where they were numerically dominant and better educated than other immigrants.

The Scandinavians became dominant in Minnesota, the Dakotas, and neighboring areas. Although representing different nations, they were nearly all Lutherans. They came as a rural people, but with an education and culture that made it possible for them to adapt quickly to the urbanization that was already occurring as they arrived. As with many Germans, ideas of social democracy were strong among them. When their societies at home developed social innovations, many were interested in bringing similar concepts to this country. (However, as the societies diverged, perhaps the Scandinavians that came here have been increasingly less attracted by events in their homelands.)

Numerically the Irish and Italians had their greatest impact on urban American society. Concentrated at the lower income levels and overwhelmingly Catholic, they changed the native American patterns of many cities north of the Mason-Dixon line, especially in the Northeast. However, this did not happen all at once: there were accommodations on both sides, and today business and finance in the states they dominate largely remain in non-Catholic hands. In New England, Irish and Italians seem to adopt the positions of the original Yankees on many political, social, and educational issues. (If so, how this came about is of considerable interest.) Other groups of non-Jewish East Europeans such as the Poles were concentrated in Pennsylvania and the Midwest and adapted to local regional viewpoints much as the Irish and Italians in New England.

The impact of the Jews has been spectacular. Devoted to education and commerce, they have achieved well in nearly every sphere, especially in arts and learning and merchandising. In the mass they are highly concentrated in a few places (New York, Washington, D.C., Miami, Los Angeles), but everywhere their influence is much greater than their numbers.

The French never settled in the country in large numbers. However, in southern Louisiana a mixed community of French origin is found. French-Canadians are also dominant along the northern edge of New England and Michigan. More important is the Spanish-speaking population of highly diverse origins. First are the descendants of the Spanish settlers in New Mexico and southern Colorado that preceded the American conquest. Second, there is the much larger post-1850 Spanish population throughout the Southwest and in some of our largest cities. With the exception of Puerto Ricans in New York City, most of this group is Mexican-American and largely of Indian racial background. There were Mexicans in southern Texas prior to the gringo conquest, but these were swamped over the years by later arrivals. The pre-United States Spanish-Americans lived, and to some extent still live, in small towns surrounded by subsistence farming plots. Post-United States Spanish-speakers arrived first as farm labor and more recently as urban labor. The early history of Chinese and Japanese in this country was one of persecution and exclusion, but after World War II a new, educated oriental population has become one of the most dramatically successful groups in our society. They are most common in or near Pacific Coast cities and in Hawaii.

Black Americans made up nearly 20 percent of our population in 1790. They lived primarily in the South (see Map 1), although there were significant numbers in the Middle states. Their percentage declined to about 10 percent in 1900 and they have since been a slowly growing part of the population. Communities of free blacks, nearly all originally slaves, developed in both the North and South before the Civil War. However, the vast majority were still plantation slaves in the deep South at the time of the war. After emancipation, Negroes remained rural and Southern until recently. Now, with the virtual disappearance of the subsistence farm and the decline of farm labor, the Negro population is more urban than the general population. For social and economic reasons almost half of the Negro population has come North, and blacks are now in a majority in some Northern cities, notably Newark, New Jersey. Thus, although Negroes constituted only 11 percent of the national population in 1970, their social visibility in the 1970s was greater than it had ever been.

American Indians have always lived in small, scattered groups with highly diverse cultures. A few Indian cultures have survived as a positive influence in the life of present-day Indian groups, particularly in the interior Southwest. However, for at least half of the presently identifiable Indian population the early cultural background has disappeared and been replaced by a negative culture based on the reservation experience of defeat, impotence, and dependency. We have yet to see whether recent cultural and political movements will change this experience. Perhaps for every individual we now recognize as Indian, another Indian has melted into the black and white populations of the country.

Americans have always been mobile. The movement west has been long-term and continuous, and has lately been augmented by another movement to a vacation-, retirement-, and aerospace-oriented Southern frontier, although the numbers are still relatively small. Movement from rural to metropolitan areas is nearly a century old, though it has recently been accompanied by a reverse movement to suburbs or new urbanizing areas. Most rural states stand still or lose population while the coasts gain.

With change and movement and growth there is surprising continuity. As Daniel Elazar has pointed out, urban living in much of the United States is not very different from rural, for in fact the movement to the cities has led to the agrarianization of many cities. As the cities grew, the percentage of owner-occupied dwellings went up and the plot size of the metropolitan dweller increased. Since internal migration has been within cultural areas, it has affected patterns of national variation surprisingly little. In general, heavy in-migration of a new people has had a reduced impact because of the "strength of the cultural bedrock once formed." However, the in-migration of radically different peoples has in recent years affected local cultures in some areas, notably in parts of Arizona, Florida, and New Jersey.[10]

# The Evolution of Regional Socioeconomic Patterns

Superimposed upon the distribution of peoples carrying distinctive cultures has been the story of the differential interaction of these peoples with a wide variety of geographical, economic, and social possibilities. The fact that the Southern and Northern peoples of the United States moved directly west, and in this movement crossed a variety of physiographic frontiers without losing their distinctiveness suggests that culture and physical environment have not been simple reflections of one another. Nevertheless, they clearly did interact.

At first New England was primarily a subsistence agricultural area. Hunting and fishing and primitive lumbering, especially for firewood, were minor supplements. There early developed a considerable craft capability that led on the one hand to a noted ability in trade and on the other to the development of industry. However, most of the people remained agriculturalists and, when better lands became available in New York and later in the Midwest, they moved out at such a rate that New Englanders were concerned, even before 1850, that the area was being depopulated.

Economic growth followed much the same pattern in the Middle Atlantic states. In Pennsylvania the original farms had often been larger and more productive, and agriculture tended to decline in importance more because of urbanization than because of the superiority of other lands. On account of differences in the class composition of immigrants and, in the early years, a greater use of slaves and indentured servants, a proletariat rapidly developed in the large cities of the middle coast. Except for agricultural religious communities, such as those of the Friends or of German groups like the Mennonites, the pressure to migrate to the West for land was less intense than in New England.

In Pennsylvania, coal mining and iron and steel production developed in the mountains in the nineteenth century to such an extent that their exploitation displaced the earlier agricultural image of the state. While old-stock Americans were common farther south, the miners of Pennsylvania were mostly recent immigrants from Wales, Ireland, or Eastern Europe. The dominance of mining in the formation of most of nineteenth- and early twentieth-century Pennsylvania was paralleled by later experience in West Virginia and Montana.

In the South there developed alongside subsistence agriculture a dominant plantation agriculture. The plantations were devoted first to tobacco and later to cotton. Sugar cane, indigo, and rice were important in some areas (cane was the primary crop of the West Indian models of plantation life). As the soil wore out in the older areas and markets expanded, cotton culture was forced farther south and west. Cotton plantations moved from the Carolinas to Georgia, Alabama-Mississippi, Louisiana, and finally Texas and the Pacific Southwest (ending in the San Joaquin Valley).

Although all Southerners have many items of culture in common when compared with the rest of the United States, we can distinguish several types of Southern physical environment and agricultural life (see Maps 2 and 3). The coastal lowlands consist of a marshy fringe that is swampy and underpopulated in most areas and a plantation belt lying inland from coastal swamp and sand. This lowland pattern starts in New Jersey and swings south through the coastal states into Arkansas and east Texas. In

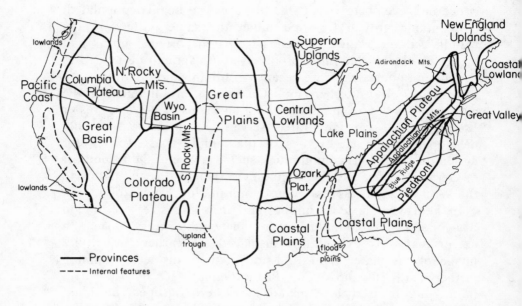

MAP 2. Physiography. Source: modified from Charles Hunt, *Physiography of the United States* (San Francisco: W. H. Freeman, 1967), pp. 7–8

between the plantations in this belt there were small commercial or subsistence farms with few or no Negroes. In later years white and black tenant farmers occupied much of the same land to form a modified plantation system. Population in the South was heaviest here, and the Negroes generally outnumbered the whites.

In the Piedmont or other upland areas, the South was originally a land of independent "yeomen," although larger plantations developed later. These areas were characterized by subsistence farms with a cash crop on the side. This was usually tobacco, but it might be indigo, wheat, or corn (or whiskey). This belt swung south from Pennsylvania through the eastern foothills of the Appalachian Mountains, rounded the Appalachians in Alabama, and then turned north on the west side of the mountains. Comparable areas not adapted to plantation agriculture form belts in Missouri, Arkansas, Louisiana, Texas, and Oklahoma and in other scattered points in the West.

Higher in the mountains covering a considerable area of West Virginia, Kentucky, and Tennessee, and in parts of the Ozarks,

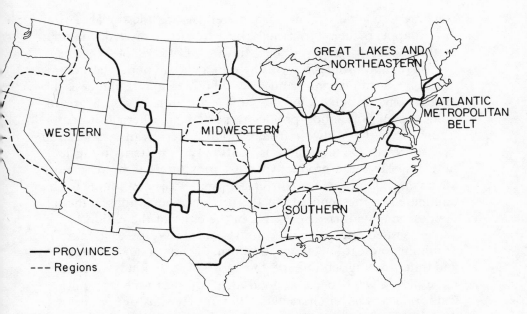

MAP 3. Economic Provinces and Economic Regions. Source: modified from Donald J. Bogue and Calvin L. Beale, *Economic Areas of the United States* (Glencoe, Ill.: Free Press, 1960), pp. xlvii, xlix

there is practically no possibility of agriculture and it is only in the last hundred years that there has been any considerable population here. Although occasionally the economy has been built on coal mining (in the Appalachian segment), to a surprising extent the people have persisted on a "hunting and gathering level" with minimal agriculture.

The Midwestern states developed first within the forested belt, but soon Northerners, Southerners, and North European immigrants learned to utilize the grasslands farther west. Finally pushing into areas of very low rainfall, they learned the geographical limits of conventional intensive agriculture. The Midwest produces the meat and bread of the country. Wisconsin has become specialized in dairy farming, as has upstate New York on the eastern fringe. As this industry became increasingly specialized and modernized, the older generation, whose farms were not thoroughly commercialized, has been forced out. However, many family farms continue to exist, with heavy investments in land and machinery generally showing poor returns for the dollar. (After 1973 it appears the returns might be generally improved.) Lumber in the northern fringe of the Midwest—portions of Wisconsin, Michigan, and Minnesota—brought in a special population dominated by Scandinavians and French Canadians. Lumber is no longer a major activity of this area, with iron having a greater influence on population profiles in parts of northern Minnesota. Elsewhere in the Midwest, from Ohio to eastern Kansas and up to eastern North Dakota, there is continuity in patterns of agricultural life. Here the productivity of agriculture has been steadily advancing. Unlike the Northeast, this area continues to be dominated by descendants of the original populations, although the descendants increasingly live in the cities of the region.

Next settled after the corn country was the West Coast. Starting as mining and cattle country, California is now a land of industry and intensive agriculture of the most diverse kinds. Although there has always been a good deal of part-time agriculture, California was never characterized by family subsistence farming. Agriculture was mostly very large-scale from the beginning and today this is more than ever true.

Oregon's Willamette Valley, on the other hand, was a family farm area. It attracted Midwesterners and Missourians, even though the climate was more like that of New England or Northern Europe. Western Washington is much like the Willamette Valley, but was from the first less an agricultural area, being more concerned with lumber, mining, fishing, and the Alaskan trade.

The western fringe of the Midwest region of settled agriculture, and especially its northern reaches, was settled after the Far West. Between the farm belt of the midlands and the Rocky Mountains there runs a strip of cattle and dry farming country from central and western Texas and New Mexico north through Oklahoma, Colorado, Kansas, Wyoming, Nebraska, Montana, and the Dakotas. (In some places, especially in Texas, sheep and goats may replace the cattle.) Although it grades into wet-land farming on the east, the open prairie offers a different type of life and it demands a different kind of people. Here farms are ranches and they are much larger than those to the east. There are many more hired hands, and the young man's ideal remains that of the movie cowboy. Culturally, there is a strong Texan influence, but this tends to die out toward the north.

Between the cattle country of the western plains and the central valleys of California or the Willamette–Puget Sound strip of the Northwest lies a vast, sparsely inhabited mountain and plateau region. Agriculture here is confined in most cases to narrow valleys where irrigation is possible, although there are a few areas of extensive dry farming—notably wheat—in parts of the Columbia Basin. Between farming areas much of the land is devoted to an extensive form of livestock grazing (and haying for livestock). The people came originally from more heavily populated areas to the east, as well as from the west coast. In New Mexico the ranching population tends to be Texan, while western Idaho was populated to a large extent from Washington and Oregon. An exception is the Mormon area. Here the possibility of irrigated agriculture and religious freedom attracted a population from upstate New York and New England rather than from closer states. Backed by high fertility, the Mormons have managed to spread over all of Utah and southern Idaho, while colonies have been established in parts of Oregon, Wyoming, Arizona, and New Mexico. In this area Mormon development has been generally on the basis of irrigated agriculture and in settled communities. As urban dwellers, Mormons are of increasing importance in Los Angeles, San Francisco, and other large cities.

Subsistence agriculture is practiced by Indians and Spanish-Americans throughout the mountain and plateau area on a scale similar to that in the Appalachians and Ozarks. Since irrigation is generally required, the technical level of accomplishment and the reward is higher than in the Appalachians. Mining has been important in parts of the Rocky Mountains. Pockets of miners are found in every state, but have been particularly important in influencing population characteristics in Montana, which has perhaps the largest number of different national groups of any of our sparsely populated states.

Since the original settlement of the country, there have been two more waves of economic change that have determined our population patterns. The first wave represented the extension of the dominance of industry and trade on the location of population, while the second has represented a growing dominance of the location desires of people on the location of economic activity. After 1800 industry began to determine population patterns outside the South. On an area-wide basis, industry became dominant in New England because western competition reduced the returns of agriculture at a time when the dominance of New England ships in international trade opened new markets and provided wealth. In terms of the technology of the era, good sites for mills along New England streams and an excellent population of surplus workers (especially farm girls) were important. Industry around Boston, New York, Philadelphia, and Baltimore also benefited from the central trading positions of these cities, and later from the tendency of cheap immigrant labor to settle first at these points.

In industrial growth the Middle States were benefited by their close proximity to iron and coal. From Pittsburgh to Minneapolis industry developed along the routes of the coal and iron exchange at points where transportation was easy. A relatively dense and productive agricultural population provided both initial labor and market. The railroads, built for agricultural exploitation, brought in another pool of workers for industry. As the national economy developed, the central location of the Midwest in the national transportation network favored its industrial growth. Another important reason for development of Midwestern industry was the type of people who settled the area. Northerners came to set up business and industry and urban centers, after having engaged in similar enterprises farther east. There was less entrepreneurial activity in the South and its western extensions. Where Southern industry did develop, it was largely with Northern leadership and capital.

Much industry has, of course, an agricultural base, whether it be farm equipment, food processing, or the processing of industrial crops such as cotton. Almost everywhere there were slaughterhouses, although Chicago had the best known. Yet the movement of people in search of jobs was South to North, and post-1800 immigrants came almost exclusively to the North. Later wage differentials and the discovery of oil attracted industries such as furniture or textiles to the South, while oil and gas attracted petrochemical and other industries. Nevertheless, the imbalance has not been made up.

Settled after American society was already industrialized, the Western states began with a larger percentage of their population urban and nonfarm than older sections of the United States away from the Atlantic seaboard. While for many years Texas remained a rural society, San Francisco became a metropolis almost overnight.

California promoters and the lure of glamourous cities began the second wave, a movement of people to climate and/or rather insubstantial "opportunity." They were so successful that there followed a movement of jobs to people based on the resulting labor supply and market. We are now in an era in which agricultural resources and strategic trade location are less important and the location of final market relatively more important. People move first, and jobs follow. This pattern leads to a spiral of growth that seems irresistible, with the large metropolitan centers sucking in population from the rest of the country. The general tendency for sheer size to attract migrating business and people is modified, however, by several other tendencies. Some migration is determined by residence preference unrelated to job or market (although the market generally follows). Movement has been out of the areas dominated by harsh continental climates and toward the seaboards. It has also been away from central cities toward suburbs. If the process of suburban sprawl thus created becomes serious enough, people will move to new areas not so afflicted, and in some places these may be far removed from current metropolitan centers.

Insofar as people continue to move into the large metropolitan corridors, these are evidently not saturated in the opinion of the movers. In this country most internal migrants have not been forced to move; they have moved because the new residence seemed better to them than the old. There is a good deal of nonsense written about the degree to which large agriculture has forced out small farmers, or the big city killed the town, or that urban crowding has produced the suburbs. In most of these cases the individuals concerned balanced their opportunities and made a choice in terms of preferred alternatives. At some point for most farm boys, and even for some of their fathers, and certainly for the women, poor districts in a city offered more of what they wanted than rural labor or the subsistence farm.[11]

The population of the metropolitan areas has, of course, changed. The first stage of growth in metropolitan life saw the influx of millions of foreign immigrants; many of them never wanted to see land again and rapidly adjusted to urban values and patterns. Although many came from rural areas, they had inherited a common hate or fear of the land and what it offered. In the United States, few rural Italians or Poles or Irish ever took up a homestead, economically one of the best chances available until World War I. Later, Negroes, Mexican-Americans, and some Southern whites had this same hatred of the land, and they have been little attracted to the suburbs even where they were available. (They might, of course, move out of a ghetto for social, educational, or security gains.) However, in the last fifty years, the influx to the cities included many Americans, old stock or post-1800 immigrants, with a love of the country and its way of life. Many of these began working in a neighboring city while living on the farm and until recently most of them have had relatives on the farm. As soon as technology and money made it possible, they moved back out of the city to uncrowded suburbs. For others, their move to the "city" has actually been to a suburb, and their later mobility is from suburb to suburb.

There has been a great deal of mixture and movement of people in the last fifty years.[12] Nevertheless, Southern cities are over-whelmingly populated by Southerners, and New England cities largely by people born in New England, although many of the latter are the children of recent immigrants. Urban dwellers in rapidly growing areas of the Far West are generally from out-of-state, but as populations grow there is an increase in the percentage native to the state in Far Western urban areas. Metropolitan growth drawing in the population of the surrounding hinterland is most characteristic of areas with relatively low area-wide growth, such as many interior metropolitan areas.

Because of the special history of social disability in the South, the American Negro has made a rapid change of residence. Nevertheless, in spite of the facts that the black is now more urban than the white and the South is the most rural part of the country, the majority of Negroes are still in the South.

Finally, with all of the freewheeling movement and the transfer of our working population from primary to secondary to tertiary economic functions, we must not be led into imagining that primary and secondary activities are not still critical to the economy. We cannot all end up teachers and researchers. A society centering around services in employment terms is still determined in size and wealth by the primary and secondary activities that its services are directed toward. Most service employment is a specialization out of an earlier, less differentiated employment in which the analogue of the service was contained in the production or extraction process. This implies that the economics of industry and agriculture will still tend to locate population to some extent as it has in the past; and to this extent the more generalized tendencies of movement will be dampened.

# Defining Basic Cultural Regions

Many geographers begin their analysis of the United States by describing its physiographic regions. Economic, cultural, and historical facts are then discussed in this framework. The regions of the country produced in this manner (Map 2) can be shown to have considerable significance. For example, Carl Kraenzel has demonstrated how misunderstanding the geography of the Great Plains resulted in a variety of social and economic problems.[13] Kraenzel's emphasis is on the particular problems forced upon this area by climate and distance. Morris Garnsey has made a similar attempt to point out the problems common to the "mountain west."[14] Analysis of this kind illustrates a use of physical geography as an organizing principle that has been overtly rejected by most geographers, although it covertly continues to shadow their work. Problem "regions" such as "Appalachia" sometimes become identified by pressure groups for government programs, but both history and geography make it impossible for them to become useful regional units except for very special purposes.

Perhaps the greatest amount of work on American regions has been done by economists.[15] The economist's regionalization (Map 3) is primarily based on patterns of commonality or difference in indices for agriculture, industry, and population. Alternately, economists and economic geographers regionalize the country in terms of economic relationships or market areas.[16] Comparison of Maps 2 and 3 will show the degree to which physiography has determined economic patterns in this country, although clearly the particulars of history and European origin account more than physiography for the economic differences of the Pacific and Atlantic coasts. The work of both physical geographers and regional economists must form one basis of any regional study, for life will continue to be affected by the physical environment and its particular economic uses and possibilities. However, we will deliberately attempt to begin our analysis of cultural regions by ignoring the physical and economic environment insofar as it does not determine the differentiation of peoples into groups with identifiable noneconomic, cultural differences.

A central purpose of the study is to provide an alternative way to look at the country. Economic and physical geographies have seen regions in terms of river basins, climatic conditions, and transportation routes or networks. In considering the sociocultural building blocks of the nation, this approach is to some extent inevitable. But the fundamental lesson of history is that different people make different uses of the same environment, and that people use material goods rather than the other way around. For example, the Great Plains was one geographical fact that was populated by a variety of different people. In the South it has been populated by Southern Baptist farmers, highly individualistic and inclined to violence. At the northern end the settlers were in large measure descendants of New Englanders and Scandinavians with a formal Lutheranism and political-economic ideals of the cooperative movement. Farther east, the New Englanders and Germans of Wisconsin built up a progressive, serious, educationally oriented society that contrasts markedly with the old American society of central Illinois and Indiana.

*This study is, in part, an extended defense of the hypothesis that it is useful to divide the country into cultural regions as defined primarily by variations in the cultures of the peoples that dominated the first settlement and the cultural traits developed by these people in the formative period (where these are significant), and secondarily by variations in the cultures of peoples that dominated later settlements, as well as cultural traits developed subsequently. Regions will be defined where there are large areas of relative homogeneity in these factors, and regional borders will be placed, when possible, where there are significant discontinuities.*

It is important to note that the study escapes triviality by suggesting the special influence of variations in old regional traditions on current behavior. Were only variations in contemporary culture involved, the study would be open to the usual criticism of the tautological nature of cultural explanation. The hypothesis should also be thought useful if it can be shown that variations among cultural regions can be extended descriptively beyond the differences in the original cultures of the people concerned to emergent regional differences in behavioral traits (Chap. II), and if recent behavior of a sort that is usually not culturally defining is predictably different in different regions (Chap. III). The reader might wish to compare from this viewpoint the usefulness of the regions developed here (Maps 4 and 5) with those of the Bureau of the Census. The hypothesis should also be thought useful if it can be shown that the regions delineated by the study provide a valuable organizing principle for developing subnational foci of awareness and commitment for elite or ordinary citizens (Chaps. IV and V).

To a considerable extent the study is based on what Wilbur Zelinsky has referred to as the "Doctrine of First Effective Settlement." [17] This is the hypothesis that the first European or American white population that established the economic and social basis of an area had a decisive influence on later patterns. This does not deny the possibility of later change or even the overwhelming of the original cultural imprint by that of a later group. In addition to first effective settlement, we also examine the origin and affiliation of the "dominant elite" (business, religious, educational, and political) in each area, for elite origins are culturally more decisive than mass origins on certain issues. The cultural regions distinguished will integrate with other geographic facts the distribution of variations in state or nation of population origin, dialects, and religious or political affiliation. (Of course, ultimately we cannot ignore the fact that economic and technological activity is also cultural activity, and physical geography will directly play its part in the following regionalization.)

This way of understanding the country is closest to that of

anthropologists such as Conrad Arensberg and Evon Vogt writing in the mid-fifties.[18] It is similar to the approach of Yale University's Directive Committee on Regional Planning, which asserted in 1947 that character values were what distinguished regions or that New England was a region because its people think it is.[19] However, the approach taken here grew directly out of the author's attempt to look at social indices from the point of view of cultural regions, starting with the wide regional variations in the homicide rate.[20]

Against this background an analysis has been developed that identifies the following cultural regions:

1. New England
2. New York Metropolitan
3. Pennsylvanian
4. South (Lowland, Upland, Mountain, Western)
5. Upper Midwest
6. Central Midwest
7. Rocky Mountain
8. Mormon
9. Interior Southwest
10. Pacific Southwest
11. Pacific Northwest
12. Alaskan
13. Hawaiian

Map 4 suggests approximate boundaries for the hypothesized cultural regions. Within regions subdivisions have been made on the basis of secondary cultural variations, induced by differences in the origin of the people, the requirements of particular geographical situations, or subsequent creativity. Most urban areas reflect fairly well their hinterlands, or are themselves an important determinant of the regional definition. Metropolitan areas that depart significantly from what we might expect in a particular region or district have also been indicated on the map. The regional borders in Map 4 are clearly only one approximation of a complex situation. A different treatment of the transitional zones found at most regional boundaries would produce somewhat different boundaries. A good case could be made that certain districts (or subregions) should be transferred from one region to another, or made into separate regions.

Although the present study is directed toward understanding the cultural regions of the country, for practical purposes social and economic relationships may be at least as important as cultural. Therefore, mapping of the country by sociocultural

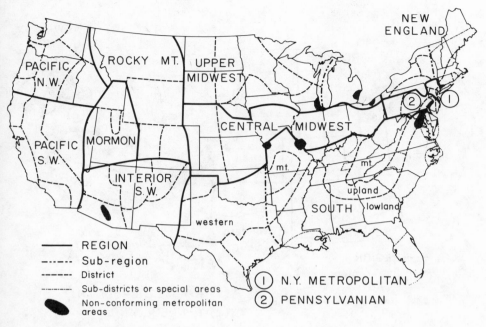

MAP 4. Cultural Regions

regions (Map 5) has also been developed. Map 5 emphasizes the importance of political boundaries and the relation of dominant metropolitan areas to their hinterlands. Clearly, many kinds of planning, economic development, and other practical work should be organized more in terms of sociocultural than cultural regions. District boundaries have been indicated on the map to suggest alternative ways of subdividing sociocultural regions for planning or other purposes and/or alternative sociocultural boundaries. In addition, areas with seriously conflicting cultural and socioeconomic relationships have been crosshatched: inclusion of such areas in neighboring regions would be expected to vary with the problems and interests involved.

The full rationale for the regional classification will be built up as the reader goes through the material. In Chapter IV regional and district boundaries will be discussed in the descriptions of the several regions. It would be useful at this point, however, to compare the regional breakdown presented here with other regional breakdowns for related or apparently related purposes.

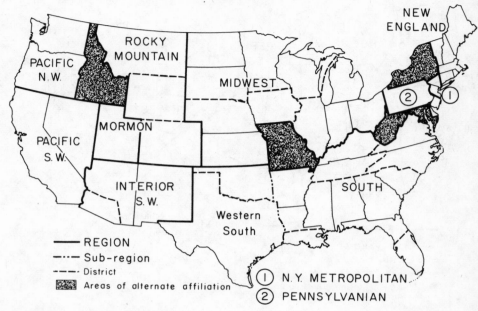

**MAP 5.** Sociocultural Regions

Comparable to the sociocultural regions are Howard Odum's six basic regions (Map 6): Northeast, Middle States, Southeast, Southwest, Far West, and Northwest (actually Western plains and mountain).[21] In order to understand Odum's classification we should note that Odum was a sociologist at the University of North Carolina who dedicated his life to the revival of the South, a regional dedication that has been common in the South and generally absent elsewhere. His major works both concentrated on a comparison of the South with the rest of the country and emphasized the needs and special requirements of the South. With missionary zeal, Odum stressed the importance of "regionalism" as a way to develop the nation harmoniously. He contrasted regionalism as he understood it with the more divisive "sectionalism," the term that Frederick Jackson Turner had used to describe much of United States history in the nineteenth century.

In spite of his generalist approach and historical and literary references, Odum's six basic regions were developed to serve planning and problem-solving objectives. The fact that the regions

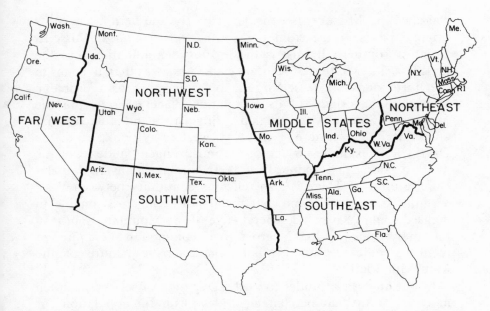

MAP 6. Odum's Six Regions. Source: based on Howard Odum, *Southern Regions of the United States* (Chapel Hill: University of North Carolina Press, 1936), p. 6

are of approximately equal size (taking both population and area into account) and established only on state lines reflects this approach. Odum considered the poverty and the social problems of the South as distinguishing regional features. Instead of differences in culture affecting social indices, he saw social indices defining culture. Thus, Odum and Moore excluded a number of states (West Virginia, Missouri, Texas, Maryland, and Oklahoma) from the Southeast because of their low Negro populations. Missouri was also excluded partly because of its higher standing in many social indices.[22] Odum's "Northwest" included all of the states between Iowa and Oregon and New Mexico and Canada. The identity here was primarily economic and emphasized density, land use, and climatic considerations.

The basis of regionalization in Map 5 is very different. While Odum could reasonably put Utah and North Dakota in one region, in our approach it would be impossible to classify together states as distinct in religious affiliation and history. In our classification Missouri is considered partly Southern because its original people came from the South; today in most Missouri counties Southern Baptist is the leading denomination and the dialect is closer to that of Kentucky and Arkansas than to states to the north or west. West Virginia presents more of a problem. However, the origins of its population place it largely in the Mountain South, with religious, linguistic, and folk culture continuity with eastern Kentucky, western Virginia, and the Ozarks. For example, to one of the most diligent students of the modern poor, "just about all of West Virginia is in the Appalachian South." [23] There is also religious continuity between West Virginia and central Ohio, but it did not seem unreasonable to make the Ohio River the general edge of the Mountain South. In this analysis the fact that Negroes are uncommon in West Virginia is not significant, for this is a characteristic feature of the Mountain South.

In our analysis attitudes toward segregation of services is much more important than percentage of Negroes in the population, for segregation of services has been a traditional feature of the Southern way of life (although its form has varied). If Odum had used this approach, his regions might have been very different. For example, if we consider the pattern of Negro institutions of higher learning and Negro enrollment in white institutions in 1929–30, we will find the South outlined as we have outlined it in Map 4, from Texas to West Virginia (although it extends over our line in the Maryland area). From Texas to West Virginia we find that below the line there was no enrollment of Negroes in white institutions, while in every state above the line there was. In every state below the line there were Negro institutions. There was also one Negro institution in southern Ohio. At the eastern end of the line we find no Negro enrollment reported in white institutions in West Virginia, Maryland, Delaware, or Virginia, and Negro institutions existed in all of these states. There were also Negro institutions in the Philadelphia area.[24]

Similar criteria to those of Odum have been used by Rexford Tugwell in his design of a new American polity with less than twenty "republics," which would largely replace states, and G. Etzel Pearcy's proposal of thirty-eight instead of fifty states.[25] Although the sociocultural regions described in our study are not meant as new states, these proposals offer instructive contrasts. Pearcy suggests thirty-eight new states defined in terms of economic community of interest and physical geography. Pearcy apparently gives no recognition to history and allegiance as suggested by present boundaries, or to the cultural affinities of the people involved. For this reason, he groups Connecticut with New York City and Rhode Island with Boston, although historically and culturally Connecticut is closer to Boston than is Rhode Island. Yet in many particulars he chooses borders very similar to those of our cultural or sociocultural delineations, notably in the division of New Jersey.

In recent years Daniel Elazar has developed a scholarly approach to the United States from the point of view of cultural regions.[26] Although his interest is in the development of a more adequate political science, his methods and materials are very similar to my own. In general terms, he breaks the country down in two quite different ways. In the first approach (Map 7) Elazar divides the nation into three *spheres* and eight *sections*. The

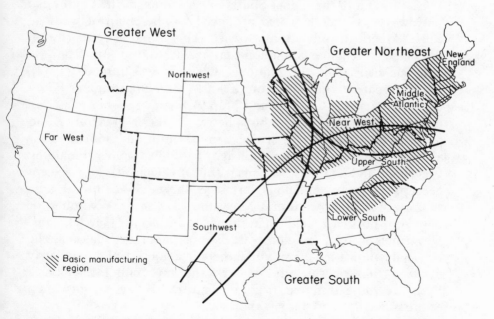

MAP 7. Elazar's Three Spheres. Source: based on Daniel Elazar, *Cities of the Prairie* (New York: Basic Books, 1970), map 7

spheres are the Greater West, the Greater Northeast, and the Greater South, with large areas of overlap (for example, West Virginia is largely in the overlap area of the Northeast and South). The "sections" are sometimes subdivisions of the spheres, but also seem to be independent of them. For example, the "Southwest" section includes Louisiana, wholly within the Greater South, and New Mexico, wholly within the Greater West. This method has the virtue of reflecting the complexity of the problem of regional definition, but the defect of not forcing the analyst to hard, rather educative, decisions. Although culture and history (Elazar's work is partly based on Turner's thinking) play a role in this scheme, economic and sociological variables appear at least equally important. To Elazar, sectionalism is "the expression of social, economic and political differences along geographic lines." [27] By placing Utah in the Far West he shows relative lack of interest in cultural factors. Thus Elazar's first regionalization is very much in the tradition of Odum, and his sections are rather similar to Odum's regions. Two differences may be noted: Elazar places West Virginia in the Upper South and Missouri in the Southwest.

However, Elazar has also produced another map of what he calls "American Subcultural Areas." This is based primarily on the maps of religious affiliation that are derived in turn from the religious census of the National Council of Churches (1952). Elazar apparently departs from Zelinsky's religious regions based on these data (see Chap. II and Map 9) when he wishes to square the religious data with both his sphere and section breakdown and the facts of migration. Otherwise, there seems little justification for a region that runs from Chicago to Philadelphia, including Cleveland and southern Michigan (but not Detroit). Nor, except perhaps in purely religious terms, is there a subcultural area running from Delaware and Maryland to western Wyoming, or one from northern California along the border to New Orleans. Nevertheless, since religion was also an important factor in the regionalization I have presented, there is a good deal of similarity between Elazar's subcultural areas and my "cultural regions." Both are quite different from regionalization largely based on economic and demographic analysis.

One of the most recent attempts to define regional boundaries in the United States has been that of Ruth Hale.[28] She contacted by mail county agents, weekly newspaper editors, and postmasters in as many counties as possible and asked two questions: "What name refers to your region of the State?" and "In what region is your state located?" Unfortunately, for the national regions the methodology was poor. First, two-thirds of the people were officials most apt to answer in official government terminology. Second, the example used to explain the concept determined the result. Since for New England respondents the example used for national region was "Midwest," there was the "surprising" result that most New Englanders identified themselves as from the Northeast rather than from New England. The tendency to reply in official terms is seen in the fact that most of the South considered itself "Southeast" rather than South. Because the respondents were not asked to name the boundaries of their region, the results are hard to interpret. In particular, the most firmly identified region was the "Southwest," which seems to include Arizona, New Mexico, Oklahoma, and Texas. But it is probable that many in New Mexico and Arizona do not see Texas in this region, and vice versa.

Nevertheless, the results in a few areas are interesting. Respondents in Oregon and Washington (Northwest) and Arizona and New Mexico (Southwest) were most consistent in regional identification. Californians were unsure of regional identification because respondents were confused between a number of terms covering a large area (Pacific Coast, Far West, West, West Coast, and Pacific Southwest). The "Midwest" included all the plains states and east to Ohio. The "South" was first choice only in Louisiana, Arkansas, and Mississippi. Kentucky went with the Southeast, West Virginia and Virginia with the Middle Atlantic. As a third exercise, academic geographers on a one-per-state basis were queried. Their responses were more traditional as regards the South and New England, although the same confusion may appear in the designation "Southwest" as in the major study.

The most recent attempt to regionalize the country is that of Zelinsky.[29] Because Zelinsky's "culture areas" are developed on bases very similar to our own, his presentation is the most directly comparable of any we have considered. The comparison is particularly important because the regional analysis in Map 4 was developed before Zelinsky's work became available. Zelinsky divides the country into five main regions: New England, Midland, South, Middle West, and West. Within these he has placed a variety of second- and third-order cultural boundaries. These sometimes overlap the main boundaries, and, especially in the West, describe cultural islands within the larger undifferentiated region.

Zelinsky defines a culture area as

a naively perceived segment of the time-space continuum distinguished from others on the basis of generic differences in cultural systems. . . . It is set aside from other varieties of geographic region [by] (1) the extraordinary number of ways in which it is manifested physically and behaviorally, and (2) the condition of self-awareness on the part of participants. . . . One must insist that if self-consciousness is lacking (and it will suffice if it is present only at the subliminal level), then we are examining something other than a genuine culture area.[30]

Zelinsky's main evidence is variation in a variety of behavioral and historic indicators such as language, religion, food habits, and so on. But Zelinsky has little evidence of degree of regional consciousness, lacking even such evidence as Hale's "Map of Vernacular Regions" based on a mail polling of local elites. Nor could he have evidence of "subliminal regional self-consciousness." I would also question the requirement that people in a culture area be conscious of it. In anthropology such classics as A. L. Kroeber's "Cultural and Natural Areas of Native North America" certainly did not inquire after the regional consciousness of American Indians.[31] However, while evidence of regional consciousness is of minor importance in cultural definition, in defining sociocultural regions for purposes of planning and vitalization, regional consciousness is a critical consideration. Most think of the Midwest as one region, so that although southern Ohio may have as much in common with the Upper South as with southwestern Michigan in basic culture, both Ohio and Michigan are socioculturally in the Midwest.

A comparison of Zelinsky's regions (Map 8) with Map 4 will suggest obvious differences in outlook. The first is that the traditional geographic categories—Northeast, Midwest, South, and West—have played a larger role in his thinking than in mine. Second, while Zelinsky strives to be a cultural geographer, the old hankering after explanation in terms of physical and economic

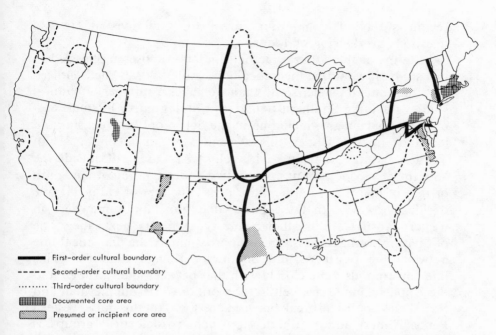

MAP 8. Zelinsky's Cultural Regions. Source: simplified from Wilbur Zelinsky, *The Cultural Geography of the United States* (Englewood Cliffs, N.J.: Prentice-Hall, 1973), p. 118

geography is hard to break. This is apparently why he did not consider the Mormon region a major cultural region (it is categorized as equivalent to the Willamette Valley), while tracing his major regional boundary north to south along the eastern edge of the Great Plains. Culturally distinct southern Louisiana is defined as a "third-order" cultural unit while culturally undefined Willamette Valley is a "second-order" unit, apparently because the valley has more traditional geographic boundaries.

However, leaving these anomalies aside, for the East Zelinsky has summarized in his regionalization and subregionalization the same linguistic, religious, historic, and other evidence that I have, and on the basis of a much greater depth of knowledge. Certainly, his treatment as a whole offers a wealth of information, no matter how one feels about the details of regionalization. In doubtful cases, he has been more reluctant to regionalize than I have, and he can only be respected for this. Zelinsky doubts the West is one region, but avoids committing himself to its subdivision. He also questions his division of Texas.

In terms of the cultural factors similar to those emphasized in this study, it would be theoretically possible to draw the Southern boundary much farther south than we have. A number of cultural studies trace the Southern boundary running north to south east of the Appalachians, including in the South only the coastal and lowland areas.[32] Under this system parts of Georgia, all of Tennessee and Kentucky, and much of Arkansas fall outside the "South." This does not fit my intuitive understanding of the South or that of many Southerners, nor does it fit that of Odum. If one decides, however, that the South does not stop somewhere in western North Carolina, then he must look for the next salient line of division. In linguistics, this is approximately the dialectical line between the Northern and Southern Midland dialects.[33] This line corresponds quite closely with that between the Cornbelt and the Appalachian Ozark belt in the work of Carle Zimmerman and R. E. DuWors.[34] The break between Northern (at this point western Pennsylvania) and Southern Appalachian dialectical groups is another salient division line between North and South. This lies just south of the West Virginia–Pennsylvania line.[35] It is significant that on the Southern Growth Policies Board set up by politicians and academics in 1971, the South included all of the states we have placed in the South socioculturally, plus Delaware.[36]

Relative to population I have distinguished more regions in the West than in the East. However, there is no reason why regions must be of equal population. The regions are defined by strong social or geographic discontinuities, discontinuities in the past that are apt to remain in the future. Because of scale and topography and climatic variations, settlement in the West has always been discontinuous and opportunity for cultural segregation greater than elsewhere in the country. Many have argued that the West, or at least the Far West, should be considered regionally as one unit. Recently Donald Meinig has suggested that while in the nineteenth century there were the several wests I have distinguished, in the twentieth these regions have tended to merge together under California's general influence.[37] However, I would argue that (1) all regions have tended toward national uniformity to about the same extent, and (2) the regions of the West have also lost links to California in recent years because in the air age San Francisco, Honolulu, New York, or Washington, D.C., are not much farther in time-distance.

The reader should not conclude that there is a right or wrong way to draw regional boundaries. The borders given to regions depend upon what the author wishes to analyze. For the purposes of this study, statistical procedures have not been used to define regions. Such procedures have been used by others for regionalization, although primarily in terms of economic variables.[38] One examination of the relationships of states by correlation coefficients representing population and agricultural variables in 1940 confirmed most of Odum's regionalization (although it placed West Virginia in the South).[39] It is significant that with the variables considered in the 1940 study, Missouri's *lowest* correlation with any neighbor was with Arkansas. For our purposes, however, Arkansas is Missouri's closest neighbor, for the first effective settlement in both states was by people sharing many of the same Southern traditions.

Border states always present problems of definition, problems that are only partially resolved by allowing regional borders to cut through a number of states. Unfortunately, migration statistics, which play a critical role in determining regional boundaries, are available only for states. Another problem with the regionalization presented here is that movement within some of the more poorly defined regions is now less common than that between regions.[40] For example, since Michigan was settled from New York State more than were states to its south, it is placed along with other Upper Midwest states; however, since the nineteenth century its relations have been more with Ohio than with states in its region. In fact, I have placed the Lake Erie coast of Ohio within the Upper Midwest (Map 4), but statistics distinguishing this area from the rest of Ohio are not available. The Rocky Mountain Region has the least regional definition in terms of intraregional migration: there is relatively little exchange between states in the region. Of the two new regions, Alaska should perhaps be included in the Pacific Northwest, but the Hawaiian Islands are the most distinctive geographical and cultural milieu in the nation. For further discussion of the precise regional lines and reasons for them, see the discussions of the separate regions in Chapter IV.

## Further Theoretical Considerations

Odum and his colleagues devoted a great deal of their discussion to academic problems of defining regions, to comparing their work with that of other social scientists, and to the development of terminology. In contrast, there will be no more theory here than is required to direct readers to the broader significance of the material and to clear up misunderstandings of intention.

The usefulness of regional analysis in organizing data either for description or explanation has frequently been called into question.[41] However, most of this criticism is not relevant to regionalism as we understand it. Regionalism does not mean that the physical environment plays a determining role, nor that the regions defined are integrated units, although some sociocultural regions are partially integrated vis-à-vis other regions. Regionalism does not imply that the nation and even the world does not have many uniformities that are better explained by other means than regional analysis. It does not deny that a careful mapping of cultural variables often shows that each variable has a unique distribution (see Chap. II). I mean only to assert that for several cultural variables of interest the distributions fall together to form similar regional patterns, and that one of the best explanations of this rough concordance will be found in variations in the cultural backgrounds of the peoples that settled in the areas in question.

"Culture" is at the same time one of the most necessary and one of the most generally abused explanatory shorthands in current use. Part of the confusion comes from the persistence of its humanistic use to refer to the higher arts or knowledge, alongside its use in social science to refer to many aspects of common daily life. The usage adopted for this study is derived from the traditions of anthropologists who popularized the latter sense of culture. Unfortunately, this usage is similar enough to the literary meaning to maintain the confusion, and many recent definitions have not helped. "Culture" will refer in this study only to patterns of learned behavior, and to *all* patterns of learned behavior that differ demonstrably from one group to another by virtue of variations in the paths and content of learning. Cultural behavior includes, of course, verbal and symbolic behavior; but unlike general social science usage, *"culture" will also be used to refer to differences in economic, political, and technical behavior.*[42] According to this definition, there is no such thing as "culture" that does not differentiate among groups of people in time and space, nor is there a contrast between the cultural and social structural aspects of a society. The discussion will not ignore the humanistic sense of "culture," for in the end it becomes more important. It is preferable, however, to refer to humanistic cultural achievements by the word "civilization" in either the singular or plural.

Cultural regions are one of several alternative, crosscutting ways of describing the culture of an area such as the United States. Zelinsky has suggested a three-dimensional way of subdividing a national culture.[43] Along one dimension people are grouped according to variations in traits such as religion, art, or language. A second approach is to make cultural divisions according to class, ethnic affiliation, occupation, life style, or age. The third approach is the regional, crosscutting both of the former. Each regional grouping also is suggested by a different pattern of emphasis along the first two dimensions.

In social science there are two main ways to develop an explanation for group differences. The noncultural explanation is that the people in Group A (class, age-group, status, community) behave differently than those in B and C because of some universal law or relationship that applies to them more than to others. For example, we might say that under certain conditions low-status people everywhere will react in certain predictable ways. A cultural explanation, on the other hand, would emphasize the similarities between low- and high-status persons in the same society and differences among societies, or it would emphasize the differences between low-status behavior in one society and that in another. Since real world situations are never strictly comparable either culturally or universally, and since both factors always play a part, there is no reason to prefer one explanation over another.

Nevertheless, if one tends to be emphasized at the expense of another, then the balance should be rectified as the data suggest. In recent studies of the United States there seems to have been an imbalance in favor of universal explanations; by concentrating on culture, the present work is an attempt to redress the balance.

The theoretical discussion I am alluding to can be seen in terms of the difference between functional and diffusional concepts of what happens in history. Most thinking today is functional. This is both the scientific and the common-sense way to think. Functional explanation assumes that necessity is the mother of invention. The diffusionist believes that usefulness and need are often less important than chance association. One way to compare these concepts is to consider how each approach would be used in analyzing the college riots throughout the world in the late 1960s. The functionalist would analyze the problems and grievances of those involved. He would notice the riots occurred many places at once and would look for uniformities in preriot situations. The diffusionist, on the other hand, would trace the history of riots in the 1960s, perhaps beginning with those at Tokyo University.[44] He would discuss the dissemination of information about riots, and the borrowing of particular details of both riots and confrontation from school to school. Closer to the study of regional differences, some historians have traced the role of the frontier in forming American character. The diffusionist would be more interested in differences between groups in response to the same frontier and the antecedents of these differences.

In addition to the regional divisions presented in Maps 4 and 5, cultural variations are sometimes best described in terms of regional cultural *cores, domains,* and *peripheries.*[45] Such an approach may be especially useful in understanding the Pennsylvanian, New England, and Mormon cultures, as well as a series of Southern cultural waves. The limits and definitions of these areas have continually changed over the course of our history; historically it is only as new cores develop on the periphery of older cultural systems that the creativity of civilization has been renewed. To some extent our national history is the story of change and stability in the locations of creativity, although the maintenance of many patterns tends eventually to shift to New York City. The fact that the centers of American entertainment industry are Hollywood, New York, and Nashville (leaving aside consumption centers such as Las Vegas and Miami Beach) tells us something about the country, and by silence also suggests where new entertainment centers might develop. The fact that a good deal of Protestant publishing also centers in Nashville tells us something else; and when we think of sports, we begin to suspect that the dominance of the Upper South in our culture and civilization, in spite of the financial dominance of the Northeast, has been greatly underrated.

In using the terms core and domain and periphery, I have in mind a model in which a bundle of cultural traits spreads in a coherent form from an identifiable area, becoming less dominant with distance. Of course, actual cores and domains do not grow geometrically, but the model is conceptually useful. In the discussions above of the course of settlement westward from New England, I was, in effect, discussing the spread westward from a New England core centering in Boston. The continued dominance of Yale, Harvard, and M.I.T. in national intellectual and educational life suggests the vitality of this core; but in this century its influence moves much less evenly and with less uniform packaging than it did in the early nineteenth century. Mormon culture was originally an offshoot of New England culture, but today north central Utah is a better example of a core region than is eastern Massachusetts. Another modern core is found in central Texas. The study discussed above of two American cultures in west central New Mexico examined peripheral extensions into the same area from the Texas and Utah cores. Of course, many cultures are intermixed, but a regional core in which there is widespread sharing of values and symbols maintains the vitality of a people. Many would argue, for example, that the Jews have become a vital people since their creation of Israel.

Understanding of core and periphery makes possible a view of American history in terms of growth and contraction of core-domain-periphery relations in our society. It suggests that we look for further creativity through the revitalization of old core cultures or the creation of new cultures at the periphery of the old. Of course, how we define core and periphery depends on our time and distance perspective. Texan culture could be regarded both as an offshoot on the periphery of Southern culture and as a center of new creativity. Boston created a new core culture on the periphery of English culture, but English culture was itself on the periphery of European culture.

In attempting to describe regional cultural variations elsewhere, students have distinguished between the "great tradition" of a cultural area and the "little traditions" within it.[46] For example, if we were to study Indian civilization, we would start with a study of Hinduism and its main derivatives. Some might study Sanskrit, while the more sociologically minded would study the "Indian population problem." India is, however, perhaps best seen as a political entity that contains many peoples and cultures, some of which bear little relation to the culture we identify with Sanskrit. Even its population problem is strongly regionalized.

In America, a study of regional cultures must initially emphasize the little traditions, the differences in dialects, housing, violence, and manners that exist alongside of certain national uniformities. Distinguishing great and little traditions is confused by the fact that there is not a centralized American society based in New York. America is not analogous to France where there is a standard centered in Paris to which most people aspire. In speech one must accept several "cultivated standards" in spite of a standardized television speech that corresponds to no dialect. Educated people from Los Angeles, Chicago, Beacon Hill, or Charleston do not speak alike and do not feel they should. The several cultivated standards have, however, much in common when compared with substandard regional dialects. The situation is further confused by the facts that much of our "great tradition" is Euro-American or "Western" rather than specifically American, and that the highly distinctive New England tradition has historically been viewed by New Englanders and many other Americans as the great tradition of the whole society.

By now it should be clear that the cultural regions outlined above for use in this book are tools for understanding, and there are alternative tools I might have used. Good arguments could be made for drawing regional boundaries in different places. But some boundaries had to be chosen; at a minimum, those I chose allowed me to organize the information in which I was interested. Some of the regions I have outlined have more reality than others and this will show up in differences in ranges of attitudes and statistical indices. Often the important cultural differences that are examined will not be in terms of the more general regions and subregions that I describe, but rather will follow other lines of division or of concentration of particular peoples. These lines may or may not have been important in developing my general regional maps.

In studying regional cultures I hope to give these cultures and the regions associated with them new meaning and respectability. This is important, for the lives of people and their surroundings need to be given more subjective significance. The effort may help self-confidence and loyalty to grow, and great communal achievements can often be traced to loyalty and self-confidence. But this does not mean that "the regions" as I describe them are the best units for enhanced loyalties; it certainly does not mean that augmenting local cultural oddities should be the goal of new regional inspiration. The greatest self-confidence and loyalty are inspired in those who see what they do locally in universal terms. New England saw its goal as the conversion and building of a continent. The Mormons have always emphasized missionary activities and the building of a new world.

As long as artists or businessmen or professors in the regional centers of the country see success as achievable only outside their region, there will be no great regional cultures. On the other hand, as long as those who remain in the "boondocks" see their task as the glorification of whatever characteristics their regions happen to possess, they will build little that is enduring. The Iranian poet Hafez was asked many times to leave Shiraz for India, where the big money was in the fifteenth-century Islamic world; but he stayed behind, where his life was. He has come down to us as a model creator of sheer beauty in poetry, while the poets who went to India are forgotten. Perhaps the greatest creativity comes from remaining at a creative distance from both great population centers and local surroundings and building a universe of one's own.

In summary, *one* approach to a cultural analysis of the United States is a regional approach that goes beyond assumptions of general uniformity. It is a good way to organize information, and much of the historical and statistical information that one wishes to use is available in this form. We can also hope to establish the degree of reality in regional boundaries for people living within them, and single out for further analysis those economic and geographical facts that make the regions salient units for cultural analysis.

## CHAPTER II

# Regional Analysis of Specific Cultural Subjects

T ERMS such as culture or subculture are useful labels with which to tag groups of cultural traits that seem to hang together and that discriminate between identifiable groups of people over time. In this chapter we will examine in some detail the distribution of particular cultural traits in the population. In addition to the intrinsic interest of the subject, this examination will illustrate the extent to which the boundaries of the regional cultures discussed in Chapter I coincide with the distribution of separate cultural traits. This should refine the reader's appreciation of both the legitimacy and the limitations of the regional classification we have proposed. The consideration of these traits will, at the same time, illustrate persistences in cultural boundaries, persistences that add significance to the regional subcultures described in Chapter IV.

## Religion

Although the United States is traditionally a Christian country, there has always been wide regional variation in both religiosity and relative denominational strength. Coupled with this has been the vertical variation in religious denomination by social status. Regional variations have proliferated with the migration west and the later immigrations.

The percentage of the population belonging to any organized church has varied throughout our history. Although ours seems to be an age of disbelief, there has been no long-term decline in religious affiliation. Affiliation has been on a downturn since the 1950s, but a higher percentage of our population is "churched" today than in 1900. More serious from a traditional point of view may be the decline in dedication to the religious dogmas of 1900, for there has been a general watering down of the major creeds. It is important to note that the newer, Western parts of the country have generally been less churched than the Eastern.

Patterns of percentage affiliated with organized religious groups have tended to remain quite stable. For example, a county by county comparison of the percentages of church membership in Illinois in 1890 with the results of the National Council of Churches study in 1952 shows remarkable continuity in the patterns of high and low affiliation.[1] This continuity has been due to persisting differences in denominational strength and general religious affiliation. Some churches have evidently been able to hold their members in the church much better than others, and some churches are much stricter in the definition of a member than others. Outside the South, areas with strong nineteenth-century foreign immigration generally have higher percentages with religious affiliation than areas primarily populated by the westward expansion of the original colonists. A weaker generalization would be that affiliation is higher where there is a dominance of one denomination rather than a thoroughgoing mixture of religious groups of more or less equal strength, as in Oregon. The dominance of the South by Southern Baptists is apparently one reason for relatively high church membership in the South.

For this discussion I will follow Wilbur Zelinsky's categorization of the country into "major religious regions." Zelinsky's work is based primarily on the National Council's 1952 census, but the discussion is updated by consideration of the more recent National Council census.[2] Because of the limitations of the sources, the discussion does not take into account those affiliated

with black churches (about thirteen million), the Eastern Orthodox churches and many native American churches (perhaps
another eight million), while the most recent survey also omitted
the Jews. The main regions distinguished by Zelinsky are New
England, Midland, Upper Middle Western, Southern, Mormon,
Western, and Spanish Catholic. (Map 9 is based on Zelinsky with
changes in the West as noted below.)

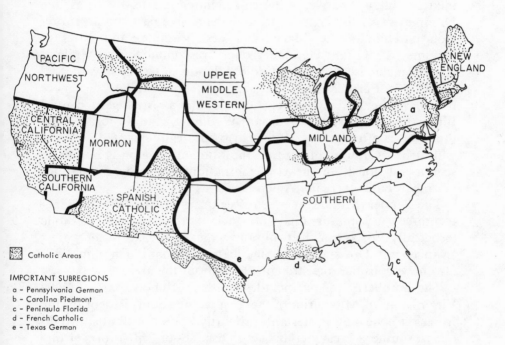

MAP 9. Religious Regions. Source: modified from Wilbur Zelinsky, "An
Approach to the Religious Geography of the United States," *Annals of the
Association of American Geographers* 51, no. 2 (1961): 193

New England is defined by its Puritan heritage. Even though
by 1971 Protestants had a majority only in Vermont and Maine,
the social and political influence of Protestant denominations
outside of Rhode Island is still so considerable as to make
Protestantism much more important in New England than
numbers suggest. The chief Protestant groups are the Congregationalists (United Church of Christ), Episcopalians, and Northern

Baptists, with the Unitarians a small but particularly influential faith.

Zelinsky's Midland Region ranges from New York State to the Rockies. The urbanized parts of this area are often Catholic-dominated, but less so as one goes west. Jews are of course of great importance in New York City. The chief Protestant denomination is generally Methodist, although there is great variation and mixture: many native American denominations such as the Disciples of Christ are strong. In a Pennsylvania German subregion (stretching into Maryland, West Virginia, and parts of Virginia), Protestant German groups are common. The Midland Region includes all of the Middle Atlantic states, Delaware, and Maryland. Farther west the shape of the Midland is more irregular, including parts of Ohio, Indiana, Michigan, central Illinois, southern Iowa, Kansas, Wyoming, and Colorado. Although it is often only a narrow strip, and is interrupted by areas with urban Catholic pluralities, the Midland Region is popularly seen as religiously the heart of the nation and its denominations are regarded as typically American.

The Upper Middle Western Region is dominated by nineteenth-century immigrants and their faiths, whether Catholic (especially Wisconsin, Detroit, and Chicago areas), Lutheran, or Evangelical. The standard American Protestant denominations also have considerable strength throughout the area.

The Southern Region includes southern Illinois, part of West Virginia, all of Missouri and the area to the south. Except on the fringes it is heavily Protestant, primarily Southern Baptist. Methodists, southern Presbyterians, and Disciples of Christ form strong minorities. Parts of the South are the most homogeneous religious areas in the country. Religious belief in this region is the most orthodox and, with the possible exception of the Mormon area, most able to maintain its strength.[3] There are islands of German influence in Missouri and Kentucky and an atypical area in North Carolina that includes Friends, Congregationalists, Lutherans, and Evangelical groups. On the Southern fringe special populations are found in the retirement areas of Florida, in the Louisiana French-Catholic area, and in the Texas Spanish-Catholic area close to the border. This latter is best described as part of a Spanish-Catholic Region including most of New Mexico and

Arizona, and part of southern Colorado. Since in this area the old Catholic majority has tended to be diluted both by Southern and Northern Protestants, the more urbanized areas such as Albuquerque or Maricopa County (Phoenix) are the more Protestant areas in the region.

The most distinct of all regions is the Mormon Region, covering primarily Utah and southern Idaho. In some counties over 99 percent of adherents to religious groups are Mormons and the population is nearly all church-affiliated. Eighty-nine percent of estimated adherents to churches in Utah, and 51 percent in Idaho, are Mormons.

The remainder of the West, an area of low religious affiliation, posed distinct problems for Zelinsky, and his classification does not master them. Therefore, instead of his "Western Region," I propose two regions (see Map 9).[4] The first would be a Pacific Southwest Region, covering nearly all of California and most of Nevada. The percentages of Catholics among adherents is high, rising above 50 percent in San Francisco and other counties. However, religious affiliation is not as common as in other Catholic areas (for example, northern New Mexico or the Northeast). The percentage Catholic has increased considerably since the early 1950s, notably in southern California. There is a large Jewish population in the Los Angeles area, and about 5 percent of the people are Mormon.

The Pacific Northwest, including Oregon, Washington, and parts of Idaho and Montana, is characterized by even lower affiliation than in the Pacific Southwest. Unlike the Pacific Southwest, Protestants dominate the region, with Lutherans, Methodists, Presbyterians, and Mormons the largest groups. Although there has been a notable gain in percent Catholic in the Northwest in the last twenty years, California, with 59 percent Catholic, is quite distinct from Oregon and Washington, with 31 to 33 percent Catholic, or Idaho with 15.

In addition to the religious regions delineated in Map 9, Alaskan and Hawaiian regions should be mentioned. Missionary activity has been quite important in both. Alaska has a strong plurality of Catholics, a high percentage of Southern Baptists, and a wide dispersion of other groups. Hawaii has a Catholic majority, with strong groups of Mormons and Congregationalists (the original missionaries).

Another way to look at regional variations as reflected in religious statistics is to look at marker groups within the population. It will be enough to mention a couple of these and suggest their significance in trying to understand a region.

Protestant Episcopal affiliation is concentrated in urban centers and along the East coast both North and South. In the poorest sections of the country Episcopal churches are often lacking. In the West, Episcopal affiliation is fairly common, even in sparsely populated areas. It may be argued that Episcopalianism forms a marker for Eastern, urban, and status-seeking social and cultural affiliation. However, what its distribution actually signifies will require more investigation.

Unlike Episcopalianism, Congregationalism characterized New England before the nineteenth-century immigration and it is still strongest there. The numerical extent of New England's penetration of the West may be seen by looking at the percentage of Congregationalists, for Congregationalism is the only standard Protestant denomination neither associated with post-1800 immigrant groups nor with the South. However, Congregationalists are surprisingly few everywhere because, for a number of reasons, their missionary zeal was reduced by the time of the western expansion in the nineteenth century. First, after the great awakening in the early eighteenth century many New Englanders became Baptists (and later Methodists).[5] Then, the breaking up of the Congregational community in New England by the Unitarian movement around 1800 resulted in the estrangement of many intellectuals. Later, the Congregationalists made an agreement with Presbyterians in the early nineteenth century not to contest Presbyterian missionary efforts outside of the East.[6] And the aggressiveness of the Presbyterians therefore reduced the significance of Congregationalist activity in the West. In addition, many Congregationalist churches on the frontier accepted Presbyterian organization without changing their beliefs.[7] Finally, the cutting edge of Congregationalism in western New York State was blunted by the revival movements that swept the area in the early nineteenth century, partly as a result of the movement into New York of Methodist missionaries from the South.[8]

Nevertheless, Congregationalists are a marker group. In Illinois in 1952 the pattern of Congregational affiliation differentiated clearly the southern edge of direct New England influence in Knox and Stark counties, although there were islands much farther south. However, by 1971 the merging of the Congregationalists into the United Church of Christ (including German Evangelical groups) had obscured this border. In Oregon and Washington it is significant that Congregationalists are found in numbers primarily in their old missionary area along the Columbia and Snake rivers and the area between.

Wherever there are Southern Baptists there is Southern culture. Even those mountain areas of the Southern Appalachians that opposed the Civil War and continued to vote Republican are now largely Southern Baptist (see Map 13). However, if we look at the less successful Southern Presbyterian movement ("Presbyterian Church in the United States"), we find that those counties in the Southern Appalachians that have been anti-South politically have also rejected Southern Presbyterian affiliation in favor of Northern affiliation. In general, the Southern Presbyterians have been less successful than the Southern Baptists in effectively extending their influence outside of the South. Since Southerners in the North often join related Northern churches, the spread of specifically Southern denominations greatly understates Southern out-migration, especially to Northern cities. However, between 1952 and 1971, there has been additional growth in the relative strength of the Southern Baptists, particularly in Missouri, Oklahoma, and Texas, as the South continues to extend its influence. In 1971 the Utah-Colorado boundary continued to restrict the eastward extension of the Mormon people, and there appeared a more surprising restriction of Southern Baptist affiliation beyond the Iowa-Missouri border. Self-selection of residence and state-related determinations of diffusion of new attitudes toward religious belief may be responsible for the apparently anomalous influence of a state border.

The actual strength of the Catholic and Southern Baptist churches in American life is considerably less than would be suggested by the religious censuses. First, the censuses lead to a downplaying of the number of essentially irreligious people. Second, people in certain denominations play a disproportionate

role in leading the community. A survey of the religious affiliations of congressmen in 1972 gives some suggestive data in this
regard. As expected, Episcopalians were greatly overrepresented.
Their primary areas of strength were eastern Virginia-Maryland-
Delaware, Colorado-Wyoming, lower Hudson Valley, Connecticut, and Washington's Puget Sound. There were no Episcopal
congressmen in California until well south of the Bay Area. In
some cases the correspondence to our regional and religious lines
was exact (for example, all five men representing Utah and
southeastern Idaho were Mormon, all four representatives of the
southern Louisiana coast were Catholic, as were the four from
southernmost Texas), but in other areas the correspondence was
fuzzier. Northern New England remained Protestant-dominated,
while in southern New England most representatives, but only two
of six senators, were Catholic.[9]

## Political Variation

In terms of the definition of culture adopted here (see Chap. I,
"Further Theoretical Considerations"), political behavior is a
special variety of the cultural behavior that distinguishes groups.
The first great exponent of a "sectional" explanation of American
behavior, Frederick Jackson Turner, was interested primarily in
voting behavior at the polls and in Congress. In addition to the
usual North-South distinction, he noted the differentiation of the
electorate into Eastern versus Western (or frontier) interests. This
approach has been criticized, and the sectional interests he noted
have been seen as rapidly disappearing with the passage of time.
Popularly, however, we continue to think in terms of his sections.
In the postwar period, several significant works have appeared on
sectional politics.[10] For the nation as a whole, the best theoretical
work on regional variation is that of Daniel Elazar, while on a
more popular level Kevin Phillips' *Emerging Republican Majority*
supports much of Elazar's work apparently without being aware
of it.[11]

Elazar finds three political cultures in the nation, with a number
of possible mixtures among them. The *moralistic* political culture

emphasizes the community, the search for the good society, idealism, even utopianism. Holders of this position are likely to be rigid and overbearing, whether they are promoting blue laws or extremely liberal and emancipated behavior. In societies with this subculture, everyone is expected to participate in politics, amateurs often attain high position, and no one is expected to take advantage of his office for private purposes. The *traditionalistic* political culture assumes a fixed hierarchical society. Politicians either belong to the elite or serve its interests. Political competition is slight and most people do not take part. However, this is Elazar's weakest category, for the elite paternalism he ascribes to it has often been absent in the South, in which he places the tradition. In some Southern areas, lack of participation and extremely individualistic and antigovernmental attitudes have been and are most characteristic.

Elazar's *individualistic* political culture really includes two subcultures that he fails to distinguish. Common to both is the idea that politics is a utilitarian device, and its achievements are necessarily compromises. However, given this, one variant of the individualistic tradition suggests that politicians should be professionals serving specialized functions—a Weberian technocratic and bureaucratic concept. In the second variant, although politics is also seen as an arena in which amateurs cannot and should not compete, politics is necessarily a "dirty game," with its players sold out to competing interests, including their own. Here compromise with evil is an accepted part of the political process. It is also confusing to the reader to note that "individualistic" political cultures are characterized by strong party organizations. "Political individualism" as popularly conceived is most likely to be present in the moralistic and traditional cultures. What Elazar means by "individualism," then, is that politics is not meant to serve the common interest, because *no* common interest is assumed to exist in an individualistic community. The individualism is that of the marketplace.

Leaving aside the confusions of his terminology, Elazar has courageously classified the nation in terms of these abstract definitions of political culture (Maps 10 and 11). Elazar has made a detailed personal study of political behavior in many places in the nation, including many more areas than those cited in *Cities of*

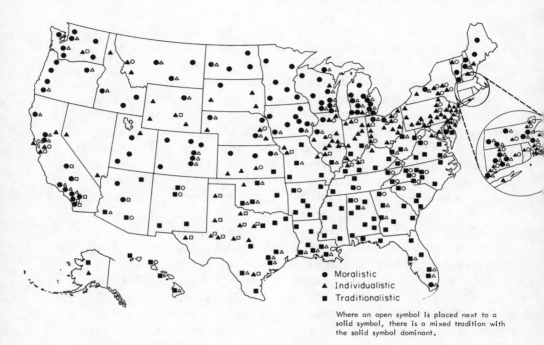

Where an open symbol is placed next to a
solid symbol, there is a mixed tradition with
the solid symbol dominant.

MAP 10. The Geography of Political Culture. Source: based on Daniel Elazar, *American Federalism*, 2nd ed. (New York: Thomas Y. Crowell, 1972), pp. 106–7

*the Prairie*, and he has a professional's knowledge of the literature. It is important, however, to note that Elazar has also made a detailed study of the movement of peoples into and within the country. Thus, his three "political cultures" reflect the three original colonial cultures, and more recent immigrants (or included peoples) are then grouped with these three. The classification by cultural "streams" is shown in Table 1.

The classification is productive and probably roughly correct. Particularly noteworthy is Elazar's suggestion that the good relations historically of Yankees and Scandinavians in Minneapolis and the poor relations of Yankees with Irish and Italians in Boston had a great deal to do with the fact that the political cultures of the people in Minneapolis were more similar than those in Boston. Because of correlations of national origin and religion, it is also reasonable to determine where peoples are largely by studies of religious affiliation.[12] However, when one

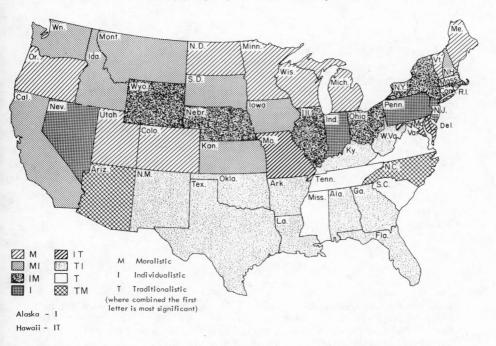

M   Moralistic

I   Individualistic

T   Traditionalistic
(where combined the first
letter is most significant)

Alaska – I

Hawaii – IT

MAP 11. Dominant Political Culture, by State. Source: based on Daniel Elazar, *American Federalism*, 2nd ed. (New York: Thomas Y. Crowell, 1972), p. 117

examines the completeness of the mapping of political cultures in Map 10 it appears that the knowledge of the background of the peoples in a particular place was used to determine its political culture as much as actual observation of political behavior. Map 10 is, then, a suggestive hypothesis as much as a report of findings.

Nevertheless, after the publication of Elazar's work, an attempt was made to see if the designations that Elazar gives to states in Maps 10 and 11 could be shown to result in statistically significant differences in political behavior. Even after controls were placed on per capita income, percent urban, and the region of the state, Elazar's designations showed some statistical significance, particularly in voter participation (naturally highest in moralistic cultural areas).[13]

In his study, *Midwest Politics*, John Fenton distinguishes between the "issue-oriented politics" of Michigan, Wisconsin, and Minnesota, and the "job-oriented politics" of Ohio, Indiana, and

TABLE 1
CULTURAL STREAMS AND POLITICAL CULTURES

| Native Streams | (Post-1800) European Streams | Political Cultures |
|---|---|---|
| Yankee | North Sea Anglo-Canadian Jewish | Moralistic |
| Middle | English Continental Irish | Individualistic |
| Southern | Mediterranean East European French-Canadian (Hispanic, Afro-American) | Traditionalistic |

NOTE: "North Sea" includes Scots, dissenting English of eastern and northern England, Dutch, all peoples around the Baltic, and some down the Rhine. "English" includes other English, Welsh, and Cornish. Source: adapted from Daniel Elazar, *Cities of the Prairie* (New York: Basic Books, 1970), pp. 166, 190, 474.

Illinois.[14] The definitions are not far from Elazar's. Fenton notes the differences in national and regional origins between these two areas, and the greater political interest and sophistication to the north. He then goes on, however, to state his amazement that Michigan, Wisconsin, and Minnesota should have evolved so similarly in recent years. He examines specific causes for this political pattern in the three states; in each he finds that since different parties do make a difference, issue-oriented politics has positive feedback for the electorate. Other than this cultural reinforcement and similar cultural origin, Fenton finds few commonalities among the three states.

Kevin Phillips' interest is in voter preference in national elections, but like Elazar he explains behavior primarily in cultural terms. Phillips uses both geographical and historical explanations of voter preference, with his main emphasis on the origin of the people in an area. Seen from this perspective, people do not blindly vote party labels for historical reasons, but vote in terms of very old regional allegiances. Phillips' concept of an "emerging

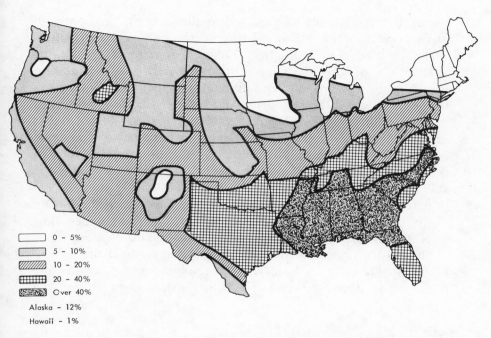

0 – 5%
5 – 10%
10 – 20%
20 – 40%
Over 40%

Alaska – 12%
Hawaii – 1%

**MAP 12. Wallace Vote Share. Source: based on Kevin P. Phillips, *The Emerging Republican Majority* (New Rochelle, N.Y.: Arlington House, 1969), p. 28**

Republican majority" is based on a shift of the old Northeast coast "establishment" from the Republican to Democratic parties, and a corresponding tendency of most of the rest of the nation to shift into the opposing camp.[15] Ideologically, as liberal causes tended increasingly to receive the endorsement of the Northeastern establishment, much of the rest of the country has looked for other havens; these often turn out to be the Republican party.

Phillips' map of the George Wallace vote share in the 1968 presidential election (Map 12) is a good reflection of the regional differentiations as we have mapped them (see Map 4), but it has a special set of meanings of its own. The Wallace vote represented differences in ideology, temperament, situation, and style. In part, Wallace appealed to people of Southern cultural background because of his accent and manner. As a populist, his appeal was widespread. He also had a special appeal to that segment of the public that had come suddenly into direct confrontation with black population growth in Northern urban areas. Nevertheless, where relationship to the New England core remained strong, Wallace's appeal fell on deaf ears. Upper north central, upstate New York, and New England also fall together if one considers the areas in which the Democrats did better vis-à-vis Republicans in 1968 than in 1960 (Map 13). Phillips' analysis suggests that some of the older areas of New England influence, such as the Mormon areas in the Mountain States, have lost a vital relation to the New England core, although the Southern style of Wallace is still not acceptable to them. The Wallace showing in the 1972 primaries might also be considered here. However, in the North, Wallace tried to change from Southern to Northern issues, thus diluting the significance of his vote as a regional indicator.

Phillips then goes on to describe the subregions of the United States on the basis of historical backgrounds and recent voting patterns. In the Northeast, he distinguishes three areas: the

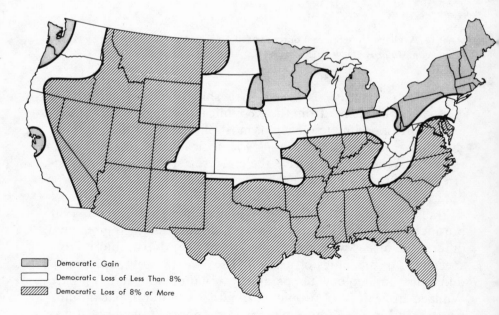

Democratic Gain
Democratic Loss of Less Than 8%
Democratic Loss of 8% or More

MAP 13. Democratic Presidential Vote, 1968 vs. 1960. Source: based on Kevin P. Phillips, *The Emerging Republican Majority* (New Rochelle, N.Y.: Arlington House, 1969), p. 29

megalopolis, the Yankee Northeast, and the non-Yankee Northeast (Map 14). The Yankee elite has so put its stamp on the
Yankee Northeast and the megalopolis it surrounds that this area
continues to attract the allegiance of Yankee-imprinted areas
throughout the nation, following whichever way it swings. Thus,
original forces and long-term allegiances are even more important
to Phillips than to Elazar. Today, the Democratic party is
increasing its strength in the Yankee area as it comes to be
identified with the establishment, but is losing its position in
non-Yankee areas. In megalopolis itself, ethnic differences are
probably more important than regional. However, even here
appeals to the Northern part of this megalopolis must be different
than to its Southern extension. The Wallace vote did not
significantly penetrate beyond the non-Yankee Northeast whether
within or without the lines of the megalopolis.

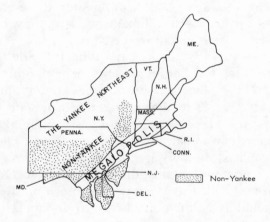

MAP 14. Political Regions of the Northeast. Source: based on Kevin P. Phillips,
*The Emerging Republican Majority* (New Rochelle, N.Y.: Arlington House,
1969), p. 47

Phillips found a continuation of patterns of voting in the South
that had been more elaborately described by V. O. Key a
generation earlier. If we look at the Wallace share of the vote, we
will find that the familiar division of the South into lowland,
upland, and mountain was reflected in the concentration of the

Wallace vote most decidedly in the lowland area, with less enthusiasm in the uplands, and least in the mountains (which incidentally has the least-educated population). However, in South Carolina the pattern was reversed and central Tennessee supported Wallace more strongly than the regional analysis would suggest. In general, the Atlantic seaboard "South" was less enthusiastic in its support of Wallace than areas farther west.

The traditionalist political pattern of the South is also found in Spanish American or Indian areas of the Interior Southwest, and some ethnic areas of large cities. It is paternalistic and antidemocratic where thoroughly institutionalized. Typical is the situation in the mountain counties of West Virginia and Kentucky, where expression of opposition to local bosses brings threat of retaliation. The critic will find the school bus no longer stops for his child, or free lunches are denied in the school.[16] In the recent past, threats of more vicious punishment, including assassination, were common in some areas against all who threatened the order. This is not to say that at its best traditionalism has not given some of the most acceptable government in the country.

In addition to Elazar's identification of the South with a traditionalist culture, the South presents several other marked characteristics. On a localistic-centralistic continuum, Elazar places most of the South in the most centralistic category. The South in this case includes Maryland (not West Virginia) and New Mexico. In the next most centralistic category, Elazar places most of the West, as well as Missouri, Illinois, Indiana, and Kentucky.[17] In another categorization, states allowing no re-election to the governorship are restricted to a nearly solid block of fifteen states in the South, including on the north Missouri, Indiana, Kentucky, West Virginia, and Pennsylvania.

Writing in 1964 on the basis of a tabulation of Southern foreign policy voting records in Congress, Charles O. Lerche, Jr., attempted to refine and even reverse the common assumption that the South was internationalist, particularly in contrast to Midwest isolationism.[18] He found that the South's internationalism was really founded on four factors: (1) the South's general historical position in favor of low tariffs, which at least until recently was in the economic interest of Southerners; (2) the strong feeling in favor of the military, and the acceptance of violence as a way to solve disputes; (3) the generally friendly disposition to help the British, for both historical and ethnic reasons; and (4) the particular attraction of the South to the policies of Woodrow Wilson, who was widely regarded as a Southern president. Lerche distinguishes this position from multilateralism. When America's international commitment moved more in the direction of helping the poor and colored peoples, and moved away from military power toward foreign economic aid, Southern internationalism declined, while internationalism in the Midwest rose relatively. The general antiforeign attitudes of the South are ascribed in a companion study of political attitudes by Alfred Hero to be based on a more pessimistic Southern view of man and a general Southern lack of experience with foreigners.[19]

The South is crosscut by further distinctions that should not be forgotten. For example, in 1960 northern Louisiana gave less than 30 percent of its vote to Kennedy, although it was a normally Democratic area, while southern Louisiana gave over 60 percent of its vote to Kennedy.[20] Religion and ethnic origin are not always strongly divisive in Louisiana, but they activated strong feelings in the 1960 election. The Germans of central Texas have remained a rural, Republican enclave since the Civil War, but they voted "wet" in prohibition times because they did not have cultural antecedents that would lead them to oppose the use of alcohol. The Mexican-American vote was largely manipulated in the past, but by the 1960s emerged as a definite force of its own. Together, however, Negroes and Mexicans number less than a fourth of the population of Texas.

The rise of the two-party system in the South, the more general enfranchisement of the Negro, the great increase in voter participation through elimination of the poll tax, and the general urbanization of the region makes it appear as though there is more change in the distinctiveness of Southern politics than has in fact occurred. The defection of white Democratic Southern congressmen from the national Democratic party accelerated in the 1950s and 1960s at the same time that the national Republican party was rejecting Northeastern direction in favor of a Southern strategy. The result has been the dislocation of old Democratic and Republican party allegiances and the increasing strength of third alternatives. The Republican party in parts of the South is taking over the old elite and business vote, which is now primarily a suburban vote, and may as a result lose the populist mountain Republican enclaves. The black vote is now solidly Democratic most places, with a resulting tendency to drive the populist white Democrats, still the great majority, into an unstructured and vacillating position. In many places, however, the apparently rapid accommodation of whites and blacks, as signaled by recent elections, may make possible the integration of Negro and white into the populist democracy at mass levels that the younger Tom Watson had hoped for, and in parallel a more respectable Negro-white union within the Republican party.

But this will not be simply a rejection of the old South. There are strengths in the black-white relationship in the South that in some ways make amity easier to achieve than in the North. Reducing the role of race may even make possible a renaissance of social distinctions. Interregional variations are generations deep: in Virginia the new Republican elite is likely to be most paternalistic, and this paternalism may be repeated in much of the lowland South; but as we move south and west or into the Uplands, we will find increasing individualism and primitive capitalist thinking among the elite and increasing independence, localism, and populism in the masses; in Texas, localism is again replaced by truly statewide politics.

As a whole, Southern politics has revolved around the Negro issue since before the Civil War.[21] The South supported the Democratic party for a hundred years because the Republicans had fought secession and because of Republican rule in the Reconstruction period. Many of the counties in the Mountain South that had opposed secession developed a Republican tradition. In general the Upland South had opposed secession in 1860–61 (Map 15); although largely Democratic, this region has maintained interests different from those of the Lowland South ever since. Populism, Protestantism, and prohibition have always been important Southern issues, but these issues have been decisive with voters in the Democratic Upland more than with white voters in lowland areas with Negro majorities. In the 1928 election, the lowlands supported Catholic and wet Al Smith; they could not allow any issue to shake their Democratic allegiance and its guarantee of continual white supremacy in black majority

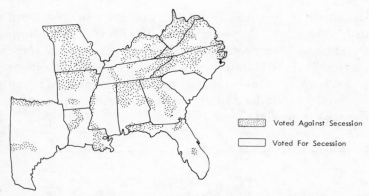

Voted Against Secession

Voted For Secession

MAP 15. Support for Secession, 1860–61. Source: based on Paul Aikman, "Southern Counties, Secession and Voting Patterns" (master's thesis, University of Washington, 1963), p. 185, and Ralph Wooster, *The Secession Conventions of the South* (Princeton, N.J.: Princeton University Press, 1962), pp. 50, 81, 102, 122, 138, 174, 206, 224

areas. To the Upland voter religion and morality were more important and he supported Herbert Hoover. In neither area did voters simply cling to party labels; they voted according to what they conceived to be a correct balance of interests and ideology.

In 1948, the Dixiecrats split off from the regular Democratic party and were supported in the lowlands. Lowlanders felt that since the national Democratic party no longer guaranteed their racial position, it must be defended in other ways. Map 16 illustrates the relation of race to the Dixiecrat vote in Arkansas, and Key shows similar relations elsewhere in the South. It is useful to also compare Map 16 with the division of Arkansas at secession (Map 15). The Dixiecrat area also provided the heart of support in the South for Barry Goldwater (Republican) in 1964 and George Wallace (Independent) in 1968. Of course, the vote for the latter candidates was made more complex by the fact that support for them was also generated in the South and nationally by nonracial issues with which Southern political leaders and voters also agreed.

Since today no national party offers guarantees on race, other issues must determine Southern white allegiances, even in Negro majority areas. The result has been the emergence of an effective Republican party in nearly all parts of the South. The rise of

Negro participation in the South on the side of Northern Democrats has polarized the white lowland South vote away from the Democratic party in presidential elections. In 1968 in some Southern states, Hubert Humphrey's vote was primarily a Negro vote. On the other hand, the continual decline in percent black in most of the South has reduced the regional intensity of the issue and nationalized it instead.

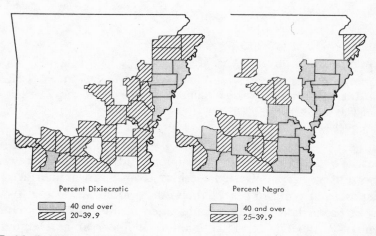

Percent Dixiecratic

40 and over
20–39.9

Percent Negro

40 and over
25–39.9

MAP 16. Relation of Percent Negro to Dixiecrat Vote in Arkansas, 1948. Source: based on V. O. Key, Jr., *Southern Politics in State and Nation* (New York: Knopf, 1949), p. 343

In the Midwest Phillips notes the New England influence in the North, extensions of Southern cultures elsewhere, and several different ethnic votes. He can point, for example, to the continuing influence of New England, German, lowland Southern, and mountain Southern cultures in rural counties of Missouri (Republican percentages by county ranging from 20 to 80 percent). Farther North, Norwegian and German communities have continued to vote very differently when issues affecting their European homelands are involved.

In the Far West Phillips divides the coastal states into a Northern Pacific belt stretching down to Santa Barbara, an interior belt east of that, and southern California. Only the Northern Pacific area is still dominated by the Northeastern core establishment. In 1960 both Oregon and California voted for Nixon. However, in California relatively heavily Catholic San Francisco County, Oakland (Alameda and Contra Costa counties), and Los Angeles voted for Kennedy; in Protestant Oregon, urban counties were all for Nixon, with only some rural counties voting for Kennedy. This was a party year, and Oregon was still voting in the old Republican, New England tradition. The next presidential election, in 1964, was ideological. Both states voted for Johnson. However, in southern California, Orange and San Diego counties supported Goldwater. In Oregon Goldwater was the victor in only two rural counties.[22]

Qualitatively there is an immense difference in both parties between elected leaders in the Pacific Northwest and those in California. California's Democratic leaders seem to cover a wider spectrum than in the Northwest, while on both state and national levels Northwest Republicans are much more liberal than those of California—Washington and Oregon Republicans are often to the left of their Democratic opponents. Many of California's Republicans remind us of Texas, those of the Pacific Northwest of Massachusetts. Elazar's map of political cultures (Map 10) gives part of the reason why, but the differences are in fact more than the map suggests.

In spite of the evidence, serious students of American voting habits or of opinion polls have often concluded that all Americans are pretty much alike, with regional differences of very little importance.[23] Most recently, Richard Scammon and Ben Wattenberg have written an excellent work on the American voter which both ignores and rejects any significant attention to regionalism.[24] The reasons for this difference of opinion are severalfold. First, opinion poll data used to supplement election results are generally available only in gross regional terms. Small national poll samples force aggregation into not more than the four census regions. However, when the country is divided into four regions, the parts seem more similar than they are. The South is the most homogeneous of these four regions, but even here Delaware and Maryland are lumped with Mississippi, the Republican mountain counties of Kentucky with the Mexican-American counties on the Rio Grande.

DeGrazia's discussion offers a good example of improper

aggregation. A generation ago he concluded on the basis of regional figures for the West that "rural-urban differences . . . are relatively unimportant," for his evidence showed that the association in much of the nation of rural areas with Republican majorities and of cities with Democratic majorities did not hold for the West. But this conclusion was only possible because of the diversity of the region the Bureau of the Census calls the "West." If deGrazia had examined his voting figures on as crude a basis as the comparison of state averages, he would have seen a different pattern. In general, the southern West was Democratic and the northern West was Republican. In Utah, Colorado, New Mexico, and Wyoming, the rural-urban difference was in the expected national direction of a more Republican hinterland, while in California there was a significant relationship in the opposite direction (Republican strength in the cities and Democratic strength in rural areas).[25] His conclusion comes from improper aggregation; since he was not thinking in terms of an adequate analysis of regions, he did not ask the right questions of his material. In addition to mistakes of aggregation, answers to polling questions are often in terms of a local context that makes them incomparable on a national basis. In 1968 Wallace in Alabama and Humphrey in Minnesota both spoke of doing "more for the Negro" but had very different "mores" in mind.

Statistical relationships between political and social factors may be either strengthened or spuriously erased by ignoring regional (cultural) effects. As two writers recently pointed out in criticism of such a study:

The differences are so great between the South and the rest of the country and the Southern states so homogeneous on many of the measures used . . . that [we are] often dealing with two distinct populations. When regions cluster in this way the correlations . . . often reflect only the social and political distinctiveness of geographical regions within the country rather than the functional relationship between variables.[26]

Although there is a growing realization of this fact, regionalism in political analysis is restricted by the necessity to consider states as units, and by the difficulty of defining the best regional breakdown for the issue in question.[27]

Ira Sharkansky has recently made an effort to determine

explicitly and statistically the effect of regional variation on the political behavior of states.[28] His approach confined him to regions defined by states, and he largely used the regional distinctions of others as his basis. However, Sharkansky considered simultaneously a variety of different and overlapping groups of states defined as regions. His most important findings showed the independence of many forms of regional variation from economic or urbanization indicators. Regional influence is especially strong on voter turnout, party competition, and education and welfare expenditures.[29] Sharkansky also found that the regions with the greatest intraregional uniformity were Great Lakes, Upper Middle West, and Mountain.[30] The Upper Middle West (Michigan, Wisconsin, Minnesota, and North Dakota) was slightly more uniform than the Great Lakes region (Michigan, Wisconsin, Ohio, Illinois, and Indiana). The Mountain region included Colorado, Wyoming, Montana, Idaho, and Utah. The least uniform regions were the largest (as expected) and the Far West, although New England also scored surprisingly low. Sharkansky found considerable variation in state government expenditure per one thousand dollars of personal income, and particularly noted seven states (the special region of New Jersey, Pennsylvania, Ohio, Indiana, Illinois, Missouri, and Nebraska) that have had very low rates of expenditures both recently and in the past.[31]

Factoring out the effect of economic variation, Sharkansky found the New England region to be remarkable for low state taxes, amateurish large legislatures, and local emphasis.[32] Public educational expenditure was low because of the importance of private schools (including Catholic). The Middle Atlantic was low on voter turnout and mental test scores, with high reliance on income tax and borrowing. The Great Lakes region showed high political competition and low per capita income tax and indebtedness. The Upper Middle West showed a high reliance on property and personal income tax, emphasis on local governments, and generous welfare payments. Plains states relied heavily on local property taxes. The Mountain states showed high scores on party competition, voter turnout, and spending, generous welfare payments, and high educational performance combined with small, poorly paid legislatures. The South scored low on voter turnout, party competition, and services in education and welfare. It relied little on the income tax, but had very active state legislatures and more centralization. Property tax was relatively unimportant. The border regions of the South resembled the South but scored relatively high on welfare services. Sharkansky argued that the border states are less transitional in the sense of change from South to North than they were representative of a continuing central state tradition.[33] I would argue that they are not so much changing to Northern patterns as simply mixed with Northern peoples.

Looking ahead, Sharkansky acknowledged tendencies for regional patterns to be erased. However, he distinguished between factors that are more subject to rationalizing influences and those that are less so. Where the federal government is deeply involved, as in highway construction, there will be more rationalization or homogenization; where federal activity is uncommon, as in party competition, regional patterns will tend to be maintained. Sharkansky especially noted the tendency of state and local officials to look for models to copy or compare themselves with in neighboring localities and states rather than further afield.[34]

In conclusion, political differentiation by region is probably one of the liveliest areas of continuing difference in the country. Not only do historical allegiances continue to be reflected in political behavior, but the sectional interests of different parts of the country continue to be diverse.

# Housing and Settlement Styles

There has been little scholarly study of variation in house styles west of the Mississippi, nor are there studies of current variation in styles. Casual observation suggests that styles of housing vary widely in the West and that there is still considerable variation nationally. Some variation is due to differences in climate and soil conditions or the availability of materials. The flat-roofed adobe of the Southwest is only possible in an area of little precipitation. The absence of basements in much of the South seems to be related to ground-water conditions, although this pattern is preserved where ground water is not a problem. (Persistences of previous cultural forms of this kind in new environments is common. For example, because of differences in cultural background we find stilt houses in Northeast Thailand in a dry area while in the Mekong Delta Vietnamese build on the ground.) In recent years developers in the East have built more "colonial" styles, while those of the Far West have built more contemporary houses. In the Puget Sound area of the Pacific Northwest there is a relatively large number of unpainted modern wooden houses and apartment buildings.

Fred Kniffen has recently summarized data on the distribution of folk housing styles in the period 1790–1850.[35] He establishes three centers of diffusion: New England, Middle Atlantic, and Lower Chesapeake. As house styles became dominant in each area, they tended to diffuse to the West (or Southwest in the case of the last two) during their period of dominance and for a few decades after, being replaced in turn by a new wave from the center of diffusion, which might have derived its new styles from England or the continent. New Englanders, building frame rather than log structures from a very early date, developed clapboarding or siding. While the New England barn style evolved little in its passage westward, house styles went through a series of modifications. First was a two-room-deep, two-story, massive, central-chimney house. This was followed by the Georgian house of the middle of the eighteenth century, formed from a central hall with chimneys at both ends. Later in the century the story and a half with central chimney became common. In the nineteenth century the classical revival led to the quite different style of frontward-facing gable with two full stories and side wings. It is significant that the distribution of the traditional New England town style for housing and public buildings such as churches was determined after 1797 in large part by the distribution of a building manual called *The Country Builder's Assistant* (see fig. 1).[36]

Middle Atlantic styles developed in the vicinity of Philadelphia and expanded over a very large region to the west and south. At their farthest expanse Middle Atlantic derivatives dominated an area from central Indiana to central Alabama. The use of logs as a mode of construction and the "I-house" were important contributions of this tradition. In this area it was the barn style that tended to evolve while the house styles were more stable.

The difficulties of adding on to a log house had a great deal to do with determining design, for many houses in this area consisted of a basic log room with enlargements. In the first extension another room might be added to the chimney end of the house forming a central chimney house with duplicate sides. Another common solution was the "dogtrot" style in which another cabin was placed one room's distance from the first, with a covered passage connecting the two (eventually the passage might become a room). This required two chimneys, one at each end (see fig. 2).

While the I-house of the Middle Atlantic region could have any number of additions, the basic style was rectangular, two stories high, one room deep, and more than one room in length. The gables were at the ends. Any type of materials might be used, and often the I-house shape was achieved through addition to the basic log cabin of the extensions described above. While there was much mixture of styles in the West, a version of the Middle Atlantic I-house became characteristic of nineteenth-century Mormon housing.[37]

Several other distinctive house styles were developed in the colonial period in the Middle Atlantic region. While log construction was used on the frontier, more developed farmhouses were often of brick or stone as opposed to New England's continued use of wood. There were two main Dutch styles developed in the New York Metropolitan region. One had a steep roof with flat-sided gables and chimneys at each end, and the other had a roof with two slopes of different pitch on either side of the ridge (a form often copied in "Dutch Colonial" today). In Pennsylvania the use of "pent roofs" or secondary roofs above the lower floors of a house with two or more stories was characteristic. "Dutch styles" from the New York area are also responsible for the characteristic porch of American house forms.[38]

The basic German Pennsylvania log barn was similar to the simple log houses of the region, and might be extended by similar additions. Moving south and west of Pennsylvania the barn decreased in size, being no longer so commonly used as an area for threshing or the housing of animals. In later years frame construction replaced logs without altering the fundamental construction.

The Tidewater South of Lower Chesapeake Bay origin had a

frame tradition and even half-timbering from an early date. Here
the evolved English cottage was the basic form. The cottage
consisted of a structure one room deep, two in length, one or one
and one-half stories high, with exterior end chimneys. It commonly had a covered front porch (see fig. 3). Additions to the rear
might duplicate the original construction on a smaller scale,
ending up with a rather cumbersome four-chimney creation.
Farther south, the structure was frequently raised on piles.
Although there was mixture along the Middle Atlantic–Southern
border around Chesapeake Bay, the line between Tidewater and
Upland South (Middle Atlantic tradition), and between frame and
log structure, was generally sharp. Barn styles, however, were
borrowed from England in the Chesapeake Bay area and from the
Upland South farther down. A distinctive Louisiana French folk
house style was the creole house with paired front doors, inset
porch, and central chimney.[39]

Although encompassing the entire area of "material folk
culture," a recent study by Henry Glassie emphasizes variations in
folk architecture on a basis similar to that of Kniffen.[40] In general,
Glassie sees more continuity than Kniffen between Lowland and
Upland South, but more of a break along the Ohio River between
South and North. Thus, Glassie distinguishes North, Mid-Atlantic, Midwest, Upland South, and Lowland South regions. It is
particularly interesting to note that he suggests a division between
the Mid-Atlantic and Upland South much as we have drawn in
our regionalization between the Pennsylvanian and Southern
regions (Map 4).

Moving away from folk styles, the plantation styles of the South
produced extended and even detached house plans. In terms of
formal architecture, it has been noted that "Jeffersonian classi-
cism" as evidenced in Jefferson's own work at Monticello and the
University of Virginia was confined in its influence to the "South"
and the extensions of the "South" as we define them rather than in
Kniffen's analysis.[41] Unlike the Georgian colonial and Adams
styles of the North and Middle Atlantic of the period, the
Jeffersonian classical style led to templelike forms. Brick was the
favored material, as it has generally remained in much of the
South. Although based on Roman rather than Greek models,
Jeffersonian suggests the Greek period that followed. Greek

revival was a national movement, but it had greater impact and lasted longer in the South (see fig. 9). The French plantation houses near New Orleans formed a distinct variant of Southern plantation architecture with French windows, immense two-story galleries, and often a railing around the top reminiscent of the New England "captain's walk."

The characteristic Southern middle- and upper-class styles of the Georgian and Greek revival period were carried westward wherever Southerners went. For example, brick or stone rural mansions of this type follow the line of Southern advance into Kentucky and southern Indiana (Madison). In this movement the Upland South (Middle Atlantic) folk tradition was overwhelmed among the well-to-do by Lowland South plantation traditions.

Later styles were developed for or had their main influence in definite areas. The "Eastlake style" (a particular version of Queen Anne showing what could be done with a lathe, a chisel, and a gouge) was popular in the West. Shingle style (a conservative Queen Anne, covered with shingles to give a New England colonial effect) was most influential in New England, but spread wherever New England styles were copied. The plain "commercial" style of many-storied buildings for business was especially popular in Chicago and the Midwest around the turn of the century. Frank Lloyd Wright's "Prairie style" was developed for the Midwest, although it was applied to designs for the Interior Southwest and Pacific Northwest. Emphasizing wide eaves, long horizontal lines, and enclosed gardens, it often appears as a rather heavy adaptation of certain Japanese forms. What we think of as "Wrightian" today was an extreme development of this style under international style influence—the result being a form that seems most adapted to the Southwest regions. A "Western stick style" and the closely related Bay Region style developed in California from a variety of influences and continues to be very influential. It was based on "simple lines, integration of outdoors and indoors, concern for view, a free flow of space, and the use of stone and textured materials." [42] Reflecting both naturalism and the local context, it was to be covered with unpainted shingles and have exposed structural members on the ceilings.

Architectural styles reflecting Spanish and Indian influence developed in certain areas and have had a regionally defined spread since.[43] Several varieties of this tradition should be distinguished: the "Monterey style" of California mixed New England and Spanish concepts to produce a two-story structure with a roofed balcony on the second level. Beginning in Monterey, California, before 1850, the style has continued to have a limited popularity in California. The "Spanish mission style," in decline at the middle of the nineteenth century, was revived later and widely imitated in California but very little beyond, although there is a more general "Spanish colonial style" found from California through Texas. The Santa Fe or "Spanish-Pueblo style" developed in California and the core area of the Interior Southwest has been an indigenous and regionally effective extension of the past in the latter area. Mixing Indian, Spanish, and occasionally modern tradition, it remains exotic outside of the Southwest (see figs. 20, 21, 25, 26).

Throughout the United States a more sophisticated and eclectic "Mediterranean style" was widely spread in this country in the 1920s. However, even at the height of its popularity, the Mediterranean style was not often found outside of the Pacific Coast, Interior Southwest, Texas, and Florida. Houses are seldom built anywhere in this mode today, even in areas such as California and Florida to which it is best adapted. While the Mediterranean style was commonly employed, often quite successfully, in finer houses of the Pacific Northwest, Spanish-Pueblo and Monterey styles are almost absent in this region.

On a more prosaic level, two types of developments characteristic of California spread from California to much of the country, but hardly to all of it. The "ranch house" and its modern adaptations seem to go back to Spanish Californian, and possibly Tidewater (see figs. 3, 26); but it can also be seen as a bungalow with the long side toward the street.[44] The style spread over most of the country. Based originally on a Bengal colonial style, the ill-defined bungalow reached its peak of popularity in California, but spread widely and unevenly.[45] Differences in the styles of builders' houses from one part of the country to another are, however, largely quantitative. One suspects that the various forms of New England "colonial" and "Cape Cod" are most common in New England and least in California, while the opposite would be true of the ranch and bungalow patterns. The

South would be likely to have a higher percentage of tract Greek Revival and perhaps English styles.

A statistical attempt to analyze folk housing in the 1930s examined 3,464 rural houses from southern Wisconsin to southern Texas in 1940. The authors found about 35 percent of the houses to be of types well represented everywhere (bungalows and one-story T-houses). About 20 percent of the houses represented types largely confined to the northern part of the cross section (a variety of two-story houses, including the pyramid), while about 40 percent were types mostly confined to the South (all one-story and small—three boarded up and down types [cf. fig. 14] and the log cabin).[46] Differences were traced to greater poverty in the South and differential availability of materials (for example, composition roofs in the North, wood shingle and metal in the South). A survey of all houses today would continue to reflect certain other variables depending on an intersection of climate and soil conditions with local expectations of what a house should be. For example, the cellar continues to be much more common in the North from the Pacific to the Atlantic oceans, as are many-storied houses and sharply pitched roofs. The basis for a survey of house styles and variations by regions has been developed, but as far as the author is aware there is no survey of this type available for recent urban and suburban housing.[47]

Contemporary house styles reflecting minority traditions such as Wrightian and Bay Region have been accepted most thoroughly along the Pacific Coast and in Arizona.[48] In the Pacific Northwest a variety of contemporary house styles in unpainted cedar is found widely, with related combinations in the more expensive builder developments.[49] However, contemporary architecture beyond housing has tended to be characterized by a uniformity of contemporary styling.[50]

Paralleling the distribution of housing styles has been the distribution of settlement patterns. Most generally rural settlement in America has been characterized by highly dispersed independent dwellings (figs. 12, 13, 14, 18), with primary exceptions in New England, among religious communities and in the Spanish and Indian communities (especially of the Southwest) (figs. 20, 22, 23).

In summarizing the evidence, Glenn Trewartha writes that

"Seventeenth Century New England . . . was described by Edmund Burke as a mosaic of little village republics. Virginia and the other planter colonies of the South exemplified almost equally well the dispersed variety [of settlement]. In the Middle Colonies the types were intermingled, though isolated farmsteads predominated." [51] The New England community was constructed as a unit. A group of people either in England or the older towns of New England banded together and petitioned for land. Once granted, the town land was divided by the group, with each family provided with a home lot (one to five acres) and a farm consisting of several parcels of land. There was usually common land for pasture and wood lot (all farms were common land in the winter). Patterns varied considerably depending on the field systems the individuals were used to in England, but generally the more cooperative open field systems lost out.[52] Farms were not of equal size, especially in the first century. Men who had contributed more to the setting up of the community financially or organizationally, or would contribute more in the future, received more, as did those with larger families. Later other families or individuals were allowed to join, but soon many towns were considered complete, and newcomers had to go elsewhere.

In the seventeenth century land was not considered a source of profit in New England as it was almost universally in other colonies. The colonizing organizations granted land to groups, not individuals. The groups had often been congregations or neighborhoods in England or, as New England expanded westward, in the older sections of New England. In an attempt to exclude outsiders, land speculation was frowned upon by town officials. Religion, as well as the relatively difficult agriculture, with its emphasis on self-sufficiency rather than a cash crop, helped to preserve community patterns, as they were to do later in Mormon Utah.[53]

Trewartha's model was increasingly disregarded with time and westward movement (cf. figs. 5 and 14). Towns were larger and people began to live on their farms. Nevertheless, New Englanders migrating in the nineteenth century repeated many elements of the early pattern. They often settled townships in the west in organized groups, being careful to set aside land for the support of church and school in the initial land division.[54] Perhaps the most explicit echo of seventeenth-century New England was in the pattern of settlement adopted by Mormon leaders of New England background. However, we must remember that the Mormon communities were set up according to an ideal plan directly related to other ideal plans of its day rather than to New England.

According to Joseph Smith's original model, "the village plot was to be one mile square, with each block containing ten acres [twenty lots to the block]. . . . A large block in the center was set aside for public buildings as the bishop's storehouse, meeting houses, temples and schools. The city would contain about 1,000 family units. . . . Outside the city would be farms." The central square with public buildings is more Midwestern than New England (see below). However, as in New England, the Mormon town allowed for common pasturing of fields after harvest. Note that the ideal town would be well above the census definition of urban (twenty-five hundred persons).[55] Whatever its size, this was a town structure that allowed for a more civilized life than was generally possible on the frontier. In establishing colonies in Utah and elsewhere in the West, the Mormons moved in groups and were provided home lots and farms in an organized fashion, if not strictly in accord with the model.[56]

Although the Pennsylvania Germans often came from organized European communities, the ability to purchase land cheaply as individuals, and the lack of common town lands in Pennsylvania, led to large farms of several hundred acres with the settler living in the middle. William Penn's moderate schemes to locate settlers close together at the edges of their domains still produced a scattered community, and were often ignored in any event.

Farther south, Virginia started without either individual ownership or agriculture. The people, largely male workers, lived in stockaded villages. Gradually small farms were allowed to develop outside the stockades. With the working out of indentures, elimination of the Indian threat, and the establishment of private rights to land, individuals fanned out to take up as much land as possible. Often the value of land was for production of a commercial crop, tobacco, rather than for the variety of uses of mixed agriculture. In early Virginia water transportation did not make even trading towns necessary. In the eighteenth century the better lands came into the hands of large plantations using Negro labor, a type of more compact settlement grew up around the mansion, and the estates became largely self-sustaining. The smaller farmers became overseers or moved west to new lands.

In the West that de Tocqueville describes in 1830, movement was chaotic and interest in land largely speculative.[57] However, there were differences between a settlement stemming from New England and one with a Southern background. As Ellen Semple says of the peopling of the West on the Northern frontier:

The New York, New England and German elements brought with them the staid, contracted ideals of the Atlantic seaboard and of Europe; they tended to settle moderate and equal-sized farms on the uplands between streams, put solid improvements on their land, reflecting sedentary purpose, while only a slow, compact protrusion of their frontier registered their advance at the cost of the wilderness.[58]

In the Carolinas and Georgia a number of religious or other planned, compact settlements developed at first. If the people were from a homogeneous ethnic and religious community, as of Friends, Germans, or Swiss in the Carolinas, they succeeded. However, the community approach to settlement was generally short-lived. The ease of getting land for oneself on the frontier was supported by the desire of the feudal grantees to get a return for their investment (or opportunity). The more settlers, the more return. People were encouraged to settle wherever they wished, and scattered small farms became the pattern followed by most of the South outside of plantations (cf. figs. 12 and 13).

Rather than looking at the overall patterns of settlement, consideration of certain specific aspects may be rewarding. In a recent article Richard Pillsbury has used the street patterns of towns in Pennsylvania as a basis for cultural mapping.[59] He distinguishes an irregular, a linear, a linear-R, and a rectilinear town. On this basis he suggests four subregions for Pennsylvania: Northern, Southwestern, Southeastern, and Central and Western. These reflect both the period of primary settlement and the type of people settling. For example, the New Englanders of the Northern tier of counties developed almost entirely an irregular form of settlement (cf. figs. 1, 4, and ultimately 24).

Of more general relevance is a recent study of the distribution of county seats with business firms facing a courthouse square situated in the middle of town. This is a pattern apparently of Pennsylvania origin which spread south and west in the eighteenth and nineteenth centuries. While very common in the Central Midwest, Upland and Western South, this form of organization was never accepted in the Upper Midwest; although there were courthouse squares in the Upper Midwest, they were not placed in the center of town.[60]

## Dialect Regions

Perhaps the most carefully studied cultural variations by region in the United States have been those of dialect. While the general outlines of differences are clear, the correct classifications and demarcations are still subject to dispute. Today scholarly attention is directed more toward class or other vertical differences, particularly since these differences often have more direct application to English teaching in the large cities. It is important to note, however, that the most important of these vertical dimensions, the black/white distinction in the central cities, is to a degree a Southern/General American dialect distinction.

The most common, baseline discussion of dialect differences recognizes seven dialects: (1) East New England, (2) New York City, (3) Mid-Atlantic, (4) Western Pennsylvania, (5) Southern Mountain, (6) Southern, and (7) General American.[61]

The dialect of East New England is focused on Boston and is largely found east of the Connecticut River and the Green Mountains of Vermont. It is characterized by distinguishing the vowel in "hot" (as in "ought") and "top" from the "broad a" in "father." But unlike most of the country, the broad a is used in "pass," "fast," and "grass," while "r" is dropped except before vowels (for example, in "car" or "hard"). The dialect of New York City is largely confined to the metropolitan area. The "r" is generally also lost here, but distinctively "curl" and "third" become "coil" and "thoid" in common speech. The Mid-Atlantic area focuses on Philadelphia, and covers southeastern Pennsylvania, southern New Jersey, and parts of Maryland. The first vowels of "forest" and "closet" are both pronounced like the first vowel of "father." The dialect of western Pennsylvania is very close to General American, but the area does not distinguish the pronunciation of "cot" and "caught" as is general, but not universal, elsewhere. Outside of western Pennsylvania this dialect is found in bordering counties of West Virginia and Maryland. The Southern Mountain dialect includes most of Kentucky and Tennessee and other fringe areas. A mixture of Southern and General American, the "r" is generally pronounced in Southern Mountain, or at the least more so than in the rest of the South. The Lowland Southern dialect omits the "r" even more generally than East New England. However, lowland Southern does not have New England's special vowels in "hot" and "top" and does not use the broad a in "grass" and "dance." The Southern dialect characteristically uses diphthongs ("yes" becoming "ye-as," "class" becomes "kla-yes"). In addition, final consonants in consonant clusters may be dropped ("find" becomes "fin' ").

Begun in 1930 and not yet complete, the *Linguistic Atlas* project has spawned a wide variety of studies of dialectical differences in pronunciation, grammar, and word usage in the United States. The dialect regions the leaders of this project have differentiated are somewhat different from those above. The major regions differentiated may be summarized as:

1. Northern
   a. Eastern New England (several dialects)
   b. New York City
   c. Inland Northern (subdialects at eastern edge)
2. Midland
   a. Eastern (subdialects)
   b. Western
3. Southern
   a. Eastern (subdialects)
   b. Mountain Upland (dialects)
   c. Central
   d. Western[62]

This classification of the atlas project differs from the first one above because of a different approach and interest. Atlas analysts were concerned with the use of different words for the same meaning and different pronunciations for the same word as one moves from area to area. Their interest has been more antiquarian, with concentration on questioning older rural people of little education.[63] The fact that most people in an area might today use a general American word, particularly in cultivated speech, was less significant to them than that a few remembered an ancient regional usage. As the linguistic atlas work proceeded westward, it focused on the traces of earlier migrations from different parts of the original thirteen colonies. Had this not been the focus, "General American" would have seemed a more acceptable way to describe the common speech of much of the country than they considered it.

It is particularly important to notice that the growth of uniformity in American speech has not been the product of any great city's dominance. General American standard has borrowed features from all the regional dialects, being closest to a mixture of the *Linguistic Atlas'* "Inland Northern" with "North Midland." The relatively low prestige of big-city pronunciation styles is related to the fact that Americans have generally distrusted the city, and particularly New York City, the national economic and cultural center. It may be noted that in a detailed study of the dialect of New York City, it was found that white New Yorkers thought that their dialect was laughed at elsewhere. As a result, middle-class white New Yorkers avoided New York dialect as much as possible. Blacks, on the other hand, liked New York speech (and especially disliked Southern dialect). Another sign of the rejection of New York speech by white society is its inability to penetrate very far even into the city's suburbs.[64]

The regions of the *Linguistic Atlas* are based on the coincidence of "isoglosses." Isoglosses are lines on a map that demarcate the prevalence of one usage from another. For each usage there will be a different isogloss. For example, in the Middle West the use of the term "corn pone" has an isogloss considerably north of that for the grammatical expression "seed" as the past tense of "see" in uneducated speech. However, isogloss lines are not distributed at random. Where many isoglosses fall fairly close together, we can speak of a linguistic boundary.

Particular isoglosses seem of greater importance than others because of their broad and continuing importance in American language. For example, Midland, Inland Northern, and most of the Southern Mountain area preserve the "r" in speech. This has been traced to the fact that the "r" was preserved in the speech of

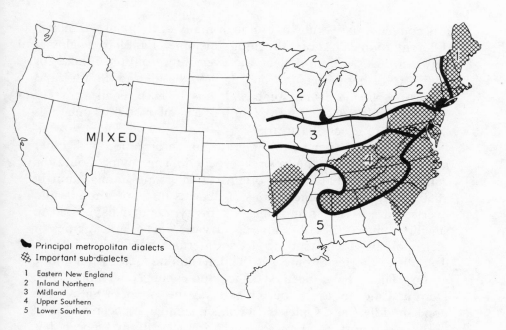

Principal metropolitan dialects
Important sub-dialects

1  Eastern New England
2  Inland Northern
3  Midland
4  Upper Southern
5  Lower Southern

MAP 17. Dialects. Source: based on Jean Malmstrom and Annabel Ashley, *Dialects-USA* (Champaign, Ill.: National Council of Teachers of English, 1963), p. 43, and other sources

Northern England, Scotland, and Ireland in the seventeenth and eighteenth centuries, but not in the south of England. The early colonists in New England and the South Atlantic coast were almost entirely from the south of England, but the Friends near Philadelphia and the Scotch-Irish who expanded rapidly in central Pennsylvania came from areas that had preserved the "r." The fact that the Scotch-Irish were the first over the mountains and dominated the early expansion of so wide an area—as well as providing Presbyterian and Methodist preachers to New York and even New England—probably accounts for "r" being retained in standard American speech.[65] Pronouncing "r" in most positions is now moving into areas where it was formerly uncommon, such as New York City.[66]

The line for the northern extension of the use of "you-all" approximates the Mason-Dixon line, or the edge of "the South" as it is conventionally known, although many of the regional dialect differentiations do not fall along this line. Familiar isoglosses between the Northern dialect and everything south are those for "pail" (Northern) versus "bucket" (Midland and South) and "greasy" (Northern and some of Pennsylvania) versus "greazy" (most of Midland and South). South of a similar isogloss one finds "barn lot" replaces "barnyard."

Map 17 is an attempt to integrate this information with other maps published in the references cited. This map should be compared with that for the origins of interstate immigration in 1850 (Map 1). The penetrations of dialects into one another and overlaps are obscured in a map of this type, but I have tried to suggest some of these by different devices.[67] The largest cities or metropolitan areas tend to have internal dialect boundaries, described in terms of blocks if the determining factor is an ethnic group. There have been specific studies of New York City, Detroit, Chicago, and other cities from this point of view.[68] An upper-middle-class, somewhat bookish, standard speech will tend also to be most common in such areas, and this speech has become widely accepted in the Far West.[69]

The longest-lasting non-English speech community outside of Spanish-American has been the Pennsylvania German ("Dutch") community and its colonies in the Midwest. While the dialectical German of these people is dying, the English of the surrounding area has been considerably influenced. Ethnic speech mannerisms seem to be able to carry on for generations after loss of the original language in Jewish, Slavic, Scandinavian, and other communities, as long as the majority of people in daily intercourse in a locality remains the same.[70]

Negro speech in the United States has often been described as a variant or a group of variants of the common or uneducated Southern dialect (or of several Southern dialects). In the North these speech patterns may tend to collapse into Negro dialects distinguished along class lines and preserving special features not found in any white dialect. Other investigators feel that Negro speech is better described as a pidgin dialect with a clear and early separation from white dialects that it only superficially resembles. One Negro dialect, Gullah, spoken on the South Carolina coast, has preserved a large number of Africanisms in vocabulary and form, handling English in a manner analogous to the Negro pidgin languages of the Caribbean.[71]

West of the Mississippi Valley the population is less settled, and language traditions are more mixed. Texas is almost exclusively a mixture of Southern and South Midland dialects, with South Midland dominant, especially in north Texas. New Mexico and Oklahoma are probably heavily under South Midland influence, with Arizona less so because of recent immigration from California and the Northeast. Study of Colorado speech has shown South Midland influences in the south contrasted with North Midland and even Northern farther north. Utah and southeastern Idaho show the most Inland Northern features in the West, while eastern Montana is an extension of North Dakota. Farther west the mixture is quite complete, with only blacks speaking a significantly different dialect. Of the coastal states Oregon shows the most influence of the South Midland dialect of an earlier period, whereas California has received the greater part of more recent migration from the South Midland.[72]

If we exclude the Southern dialect and its extensions, it might be possible to think of a differentiation of language patterns into East, Midwest, Mountain, and West Coast. This possibility has been obscured because questions in the *Linguistic Atlas* were oriented toward mapping the Western expansion of East Coast dialects. In the western vocabulary the atlas project could find that "corral" and "arroyo" replaced eastern words for barnyard and small canyon because these were concepts that it started out to explore.[73] It could not discover differences such as those illustrated by New England words such as "frappe" for milkshake and "tonic" for soda pop. Often regions are marked by particular word usages stemming from the local cultural situation. Thus, in the Mormon region, "gentile" refers to any non-Mormon, while in the core of the Interior Southwest "Anglo" refers to any person not of Spanish or Indian background. As far as I know, no study of truly contemporary differences in regional dialects has been undertaken.

Closely related to regional dialectology are studies of particular classes of words that investigators have proposed as cultural indicators. For example, in a detailed study, Wilbur Zelinsky has examined the variation of English male forenames in several eastern counties of the United States in 1790 and 1968, using official census or tax lists and telephone directories.[74] He discovered definitely different New England and Southern groups of names in both years, but with considerably less difference in 1968. There was little evidence of a distinctive Mid-Atlantic pattern, but in 1790 there was a distinctive Charleston pattern of names. There was relatively little evidence of rural-urban differentiation. Perhaps most significant was the fact that while the Southern counties showed little change over time, the difference between the 1968 New England counties and the 1790 New England counties was almost as great as any of the differences in the study. Thus, while the South slowly evolved, New England changed from one set of New England names to another.

## MALE NAMES DISTINCTIVE OF TIME AND PLACE

| Colonial America as a Whole | Old New England | Modern New England | Modern North | Modern South |
|---|---|---|---|---|
| Thomas | Amos | Harold | George | Jim |
| John | Asa | Albert | Robert | Bob |
| William | Timothy | Norman | Charles | Joe |
| Isaac | Elijah | Lawrence | James | Jack |
| Jeremiah | Josiah | Donald | Hugh | Willie |
| James | Ebenezer | Stanley | Richard | Clyde |
| Solomon | Abel | Arthur | Francis | Jerry |
| Samuel | Israel | Kenneth | Lewis | Ray |
| Benjamin | Simon | Herbert | Clarence | Eugene |
| Matthew | Ephraim | Raymond | Frank | Harvey |

In a similar effort Meredith Burrill has made a detailed comparison of the occurrence of descriptive geographic terms on maps in different parts of the country.[75] For example, "brook" occurs on topographic maps consistently in the New England region (including upstate New York), most of New Jersey, and the Philadelphia area. It is found less frequently in a band to the south and west of this area (reaching farthest directly west to beyond Minneapolis) and is scattered elsewhere. "Stream" is used as a map designation frequently in northern New England and the Northeast, but then dies out much faster than brook. "Wash" is especially common in the Pacific Southwest, Utah, and the Interior Southwest. "Slough" occurs widely, but is rare in New England. "Pond" is uncommon in the West but frequent in New England.

## *Additional Variations*

Common experience suggests that there are many other regional variations that further investigation might discover. Some of these are frivolous, others impart a great deal to the texture of life.

Compared to the eastern parts of the country, middle-class homes in the Pacific Northwest and perhaps Pacific Southwest are seriously landscaped in a manner quite uncommon in the rest of the country. In most of the country, the middle-class home has a lawn while the rest of the landscaping is largely a lawn edging. Traditional vegetable and flower gardens without landscaping are common in the Midwest. In the South the lawn may receive less emphasis because of the difficulty in growing good lawns there. As is so often the case, the Pacific Northwest or Far West emphasis on landscaping and ornamental garden is based partially on the climate and the topography, but these have in turn developed traditions and expectations, while the Japanese gardening tradition has played a part.

Folk singing is another aspect of culture that is regionally specific. Leaving aside the many survivals of non-English folk traditions in America, Alan Lomax has roughly mapped the country in terms of basic folk styles.[76] The four basic styles are: Northern, Southern White, Western, and Southern Negro. The Northern was found north of a line from Montana to Missouri to southern Pennsylvania. It was characterized by an unaccompanied solo in a hard, clear voice. Surprisingly, Lomax feels it was more British and less puritanical than the Southern White tradition. The Northern tradition largely died out by the middle of the nineteenth century.

The Southern White tradition was dominant in all areas of the South, but was especially developed in the mountains. Toward the west it did not go farther than the edge of the Ozarks and eastern Texas. It was an unaccompanied, highly ornamental solo, often sung in a nasal, high-pitched voice. Although the theme was melancholy, violent, and steaming with emotion, the singer was to be impersonal and withdrawn. In its original form such singing is rare today, especially because of the general acceptance of instrumental accompaniments and the effect of popular music. Yet, as Lomax points out, "poverty and isolation permitted this backwoods music to develop on its own for more than a century. Thus it grew strong enough to absorb urban influences and produce a regional style (hillbilly) which has attracted a vast city audience." [77]

The Western style is a mixture of Northern and Southern White, but is primarily a development out of the Southern White style on the basis of its evolution in the Ozarks and eastern Texas. Compared to the Southern White tradition, it is less intense and nasal, perhaps more open.

The Southern Negro style grew out of the interplay of European religious and popular music with African traditions. Unlike the white styles, Negro music was originally choral and instrumental. Always emotional, at times erotic, the music completely involved every part of the performer's body. While the white folk styles emphasize the meaning of the words, Southern Negro styles emphasize the music, occasionally to the point where words are used purely for their sound. Today, the spread of this style both directly and indirectly to the North and West has gone well beyond Negro circles.

Popular music is an area in which there are important differences in regional popularity, although as a consumer product these are less pronounced. Modern cowboy songs *are* more popular in ranching areas. Like jazz, country and western music could become nationally popular only when persons from the South migrated to form communities in the metropolitan areas of New York, Chicago, Detroit, or California. The recent spread of Negro styles has a similar background. While originally introduced outside of the South for people of Southern background, Southern musical styles have taken root in the North. The

Western style has currently spread very widely. The Lawrence Welk brand of popular music has, on the other hand, a German-Polish character and has achieved its greatest influence where people of this background are dominant.

Food styles also vary widely. As a recent article on the McDonald's hamburger chain points out, outside of the New York City area the hamburger replaces the hot dog as the national food. Although the McDonald's chain tries to offer exactly the same food everywhere,

a few small variations are permitted to suit regional tastes: On Long Island no mustard is served on regular hamburgers; in Memphis more mustard is served and less ketchup; in Texas even more mustard and less ketchup. In parts of New England a coffee milkshake is added to the regular line-up of chocolate, vanilla and strawberry. In parts of the South, Dr. Pepper is served as a fourth soft drink.[78]

Recently, *Time-Life* has put out a small series of cookbooks on regional American cuisine. Published so far are volumes on New England, Southern, and Northwestern (Odum's Northwest plus the Pacific Northwest, Western Canada, and Alaska). The "Northwest" emphasizes fresh, often wild foods and is heavily influenced by the Orient.[79] A study of Southern food habits has concluded that many of the traditional Southern foods were originally frontier foods in both North and South. However, in the South, dependence on pork products, corn and cornmeal, and simple crops such as turnips and greens lasted through the nineteenth century and into the twentieth.[80] Southern cooking has also been augmented by crops that were more available in the South or parts of it because of the climate. These include rice in certain areas, shrimp in Louisiana, and sweet potatoes rather than Irish potatoes.

Regional variations in food-buying habits illustrate important differences even after we factor out differences in income. Using the four standard census regions, we find that in 1967 the average Southern household spent about three times as much on cornmeal and lard as families elsewhere and twice as much on flour, fresh snap beans, frozen lima beans, and cola drinks. The Northeast spent three times as much on ginger ale and twice as much on macaroni-spaghetti-noodles, seafood, frozen spinach, and frozen green beans. The Western family spent about twice as much as most regions on rice, and four times as much as the Southern household on nonwhite bread. The Northeasterners spent two and one-half times as much on blended whiskey as the Westerner, but the Westerner spent 40 percent more on bourbon, scotch, and straight rye.[81]

In several expense categories other than those for food, cultural differences are apparent. The South spent two and one-half times as much as other areas on tobacco other than cigars and cigarettes and more than others on insect sprays. The Northeastern household spent five times as much for hats for girls sixteen and seventeen years old as the Western household, while Westerners spent four times as much on motorcycles and scooters. The Northeast was far ahead in expenditures for concerts and plays and newspapers, but the West was ahead in books and electric blankets. It is interesting, however, that the South is somewhat above both the Northeast and North Central areas in the purchase of hardbound books.[82] Outside of a few areas, however, sales to schools and college students may determine the size of both Southern and Western hardbound book sale statistics.

The distribution by states of membership in truly voluntary associations and of the circulation of special interest magazines has been recently studied by Zelinsky.[83] Unfortunately, since Zelinsky's interest was in factorial analysis of the results, he did not present the raw data directly. From his data we can infer, however, that in 1970–71 *Playboy* magazine had relatively high circulations in the areas of the country attracting recent migrants and relatively low circulation in the Midwest. On the other hand, magazines such as *True Confessions* or *Secret Romances* were read more commonly in the South. The states of the megalopolis, together with Illinois and California, had the higher percentage of readers of *Saturday Review*, *New Republic*, and the *National Review*, while people in the West as a whole (and Minnesota) would be more likely than those elsewhere to read *Camper Coachman*, *Camera*, or *Trailer Life*. Magazines such as *Saddle and Bridle*, *Hounds and Hunting*, and *Shooting Times* found relatively higher circulations in the South. Among organizations the War Resisters League and Common Cause were found in the more sophisticated areas, the International Arabian Horse Federation in the less. The National Council of State Garden Clubs was strong in the South, the American Bowling Congress in the Midwest. It is to be hoped that Zelinsky may publish his data by states, journals, and organizations, so that a more informed picture of regional variation in personal preferences of this type can be developed.

The American agricultural county fair developed in western New England was quite different than those known elsewhere in the world.[84] The emphasis, as in things New England, was on education and information rather than commerce. At the first climax of the county fair pattern in 1820, fairs were limited almost entirely to New England (including upstate New York). By 1858, county fairs were spread widely in the Midwest and upper South. The Civil War eliminated such fairs temporarily from the South, but they became established at this time in Utah. By 1949, they had spread throughout the country, but were still not common in the lowland South, Texas, or the Interior Southwest. The map of fairs suggests that, in addition to division along old cultural lines, the fair was adopted most easily where there was a core of fairly prosperous family farms practicing mixed farming.

In his study of kinesics, or body motion communication, Ray Birdwhistell has in passing noticed regional variations in smiling in the middle class. He found the lowest frequency for western New Yorkers, then upper New England and the central Middle West. He noted the highest frequency in the South, but in the Mountain South smiling was much less frequent than in lower areas. It is appropriate for a young lady to smile at strangers on the street in Atlanta, but inappropriate in Buffalo, where the meaning of the smile would be very different.[85]

# CHAPTER III

# Regional Variations in Common Social Indicators

C HAPTERS I and II developed the bases upon which one
could distinguish the cultural regions of the United States.
It was shown that different popular origins, histories of
settlement, and emergent ideals led to lines of differentiation in
dialect, religious affiliation, voting behavior, and other traits.
Where these lines roughly coincide, it is possible to establish the
borders for cultural regions. Chapter I included several maps of
suggested cultural and sociocultural regions, but the main point of
the discussion to this point has been the possibility of the
enterprise, not the particular regionalizations. In this chapter, I
shall turn the question around and see whether differences in
regional culture produce differences in social statistics. If there is
social significance to regional differences beyond antiquarianism
and symbolic affiliation (for example, to party or religious sect),
then it should be possible to demonstrate this through the
examination of social statistics.

There have been several factor analyses that have attempted to
regionalize the country in terms of "families" of correlated
variables. In the first, John Cole and Cuchlaine King describe the
distribution for those factors found in considering the correlation
of twenty-five variables in the United States.[1] Unfortunately, the

variables are largely those common to demography, economics, and physical geography, and it is hardly surprising that their results provide a map similar to that of the Census Regions. In these terms the cultural identity of the South is expressed, but also the culturally irrelevant identity of a mountain group of states that includes the very different cultures of Nevada, Utah, and New Mexico. Satisfying neither the conventional view nor the cultural is a method that also closely relates the Dakotas and Alaska.

More innovative and ambitious is a recent regionalization by Zelinsky on the basis of a factor analysis of membership in voluntary associations and the circulation of special interest magazines.[2] While the information gathered is potentially of great interest, its amalgamation into regions by "cluster analysis" is not very useful. There is simply too much variation.[3] For example, while Washington and Oregon are included with California in the same western region, in Zelinsky's composite map they are in distinctively different quintiles from California for four out of the seven factors analyzed, including the factor accounting for the most variance. Texas is also one of the eight states in Zelinsky's "West," and it is distinctively different from California in three or four measures, including the most significant. Texas does not fall into the same quintile with Washington and Oregon for *any* of the seven factors taken separately, and only once does one of the two Northwestern states fall into a neighboring quintile on the separate factors. The nature of the data is also open to the general objections to the ecological fallacy (see below for homocide), for circulations and memberships considered often involve very small percentages of the population in any state (for example, membership in the War Resisters League or the Soaring Society of America).

More useful for our inquiry is the work of David Smith with aggregated indicator measures for states and cities. Providing some confirmation of the behavioral significance of the regions I have distinguished, he states: "Three major regions can be identified: the belt of states from the Pacific Northwest to the Great Lakes, with its outlier in New England, as the regions of high social well-being; the South from Texas to Virginia, as the region of low social well-being; and the transitional zone virtually continuous from California to New York."[4]

Smith has produced two maps as the basis for this generalization.[5] In the first (Map 18), he placed states in four categories: (A) relatively low social pathology and high socioeconomic well-being; (B) better performance on well-being than on reducing pathology (Pennsylvania, Ohio, Delaware, Rhode Island, Colorado, and Michigan are actually fairly close to average on both of these dimensions); (C) average on both dimensions, that is, less well-off than Group B and much more pathology than A (Indiana could have been placed in Group A); and (D) low in social well-being and variable in pathology. On Map 19, which combines the scores on general well-being and social pathology, it is particularly important to note state-to-state continuities and discontinuities. The Pacific Northwest stands out as a remarkably uniform area, as do Wisconsin and Minnesota in the Upper Midwest. Although percentage black accounts for a good deal of the variation, note the scores of white West Virginia and Oklahoma compared to their Midwest or Northeast neighbors.

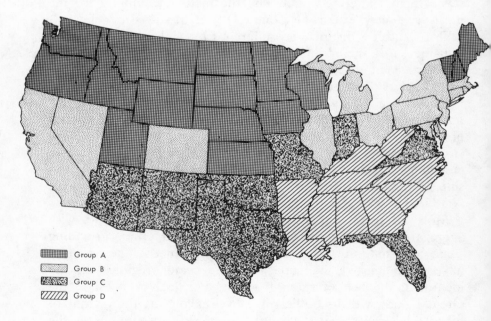

Group A
Group B
Group C
Group D

MAP 18. Patterns of Social Well-being. Source: based on David Smith, *The Geography of Social Well-being* (New York: McGraw-Hill, 1973), p. 100

MAP 19. Social Well-being Scores. Source: based on David Smith, *The Geography of Social Well-being* (New York: McGraw-Hill, 1973), p. 100

Again the figures for the Central Midwest hide a considerable intrastate variation north to south that is independent of percentage black. For an example of how this gradation might appear, the reader should consider Smith's "Community Efficiency Index" (housing, health, crime, and poverty) for Ohio counties (Map 20).[6] There is a steady lowering of performance in terms of these indicators north to south.

There have, of course, been a number of attempts to show how social indicators vary by states, cities, or regions. These efforts consistently suffer from two kinds of defects, defects only partially avoided by Smith. First, although the social indicators "movement" is ostensibly a reaction against overdependence on economic indicators, most aggregated indices for states include purely economic indicators such as per capita incomes or retail sales. In addition, there is an unwillingness to stick with output indicators because of their paucity. Analysts are led to include in educational excellence inputs such as average salary for teachers,

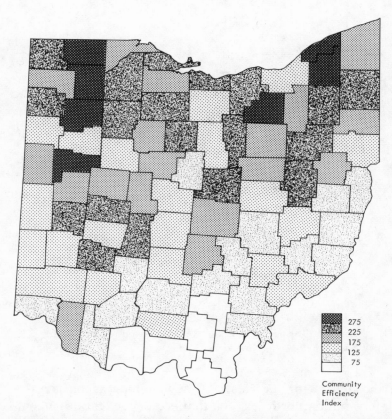

275
225
175
125
75

Community
Efficiency
Index

MAP 20. Community Efficiency in Ohio Counties. Source: based on David Smith, *The Geography of Social Well-being* (New York: McGraw-Hill, 1973), p. 16

or in excellence in health care the relative number of physicians, dentists, and lawyers. Second, there is reason to doubt the sense of putting together overall "goodness indices" that mix a variety of health, education, welfare, and crime indices.[7] In addition, few studies of regional indicators make any attempt to use statistical procedures to isolate the influence on outputs of differences in regional cultures as distinct from differences in the other more obvious socioeconomic variables.

This chapter presents studies of the significance of variation by region for three types of social statistics: violent crime, education, and health. For violent crime, only homicide is considered because of the general lack of comparability of other crime rates. Emphasis is placed on relative influence of Southern culture in the several states. For the social indices considered, this is likely to be the most significant influence. Yet as we move away from homicide, we will see that there are several other more positive regional influences that modify this basic contrast. It should be stressed again that this chapter addresses the question of the behavioral significance of old cultural influences on current behavior; this behavior is *not* a primary way of defining cultural regions.

# Homicide and a Regional Culture of Violence[8]

A number of theories have been advanced on why the homicide rate in this country has historically been higher than that of other economically advanced nations. This is particularly important today because homicide is considered to be an indicator of the violence that some critics believe characterizes our culture. Meanwhile, it has been known for a long time that homicide rates among Negroes and Southern whites are well above national averages. The evidence suggests that it is a predisposition to lethal violence in Southern regional culture that accounts for the greater part of the relative height of the American homicide rate. This regional culture was already developed before 1850. Popularly mentioned causes of violence such as poverty or inequality or ignorance seem of relatively less importance, at least as far as the historic homicide rates are concerned.

Although there have been few studies of homicide, reference to a broad spectrum of research may be found in Marvin Wolfgang and Franco Ferracuti, *The Subculture of Violence.*[9] In a less theoretical manner Marvin Wolfgang's *Patterns in Criminal Homicide* summarized what was known up to that time, and presented a detailed study of a series of homicides in Philadelphia.[10] Perhaps his most controversial finding was that murderers are generally people who have been involved in crime previously, as are a large proportion of their victims. He confirmed the general impression that most murders are intraracial, which is related to the evidence that they are among those known to one another. (Since this evidence allows cross-checking with *Vital Statistics* for murder rates, investigators can examine these rates with more assurance than any other criminal rates.) It is generally established that in the United States murder is more often committed by blacks than whites, by lower class than middle class, by men than women, by Southerners than Northerners.

Wolfgang offered evidence that Negro rates in Philadelphia could not be accounted for on the basis of social class alone.[11] Although most murders are committed against persons known to the murderer, and often within the family, murderers and victims tend to be engaged in criminal activities or living within a seriously disturbed, criminal milieu. However, criminal activities and disorganization are associated with murder much more in some groups than others. The Irish, for example, have long had a reputation for a great deal of scrapping, but this very seldom results in murder. While alcohol has been shown to be highly correlated with murders in Philadelphia, the heavy drinkers of Ireland today are little inclined to murder no matter how drunk they get. We should not be surprised by this result, for we have learned that behavior, rational or irrational, is almost always patterned in terms of the culture of the actors.

The remarkable height of the murder rate for the United States can be established by considering Table 2. It should be noted, however, that United States rates are high only for a developed country. Comparison of figures for the British Isles with those for Australia or Canada suggests that we should expect the settled colonies to have about twice the rates today of their original homelands. However, Chile, Argentina, and the United States, all relatively developed countries in the Americas with little remaining Indian population, have rates severalfold higher than their homelands. The United States rate for whites alone in 1966 was 3.1, still about three times what we should imagine it should be in terms of the general experience of the developed world.

There have been a number of studies of the differential between Northern and Southern behavior in homicide statistics (cf. Tables 3 and 4). These include works by Frederick Hoffman, H. C.

TABLE 2
SOME REPRESENTATIVE HOMICIDE RATES
(Rate per 100,000, 1966)

| Nation | Rate (1966) | Nation | Rate (1966) |
|---|---|---|---|
| Colombia | 21.2 | Canada | 1.3 |
| Mexico | 18.7 | Scotland | 1.1 |
| Thailand | 14.9 | West Germany | 1.1 |
| Philippines | 10.0 | Italy | 0.9 |
| Venezuela | 8.7 | Sweden | 0.8 |
| Chile | 6.4 | France | 0.7 |
| United States | 5.9 | England and Wales | 0.7 |
| Argentina | 5.8 | Northern Ireland | 0.5 |
| Japan | 1.4 | Ireland | 0.4 |
| Australia | 1.3 | Spain | 0.2 |

SOURCE: Data from *World Health Statistics Annual, 1966* (Geneva: World Health Organization, 1969). 1965 data were used for Italy.

Brearley, Austin Porterfield, Lyle Shannon, and Stuart Lottier.[12] Hoffman was particularly concerned by the high American rates compared to the rest of the world, going back at least to 1910. He noted that this was not at all a rural phenomenon, pointing out in particular the city of Memphis, which led the nation for a number of years with murder rates as high as 88 per 100,000. Brearley, a Southern scholar, seriously explored the reasons for differences between Northern and Southern states, developing figures for the twenties comparable to those found today. Qualitatively, he was also interested in the traditions and texture of life that might be responsible.

In a recent review of the problem of Southern violence, Sheldon Hackney refuted several noncultural explanations.[13] He pointed out that many theories attributing homicidal tendencies to certain child-training practices or higher levels of adult frustration do not hold up under examination. For example, it is the less competitive, less commercially minded rural South that has historically been the source of high homicide rates. European countries with relatively rigid child-training practices have much lower rates. In this country, economic and status positions in the community cannot be shown to account for differences in rates between whites and Negroes or between Southerners and Northerners. While the possession of firearms does contribute to actual murder statistics, laws against firearms often seem ineffective in the South, and differences in aggravated assault rates reflect the murder differentials in any case. After the original publication of my own data below, I became aware of a very similar study by John Shelton Reed.[14] After reviewing the homicide data, Reed brings forth considerable evidence from a variety of opinion polls in support of the thesis that there is an important difference between Northern and Southern attitudes toward violence.

A less decisive study of attitudes justifying violence has been made by the Institute for Social Research of the University of Michigan.[15] This study finds weak correlation between a Southern or border background and a positive attitude toward social violence. However, the border and Southern respondents were definitely overrepresented in those small groups with extremely violent attitudes, the study's "warriors" (who would use violence for both social control and change), "anarchists," and "vigilantes."

These findings suggest that a cultural explanation be given particular emphasis in explaining American homicide rates, and that this explanation must be primarily based on an understanding of the influence of Southern regional culture. Psychological, societal, and cultural explanations have been advanced in a number of forms, and each "explains" part of the evidence. For example, Andrew Henry and James Short tried to tie the first two together by viewing murders as aggressive reactions to frustration, with differences in rates stemming from variations in the social situation of groups or classes.[16] Cultural explanation can be related to general theory in criminology by pointing out that cultural differences both produce and result from "differential association." [17] This is particularly true if "culture" refers to all group-related differences in learning.[18] In groups with high murder rates, individuals have on the average (or a few regularly have) a different set of learning experiences than those in groups with lower rates. There is a different balance of culturally defined rewards and punishments, and these are determined by differences in the subcultures of the respective groups.

The following discussion will support the case that persistent differences in homicide rates seem best explained by differences in regional culture. Qualitatively a number of elements in Southern life and very early references to a Southern tendency to lethal violence lend support to the cultural explanation. With the mingling of the American population through internal migration, the Southern tendency to violence has diffused broadly; but the differences between sections of the country in homicide rates can still be related to an inferred degree of "Southernness" based on migration patterns.

Before turning to the evidence, we must consider the limitations on both differential association and cultural variation as explanatory concepts. Both Sutherland's theory and the theory of a regional culture of violence advanced here are suggested as explanations of the epidemiology of crime or of a particular crime.[19] Neither predicts how an individual will behave, but both suggest that past rates in a group are the result of, and result in, a continuing cultural tradition that will tend to produce similar rates in the future, and that external changes in the context of a group will be only slowly reflected in changing behaviors. Whatever the problem of the individual—psychosis, marital troubles, personal danger—the outcome for that individual is more likely to be homicide in a group with a cultural tradition of lethal violence than in another group.

There should be no attempt in any social science theory to suggest that *all* of anything categorized so loosely as "crime" or even "murder" can be explained by a single theory, particularly an epidemiological theory. The relative heights of age-standardized murder rates are determined by four additive and interactive conditions or states: (1) the universal conditions of social life; (2) the rates of certain other criminal activities; (3) the extent and severity of "disorganized conditions"; (4) the culture or subcultures of the population (these vary in the extent to which the first three points lead to lethal violence). Although these overlap, it is primarily with the fourth condition that cultural explanations such as differential association should be concerned, while many other sociological and psychological explanations are primarily concerned with the first three.

Without going deeply into these other factors, it is suggestive of universality that as murder rates go down, relatively more murder is committed by females and those in middle and upper classes.[20] However, the low murder rates of areas such as the British Isles (Table 2) suggest that less than a tenth of United States rates could be explained as a universal accompaniment of social life. Since in Wolfgang's study murder was associated with more general criminal careers for over half of his sample, there is probably some relation of murder to other crime.[21] In the last few years, with rapidly rising general crime rates in the nation, homicide rates have also been edging up, probably because of their ties to other types of crime. However, only a small part of the historical experience of homicide rates can be explained in this way. The areas of highest crime rates have often been areas of relatively low homicide rates and vice versa.[22] Turning to the third general category of explanation, in the United States disorganized conditions such as those found on the frontier and in the skid roads of central cities have been related to high murder rates.[23] In these situations there is a high ratio of males to females, relatively few living in organized families, high mobility, and an anonymity that tends to attract people with criminal tendencies or psychological abnormalities.[24]

The theory of a subculture of violence advanced by Wolfgang and Ferracuti is similar to that of a "regional culture of violence" advanced here. There are, however, several differences. The concept of a subculture of violence is explicitly based on a definition of culture that stresses norms and values, while the concept of culture used here (see Chap. I) is not.[25] Violent people do not necessarily develop a culture that condones violence. A violent tradition may be one that in a wide range of situations condones lethal violence *or* it may be a tradition that more indirectly raises the murder rate. For example, the culture may put a high value on the ready availability of guns, or it may legitimize actions that lead to hostile relations within families or between classes, and these in turn may frequently lead to lethal violence. The concept of culture used here stresses persistence over time and intergenerational reinforcement more than the subcultural concept of Wolfgang and Ferracuti. As an additional note, in this paper "violence" means "lethal violence," while Wolfgang and Ferracuti seem at times to have a broader definition. In any event, differences in the lethality of violence among groups should not be obscured. If "subculture of violence" were given a broader definition of culture, but was limited to lethal violence, then the concept would be fully complementary to what is being advanced here.

In our terms, a society characterized by a regional culture of violence would likely also be characterized by (1) more extreme subcultures of violence and/or a larger percentage of the population involved in violence (with less limitation by class, age, or race); (2) lethal violence as a more important subtheme in the general culture of the region; and (3) weapons and knowledge of their use as an important part of the culture. The concept of a regional culture of violence will help to explain why subcultures of violence do not develop equally everywhere under apparently similar conditions, and will go part of the way toward explaining the particularly lethal subculture among black Americans.

After establishing the theoretical context, let us return to a more detailed examination of the evidence for a regional culture of violence. If Southern culture is primarily responsible for the high murder rates in the United States, then at what time and in what way did Southern culture come to support such a remarkable tendency? John Hope Franklin has diligently explored the Southern tendency to violence in the period before the Civil War.[26] He shows in full the existence of the traits found after the war by such men as Redfield or Brearley, from the continued institutionalization of the duel long after it had been given up in the North to the love of casual violence on much lower levels of society. The rulers of the South were seldom any longer the more truly aristocratic Southerners of Virginia who ruled during the golden age of the republic. Other than carrying the Southern-Northern difference back to 1800, Franklin also documents the relation of Southern violence to an expansive foreign policy and to the deep Southern interest in everything having to do with military training and display.

More important is the fact that large landholders generally came to the South for easy wealth so as to establish for themselves the type of feudal estates that were not available to them in England. In the nineteenth century their vision remained that of the exploiting, seventeenth-century rural aristocracy, and many reached their goal through the availability of poor, indentured whites and then blacks. Extreme class differences were expected from the beginning, and the poor white and black fit into this picture, as did the acknowledged fact that such societies had ultimately to be maintained by violence. It is also important to remember that more whites in the South came from a lower status in England than was true in New England. Perhaps more important is the fact that the South remained a frontier society geographically for a much longer time than the North (see Chap. IV).

In a magnificent study by an amateur, H. V. Redfield examined the difference between murder rates in the North and South in the 1870s.[27] A native of Cincinnati, he traveled widely in both areas, but particularly the South, gathering data from official statistics and developing complete newspaper files. As close to the Civil War as he was, he believed that the Civil War was not an important cause of Southern violence, for the patterns considerably antedated the war. He compared rates for "old states" North and South and for frontier states, finding that South Carolina was as much in excess of New England as Texas over Minnesota. In both cases he estimated well over ten times as much murder per 100,000 in the South as in the North. He clearly saw that Texas was populated largely by the old South and Minnesota by the North. By comparing counties in Ohio, Indiana, and Illinois, he felt that the line between North and South ran through these states, while Iowa was characterized by northern rates.

Redfield identified a number of different patterns of Southern murder. People were killed because of "difficulties" of several sorts. Drunken brawls might not be too different than in the North, yet they more often led to murders, both because of attitudes and the practice of carrying guns or knives. Murder might also occur to redress insult to personal honor, or because of a tough's desire to show off. Groups, whether they be gangs or clans, often attacked rival groups out of animosity or for political ends. "Feuds" as such play less of a part in his analysis than we might expect of one so familiar with the situation in Kentucky.

Redfield illuminated two aspects of history that we understand today rather differently. First, the Western street duel of later romance was described as Southern, as characteristic of South

Carolina as of Texas. Second, the stealthy night killing by an organized group or mob was common throughout the South, though especially in Texas. Murder of this type might be accomplished by ambush, by a raid on a house, including the wiping out of the whole family as in the recent Yablonski case, and might include a lynching. It is important to realize that the patterns of terror we associate with Ku Klux Klan attacks on Negroes was a white-against-white pattern as well.[28]

It is useful to consider what Redfield regarded as the forces that maintained the tradition of violence in the South. Most generally he believed that there was a lack of regard for human life. He thought an exaggerated sense of honor contributed, as did the unnecessary carrying of weapons (apparently much more common then in the South than it is today). In many rural areas he pointed out that a lone law officer was often powerless or afraid to intervene (the rate of death by violence to peace officers was very high at this time, particularly in Texas). Even if caught, the murderer probably would not be convicted or would be given a light sentence. In these cases several factors seemed to be influential. The jury was not likely to take the crime as seriously in the South as in the North. Jury members were more likely to accept the reasons given as justifying the killing. The jurors themselves had often been involved in violent affrays and might be again, and they feared the possibility that a relative or friend of the accused might be on their jury in the future. If they convicted the murderer, they feared retaliation by his relatives. The murder might have been committed for reasons they directly or indirectly approved. Redfield gives many examples of his belief that murder was seldom punished as severely in the South as in the North, including a number of cases of men being brought to trial for murder who had committed several murders previously.

After Redfield, the basic data on Southern-Northern homicide differentials have been presented a number of times (cf. Tables 3 and 4). The spatial arrangement of the rates is depicted by Map 21, in which homicide rates have been averaged for 1964–65.

In spite of considerable work, there has been relatively little attempt to see how much of the Northern-Southern differential could be attributed to factors other than a separate, identifiable homicidal trait among those of Southern background. In attempting to apply the multiple regression approach to this problem, I tried to include evidence relating to a number of alternative hypotheses. It has long been thought that homicide in this country was associated with factors such as low education and low

TABLE 3
HOMICIDE RATES IN THE TWENTIES
(1920 and 1925 per 100,000 pop.)

| State (Rank order by white homicide rate) | White | Nonwhite |
|---|---|---|
| Florida | 12.5 | 62.9 |
| Kentucky | 8.7 | 49.0 |
| Louisiana | 8.7 | 35.0 |
| South Carolina | 8.6 | 18.5 |
| Mississippi | 8.3 | 32.0 |
| Tennessee | 8.0 | 48.8 |
| Alabama | 7.4 | 34.4 |
| Illinois | 7.2 | 72.4 |
| California | 7.1 | 27.5 |
| Missouri | 6.9 | 66.9 |
| Virginia | 6.7 | 20.0 |
| Ohio | 5.1 | 70.1 |
| Washington | 4.8 | 26.0 |
| Michigan | 4.7 | 88.9 |
| North Carolina | 4.7 | 20.8 |
| New York | 4.4 | 28.7 |
| Pennsylvania | 4.4 | 26.7 |
| New Jersey | 4.1 | 20.9 |
| Indiana | 3.9 | 65.0 |
| Kansas | 3.8 | 36.9 |
| Maryland | 3.2 | 21.2 |
| Delaware | 3.0 | 9.8 |
| Massachusetts | 2.3 | 12.8 |
| Wisconsin | 1.8 | 28.4 |

SOURCE: H. C. Brearley, *Homicide in the United States* (Chapel Hill: University of North Carolina Press, 1932), p. 99. Brearley excluded states for which he had too small a sample of nonwhite homicides or no data at all for 1920 and 1925 (averaged). It must be remembered here and below that for a number of states, especially Washington, nonwhite is significantly affected by other than Negro populations.

income. In particular, the positive relation of "low status" to homicide suggested by Henry and Short may be checked by including these factors. Popularly it is believed that crime is related to urbanism or the large city environment, while others have pointed to its rural affinity.[29] It is obvious that variations in the percentage each area contained of people at the ages with high murder rates (20–34 or 18–45) would also be responsible for much

TABLE 4
CRIMINAL HOMICIDES PER 100,000 POPULATION 1960 BY STATES

| State | White | Non-white | Total | State | White | Non-white | Total |
|-------|-------|-----------|-------|-------|-------|-----------|-------|
| Ga. | 4.4 | 27.3 | 10.0 | Mich. | 1.8 | 20.4 | 3.6 |
| Ala. | 4.2 | 25.3 | 10.5 | W. Va. | 3.1 | 13.3* | 3.6 |
| S.C. | 4.9 | 19.5 | 10.0 | Hawaii | 2.5* | 3.9* | 3.5 |
| Va. | 6.9 | 20.2 | 9.7 | Ohio | 1.9 | 21.3 | 3.5 |
| Alaska | 6.3 | 19.2* | 9.3 | N.Y. | 1.8 | 18.7 | 3.3 |
| Fla. | 3.8 | 34.4 | 9.3 | Ind. | 1.8 | 22.6 | 3.0 |
| N.C. | 3.9 | 24.9 | 9.2 | Kans. | 2.2 | 18.7* | 2.9 |
| La. | 3.1 | 19.1 | 8.3 | S.D. | 1.7* | 33.3* | 2.9* |
| Nev. | 7.2 | 18.2* | 8.1 | Pa. | 1.5 | 18.0 | 2.7 |
| Miss. | 2.5 | 15.5 | 8.0 | N.J. | 1.6 | 13.8 | 2.6 |
| Tenn. | 3.7 | 27.0 | 7.6 | Wash. | 2.2 | 12.8* | 2.6 |
| Texas | 4.3 | 30.7 | 7.6 | Ore. | 2.0 | 27.0* | 2.5 |
| Ark. | 3.7 | 21.7 | 7.5 | Utah | 1.8* | 17.6* | 2.1* |
| Ariz. | 4.5 | 27.3 | 6.8 | Conn. | 1.2 | 18.0* | 2.0 |
| Ky. | 4.5 | 27.1 | 6.1 | Neb. | .87* | 40.5* | 1.9 |
| N.M. | 4.8 | 22.9* | 6.1 | Maine | 1.8* | 0.0* | 1.8* |
| Okla. | 4.0 | 23.2 | 5.8 | Idaho | 1.1* | 30.0* | 1.5* |
| Md. | 2.5 | 21.3 | 5.6 | Wis. | 1.3 | 12.9* | 1.5 |
| Del. | 2.3* | 24.2* | 5.4 | R.I. | 1.3* | 4.8* | 1.4* |
| Wyo. | 4.3* | 42.9* | 5.2* | N.D. | 1.0* | 23.1 | 1.4* |
| Ill. | 2.3 | 25.1 | 4.7 | Mass. | 1.1* | 10.4* | 1.3* |
| Mo. | 2.8 | 22.9 | 4.6 | Minn. | 1.1* | 16.7* | 1.3* |
| Calif. | 3.3 | 18.3 | 4.5 | Iowa | 0.9* | 10.3* | 1.0* |
| Colo. | 3.0 | 32.1* | 3.9 | N.H. | 1.0* | 0.0* | 1.0* |
| Mont. | 3.1* | 25.0 | 3.9 | Vt. | 0.0* | 0.0* | 0.0* |

SOURCE: *Vital Statistics of the United States, 1964*, Vol. 2, pt. B, "Mortality Rates by Race" (Washington, D.C.: U.S. Public Health Service, 1966).
* 20 or fewer homicides

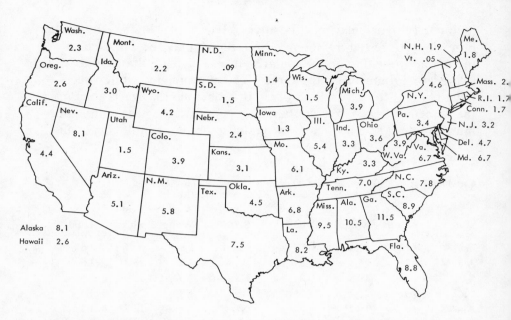

MAP 21. Murder and Nonnegligent Manslaughter (1964–65 Averaged), per
100,000 Population. Source: based on data from *Statistical Abstract of the United
States, 1967* (Washington, D.C.: Bureau of the Census, 1967), p. 151

of the difference in the reported rates. Since murder rates reflect
victim survival rates, a decline in murder rates has been associated
with improving medical services; it seemed reasonable to suppose
that differences in the availability of medical services might affect
murder statistics.[30] One could only discover the influence of
"Southernness" while controlling for such factors. Of course, even
if it appeared that the apparent influence of Southernness on
homicide rates could be explained by those common sociological
variables such as low education and income that are also
associated with Southernness, one could imagine that Southern
culture "caused" them all. However, there would not in this case
be a separate regional cultural trait for homicide, and the claim of
Southern cultural influence on the rate would be much harder to
make convincing.

It is difficult to define exactly where and in what proportions the
influences of Southern and Northern culture are to be found
today. In order to examine the relation of homicide to Southern-

ness we must, however, give a numerical value to its cultural influence in the states, or other units, we wish to examine. For this purpose an index of Southernness (Map 22) was constructed on the basis of available evidence, with a high score of 30 given the most purely Southern states and a low score of 5 to the least.

MAP 22. Index of Southernness

Six rules governed construction of the index of Southernness. (1) Virginia, West Virginia, Kentucky, Tennessee, North Carolina, South Carolina, Georgia, Alabama, Mississippi, Louisiana, and Arkansas were given scores of 30. If we define Southern culture in Redfield's terms to include the culture of both lowland and mountain South in the nineteenth century and to grade South to North in the Central Middle West, then the elite and the general population of these states has up to now been under overwhelming Southern influence. (2) States with only indirect Southern influence and virtually no white Southern population were given scores of 5 (New England and most Upper Midwest states). (3) States with about half of the population of Southern background and/or a Southern majority at time of first settlement were accorded a score of 20. This score indicates states felt to be of half, or slightly more than half, Southern background. (4) States with overwhelming Southern background and a white population primarily from the South, but with strong non-Southern minorities that have preserved some independence from this heritage by virtue of a separate existence or recent movement to the area were rated at 25. (5) Definitely non-Southern states with a strong representation of Southern population in either the formative period or more recently scored 15. (6) States overwhelmingly non-Southern, but with a weak Southern representation in the population or a Southern cultural influence in the formative period were given 10. It should be noted that a purely Southern state would score 35 and a purely Northern score 0, but no state qualifies for these categories.

It will be seen from Map 22 that the index largely reflects the cultural regions as I have defined them (Map 4). Such "typical American states" as Kansas, Colorado, and California received scores of 20. These states are not more than half Southern, but among those classes or social positions that contribute most to homicide, Southern culture was felt to be very important. West of the Plains, Southern influence is rather evenly spread because of the original dispersion, the later dispersion of Texas culture, and the recent dispersion to Western cities from West South Central states. In Ohio, Indiana, and Illinois a detailed map would show a gradation from 5 in some northern fringe counties to 30 in some Southern counties, but these are averaged out in state index values. With urbanization many Southerners have crossed over the graded area to Detroit but not to Milwaukee. This difference in recent migration does show in the figures. Idaho represents a combination of counties in its northern and central areas that should be scored 20 and others in the southeast that should be scored 10.

Many of the index scores could be questioned. However, it would be difficult to reverse the relationship of a state to its neighbors or change greatly the extremes. The index can be confirmed or refined by looking at both Bureau of the Census material in successive censuses on state of birth[31] and at qualitative studies of the antecedents of elites, as well as studies of current cultural foci on elite and popular levels. The religious and linguistic data we have used in previous chapters were also used as basic sources. An excursion with a quite different index of Southernness (generally reducing the Southernness of border and Western states) explained less of the variance (27 percent) using the Table 6 variables, but index of Southernness was still the most significant of the variables considered.

Applying standard techniques of multiple correlation to the murder statistics, the results of Tables 5, 6, and 7 were obtained. Table 5 presents simple and multiple correlation data of the forty-eight continental states with homicide rates in 1960. Index of Southernness explains a great deal—indeed, more than any other

TABLE 5
RELATION OF CRIMINAL HOMICIDE TO SELECTED VARIABLES
(By 48 states, 1960)

|  | Percent Variance Explained | Partial Correlation at Entry | Simple Correlation |
|---|---|---|---|
| Index of Southernness | 74.6 | (.86)** | .86** |
| Percent Negro | 82.5 | .56** | .87** |
| Percent 20–34 | 87.3 | .53** | .57** |
| Median income (adjusted), inverted | 88.4 | .29* | .43* |
| Percent urban | 88.7 | .16 | −.15 |
| Physicians/1000, inverted | 89.1 | .20 | .46** |
| Median years of school completed, inverted | 89.2 | −.09 | .51** |
| Hospital beds/1000 | 89.4 | −.13 | .48** |
| Population | 89.4 | −.05 | .05 |
| Percent in cities over 300,000 | 89.4 | .02 | .001 |

SOURCES: In addition to the data in Table 4, most sources for the variables may be found in the references to Table 8. The figures for physicians and hospital beds were taken from the *Statistical Abstract of the United States, 1962* (Washington, D.C.: Bureau of the Census, 1962), p. 80.
NOTE: The program (U.C.L.A. biomedical data) is such that the variable with the highest single correlation to the dependent variable is entered first, the one with the highest remaining partial correlation entered next, and so on until there is no remaining significant partial.
** Significant at .001 level
* Significant at .05 level

variable does—of the variance. (With all fifty states, including
Alaska and Hawaii where our approach makes the least sense, the
total variance explained drops to 88 percent and that explained by
index of Southernness to 71 percent.) It is characteristic of this
form of regression that the relative influence of the first variable
entered appears to be more than it is, even if there are low
intercorrelations. It will be noted below that we have made several
attempts to get around this difficulty, although a factor analysis
was not done. The high correlation of index of Southernness with
percent Negro, low education, and low income must be noted
(intercorrelations of .71, .52, and .47, respectively). As elsewhere,
since the index of Southernness and percent 20–34 are not closely
correlated (intercorrelation of .39 is higher here than is usual),
they add quite separately to the variance explained. If index of
Southernness is forced last in the multiple regressions, it still has a
highly significant partial correlation.[32]

TABLE 6
RELATION OF WHITE CRIMINAL HOMICIDE
TO SELECTED VARIABLES
(By 50 states; 1960)

|  | Percent Variance Explained | Partial Correlation at Entry | Simple Correlation |
|---|---|---|---|
| Index of Southernness | 52.0 | (.72)** | .72** |
| Percent 20–34 | 70.0 | .16** | .60** |
| Percent nonwhite | 73.6 | −.37* | .38* |
| White population size | 74.7 | −.20 | −.12 |
| Physicians/1000, inverted | 75.0 | .10 | .47** |
| Percent urban | 75.7 | .17 | .10 |
| Median income (adjusted), inverted | 75.9 | .08 | .15 |
| Hospital beds/1000 | 75.98 | −.06 | .51** |
| Median years of school completed, inverted | 76.09 | −.07 | −.03 |
| Percent in cities over 300,000 | 76.2 | −.07 | −.12 |

SOURCES: See sources for Table 5.
** Significant at .001 level
* Significant at .05 level

If we take white homicides alone, in Table 6, the correlation of Southernness and homicide is somewhat reduced, although still remarkably high and significant. Percent nonwhite has significant positive correlation with homicide, although it adds little additional to the variance explained. However, if we look at the partial correlation of *percent nonwhite* after index of Southernness is entered, it falls to .07; after both Southernness and percent 20–34 have been taken out, it becomes − .37. This indicates that having nonwhites in a state certainly does not add to tendencies to white homicide, as a theory of generalized conflict might predict. Omitting percent nonwhite entirely in an excursion did not reveal any other significant variable that had been submerged by its presence. Forcing index of Southernness last in this case gives a considerably more decisive result than for all homicides. Here the index adds in this last position 16 percent to the variance, and its partial correlation after everything else is accounted for is almost as high as the original correlation.

It seemed useful to try to investigate the degree to which index of Southernness was "explained" by the other variables when it became the dependent variable. The correlation of Southernness with homicide and percent Negro was obviously high, so we dropped these variables from the regression (Table 7). Sixty-five percent of the variance in index of Southernness is correlated with variables such as education and medical facilities, although "explanation" probably goes the other way. The high negative correlations of medical services with Southernness suggest that the contribution they make to lowered death rates after criminal assaults (as predicted) was *not* the reason for their contribution.

Some evidence of the relation of Negro homicide to Southern homicide was examined. For example, Thomas Pettigrew and Rosaline Spier found that the highest positive correlations by states of Negro homicide rates were with a "homicidal culture index" of Negro offenders and with the white homicide rates.[33] Correlation values were .55 and .50, respectively, both significant at the .01 level. The homicidal culture index was prepared on the basis of the white homicide rates of the states of origin of the Negro offenders. There were also high correlations with Negro mobility when the homicidal culture index was held constant. However, my own work and census information would suggest

TABLE 7
RELATION OF INDEX OF SOUTHERNNESS
TO SELECTED VARIABLES
(By 48 states; 1960)

| | Percent Variance Explained | Partial Correlation at Entry | Simple Correlation |
|---|---|---|---|
| Percent Negro | 50.2 | (.71)** | .71** |
| Hospital beds/1000, inverted | 67.2 | .59** | .61** |
| Percent 20–34 | 70.4 | .30* | .39* |
| Median years of school completed, inverted | 74.2 | .36* | .52** |
| Percent in cities over 300,000 | 75.4 | .22 | .04 |
| Percent urban | 78.0 | −.32* | −.24 |
| Median income (adjusted), inverted | 78.4 | .13 | .47** |
| Physicians/1000, inverted | 78.5 | −.04 | .48** |
| Population | 78.5 | −.02 | .05 |

SOURCES: See sources for Table 5.
** Significant at the .001 level
* Significant at the .05 level

that this may reflect the contribution that a relatively large percentage in the 20–34 age bracket makes to the variation, and the fact that high mobility may be related to an underreporting of the population base, particularly of the urban Negroes.

Redfield believed that Negro homicide rates in the South were lower than white. Although many more Negroes were killed by whites than vice versa, his data showed there were fewer Negroes murdered per hundred thousand than there were whites. In the South he had to rely on a detailed compilation of newspaper reports; generally these seemed to be remarkably complete, especially in states with one state-wide newspaper. But it may be that black deaths tended to be ignored by the white newspapers to a considerable extent, either out of lack of interest or a desire of the blacks to keep their difficulties to themselves. If this is not the case, then there has been a tremendous change since the 1870s, a change already well along by the 1920s. One explanation may be that the Negroes were so poor in the 1870s that guns and even knives in Negro possession were rare (as well as sometimes unsafe and illegal). With fewer weapons, the same amount of Negro violence might have resulted in relatively fewer homicides than today. It is remarkable that neither in the twenties nor in the sixties have the highest Negro rates been in the heartland of the South, but Wolfgang's study of murder in Philadelphia suggested that the highest rates were among recently arrived Southerners.[34] It seems likely that differences in age and sex ratios play a part in his results.

As an excursion to the manipulation of the data correlated in Table 5, percent Negro was forced last. It was important to know if blacks could be considered as indistinguishable from other groups of relatively uneducated and poor persons of Southern background. In the stepwise regression, percent Negro in last position added 5 percent to the variance explained and, when entered, had a highly significant partial correlation of .58. The small influence of percent Negro on white rates suggests indirectly that the Negro tendency to higher homicide rates is not simply a heritage of general, backward Southern culture. (It is likely that there are other Southern subcultures that would appear to diverge in the same direction.) This is clearly a question which should, however, be investigated by other, more adequate means.

Detailed examination of results and further statistical excursions suggest that it would be possible to create an index of Southernness that would correspond both more closely with the homicide rates and with the historical backgrounds of the people in the several states. Examination of residuals suggests that there should be a reduction in extent of ascribed Southernness above the North-South regional frontier; on the other hand, Texas and Florida act like extreme Southern states. We should also examine where for historical reasons we might make changes in the index of Southernness, although it would not help the correlations. For example, New York should perhaps be treated as a New England state in terms of Southernness. However, it is more useful to stay with the original fairly clean index developed largely independently of knowledge of homicide rates.

Homicide rates in Puerto Rico and Mexico (Table 2) suggest that Spanish-speaking Americans would be likely to increase greatly homicide rates where they are in significant numbers.[35]

Perhaps the Puerto Ricans in New York City have such an effect, but a detailed look at states and localities in the Southwest with large Mexican-American populations suggests behavior rather similar to that of the Southern whites in their area. Nor does a look at other minorities such as the Indian suggest either direct or indirect influence.

In conclusion, it seems established that there is a significant relationship between murder rates and residence in the South. This relationship can be traced back to differences between the North and South that were already observable before the Civil War. It can be shown that outside of the centers of Southern and Northern society, state homicide rates grade into one another in rough approximation to the extent to which Southerners have moved into mixed states. While differences in standard demographic or economic variables such as age composition, median education, or median income account for a good deal of the variance among sections of the country in murder rates, there is a significant remainder that may be related to "Southernness" alone. There seems, then, on both qualitative and quantitative grounds to be evidence that the culture that developed in the Southern states in past centuries leads to high murder rates. Looking at international and state comparisons, it also seems likely that this specifically Southern culture accounts for most of the difference between the murder rates of the United States and those of comparable countries such as Canada or Australia.

# The Relationship of Regional Cultures to Educational Performance[36]

In most attempts to examine educational indicators in the United States, the country as the whole is generally taken as the relevant unit, with occasional breakdowns by race, age, class, or rural-urban residence. It is exceptional to find analysts discussing figures in terms of the four census "regions." In a recent study of educational indicators, Abbott Ferriss does not make any regional breakdown, although he mentions the possibility of doing so.[37]

There are many reasons for ignoring region, including the politics of data release.

To say that there are regional differences in culture and behavior and to expect these to influence educational performance is only one version, but an often ignored version, of the evidence that family background, educational and achievement values, and teacher quality (as opposed to methods) determine performance.[38] Regional differences might be considered macrovariables, while most studies have considered microvariables that directly influence individual students. Both approaches emphasize the difficulty of making large-scale changes in relative educational performance among students of different backgrounds and in different surroundings. Exceptions are found when populations with high achievement cultural potential but temporary barriers such as language or extreme poverty are considered (for example, the Japanese and Chinese).

As has been pointed out, the North has historically been the more educated part of the nation. In the South education grew very slowly for two reasons. First, the people who came there originally were probably less educated and less interested in education than those who came to the North. However, more important in the long run was the pattern of life, which encouraged isolation, with remarkably little development of town, school, church, or city until very late. The New England pattern was almost the antithesis of the Southern. Towns, churches, and schools were established initially, and people frequently moved west as organized communities. As organized religion lost its grip on New England intellectuals in the nineteenth century, many from this background developed an almost equally fervent interest in education for its own sake. In addition, money and motivation made it possible for New England culture to establish a pattern of influence in areas where New Englanders were always a minority. Only in one part of the West, Utah and southeastern Idaho, did people of New England background dominate the period of first effective settlement. In much of the North the New England pattern has been supplemented and reinforced educationally by the essentially urban and cosmopolitan interests of many of the peoples of the post-1800 immigrations.

In attempting to determine what influence such regional

cultural differences may continue to have on education, it is convenient to consider regional variation on two levels: (1) the level of minimum basic education, and (2) the level of elite or professional education.

On the first level there is a historical pattern of difference between North and South in illiteracy rates. Of the forty-eight original states, Louisiana had the highest illiteracy rates in both 1900 and 1960 (39.6 and 6.3 percent, respectively) while Iowa was at the bottom of the list in both years (2.7 and 0.7 percent, respectively). All states above 10 percent in 1900 and above 4 percent in 1960 were in the South; all states under 4 percent in 1900 and under 1 percent in 1960 were in a broad band from Iowa to the Pacific Northwest.[39] Although schooling is not a performance measure, it has been historically related to literacy. Map 23 shows the percentage of the population over twenty-five years of age with less than eight years of school in 1960.

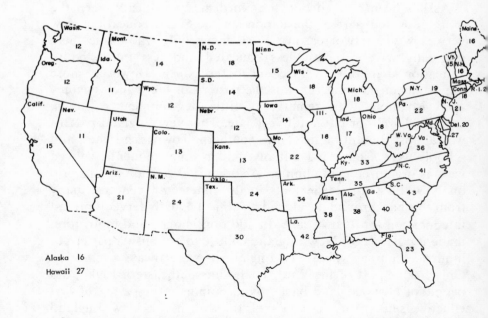

Alaska  16
Hawaii  27

MAP 23. Minimum Schooling Deficiencies: Percentage of Population 25 Years Old and Above with Less Than 8 Years of Schooling (1960). Source: based on data from *Statistical Abstract of the United States, 1970* (Washington, D.C.: Bureau of the Census, 1970), p. 112

Other indices of mass education above the literacy level also change slowly, and comparative relationships persist even among the young. If we look at the percentage of the population in 1960 between twenty-five and twenty-nine with a high school education, we find a range from the low forties to the low seventies, with relationships in 1960 generally reflecting those in 1940. The gap between the highest and lowest has narrowed slightly, but mostly because of the more even distribution of Southerners, especially Negroes, in the North. In 1960 Kentucky still had thirty-two counties with less than 15 percent of the population having a high school diploma, whereas Utah had no counties with less than 35 percent. It is notable that evidence of extreme educational deprivation seems to persist primarily in certain isolated areas of Kentucky and Tennessee (incidentally in a white population).[40]

Among the few measures of educational quality for which a breakdown by states is available are the failure rates of the Armed Forces Qualifying Tests.[41] Questions can be raised as to the usefulness of the failure rates; in particular, since the same individuals may in some cases take the tests more than once, the greater Southern interest in the military might mean higher Southern failure rates.[42] There may be some deliberate failure. However, comparison of failure rates with the data presented above suggests they are not greatly out of line for our purposes. The rates are mapped by state in Maps 24 and 25. It is significant that the same band of states that has traditionally had the least illiteracy also had the fewest test failures, even though most illiterates were in a different age group from those taking the tests.

Intuition and input indicators would have suggested that New England, New York, and California should have had relatively lower failure rates than they did.[43] In fact the rates correspond very closely with the data on percentage of the population with less than eight years of school in Map 23. The unsatisfactory performance of the most advanced parts of the country is in part due to a relatively large proportion in these areas of white people, or people classified as white, that have not become thoroughly integrated in our society or have not accepted white American educational culture. This especially includes Spanish-speaking Americans.[44]

In mass education, differences between North and South are

MAP 24. Percentage of Failures on the Armed Forces Qualifying Test, 1958–65.
Source: based on data from *American Education* 2 (October 1966): 1–9

reflected in many qualitative and quantitative indices. The under-
lying cultural factors, rather than the more measurable and
superficial educational inputs, seem to be determinative. However,
the test failure figures used here were presented in *American
Education* in juxtaposition to comparative input figures such as
educational expenditures per pupil, pupil-teacher ratio, average
teacher salary, and percentage of teachers receiving $6,500 or
more a year. The purpose of including these data was to show that
"the price of poor school support is poor education." [45]

To test the counter-hypothesis that general culture was more
important than the quality or quantity of educational input, a
multiple regression technique was used, with white failure rates,
1964–65, as the dependent variable (Table 8). The primary
variable introduced in addition to those mentioned above was the
index of Southernness. It is significant that the index was
developed for examining variations in homicide rates (see above)
and is incorporated here without change. Median education of
those over twenty-five, the second most explanatory variable, is

MAP 25. Percentage of Failures (Whites Only) on Armed Forces Qualifying Test, 1965. Source: based on data from *American Education* 2 (October 1966): 1–9

closer to education than the index, but itself reflects previous culture, and is very difficult to change quickly. Regressions were also run using AFQT failure rates 1958–65 and 1969 for all races.[46] Percent Negro was easily the first variable to enter and total variance explained was 94 and 84 percent, respectively. Here index of Southernness had simple correlations of .76 and .66 and percent completing less than eight years of school was slightly more predictive than median education.

As mentioned above, in interpreting Table 8 it would be a mistake to imagine that index of Southernness was relatively as important as the figures suggest, for the first variable to enter the stepwise regression appears to be more significant than it is. Particularly in this case, the variables used are so interrelated that great caution must be exercised. Nevertheless, this evidence would suggest that general cultural factors are more important than particular educational inputs, a result that agrees with the Coleman report.[47]

The interrelations of the variables in the regression point to one of the difficulties inherent in an attempt to discriminate statistically the influence of regional culture *per se* from other influences on a pattern of behavior. For if there is a regional culture, it will

TABLE 8

RELATION OF WHITE AFQT FAILURES TO SELECTED VARIABLES
(By 50 states, 1964–65)

|  | Percent Variance Explained | Partial Correlation at Entry | Simple Correlation |
|---|---|---|---|
| 1. Index of Southernness | 50.0 | (.71) | .71 |
| 2. Median education (white) | 62.2 | −.49 | −.53 |
| 3. Percent 20–34 | 65.2 | .28 | .18 |
| 4. Education expenditures/pupil | 69.6 | −.36 | −.53 |
| 5. Percent in cities over 300,000 | 71.5 | .25 | .03 |
| 6. Median income | 73.1 | −.24 | −.56 |
| 7. Percent urban | 74.5 | .22 | −.24 |
| 8. Percent voting (1968) | 75.2 | .17 | −.62 |
| 9. White population size | 75.5 | .11 | .03 |
| 10. Percent with under 8 years education | 75.6 | .08 | .70 |
| 11. Percent teachers earning over $6500 | 75.8 | .08 | −.42 |
| 12. Average teacher salary | 76.1 | −.02 | −.43 |
| 13. Pupil/teacher | 76.2 | .05 | .57 |

SOURCES: (1) index of Southernness: see text; (2) median school years completed 1960 (white population 25 years or more): *Statistical Abstract, 1969* (Washington, D.C.: Bureau of the Census, 1969), p. 109; (3) Percent of the total population in the age group 20–34 (calculated from population figures): *Statistical Abstract, 1969,* p. 27; (4) estimated expenditure per pupil: *American Education* 2 (October 1966): 1–9 (adjusted in terms of the consumer price index constructed from the "Consumer Price Index of Selected Cities" in *Statistical Abstract, 1962,* p. 350, and "Annual Costs in a Moderate Urban Living Standard for a Four Person Family: 1967," *Statistical Abstract, 1969,* p. 348); (5) percent of total population in cities of 300,000 or more, 1960: *Statistical Abstract, 1962,* p. 22; (6) median money income of families, 1959 (adjusted in terms of consumer price index [see no. 4, above]): *Statistical Abstract, 1962,* p. 333; (7) percent urban: *Statistical Abstract, 1969,* p. 17; (8) percent of registered voters voting in 1960: *Statistical Abstract, 1969,* p. 270; (9) white population size: *Statistical Abstract, 1969,* p. 27; (10) percent with less than eight years education: *Statistical Abstract, 1970,* p. 112; (11) percent of teachers earning $6500 or more: *American Education* 2 (October 1966): 1–9; (12) average salary, elementary and secondary instructional staff: *Statistical Abstract, 1962,* p. 127; (13) pupil/teacher ratio: *American Education* 2 (October 1966): 1–9.

influence many of the measures included in a regression of this kind. For example, most areas of the South are relatively poor and have poor schools, which produce relatively poorly trained people who grow up to teach in or support the schools of the next generation. It is quite likely that there are certain features of Southern regional culture (for example, a relatively disorganized life style) that account for economic and educational poverty. Only to the extent that the educational performance of a region is unconnected to its economic performance will regional culture have a separate value of its own. Obviously, the difficulty of having a separate explanatory cultural variable is enhanced when variables such as median education are added to the list of explanatory factors for educational performance. Nevertheless, educational variables were added in an attempt to contrast in some degree particular and universal types of explanation.

In education at a higher level many of the same patterns are

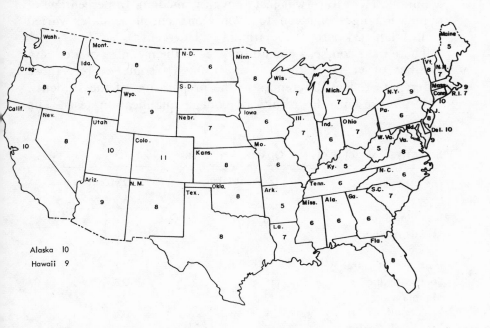

MAP 26. Higher Education Attainment: Percentage of Population 25 Years Old and Above with 4 Years or More of College, 1960. Source: based on data from *Statistical Abstract of the United States, 1970* (Washington, D.C.: Bureau of the Census, 1970), p. 112

found, yet there are important differences. Map 26 gives the percentage of the population twenty-five years of age and over with four years of college or more in 1960. It will be noted that there is much less state-to-state variation in higher education than in the percentage with zero to seven years of schooling (Map 23). The highest state has only slightly more than twice the percentage of the lowest. The high states are in general not those with the lowest percentage with less than eight years of education. While Iowa was a leader in mass education, in higher education Iowa is one of the lower ranked states. Thus, the Northeastern seaboard and California have greater extremes in education than do the less complex states with a high standard of mass education. This is, however, partially because the best educated in the states with high minimal standards move away. A study of full-time remaining enrollment at four-year colleges by state in 1963 showed the top five to be Utah, Arizona, North Dakota, Kansas, and Montana. Here Iowa was just above the median. In percentage of population ages eighteen to twenty-one enrolled, states varied from Utah's 34 percent to Virginia's 11 percent.[48]

There is, of course, a great difference in the meaning of a certain number of years of higher education. To some degree, those differences reflect differences in the preparation of the students. Table 9 presents the results of college qualification tests. The

TABLE 9
SELECTIVE SERVICE COLLEGE QUALIFICATION TEST (1966)

|  | Percent Highest Category | Percent Lowest Category |
| --- | --- | --- |
| New England | 26 | 7 |
| Middle Atlantic | 25 | 9 |
| Pacific | 22 | 13 |
| East North Central | 17 | 12 |
| South Atlantic | 15 | 22 |
| Mountain | 13 | 22 |
| West South Central | 9 | 32 |
| East South Central | 7 | 47 |

SOURCE: *American Education* 2 (November 1966): back cover. The West North Central figure is not given. Tests were given to those ranging from high school seniors to graduate students, but the bulk are college freshmen and sophomores.

reader will note that variation in higher education is more extreme than Map 26 suggests. Again, score differences between the North and South are congruent with the Coleman report.[49] However, other test results cast some doubt on the significance of the college qualification scores.[50]

Another way to look at differences among states in the quality of higher education is to examine the number of students who go on from college in that state to attain doctorates.[51] Map 27 gives the number of Ph.D.'s granted between 1920 and 1961 to individuals with baccalaureates from each state per 100,000 state population in 1950. Since the median doctorate was received after 1950, the median undergraduate education was received in the forties. It should be noted that because of rapid population growth, the figures for Florida, Texas, New Mexico, Arizona, Utah, Nevada, Washington, Oregon, and California would all be relatively higher if the base population were 1940. States such as

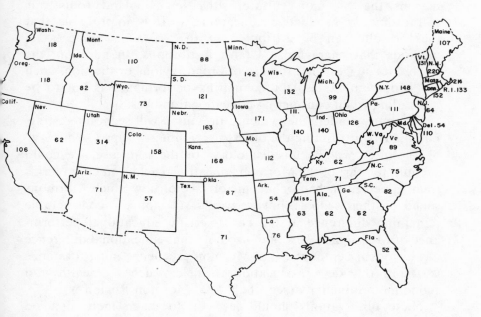

MAP 27. Baccalaureate Origins of Doctorates by States, 1920–61 (per 100,000 Population, 1950). Source: based on data taken from the National Academy of Sciences/ National Research Council, *Doctorate Production in the United States Universities, 1920–1962* (Washington, D.C.: NAS/ NRC, 1963), pp. 28–29, 198

Idaho or Delaware are low both because their students go elsewhere for baccalaureates and because there is very little doctorate work offered in these states. Massachusetts and New Hampshire have high scores because they have large numbers of students from other states coming for baccalaureates, and their out-of-state students are of a quality most likely to subsequently achieve doctorates.

Map 27 shows that Southern universities have produced relatively few candidates for doctorates. On the other hand, Utah's pre-eminence is outstanding. Utah draws Mormons from all over the country to its schools, but the fact that so many of them should go on to receive doctorates is remarkable. Utah's universities could be granting inferior doctorates. However, there were only 640 doctorates given in Utah in these years while its baccalaureates were receiving 2,125 doctorates, mostly in the natural sciences.[52] It would appear that for as yet unexplained reasons the Mormon culture with New England roots was extraordinarily productive educationally. It is improbable that these results can be attributed to the particular educational methods that characterize Utah's institutions. In addition, the Utah data suggest that the use of broad regions or divisions such as "Mountain States" for comparing performance is apt to be misleading when considering educational indices.

For many readers the evidence presented will seem interesting, but vaguely attributing the differences among groups to "history" or "culture" will be unsatisfactory. In the last case, we could account for part of the Mormon educational achievement in terms such as percent urban or income or race or how much Mormons spend on their schools, but we would still notice a considerable remaining difference in the characteristic educational performance of Mormons. We would also note that educational difference has historical depth, and that Mormon excellence in performance is found outside of education in fields such as health and economic productivity (see Chap. IV, "Mormon Region").

These observations should lead us to make more detailed examinations of the causes of Mormon success in education, but I do not want to pretend that I know what the answers will be. It is significant that in basic "value orientations" as expressed in test results Mormons and Texans in the "Five Cultures Area" of New

Mexico were much more similar than a comparison of the respective communities and the behavior patterns of their members led the investigators to suspect.[53] Apparently Mormon institutions both compelled and made possible the achievements of its individuals, and perhaps characteristic Mormon behavior was learned on levels below that of value orientation. Steady work habits and a particularly high value on work no doubt carry over into educational performance. More examination may suggest Mormon performance could be traced to something as direct and autonomous as a generalized, high achievement pattern of expectations in the educational area that began fortuitously, but has been sustained by the pattern of rewards in our society. Mormon performance in education might also be attributed to something as indirect as a characteristic self-confidence and stability of Mormon personality that in turn is inspired by community, church, and family support. This, in turn, would make success likely in whatever direction an individual moves. Of course, our interest is in the Mormons because they stand out regionally; there are many other subcultural groups characterized by particular patterns of educational performance that need equally to be studied.

In conclusion, I have tried to demonstrate that persistent long-term cultural differences have a significant influence on educational outcomes, given a reasonable standard of contemporary educational performance. The particular types of cultural differences examined were those that could be demonstrated by looking at geographically presented statistics. In the process of making this case, I have described those regional variations in education at minimal and higher levels that have characterized the United States in the past and are likely to continue to be influential for the foreseeable future.

# White Infant Mortality and Cultural Regions

The arrested rate of decline of infant mortality rates in the United States in the 1950s and early 1960s has been a source of considerable concern and investigation. The fact that a number of European countries with higher infant mortality rates in the thirties continued to reduce their rates in the 1950s until they were considerably lower than United States rates by the mid-sixties suggested a serious failing in the development of health services in the United States.[54] I cannot directly explain why our rates did not fall significantly in the 1950s, but by looking at regional differences in rates within the United States, I can offer new insight into the problem. The regional approach should also eventually improve the basis upon which state and local medical services are compared.

Social indices, such as the infant mortality rate, often reflect an interaction between the possibilities of the technical culture of the time and the general culture of those who use or are affected by that technical culture. In other words, social indices are affected both by what is available to do and what is done. "What is done" in the medical area refers both to how medical services are organized or made available *and* to how people respond to their own medical problems, or use available information and services. A preliminary investigation suggests that infant mortality rates are significantly influenced by regional cultures in the United States. However, infant mortality rates are a good deal less clearly related to Southern-Northern or other gross areal distinctions than are homicide rates. In addition, differences have been declining among regions rapidly in the last thirty years, probably because medical as opposed to premedical care has become more and more determinative of the rates. The current situation is given in Map 28 for white infant death rates. Because of the special health problems of Negroes, Indians, and other nonwhite races, these groups have been omitted. (If they were not, differences in rates would largely reflect differences in percent black.) It will be noted that with few exceptions the relative position of states in 1967 was the same as in 1960, although there has been considerable improvement almost everywhere in the 1960s.

The results of comparing statistically infant mortality rates and the index of Southernness developed for homicide (above) are given in Table 10. In addition to Southernness, Table 10 contains a number of other variables that are commonly thought to explain part of the variation in infant mortality. Percentage Roman

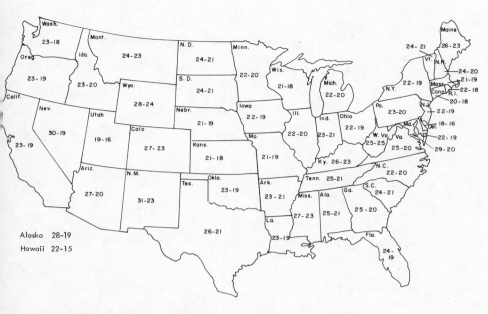

MAP 28. White Infant Death Rates, 1960 and 1967 (per 1,000 Live Births). Source: based on data from *Statistical Abstract of the United States, 1970* (Washington, D.C.: Bureau of the Census, 1970), p. 57

Catholic was added because of the evidence of earlier experimental regressions and the former emphasis of some priests on child-bearing even when under less than ideal conditions. The analysis is confused because many of the more important of the variables in this regression are also directly a part of the cultural complex labeled "Southernness." Attitudes characteristic of Southernness result in less interest in education, in making money, or in providing health facilities. There were again high intercorrelations among these variables so that what appears first is said to "explain" relatively more than it does (see also the discussion of homicide above).

In 1960 Utah had the second lowest white infant mortality rate. Examination of the residuals of the foregoing regression suggests that Utah is one of the states furthest below its predicted value in terms of the relationships of the variables in Table 10 to infant mortality. Since Utah had the lowest infant-mortality rate in 1959 and was third lowest in 1957 and 1958, its 1960 position was

TABLE 10

RELATION OF WHITE INFANT MORTALITY TO SELECTED VARIABLES
(By 48 states, 1960)

|  | Percent Variance Explained | Partial Correlation at Entry | Simple Correlation |
|---|---|---|---|
| 1. Physicians/1000 | 16.3 | .40*** | −.40*** |
| 2. Percent 20–34 | 24.9 | .32** | .30** |
| 3. Percent rural | 28.0 | .20 | .30** |
| 4. Percent Roman Catholic | 31.6 | .22 | .09 |
| 5. Government health expenditures | 35.2 | .23 | −.06 |
| 6. Index of Southernness | 39.1 | .24* | .38*** |
| 7. Median education | 41.2 | .19 | −.02 |
| 8. Hospital beds/1000 | 42.1 | −.12 | −.30** |
| 9. Percent in cities over 300,000 | 42.4 | .08 | −.13 |
| 10. White population | 42.7 | −.07 | −.24* |
| 11. Median income | 42.8 | −.06 | −.28** |
| 12. Fertility | 42.9 | −.04 | −.28** |

SOURCES: Infant mortality rate: *Vital Statistics of the United States, 1960*, Mortality, Part A (Washington, D.C.: U.S. Public Health Service, 1963), Table 3-E, pp. 3–8; (1) physicians/100,000: *Statistical Abstract, 1962* (Washington, D.C.: Bureau of the Census, 1962), p. 80; (2) percentage of the population between the ages of 20 and 34: *Statistical Abstract, 1962*, p. 27; (3) percent rural: *Statistical Abstract, 1969*, p. 17; (4) percentage of the white population belonging to the Roman Catholic church: *Churches and Church Membership in the United States*, Series A, no. 3; (5) state and local expenditures/capita, health, and hospitals: *Statistical Abstract, 1961*, p. 411; (6) index of Southernness: see text; (7) median school years completed by white population 25 years or more): *Statistical Abstract, 1969*, p. 109; (8) number of hospital beds/100,000 population: developed from number of hospital beds (*Statistical Abstract, 1962*, p. 80) and total population (*Statistical Abstract, 1969*, p. 27); (9) percentage of state population residing in cities of 300,000 or more: developed from city population (*Statistical Abstract, 1962*, pp. 22–23) and state population (*Statistical Abstract, 1969*, p. 27); (10) white population: *Statistical Abstract, 1969*, p. 27; (11) median money income of families, 1959: *Statistical Abstract, 1962*, p. 333 (corrected by a consumer price index constructed from "Consumer Price Index of Selected Cities," *Statistical Abstract, 1962*, p. 350, and "Annual Costs in a Moderate Urban Living Standard for a Four Person Family: 1967," *Statistical Abstract, 1969*, p. 348); (12) fertility rate: calculated from *Vital Statistics, 1960*, vol. 2.

NOTE: The program used (U.C.L.A. biomedical data) is such that the variable with the highest simple correlation to the dependent variable is entered first, the one with the highest remaining partial correlation entered next, and so on until there is no remaining significant partial.

*** Significant at .01 level
** Significant at .05 level
* Significant at .10 level

probably not a chance occurrence; in 1967 Utah was holding its position, with only Delaware and Hawaii below.[55] If we look somewhat further back at the historical record, we will note that Utah has not always been in such a good position nationally; for example, the Pacific Northwest states of Washington and Oregon had lower rates in the 1930s.[56] In examining the decline of infant mortality rates in the United States since 1930, at least three patterns may be distinguished. Many states followed the overall pattern of a rapid drop starting in the 1930s, then a leveling out in the early 1950s, with some states actually having higher rates in the late 1950s. Another pattern is found for most states that had relatively very high rates in 1930. Generally these states still were well above national averages in 1950. They continued to lower rates in the 1950s, although most still had relatively high rates in 1960. Colorado, New Mexico, and many Southern states fall into this class. In addition, there were a few states with fairly low rates in 1930 or 1950 that also managed to lower these still further in the 1950s—Utah and Delaware are notable examples.

To detail more specifically the influence of regional cultures as contrasted to interstate variation, an examination was made of the distribution of infant mortality rates 1951–60 by county for Utah, Idaho, Wyoming, and Colorado.[57] The data suggested first of all that the more sparsely populated counties varied more widely; however, their small populations probably made it more difficult to iron out chance variations in infant mortality. On the average, these counties also had higher infant mortality rates (see Table 11). Lower education and income in rural areas is one reason, but sheer lack of doctor availability in crises is probably important.[58] The most significant areas of low infant mortality rates (below 21/1,000) were the five most heavily populated counties in northern Utah, a group of counties in southern Idaho, and a third group of sparsely populated counties in eastern Colorado.

The comparison of Mormon Idaho with non-Mormon (western and especially northern Idaho) is instructive. The data suggested that it was not just special characteristics of the state administration of health services in Utah that resulted in lower infant mortality; nor were deficiencies in Idaho services necessarily responsible for higher Idaho averages. In Colorado among heavily populated counties only university-dominated Boulder County

TABLE 11
METROPOLITAN AND NONMETROPOLITAN COUNTIES,
1950, 1955, 1960
(White deaths under 1 year per thousand live births)

|  | 1950 | 1955 | 1960 |
|---|---|---|---|
| United States |  |  |  |
| Total | 26.8 | 23.6 | 22.9 |
| Metropolitan counties | 24.5 | 22.6 | 22.2 |
| Nonmetropolitan counties | 29.7 | 25.0 | 24.1 |
| Utah |  |  |  |
| Metropolitan counties | 20.1 | 19.9 | 17.4 |
| Nonmetropolitan counties | 25.8 | 20.2 | 21.9 |
| Colorado |  |  |  |
| Metropolitan counties | 30.6 | 29.3 | 25.4 |
| Nonmetropolitan counties | 38.9 | 31.0 | 30.0 |
| Idaho |  |  |  |
| (No metropolitan) | 27.0 | 20.7 | 22.7 |
| Wyoming |  |  |  |
| (No metropolitan) | 30.9 | 26.5 | 27.5 |

SOURCES: *Vital Statistics of the United States, 1950*, vol. 2, Table 14 (Washington, D.C.: U.S. Public Health Service, 1953); *Vital Statistics of the United States, 1955*, vol. 1, Table 20 (Washington, D.C.: U.S. Public Health Service, 1958); *Vital Statistics of the United States, 1960*, vol. 2, pt. B, Table 9-2 (Washington, D.C.: U.S. Public Health Service, 1963).

had very low rates. Very high rates in south-central Colorado reflected the old Spanish-American population in the area. The fact that high rates extended to the Kansas border in the south probably also reflected the relatively heavy influence of Southern culture in all of southern Colorado. Elsewhere, high rates in the relatively heavily populated stretch from Arapahoe and Denver counties in Colorado to Laramie County (Cheyenne) in Wyoming presented a considerable contrast to the comparable populated strip in Utah. In this Colorado piedmont there is a mixed population, including Spanish and Anglo-Texans.

Although only a small population is involved, notice should be taken of the low infant mortality along the eastern border of Colorado with northern Kansas and southern Nebraska. In particular, the situation in Kit Carson County has been the subject of considerable study.[59] Here a more detailed study of a ten-year period (presumably 1950–60) estimated a rate of 10.0, giving it one of the lowest infant mortality rates in the decade, an achievement particularly remarkable in a rural county with no more than average living standards. Clearly there was something particular in the health capabilities and attitudes of this county that made it very special. However, that Kit Carson and counties to the north should have had relatively lower rates than the rest of Colorado is not surprising. Kansas and Iowa both averaged considerably below Colorado in the 1950s. In terms of religious affiliation these counties form a continuation of the pattern found to the east, a pattern that breaks up immediately to the west.[60] Religion, of course, is not the issue, but rather the cultural affiliations represented by religion.

Returning to the Mormon cultural area, other statistics suggest that creating a particularly good physical environment in American terms for an infant is by no means an isolated phenomenon for Mormon culture. For years Utah has had one of the highest birth rates in the continental United States, and often the highest; this is even more clearly true if we consider whites alone. In the late 1960s Utah continued to maintain its leadership.[61] Only partly as a consequence of its low infant mortality rate, Utah's total death rate has generally remained below 7.0 in the 1960s, making it one of the lowest in the world. Perhaps most closely related to the infant mortality rate is the fact that Utah had the highest percentage of households that were classified as "husband-wife" in 1969.[62] Thus, Mormon family values seem to support both high fertility and low infant mortality (see Chap. IV).

Other regional or cultural considerations may be combined with an analysis of the residuals of the regression of Table 10 to improve understanding of the relation of health services to infant mortality rates. States that had considerably higher rates than that calculated by the regression included Maine (also reflected in New Hampshire and Vermont), Colorado, New Mexico, Texas, Wyoming, and Nevada. Spanish-Americans apparently account for a portion of the problem in Texas, New Mexico, and Colorado, while distance and remaining features of frontier culture or other special factors are operative in Wyoming and Nevada. Perhaps particular problems in offering or receiving health services that relate to French-Canadians are reflected in the results for Upper

New England. Other than Utah, exceptionally low rates in terms of residuals are found for Delaware, Louisiana, and North Carolina. If one notes that these states also have much higher Negro infant mortality rates in 1960 than neighboring states, we are less impressed. In terms of the regression this means that one reason for the discrepancy is that the figures used underestimated the medical facilities provided primarily for whites (that is, a greater percentage of physicians were serving primarily whites in these states than in neighboring states). The low white rate in Delaware (resulting from a very low rate in the Wilmington SMSA) should, nevertheless, be looked into further. A final way to use this evidence is to note that in terms of the factors considered in the regression, including culturally adjusted national norms for white infant mortality, Connecticut's rate of 20.0 per 1,000 live births and South Carolina's 23.9 suggest equal achievement by health services.

If we compare the present discussion with the work of Shapiro, Schlesinger, and Nesbitt cited above, several points stand out. First, as is so common in discussions of social statistics, regional differences are discussed in this work primarily in terms of the broad geographic regions of the census.[63] This approach naturally obscures the kind of phenomenon found here for the Mormon cultural region or for the Spanish-American regions within the mountain division (although Shapiro et al. mention the latter in passing). Since the regional approach suggested in this paper is only another way to consider cultural effects on infant mortality, several facts congruent with a cultural hypothesis but not proving it (because of alternative explanations) in the Shapiro text should be mentioned. First, the neonatal period, the period most under the influence of medical technology, shows white and nonwhite mortality rates to be much more similar than rates for the postneonatal period. Differences among regions and races were also higher in the one- to four-year period and for accidents than in the neonatal period.[64] In addition, Negro neonatal rates were found in a special study in New York City to be considerably higher than white rates for each occupational class, with Negro professional and managerial people having the rates of white service workers and laborers.[65] (The tendency for culture to determine to some extent occupational choice and opportunity reinforces this pattern.) Finally, the very low infant mortality rates of Chinese and Japanese in the United States in 1959–60 (14.9 and 14.2) suggest the opposite type of cultural influence. Probably not coincidentally, Japan and Taiwan both have had rates below those of the United States in recent years; Hawaii, heavily under oriental influence, had the lowest infant mortality rate in the country in 1967.[66]

It is also useful to compare the present study with the more general search for the explanation of variations in the mortality statistics of the several states by Richard Auster, Irving Leveson, and Deborah Sarachek.[67] Using data similar to that used for Table 10, and for the same period, they found that while high education went with lowered mortality, high income was associated with high mortality, as were cigarette and alcohol consumption. We did not find this relation to income, probably because medical care is more closely related to infant mortality than is general mortality. (General mortality rates are influenced by population distribution and aging.) However, it appears that the regional approach suggested here might have led to additional insights into their problem. For example, if they had looked at a map of income and educational variables, they might have noted that low-mortality northern rural states of modest median income but with few very poor were depressing mortality rates relative to states with higher median incomes but many poor. Income differentials are strongly influenced by traditional regional patterns. They might also have noted that Utah's contribution to the correlation of low mortality with less use of alcohol and cigarettes is dependent on a third factor, the strict Mormon prohibition on the use of either.

In conclusion, it has been possible to show that cultural differences account for part of the variation of infant mortality rates in this country, and that some of these differences can be seen in regional terms. Medical inputs are likely, then, to be taken up less rapidly and less thoroughly in some areas than others. The effect of general North-South cultural differences is, however, now small, with other regional cultural differences of more importance. In particular, the Mormon region was discussed as one with lower rates in the 1950s because of particular cultural factors. The inclusion of regional cultural factors takes into explicit considera-tion the fact that different people will respond to the same knowledge and service in different ways. Thus, by potentially increasing comparability, these factors make possible a better understanding of which localities or states in the nation are doing a particularly good or poor job of providing medical services relevant to the reduction of infant mortality rates.

# CHAPTER IV

# The Cultural
# and Sociocultural Regions
# and Their Subdivisions

I N CHAPTER I the argument was advanced that it would be
useful to think of the country as composed of a number of
cultural regions. The proposed regions were presented in Map
4 and briefly defended, while alternative sociocultural regions
were presented in Map 5. Chapters II and III offered substantial
support for the usefulness of cultural regionalization, as well as
other evidence for a real cultural differentiation. In this chapter,
the cultural regions mapped in Chapter I are examined in more
detail. Before proceeding, the reader should refer again to Maps 4
and 5 and the accompanying text on the basis of justification for
regional definition. Useful regional sources in addition to those
mentioned in Chapters I–III are given at the end of the book, in
Regional Bibliographies for Chapter IV. The following presenta-
tions are only sketches, starting points for an analysis, but I hope
they will suggest the problems and alternatives the approach
raises, and the possibility that it may be used constructively for
the development of a more vital national life.

In presenting the following regions, I have based much of the
picture on a consideration of population origins, which for the
early periods may repeat material already considered. The analysis below is also supported by detailed consideration of census

migration data from 1870 to 1970, and, as pointed out in Chapter I, greatest attention is given to the background of the peoples that dominated the first effective settlement.[1] Life creates its own continuity; once the patterns of life are established, there is an increasing tendency for those who move to an area, or decide to stay there, to be predisposed in favor of the area before the move, or to assimilate its culture willy-nilly. While in a few places there has been rapid change since 1960, we can presume this process of regional selectivity will have shaped most of this change. After contrasting Oregon with the rest of the West, and particularly California, a recent writer points out:

Those who leave California to live in Oregon are making a sharp change, and they usually are aware of it. . . . They cite California smog and congestion, and the desire to raise their children in a smaller community. . . . Those who later return to California—and they are not insignificant in number—talk mostly of their depression at heavy Oregon rainfall and a sense of remoteness, and their nostalgia for the live-and-let-live freedom of California.[2]

In other words, some of those who return note at least subconsciously that Oregonians are not "their kind of people."

# New England

## Population

In 1970 there were about twenty-two million people in New England. The area (see Map 29) was growing spottily, with a slightly lower overall growth rate than that of the nation as a whole in the 1960s. Except for a few Dutch and Germans in the eastern part of New York State, the original settlers in the region were primarily English of Puritan background. However, in the seventeenth-century Puritan amalgam that populated the area, there were some English of non-Puritan background, Scotch, Scotch-Irish, and French. In upstate New York the New England settlers of the next century overwhelmed the earlier community of Dutch and Germans. After its settlement, this expanded New

REGION
Sub-region
DISTRICT
Sub-districts or special areas
Non-conforming metropolitan areas

MAP 29. Northeast Cultural Regions and Districts

England experienced the full force of subsequent migrations to this country, particularly those of the Germans, Italians, and Irish in the nineteenth and twentieth centuries. This period also saw a considerable movement into the region from French Canada. A few thousand American Indians remain, particularly in upstate New York and Maine. More recently a significant urban Negro population has developed, but not to the extent farther south or west. New England has had a long record of heavy out-migration, with a comparatively stable native population. Out-of-state natives are generally from other states within the region.

## General Description

In the west the New England region is physiographically a continuation of the area to the southwest. Most of the region is hilly, with the highest mountains in the Catskills and Adirondacks of New York, the Green Mountains of Vermont, and the White Mountains and their companion ranges in New Hampshire and Maine. Only one or two peaks exceed six thousand feet. Lowlands spread out from the edges of Lake Erie and Lake Ontario. Most of Connecticut, Rhode Island, and eastern Massachusetts is also quite low, if sometimes rough. The most notable river valleys are the upper Hudson River valley and its western offshoot, the Mohawk, the upper reaches of the Susquehanna, and the Connecticut River valley.

There is a variety of different climates in the area. Along the Great Lakes and the Saint Lawrence a cold winter is followed by a dry summer, with temperatures quite warm toward the southwest. In the mountainous regions cold, snowy winters are followed by cool, wet summers. In the lowlands to the east and south relatively mild, wet winters are followed by warm, humid summers—with both heat and humidity decreasing toward the north and east.

## History

About a decade after the first settlement at Plymouth in 1620, settlers swarmed into Massachusetts Bay to establish family farms or engage in urban pursuits. The newcomers were mostly Puritans from north and east of London and they absolutely dominated the life of the colony. The Puritans were middle-class Calvinists in close communication with Dutch Protestants and Scottish Presbyterians.

The growth of the community was fairly rapid and steady. After the first decades there was continual war on the frontier with Indians, who were often encouraged by French support. At first, serious attempts were made to convert the Indians, and communities of "Praying Indians" developed. However, in King Philip's War in the 1670s many Praying Indians were killed on both sides, and the attitudes of Indians and whites stiffened. The reasons for the war suggest an equal apportionment of blame: loss of land by the Indians, who gave the land rather willingly at first but then begrudged it later when the results were seen; threatened loss of control by chiefs over their people; abandonment of the old ways; drunkenness; and desire for plunder by Indian bands. As the colony expanded, increased interest in land speculation and the tendency of settlers to establish isolated dwellings both exacerbated the conflict and increased the temptation for the Indians. Finally, on the advancing frontier continuing atrocities on both sides developed a depth of hatred and desire for revenge and extirpation that led to the essential elimination of the Indians in most of the six eastern New England states. Remembering the result, we are apt to forget the importance of the struggle. At the time of King Philip's War, and again in the eighteenth century, Indian attacks caused the abandonment of large areas of eastern New England, which were subsequently only slowly reoccupied, particularly in Maine.

In upper New York State the story was considerably different, for the Iroquois were better organized and more able to compete with the white man on his own terms. For one thing, they had had a much longer time to adjust to European civilization before the flood of settlers began. From their homes in central New York elements of the Iroquois League had destroyed Indian groups in every direction both before and after the arrival of the white man. With the French and Indian Wars and increasing pressure, however, the league tended to fall apart. Its fate was sealed when most of the tribes supported the British in the Revolutionary War. Some moved to Canada, others were gradually squeezed onto reservations. There were never many Iroquois, perhaps twenty thousand; but to a degree they have managed to maintain their identities and numbers down to the present.

The New England frontier was pressed back in all directions from the Boston-Salem-Plymouth core. Although forward movement was comparatively steady and solid, settlement skipped over some intervening land to develop the Connecticut Valley. After filling in the intervening area, settlement continued its advance. To the south, New Englanders moved onto Long Island and then into northern New Jersey. By the time of the Revolutionary War they had moved north into New Hampshire and portions of Vermont and Maine, while to the west they were moving across the New York border along its entire length. At this time New York had fewer inhabitants than New England, and many of these inhabitants were former New Englanders. Upstate, only small groups of settlers around Albany and along the Mohawk and at scattered points to the south existed outside of the New England sphere. After the revolution New England continued to expand to the north, but most of the movement was west, until by 1830 New Englanders had engulfed most of New York, and their sons were seeking lands still farther west.[3]

Although largely agricultural, almost from the beginning New England was ruled by urban leaders and urban values. The leaders of the community formed an intellectual-theological elite with international connections, and they managed for three generations to maintain an independent political-religious system. Puritan leaders did not believe in separation of church and state, but rather in their virtual identification. The "meetinghouse" they created in the New World was explicitly not a church, for it should serve both religious and secular purposes. When Puritan leaders saw that they could not rule England, some came to New England in the hope of establishing a nation they could rule. They strove to create an ideal community of one belief, free from controversy. Although an English colony, New England was to a surprising extent free of English rule. There was no Church of England for generations, and it was not until the late 1680s that the British were able to compel the area to accept a governor appointed by the king. Sometimes church leaders were also political officials, but more commonly they were sources of advice, advice that came close to direction because of their power to exclude citizens from the church.

The design of the community was formally unstructured, requiring prestige and intellectual superiority rather than force to hold it together. Each congregation had absolute control over its own affairs, and attempts to unify the system in the manner of the Presbyterians were regularly rejected. Only individual congregations could ordain a minister, and only with his congregation's permission could he leave to take another post. In the 1630s Harvard College was established to train the clergy, and from this point on the clergy were largely trained and ordained in New England. At Harvard College, and by means of the churches and printers of Boston, the elite established its pre-eminence, issuing guidelines that were generally accepted both religiously and politically in the seventeenth century. However, this elite could not compel the obedience of congregations, and ministers in western Massachusetts, Connecticut, and elsewhere published differing opinions, with which Boston contended not always successfully. Although the churches ruled, many of the people were not admitted to the church. Using the term "Brahmin" to describe the seventeenth-century elite of Massachusetts Bay has some justice. To some extent the priesthood was hereditary in family lines, it was dominant without ruling, and dominant over a religious society in which many were outside the religious pale.

Members of the church were called "saints" and they made all secular and religious decisions. As T. J. Wertenbaker explains:

It was fundamental to the congregational conception of a true church that none but saints be admitted. "By saints we understand such as have not only attained knowledge of the principles of religion and are free of gross and open scandals, but also do, together with the profession of their faith and repentance, walk in blameless obedience to the Word. . . . Nothing can be more fatal to the interest of religion than to constitute churches of unsanctified members." [4]

This was a controlled community in which frivolity and idleness were outlawed. To each ten families in some communities a tithing man was appointed to see if any were avoiding private worship, using profanity, or idling. Drinking was not prohibited as in a later puritan tradition, but drunkenness was a crime.

Although maintaining social distinctions was seen as a means of maintaining values, the New England town represented a great increase in democracy for the average immigrant. As one historian says:

For the first time in their lives, the inhabitants of an English town were assuming that each adult male would be granted some land, free and clear. [The settler might be] shifting from a village in which half the adult males were landless laborers, and the other half tenants paying yearly rents and feudal fees, to a Massachusetts town in which he had the power to grant land to all inhabitants according to "estates and persons." [5]

Although for some purposes many were excluded from decisions, in fact most people had from the beginning much more say than they had had back home.

As time passed, the original Puritan society evolved. The children of the pioneers were often unable to show the required evidence of personal conversion. When this resulted in a lower percentage of church members, the elites were forced to admit less consecrated persons into the churches. As London exerted more direct control, property qualifications became more important than religious qualifications for political participation. With pressure on the land and the growth of cities, class distinction became more important and political issues were separated from religious. Disputes within the church led to the establishment of rival intellectual centers such as Yale. Liberal thought from England mediated through Harvard, along with the reassertion of London's control, created a liberalized attitude toward religious differences. Presbyterians, Baptists, Anglicans, Friends, and Roman Catholics were grudgingly given a place. Religious emphasis began to switch from severe Calvinist rationalism to emphasis on good works, on emotional goodness. This evolution allowed many New Englanders to go over to Methodism or Presbyterianism, especially among New England emigrants. Most decisive in the breaking up of the community of God was the adoption of Unitarianism by the elite intellectuals of Harvard at the beginning of the nineteenth century. This evolution led to a variety of sects, notably transcendentalism among a few intellectuals, Mormonism among rural New Englanders, and Christian Science among the urban bourgeoisie.

The descendants of the Puritans continued to emphasize towns, education, and religions. New England communities educated so many native New Englanders in the nineteenth century that they became the teachers of the rest of the country from kindergarten through college. Yet, Boston's influence decreased with distance. As society moved north and west, towns were less carefully and consistently laid out, and religion less central. Even before New Englanders were affected by the arrival of new immigrants or mixed with other peoples in the West, these changes were occurring. Perhaps nowhere else is the relation between core and periphery as easy and regular to trace in a cultural area: intensity of New England patterns regularly lessens with time and distance from the core.

In the nineteenth century waves of immigration changed the heavily populated portions of New England into Irish-, Italian-, and French Canadian–dominated sections. Most New Englanders are now Catholic. Yet the change was gradual enough and the prestige of the elite held on so well that the New Englander today is still more under the influence of New England tradition than are Americans elsewhere. Senator Kennedy is Catholic and Senator Brooke is black, yet in their public attitudes and positions they represent a continuation of New England tradition.

Subsistence agriculture was the foundation of colonial New England, although there were some exports of wood and agricultural produce. Because it was never a really good agricultural area, maritime activities—fishing, whaling, shipbuilding, international trade—were important from a very early period. The authoritarianism of the ship made a poor school for democracy. The form of New England life, the independence and local democracy that imparted so much to the rest of the nation, grew out of the farming community. In the early nineteenth century, agriculture began to die out because of western competition, although sheep and wool production gave a brief autumn, and Maine potatoes and other specialty crops were important early in this century. Shipping and shipbuilding declined rapidly after 1860 because the region's love affair with the clipper ships made it hang on too long to the sail. Manufacturing based on textile mills established along New England's rivers dominated urban growth in the nineteenth century. With the decline of textile, footwear, and related industries, high-technology industries such as electronics and machinery manufacture have come to occupy an important place in the economy of the region after World War II.

# Regional Characteristics

Many attempts have been made to describe the New England character. One of the best is that of Samuel Eliot Morrison:

It was Yankee, a new Nordic amalgam on an English Puritan base; already in 1750 as different in its character and its dialect from the English as the Australians are today. A tough but nervous, tenacious but restless race; materially ambitious, yet prone to introspection, and subject to waves of religious emotion. Conservative in its ideas of property and religion, yet (in the eighteenth century) radical in business and government. A people with few social graces, yet capable of deep friendships and abiding loyalties; law-abiding yet individualistic, and impatient of restraint by government or regulation in business; ever attempting to repress certain traits of human nature, but finding an outlet in broad, crude humor and deep-sea voyages. A race whose typical member is eternally torn between a passion for righteousness and a desire to get on in the world. Religion and climate, soil and sea, here brewed of a mixed stock a new people.[6]

After dismissing many oversimplifications, George Pierson concluded that there was a New England culture because (1) the original settlers came as a peculiar people endowed with extraordinary will and talent for concerted effort illustrated by three great creations—the congregation, town meeting, and public school system; (2) for two hundred years they maintained a high degree of exclusiveness, forming a culture by exclusion; and (3) they have generally been recognized as different, as almost un-American—pessimist not optimist, introvert not extrovert, frugal not wasteful. Feeling outnumbered, nineteenth-century New England developed the "area grievance" required by regionalism and set forth on three campaigns: to Christianize and control the West, to reform the South, and to industrialize and capitalize the East. In the 1950s Pierson saw a revived New England in which regional feeling persists, educational leadership remains, and independence of mind and moral idealism are still taken very seriously.[7] Restraint with idealism is also a characteristic of the best of New England.[8] To me the primary inheritance from nineteenth-century New England is emphasis on the importance of words, ideas, and theories as opposed to the simple calculation of the interest of different groups in society. (Compare the discussion of Elazar's moralistic political culture in Chapter II.)

Of course, there has always been a variety of New Englanders—of the sea, of the city, of the countryside, of trade, and of factory. At least four different levels of culture should be distinguished here: (1) farmer; (2) trader, craftsman, and merchant; (3) intellectual elite; and (4) industrial proletariat.

Since New England society and its emigrants at the time of its later dispersal were made up mostly of farmers, almost down to the present, farm life may be regarded as the backbone of the popular culture. Although farm life in New England has always been characterized by the independent proprietor, the original community was in many respects a utopian peasant commune. Its small, rocky subsistence farms were quite unlike those of colonial Pennsylvania. Toward the west, the New England farm became larger with changing standards of living and better land. The farm itself had at first been separated from the dwelling plot of the family in the tight community (see Chap. II, "Housing and Settlement Styles"). When later settlements and the disappearance of the Indian threat separated the houses, the community was still quite cohesive, well integrated with its church and school.

The principles of life were sobriety, hard work, order, and self-reliance. Consensus was more the key than democracy. Compared to similar subsistence farms in the South, the New Englander worked harder, ate a more varied and plentiful diet which produced better health, and was more regular in church and school attendance. Although he had a gun for hunting, the farmer was almost never involved in violent quarrels and there was relatively little crime. True to the restricted emotional tone of the community, religion was traditionally less violent than in the South or West. The Salem witch trials may seem an exception; yet it is characteristic of highly controlled societies to have occasional outbreaks of this sort. The comparatively intense and quiet Pueblo communities of the Southwest have also been marked by outbreaks of concern with witches. However, one should note that the Salem witch trials were relatively sober judicial proceedings and by no means lynchings.

Lura Beam's description of the people of a Maine hamlet may give some of the feeling for the way of life of the common rural people around the turn of this century:

The success of their lives in a cold country on stony ground is very English; so is their reserve toward the arts. Spirituals, dancing, and island arts produced in isolation came from other climates, conditions and temperaments. These people were too set on subsistence goals, too reined in emotionally. . . . Its citizens were striving for conduct, not art. They were creating themselves, by rules, by conflict, by appreciation, by recognition. Many of these unknown lived well and died well—silent, consistent, and organized to the end. Some of them talked well. . . . Everyone could do something in the practical arts, men in farm crafts, women in household arts. Everyone was supposed to excel in one or two of the tasks of his routine. Those who did not were called "gormless," which means lacking in sense of form or in an ability to achieve it. The standard of the ordinary task included the organization, skill, finish and style that mark the artist.[9]

The trader and artisan class of Paul Revere and the young Benjamin Franklin was freer of conventions, less under the thumb of the church in traditional New England. Although industrious and conscientious in the New England manner, traders seemed to feel they had a right to reject the severe morality of the farmer who prided himself on not being small in his dealings. The "Yankee peddler" often cheated his customers, regarding his relationship to them as a kind of game. "Sharp" or dishonest business practices were understood, if often resented. As time passed, many of this level rose to be great merchants or financiers. Their interests, and the growing cultural cleavage of worker and owner, made them hardly the proponents of democracy.

All elements held the intelligentsia in considerable esteem, and it was the intelligentsia that was able to bind the parts together. The New England elite was hard-working, but more remarkable was the degree to which it emphasized intellectual attainment and teaching. The importance of Harvard in the administrations of Franklin Roosevelt and John Kennedy was merely one of the many recurrent attempts of this elite to dominate a nation in which its ideals are accepted by only a small minority.[10] Since creative minds are seldom easy to classify, it is hard to find generalizations that fit New England intellectualism. It is persistent and self-satisfied, highly moral, especially about the faults of others. Henry Adams describes his classmates of 1858 as "singularly indifferent to display, artifice, florid expression, . . . distrustful of themselves but little disposed to trust anyone else; with not much humor of their own. . . . They never flattered, seldom praised, . . . their attitude was a law of nature; their judgment beyond appeal. . . . Each individual was satisfied to stand alone . . . yet to stand alone is quite natural when one has no passions." [11]

Here is the rural New England farmer in intellectual clothes, but also much of the rationalistic, Puritan minister of two centuries before. The literary achievements of New England society in the mid-nineteenth century were still the products of a remarkably homogeneous society. New immigrant peoples were coming in, but they did not play a part in the intellectual world. These New Englanders were open to the ideas of the world, just as the Mathers had been in the seventeenth century; but they persisted in seeing these ideas in their own terms. In common with the older Puritan tradition, they believed in themselves and their mission. As Van Wyck Brooks says of the intellectuals of Boston, Cambridge, and Concord, "that New England was appointed to guide the nation, to civilize and humanize it, none of them ever doubted." [12]

The proletariat underclass always existed in New England, but at first it was small. Relatively few indentured servants were brought to New England and there were few slaves. In early industrialization there was a deliberate attempt not to create a proletariat. The Lowell Mills of the early nineteenth century employed girls off the farms in a highly paternalistic manner, with an emphasis on education. Soon native New Englanders could not be found to work in the factories and man the ships for New England's industrial and mercantile expansion. The new proletariat imported to do the work of the community represented very different values. In time these new peoples developed a political and cultural leadership that could successfully compete with the old aristocracy. However, this leadership has also merged with the old aristocracy to form a new New England elite.

With the decline of religion as the avenue of communication from top to bottom of society, there is perhaps a greater gap today in New England between the thinking of the elite and masses than there has ever been, a gap affecting both Catholics and Protestants. Yet its prestige remains, and the intellectual elite continues to lead the region as nowhere else in the country. It is this elite that makes Massachusetts the most liberal state politically in the union, especially on national and international issues.[13]

The "town" as the essence of New England popular culture has its equivalent only in descriptions of the Midwest regions. Its sense of harmony, of man and nature in equilibrium has often been evoked in studies of the area. Today, with emphasis on suburbia and exurbia, the town as a new focus of life for people with quite ample incomes and metropolitan interests continues to feed the popular mythology. In 1971 two of the more popular new nonfiction books were based on contemporary New England villages (Anthony Bailey's *In the Village* and Edmund Wilson's *Upstate*). The "natural world" bordering urban areas in such locales may seem so populated as to be quite "unnatural" to a citizen of the Rocky Mountain or Pacific Northwest regions. Yet we must remember that Thoreau's nineteenth-century Walden lay only a few miles from Concord and quite close to a railroad track. He regularly walked to town to spend the day.

New England dominated American literature in the nineteenth century. The rest of the nation had distinguished writers, but the New England group of Thoreau, Emerson, Hawthorne, Lowell, Longfellow, Dana, Prescott, and the others was outstanding. The intellectual dominance of New England, expressed and abetted by its high production of schoolteachers and college professors, led many Americans brought up far from New England to identify New England with Colonial America. Perhaps the celebration of Thanksgiving ("New England Day"?) best symbolizes this identification. Although Robert Frost wrote strictly as a regional poet, the identification of New England with the whole nation that has been achieved through literary dominance made him seem a national poet to the mid-twentieth-century American.

In the twentieth century, however, Southern, Mid-Atlantic, and Midwest writers have achieved at least equal prominence, especially outside of poetry. The greatest shift in the balance of intellectual forces against New England has been achieved by the immigrant populations, particularly the Jews, who have risen to high positions throughout the intellectual establishment. Their unsentimental, urban, and urbane attachment to learning and position wherever support can be found, together with their sentimental and cultural attachment to New York City, has greatly reduced the dominance of New England intellectual culture. Nevertheless, New England is far ahead of the rest of the nation in both the quantity and the quality of its higher education and research. Its greater reliance on private institutions and the gradual Americanization of the American Jewish community may make it possible for New England to co-opt this challenge as it has those of the past. The establishment since World War II of Brandeis University near the Harvard-M.I.T. complex both symbolizes and promotes this process.

# Districts, Subdistricts, and Sociocultural Subdivisions

In New England, sociocultural borders are in general identical to the cultural (see Map 29). The region naturally falls into two subregions: Eastern and Western. The primary basis for distinguishing the districts within Eastern New England is that of historical development from a single core. The *Core District* covers most of Massachusetts and Connecticut, as well as southeastern New Hampshire and the southern tip of Maine. Within the region it represents the area of most seventeenth-century settlement outside of Rhode Island, and is today a highly urbanized area of mixed population.

The *Old Frontier District* includes most of Maine and New Hampshire, all of Vermont, western Massachusetts, and a small area of Connecticut and New York. Although the central Connecticut Valley portion of this district was settled in the seventeenth century, it exhibited from the first a frontier attitude, a democratic egalitarianism not found on Massachusetts Bay. This distinction has been important ever since. Vermont was founded in part by free thinkers, and later produced the founders of the Latter Day Saints. Maine has been a home of Baptists and has had the longest experience of any area with the prohibition of alcoholic beverages. Even in New Hampshire, only the southeastern corner is under metropolitan influence.[14] The Old Frontier District has always been much less thickly settled than the core. With ease of access, the area is at least making a population comeback as a vacation land and site of specialized industry. However, this development still has not touched the district's interior and has barely entered Maine. Along its northern edge, the French Canadians have become dominant in a considerable area (marked in Map 29 as a special area), but as a whole the district is more Protestant and native American than the urbanized core.

The *Rhode Island District* is historically part of the original core area, yet from its founding Rhode Island has followed its own way. When most New Englanders speak of New England, they ignore Rhode Island. For example, in the collection *We Were New England*, a wide variety of selections include essentially nothing on Rhode Island.[15] Vermont is mentioned very little because it is a new state, but it is within the pale as Rhode Island is not. In the eyes of Boston, the sacred New England community was never established in Rhode Island. The result of Roger Williams' stand on the religious issues of his day was to allow Friends, Anglicans, Roman Catholics, and others a berth long before they could enter the body of New England. Newport looked south. In the nineteenth century it was a favorite resort of the wealthy from New York City and the South. The slave trade was important to Newport as it was not to Boston. First to industrialize, Rhode Island came to be more dominated by immigrant Catholic cultures (French Canadian, Irish, and Italian) than was the case in the rest of New England. It is significant that in 1971 there were many more Congregationalists (United Church of Christ) than Episcopalians in all states of eastern New England except Rhode Island, where Episcopalians outnumbered Congregationalists three to one.[16] The proudest relics the tourist sees in Rhode Island are the Newport mansions from the time this area was a playground of the wealthy of New York City. Although it participated in the elite literary development of New England to some extent, liberal tradition and cosmopolitan society did not produce the intellectual or artistic flowering in Rhode Island that might have been expected. It is not surprising that a small survey of college students recently showed Rhode Island ranked lower than other New England states as a place to live.[17]

The traditional New England of the six states requires little defense as a region. However, the inclusion of upstate New York as well as a broad strip of Pennsylvania in an expanded New England cultural region is open to a great deal of question. This is the home of what might be called "third-wave New Englanders." But it is also the home of many nineteenth-century immigrants of other backgrounds.[18] It would be possible to see upstate New York, or at least the western half of the subregion, as a part of the Upper Midwest. With every step westward tradition becomes more "Midwestern," and Cleveland is not too different from Buffalo. Although historically the New England inheritance is much more solid in the subregion than anywhere to the west, centers of New England excellence are more to be found in Michigan and Wisconsin than upstate New York. The massive

Albany Mall of Rockefeller is New York City style, not upstate. Edmund Wilson writes:

> I come to feel, when I have been here for any length of time, the *limited* character of upstate New York. It does not go very far into the past and it does not come very far forward into the present. A phase of American life is preserved here and still flourishing; and yet, there is still about the better-class life a sort of cold-storage quality. The people have been nice here and decent, more amiable and outgoing than they are in New England, serious-minded and moderately cultivated; but there is no great liveliness of interchange, no density of the "spiritual" life. Religion now hardly exists.[19]

The Chautauqua Assembly established in 1874 on Chautauqua Lake in far western New York State was originally a summer school for religious studies, but for most of the country the Chautauqua Assembly was the forerunner of the general summer school and symbol of the lecture circuit for cultural uplift. At the same time, Chautauqua had the flavor of the fun and culture attitude toward mass education that is much more characteristic of areas to the west than of New England. To me, Chautauqua symbolizes the far edge of New England. Institutions of higher education, such as Colgate and Cornell, remind one of New England; the larger Syracuse, Buffalo, and Rochester universities more of the Midwest or New York City. The final cultural placement of this region awaits better regional analysis. Socio-culturally that part of the region in Pennsylvania should be considered Pennsylvanian, while upstate New York may alternately be grouped with the New York Metropolitan Region, its other neighbors, or treated separately.

Western New England can be divided into several districts. The most important and urbanized are the *Hudson-Mohawk* on the east and *Western New York*. The Hudson-Mohawk contains the remnants of prerevolutionary upstate culture and the Southern Adirondack playgrounds of New York City. Western New York contains the larger, newer cities of New York; it has the most industry, best farms, and best schools of upstate. A *Saint Lawrence District* in the far north contains many French Canadians, and is as much oriented to Vermont and Canada as to New York. An *Appalachian District* contains primarily the parts of the region that are oriented southward, especially toward the Susquehanna and Delaware river valleys. This area is Protestant-dominated, almost a refuge area for the native Americans who have been overwhelmed elsewhere in the subregion.

## Problems and Potential

The sense of mission of the New England elite still animates its great educational institutions and many of its business institutions. But the sense of commitment of more ordinary people may have fared less well. There must be developed channels of communication and mutual understanding that allow all of the people to participate in and support the missions of the future. One cannot help but think that its great universities would also be improved in this way. It might be useful if the intellectuals of Harvard, Yale, and other institutions in their sphere knew more of the life of the people around them, more of the regional role of their predecessors, and more of the historic role of the region in the nation. Their persistent claim to universalism and civilization is worthy of respect, yet from the regional point of view they claim both too much and too little. In one sense Athens spoke to the world, in another primarily to Athenians.

Only the South has the sense of regionality that New England has, and of the two, only New England is small and unified enough for regional planning and promotional activities to have an important impact. Regional organizations such as the New England Council consciously direct their activities toward developing a regional sense, while other economic and political regional organizations work toward more immediate ends.

Economically New England is likely to remain a slow-growth area. Movement in the nation continues south and west, and both fertility and immigration are now suppressed nationally. In these conditions the "hinterland" that is most apt to affect New England culturally is French Canada. Higher birth rates and a new migration from Canada might give the majority of northern New England states, at least, to the French. Unlike other immigrant waves, the French Canadians, closely related to a contiguous homeland across the border, may have a more lasting cultural impact than the immigrants before them. Imbued with cultural nationalism, they are less likely to fall under the influence of the old New England elite than are other immigrants to the region.

Slow growth should not be seen as an evil in the next period of New England. The influence of New England outside of the region has always been more qualitative than quantitative, and preserving and expanding its qualitative mission offers quite enough challenge. The nation still needs more *good* teachers and *good* ideas than New England produces.

New England never did as well at educating the new immigrants into its cities in the late nineteenth century as it did in educating the rest of the country through the emigration of the preceding Puritan generations. Today, with another immigrant group, the Negroes, it seems likewise to be doing more poorly than it should. In part the problem is stagnation, an inability to make the transition from the elite educational standards of the nineteenth century to the mass standards of the twentieth; in part it is the unwillingness to adapt New England culture to immigrant cultures; in part it is the natural hostility of one wave of immigrants toward those that follow.

For whatever good or human reason, until recently mass education has been neglected. Elite standards were high, and those who failed to meet them were ignored, their education given over to the poorly educated, prejudiced, and poorly paid. In this area, as in no other, New England should exert itself—not to copy national trends and values, but to create new and more adequate answers to the need of all for meaningful education that places them within rather than outside of the community. The nation still needs the examples of hard work, simplicity, education, taste, and moral fervor that New England society at its best has always represented. Controlling growth, New England can also maintain and improve upon a panorama of quiet beauty unknown in the rest of the country. It can certainly do more toward preserving the beauty and meaning of its historical heritage. As Ada Louise Huxtable points out, even the milltowns should be looked at again.[20] New England of all places should stand against the grain, even if only for the sake of resisting the uniformity and flatness of modernity.

Both Rhode Island and upstate New York have problems of

regional identification. Rhode Island can either develop its image as a particularly liberal and cosmopolitan New England, or it can try to change its image to that of an autonomous culture in its own right. Finally, it may choose to be an outlier of the New York Metropolitan Region. Upstate New York has a more complicated choice in whole or in part. The people of the subregion, or its separate districts, may decide to strengthen their New England affiliation or gradually to replace this with other affiliations—a distinct possibility being the evolution of an upstate cultural region. If the latter does not occur, it is likely that the subregion will be drawn apart, to be metaphorically divided among surrounding regions. Politically, further integration into the New York Metropolitan Region would be easiest. Yet the traditional upstate need to balance off the city also forms a basis for sharpening rather than dulling the cultural cleavage.

# The New York Metropolitan Region

## Population

In 1970 there were over seventeen million people in the New York Metropolitan Region (see Map 29), making it the most densely populated region in the country. Growth rates were considerably below national averages, although suburbs continued to expand. The region has always been characterized by a high percentage of recent immigrants and it continues to have the highest percentage of foreign-born in the nation. New York draws relatively little on the rest of the country. About 85 percent of the native whites in the region were born within it; most mobility in the 1970s was between northern New Jersey and New York City. By 1960, 63 percent of the blacks in New York City were born there, with the rest drawn almost entirely from the South Atlantic states. The overwhelming majority of Puerto Ricans resident on the mainland live in the metropolitan area.

## General Description

The Piedmont narrows and nearly disappears in the New York City area. A flat, sandy coastal plain occupies the area to the south and east of New York City. To the west and northwest, a swampy lowland is succeeded by rolling hills that rise into the Appalachians at the southern edge of the Catskills. To the north the rocky roughness that characterizes Manhattan Island continues up both sides of the Hudson, and is responsible for a remarkable preservation of forest cover. Because of physical geography, travel and trade have always moved either north up the Hudson, or northeast to southwest along the line of the megalopolis. Most of the region has a mild climate slightly warmer than that of Boston.

## History

New York was settled by the Dutch shortly after the establishment of the Plymouth Colony. But the settlements were largely for trade with the Indians, and so remained quite small. The Dutch developed a system of feudal grants that was confirmed and extended by the British, although it was abandoned early in New Jersey because of a confusion of ownership that resulted in overlapping grants. For generations the difficulties of obtaining land of one's own in New York held down development and deflected migration to Pennsylvania and New Jersey. In the early eighteenth century New York City still had a relatively underdeveloped hinterland to the north. The number of Dutch was never large; many were actually "Dutchified" French Huguenots, Germans, or others. When the English took over in 1664 the province of New York contained only eight thousand people, of whom perhaps two-thirds were Dutch. Because of the strength of the Dutch Reformed church and the fertility of the people, they remained an important force in several parts of the region, with the use of Dutch in many churches continuing into the nineteenth century. Nevertheless, the dominant people by 1700 throughout the region were English, although of several different kinds. Most important were the New Englanders who moved into the city,

onto Long Island, and into northern Jersey, and westward from
New England toward the Hudson River along its entire length. In
New York City there was also a mixed English population in
which the Anglicans were socially dominant.

Until the early nineteenth century New York was only one of a
number of Atlantic port cities of comparable importance, and
there was no unified national economy. Economically each city
relied for trade primarily on the enterprise of its mariners and the
production of its nearby farmers; and in these respects New York
was not particularly favored. By 1800, however, the destruction of
the power of the Iroquois had opened upstate New York, and
trade flowed down the Hudson. With the opening of the Midwest,
the Erie Canal was built as the only effective means of bulk
transportation other than the Mississippi River. Rapidly New
York City became *the* city. Its harbors were deep and accessible,
and most railroads chose the terminal whose importance had
already been established by barge traffic. Thus in spite of the early
lead of Philadelphia and the fabled enterprise of New Englanders,
New York City attained a primacy it never lost, for the first city to
centralize an economy obtains an almost unbreakable grip.

The development of the city was in stages that are still
preserved by the names of its subdivisions. Until nearly the end of
the nineteenth century New York City was restricted to Manhattan Island, while other large cities, notably Brooklyn, grew
nearby. The boroughs of New York have remained subcities to a
degree not found in other cities in the country. In more recent
years, attempts to establish a much larger unit of metropolitan
government have been balanced by attempts to decentralize
control, especially of the schools.

# Regional Borders and
# Regional Characteristics

Wherever the feudal tenures were broken, the New Englanders
established villages and towns in the metropolitan area that
contrast with the large independent farms that characterized the
Pennsylvanian Region to the south. With the growth of the city

and the ring of urbanized life that surrounded it, the New England influence was submerged in the nineteenth century. Today, all of Long Island is in the metropolitan region culturally, as is a part of Fairfield County, Connecticut. New York City influence now extends up the Hudson as far as Dutchess County and on the west into the southern Catskills. To the west and southwest the region is demarcated from the Pennsylvanian Region by a line running roughly southeastward from Warren County, New Jersey, through Princeton to the Atlantic Ocean somewhere in Ocean County. The line is approximately that established between East and West Jersey in 1676. However, even more than other regional boundaries, that of the New York Metropolitan Region has been a moving boundary that cannot be defined precisely.

We think of New York as the center of American civilization. Indeed, it is where money is and where most people with talent gravitate. There immigrant talent in all the arts and in many of the professions is most likely to find a home. Great musical organizations, museums, the theaters, and nearly all of the major publishers are located in the city. Yet if we consider its potential richness, the metropolitan region has been surprisingly uncreative. Although New York City has given us Irving, Cooper, Melville, Whitman, and Wharton, the metropolitan area has not dominated American literature as Paris has dominated the French. New England and the South have equally significant literary traditions.

New York City plays an anomalous role in the country because it is culturally the most distinct from any considerable hinterland. The city has historically had one of the seven distinct dialects in the country (see Chap. II, "Dialect Regions"). It is the only region where Jewish culture plays a dominating everyday role in life from high art through popular art to the foods available on the street. Prime-time national television is infused with New York City culture, beliefs, and attitudes, particularly those of its highly literate Jewish community. (In public television New England's WGBH shares influence, but this affects only a small minority.) Outside of prime time, the more general American influence of Hollywood, Southern influences in religion and music, and the non–New York addiction to spectator sports play a larger role in television and radio. New York has almost complete control of elite thinking in the country through its control of the *New York Times* and the *Wall Street Journal*, as well as the *National Review* on the right and numerous journals on the left.

With all of its power and its control of the media, New York does not run the country (nor, certainly, does Washington, D.C.). Franklin Roosevelt's Hyde Park seems to be about as close as a man can live to New York City to be elected president in recent times. Leading congressmen are relatively seldom from New York State, partly because the volatility of its public makes it hard to build seniority. The great foundations are centralized here, but New York's universities do not dominate higher education, nor are its research institutions the most renowned.

Yet it is a center of quality. Thomas Griffith, a man from Seattle, explained it well:

Out of the congested streets of New York comes a toughness and resilience of character that knows what it wants and is unsentimental in demanding it. Its most familiar product is that pushing, fast-talking, ruthless fellow who will step on faces to get where he wants. The quality manifests itself also in that mordant, unsparing wit that is the style of those big-time comedians who honed themselves on hecklers on the borscht circuit in the Catskills; it is also to be heard among thousands of New Yorkers, cab drivers and delivery boys, who pass off their daily complaints in the same rhythm of caustic wisecrack and deadpan response, as if wit would be spoiled if given too good a reception. Economy of words, and those slurred, is the New York speech; courtesy, consideration and sympathy are carefully rationed: "So what? We all got problems."

The unsentimental, demanding metropolitan quality that is New York's gift to the rest of the country has its origins in harsh circumstances and European beginnings. Here there is none of the West's sunny benevolence conferred on all but on none deeply: Old World families, a unit to themselves, are capable of strong feeling within it, but against everyone else are armored like armadillos. Among these people—the Italians, the Poles, the Russians, but above all the Jews—humor is never far from melancholy. They seem to have been born generations ago, and never to have passed through naivete. They know the price of things, and think you a fool if you do not. They demand value. They know that they must work to get ahead, and are not indulgent of those who plead their charm to escape being judged on their merit. It is not only the poor who have this severity of judgment; among Jewish intellectuals, among wealthy Jews, among other European groups in New York are inherited standards in music, in art, in medicine, in science: if you would claim a special distinction, then deserve it. I do not mean that all Jews, all

Fig. 1. New England house and church styles, Hainesville, N.H. *Photo by Dick Smith, courtesy of State of New Hampshire Office of Vacation Travel*

Fig. 2. "Dogtrot" house, Great Onyx Cave, Ky. *Courtesy of the Library of Congress*

Fig. 3. Sam Houston's home in Huntsville, Texas, an example of the tidewater house style. *Courtesy of the Texas Highway Department*

Fig. 4. A rectilinear plan in difficult topography. Wilmerding, Allegheny County, Pa., 1887. *Courtesy of the Library of Congress*

Fig. 5. New England town settlement, Lincoln, Vt., 1940. *Courtesy of the Library of Congress*

Fig. 6. "Its harbors were deep and accessible. . . ." New York City with Jersey piers. *Courtesy of the New York Port Authority*

Fig. 7. "The exceptional fertility of Southeast Pennsylvania." York County, Pa., 1939. *Courtesy of the Library of Congress*

Fig. 8. The Pennsylvania Amish helping a neighbor build a barn. *Courtesy of the Pennsylvania Department of Commerce*

Europeans, have good taste (any more than all Negroes have rhythm) and if it is tawdriness they want, they can be just as demanding of value. But there is in New York City a sophisticated nucleus centering around them that makes for exacting critics and appreciative audiences. This is not the world of the Western United States, pleased to have heard an evening of chamber music at all: New Yorkers insist that the performance must measure up, and from their ruthlessness come the big city's standards of quality, the seeming heartlessness that sets it off from the rest of the country.[21]

Conceiving themselves as living in the nucleus of the country, New Yorkers write national histories while writers elsewhere write regional histories, or national histories from regional viewpoints.[22] New York City has been the center of American cosmopolitanism for a long time. A study of the press in the colonies before the Revolutionary War found that the newspapers of New York and Philadelphia were most inclined to print news about the European continent and least likely to print news of their own colony. The Southern papers were most apt to print news of the colonies as a whole, while Boston papers printed the largest proportion of their news about Massachusetts and Great Britain.[23]

Although the New York Metropolitan Region is more authentically heterogeneous in its cultural makeup than any other region in the country, New York is less a reflection of the country as a whole than the Pacific Southwest, or even southern Florida. The heterogeneity of post-1800 immigrant groups, especially the smaller ones, is more entrenched in the region than elsewhere. The melting pot has perhaps been least successful here because of the continual infusion of new compatriots from the homeland, and the sheer size of the many nationality groupings.

Perhaps the effect of New York City upon northern New Jersey has been destructive. In any event, the state of New Jersey illustrates nearly all of the currents and trends in American history, and particularly its problems. Torn apart by ties to two major centers, both outside of its borders, it has never been able to create a guiding sense of statehood. Its southernmost county, Cape May, looks back proudly on a New England heritage, while to the north its largest city, Newark, is black. Historically, the older population of Dutch, New Englanders, Quakers, Scotch-Irish, and Swedish was inundated by Irish Catholics and Germans, while these were again overrun by Italians, East Europeans,

Hungarians, and Jews, and again by Southern whites, Negroes, and Puerto Ricans. Before 1900 the people of the rural white Protestant counties were outnumbered by more recent immigrants and in many places these in turn have been twice overrun by even more recent migrants. Feeling little sense of community, these groups have repeatedly clashed.

The result has been a hollowed-out society, without leadership, style, or purpose. Organized crime has been most successful here, and pollution is the most intense. Northern New Jersey thrives on its location and its pool of highly skilled industrial labor. But this is not enough. Perhaps nowhere else is it so important for a population to be encouraged to develop a feeling for the direction of their loyalties and their identities. Nowhere else is it so imperative that a people be allowed to catch its breath, to emphasize quality rather than quantity. But again, this cannot be done without a sense of identity—and this may not be achievable along state lines.

## Subregions, Districts, and Sociocultural Subdivisions

Within the New York Metropolitan Region, several districts may be identified. The *Metropolitan Core District* should include the city plus continuously developed areas as far north as central Westchester and as far east as eastern Nassau, as well as an area immediately across the George Washington bridge. The *Hudson-Essex District* includes the heavily ethnic and black areas of Newark, Jersey City, Bayonne, Elizabeth, and their immediate environs. While to some extent a continuation of New York City, this area has had a somewhat different history. Newark is more than another borough of Manhattan, as the census suggests by considering it a separate metropolitan area. *Puritan New Jersey* includes the remainder of the state that is within the New York Metropolitan Region. Although the presence of New Englanders here has marked the area off within the region, their continuing influence is less than in the Western subregion of New England. Other districts are the *Eastern Long Island* and *Northern Periphery*. It is characteristic of the last three districts that, while heavily impacted by New York City culture, they retain some of the flavor of the population that settled the area in colonial times. Puritan, Scotch-Irish, and Dutch influences still play a more significant role than in the City.

In sociocultural terms the separation between the history of New York City and New York State has made the problem of regional differentiation more than ever complex. As Map 5 illustrates, both New Jersey and upstate New York are sociocul-turally transitional areas. In some senses "upstate" should be considered as multiregional, for it faces in several directions. Upstate New York's cultural ties are more with New England, but its political, and often elite, ties have been with New York City. It also has close relations with Canada, Pennsylvania, and the Upper Midwest. As I noted above, New Jersey is a state without a focus of its own, torn between two metropolitan centers outside its boundaries.

## Problems and Potential

The problems of the region are to a considerable extent those of struggle for space, privacy, and the preservation of the wide variety of local life forms. The size of the New York market, combined with the increasing influence of market size rather than raw materials on economic opportunity, means that economically the region as a whole is apt to remain reasonably sound, at least in the short term. This does not necessarily help the cities. Pressure to leave the dangerous inner cities is increasing. The result is suburban occupation of more and more of the countryside, and the impoverishment of the amenities for which cities are famous. Recent proposals to reduce zoning regulation for egalitarian reasons may cause a further and more chaotic suburban expansion. People will gradually cease to support what they can no longer easily or safely reach. New York City has the most thoroughly urbanized population in the country, partially because many of its immigrants in the last hundred years either were thoroughly urban when they came or came from peasant peoples with little love of the land (especially Irish and Italians). Yet New Yorkers continue to leave. Lack of safety in the schools, in housing projects, or for the old is often cited as a reason. The more families that leave the city, the worse the problem becomes.

Yet it is easy to lose perspective. Recent reports indicate that the New York SMSA scores higher than most metropolitan areas in the nation on many indicators: scores were particularly high on social equality, mental health (very low suicide rate), and transportation (the study obviously favored mass transit), but low on housing, public order, and community concern. The people are apparently optimistic about their future and rank their city generally far above competitors in quality of life.[24] The problems of New York have been immense for over a hundred years, and many of the peoples that formed a wretched underclass in the past have used the city to rise to affluence.

A critical question that this leading region in the nation has not really faced is whether it wants to keep growing. Although many see Manhattan and its surrounding "barrens" as a fearful wasteland, the planners of the city urge further growth. They could be right. It is possible to have more and more, better and better, and this projection is one way to pay for current necessities. Yet, it is also possible that a change in focus away from more and more as the way to solve problems generated by past growth would lead to superior solutions.

Five major land uses in the region may be distinguished: dense residential, commercial, suburban residential, agricultural, and wildland. Over the last two generations the first three have increased in acreage at the expense of the last two. For a while yet this may continue, but with overuse wildland becomes wasteland; its nature changes even as it increases in acreage. Might it not be possible to slow the growth of suburbs and preserve more? Another challenge is the much-discussed quality of life in the suburbs. For a wide variety of value systems, it declines as suburban populations increase. Perhaps the "neighborhood life" of the city can be re-created in the suburbs, but this means a different attitude toward living patterns and restrictions than is currently fashionable in the drive for general homogenization of life patterns.

New York City has managed to maintain its viability in the face of great pressures. Proudly, it claims to be the only old American city to rebuild its central business district since World War II without federal aid. In office space the city has continued to build its advantage over the rest of the country. The fabulous apartment rents of downtown Manhattan combined with the reliance of the well-to-do on expensive private schools makes possible the continued concentration of the wealthy in the city.

New York built its greatness at least partially on the requirements of the transportation and communication systems of the past. Today transportation patterns and capabilities are changing, and communication advances may make possible face-to-face contact without travel. If the unique bringing together of skills and abilities that has made Manhattan grow should become less important, the city may lose the critical edge that has offset its declining amenities. Internationally, the rise of Japan and the Far East means that in the future West Coast ports may compete on a more even basis for the trade of the country. Nationally, the steady shift of population and production to the South and West reduces the advantage of New York's location, while the increasing importance of federal government activity in the economy tends to displace action from New York to Washington, D.C.

# *The Pennsylvanian Region*

## Population

In 1970 there were about thirteen million people in the Pennsylvanian Region (see Map 29). Growth rates for the region in the 1960s were well below the national average. While the Philadelphia area grew relatively fast, and Wilmington and Trenton were above the national average, population in the west declined. The region has historically been characterized by a high percentage of foreign-born, but in recent decades it has not been a major destination for immigrants. Even the fast-growing Wilmington area had a lower percentage of foreign stock (first- and second-generation immigrants) than the nation as a whole. Few of the native whites of the region have been born outside the region; with primarily intraregional mobility, 89 percent of the whites in

Pennsylvania in 1970 had been born in the state. At about 10 percent, the black population of the region is lower than that of the New York Metropolitan Region and is concentrated in a few cities.

## General Description

Physically the region is dissected by extensions of the same series of ranges running southwest to northeast that is found in the South. Starting from the east, a coastal plains area of pine barrens and truck farms covers most of southern New Jersey. The major cities of the megalopolis are sited either on or adjacent to the slightly higher and more rolling piedmont level to the west of this plain. Behind the piedmont the Appalachian Mountains and valleys and their outliers on either side cover nearly half of the region. On the western side of the mountains the rough Allegheny plateau completes the region. The headwaters of the Ohio River are in the west; the central-eastern portion of the region is dissected by the southern-flowing Susquehanna and Delaware rivers. As a result of the topography, movement directly west through the region has historically been very difficult. Precipitation varies generally between thirty-five and forty-five inches, approximately the same as in all the major Eastern cities. The climate of the coastal and piedmont areas is milder than that of Midwest areas at similar latitudes, while the climate of the mountains and western plateau of Pennsylvania is a good deal cooler.

## History

The Pennsylvanian Region was the last coastal region to be settled. In Pennsylvania and West Jersey the dominant English were Quakers and Anglicans. Their tolerance and the agricultural character of the country attracted a very large and mixed German and Scotch-Irish population. After further heavy early nineteenth-century settlement of Germans throughout the area, and of Irish in the cities, the region received a portion of the later influx into the country of East Europeans, Welsh, and Cornish, as well as Italian, Irish, and other immigrants.

In common with most of the Southern colonies, the Pennsylvanian Region was originally characterized by large proprietorships, which began with grants of whole colonies. In Pennsylvania and most of New Jersey the feudal system was almost immediately replaced by the sale of land to farmers, frequently at very low prices. William Penn was more interested in the health of his colony than in profit, and since the best farmland in the North was in colonial Pennsylvania, the pressure to abandon the feudal system was intense. In many cases the settlers in the region set up farms on the basis of poor or nonexistent deeds and struggled for title later.

At the mouth of the Delaware River the Swedish and Dutch established small colonies of a few hundred in the middle of the seventeenth century. Most of the people were Finnish Lutherans. After the Dutch defeated the Swedish, the English defeated the Dutch in the 1660s and English Quakers settled on the Jersey side of the Delaware. In the core area of southeastern Pennsylvania and southern New Jersey the opposition of the Delaware and other Algonquins was as feeble as it had been in the settlement of the New York Metropolitan Region. Both internal Indian weakness and the destructive influence of the Iroquois on neighboring tribes accounted for this lack of force. Later, Iroquois raids along the region's northern frontier became an inhibiting factor until after the Revolutionary War.

In the 1680s William Penn established Pennsylvania as a Quaker colony. Although we think of his colony as what is now southeastern Pennsylvania, he was also in control of modern Delaware and portions of New Jersey. Penn was ostensibly a landed proprietor concerned with long-term gain, but his ideological goals were at least as important as his economic interests. Socially and intellectually (if not morally), Pennsylvania was to be a liberal colony that frowned on slavery and was open to all religions. Combined with the exceptional fertility of southeast Pennsylvania, this policy caused the colony to become a favorite home for the second wave of immigrants to America. The four dominant groups in the early population of Pennsylvania were Quakers, other English and Welsh, Germans, and Scotch-Irish (including Scotch and Irish as well). The first two groups were strongest in Philadelphia itself, where they developed a remarkable number of the leading intellectual figures of the day.

The Germans were chiefly rural; although called "Palatine," they represented a variety of western German peoples, including Swiss. The importance of the Moravian, Mennonite, and Amish communities suggests the pietistic Protestant bent of the immigrants. Coming later, after the Germans and English had settled much of the best land, the Scotch-Irish often settled on the perimeter of the early colony, or after a period of indenture migrated to the perimeter—and rapidly moved farther afield. An important part of the story of Pennsylvania in the last half of the eighteenth century was the movement of the frontier westward by the descendants of the mixture of peoples in Pennsylvania. The expansion of the Pennsylvania frontier initially southwestward into the Upland and Mountain South was due in part to the reluctance of the Quaker-dominated government either to protect the frontier against the Indians or to displace the Indians, and in part to the difficult topography, with the direction of the valleys turning migration to the southwest.

Quaker power was shaken in the 1750s, but until the American Revolution the Quakers managed to remain the major political grouping in Pennsylvania, although outnumbered by as much as eight to one. They did this through the allegiance of the politically uninvolved Germans and restrictive franchise laws backed by the British government and its governors. In spite of political and economic power, many colonial Quakers frowned on education beyond the secondary level. They were late in developing institutions of higher education because the Quaker meetings did not require a highly educated, elite ministry. The association of Quakers with higher education was largely a product of the nineteenth century.

Shortly after 1810 New York City was able to displace Philadelphia as the largest and wealthiest city in the country, and Philadelphia lacked the special attributes of Washington (politics) or Boston (education and culture) that allowed these cities to compete in esteem. The opening of the West found Philadelphia poorly situated, particularly in the canal era. While it continued to have the most productive local agricultural hinterland, in 1820 its isolated position relative to the larger world to the west caused it to lose out.

With the later nineteenth century and the new immigration, the complexion of Pennsylvania changed again. Now it became the workhorse of the country. As a center of fossil fuel production, the state became the great iron and coal center of the nation. Perhaps nowhere else were so many fortunes produced by the industry of the age. To do the work Slavs and Italians and Arabs, the poor but hard-working of the world, were added to the population. But by the middle twentieth century Pennsylvania was again in a slump of worked-out mines and technically backward industry.

## Regional Borders and Regional Characteristics

As usual, the borders of the Pennsylvanian Region are not sharp. On the southwest, the border of the region might be placed either within the southern tier of Pennsylvania counties or far down, halfway through West Virginia. In determining regional lines (see Map 29), I have taken into account the development and spread of several cultural cores related to the area. These are the Virginia tideland, the Chesapeake Bay, the Southeastern Pennsylvanian, the New York City, the New England, and the Southern Appalachian. As each of these expanded and met the others, a rough pattern of cultural areas was carved out. The Chesapeake Bay culture expanded westward a short way, but was quickly pinched off by the northwest migration of Virginians and the southwest migration of Pennsylvanians. Tideland Virginian culture expanded northwestward, until it penetrated the southwestern part of Pennsylvania. West of the Susquehanna River there developed a "frontier Pennsylvania" or Appalachian cultural core. Although the people represented the same elements as the southeastern Pennsylvanian culture in somewhat different proportions, the challenge of the mountainous frontier selected out a less educated, less religious, more adventurous, more violent, and less community-minded strain from among those who were migrating to and through New Jersey, Delaware, Maryland, and Pennsylvania after 1700.

The resulting Appalachian people struggled with the southeastern Pennsylvanians for control of the state at the same time as
their neighbors were moving rapidly south and west into Virginia
and North Carolina, Kentucky, and Tennessee. More slowly they
moved westward across the Appalachian ridges. In central and
western Pennsylvania, Appalachians continually mingled with
representatives of southeastern Pennsylvanian culture, and to
some extent New Englanders. In this competition the dominant
Presbyterian element maintained and developed a more civilized
pattern. Their intellectual light became Princeton University. But
those Appalachians who went south found themselves intermingled with, and eventually perhaps outnumbered by, poor lowland
Southerners who had few pretensions beyond survival. The poor
Southerner reinforced rather than meliorated the violent atomistic
nature that the frontier had helped to foster in northern Appalachia. North of the Pennsylvanian Region New Englanders continued to move westward after the revolution until they had
occupied all of New York State and the northern tier of counties
in Pennsylvania.

It is generally along the east-west dimension that the regionalization of this study has had its greatest difficulty. Pittsburgh is in
many ways still the beginning of the West that it was in 1780. Yet,
the historical experience of Pittsburgh ties it more to Central and
Eastern Pennsylvania than to Ohio. Nineteenth-century Ohio had
its patterns much more set by agriculture, much less by coal, iron,
and steel. Pittsburgh and Pennsylvania are more dominated by
nineteenth-century immigrants than is the more "native" Ohio.
New England influence has been greater in Ohio, while the
influence of southeastern Pennsylvania and Princeton University
has been less. A separate dialect has been identified for Western
Pennsylvania, while no further dialect boundaries have been
defined to the west (see Chap. II, "Dialect Regions").

Philadelphia has had two great periods of artistic and intellectual creativity. The first began with the men around Benjamin
Franklin and ended after the War of 1812. It was the period of the
establishment of what was to become the University of Pennsylvania and of the American Philosophical Society. These were the
years in which Philadelphia's Benjamin Rush was our leading
medical doctor, and the city's publications were the most impor-

tant in both the arts and the sciences. It was the period when
Pennsylvania led the world in prison reform. The second period of
creativity was in the last part of the nineteenth century, when S.
Weir Mitchell led a circle of outstanding ability. A renaissance
man in Franklin's mold, Dr. Mitchell published widely in
medicine (including a work on hysteria that was to influence
Freud), was highly successful in both his practice and society, and
published many volumes of verse, stories, and a dozen novels.
Within his circle were the novelist Owen Wister *(The Virginian),*
the publisher and historian Henry Charles Lea *(History of the
Inquisition of the Middle Ages),* and the artists Thomas Eakins and
Mary Cassatt, as well as other outstanding scholars and architects.

Over the years Philadelphia has been proudest of its conservative and ancient elite, its doctors, architects, and lawyers. The city
has perhaps more excellent architecture per capita than any in
America. Yet withal, this has been a surprisingly nonintellectual
elite, and one most indisposed to participate in national government, even when asked. The "Philadelphia lawyers" have produced no supreme court justices, in part because of their
disinclination to abstract thought (which intersects in turn with
the lack of an educational institution of the stature of those in
New England). It has also been suggested that the principled
inability of Quaker leaders to take responsibility in the face of
Indian threats or British repression carried over into a reluctance
of their Anglican elite descendants to get involved.[25]

Writing in the last half of the nineteenth century Henry Adams
characterized the cultural role of Pennsylvania as follows: "When
one summed up the results of Pennsylvania influences, one
inclined to think that Pennsylvania set up the government in 1789,
saved it in 1861; created the American system; developed its iron
and coal power; and invented its great railways. . . . The
Pennsylvania mind . . . was not complex; it reasoned little and
never talked; but in practical matters it was the steadiest of all
American types; perhaps the most efficient; certainly the saf-
est." [26] Somewhat different was a description of typical letters of
introduction for young men from Boston, New York, and
Philadelphia. The letter from Boston was said to emphasize the
applicant's educational attainments, the letter from New York the
applicant's activity and drive, but the letter from Philadelphia his

social connections.[27] This traditionalism seems to have characterized even the era of rampant capitalism of the nineteenth century
in which Philadelphia played an important part.

The remarkable lack of creativity of Pennsylvania as a whole
since the eighteenth century, in both statesmen and writers, has
been noted by Zelinsky.[28] In addition to the nonpublic role of the
Philadelphia elite, it would appear as though the Pennsylvanian
rural ethos moved against excelling in any way and against change
of any sort. It is significant that only in this American home and
its western extension could the conservative Amish thrive, while
the movement died out or merged with other groups in Europe.
Yet in our day there may be a revival, signified by the importance
of John Updike in letters and the Wyeths as painters. The Wyeths
are not the kind of artists a cosmopolitan center such as New
York would produce, but for this reason they are perhaps a more
legitimate regional expression. On another level there has been a
considerable revival of intellectual life through the recent activities of the Quakers and the rising status of several colleges and
universities.

## Subregions, Districts, and Sociocultural Subdivisions

An atypical *Coastal Fringe District* may be identified on the
ocean from north of Atlantic City to Cape May. West of this the
*Pennsylvanian Core District* covers most of southern New Jersey,
the Wilmington area of Delaware, and the southeastern counties
of Pennsylvania (with the dividing line probably somewhere in
Berks and Lancaster counties). West of this there is the *Central
Pennsylvania District* under strong German, but a little old
Anglican or Quaker, influence. This is also the hearth of the
southern Appalachian or Mountain South culture. However, the
Scotch-Irish people who gave birth to this culture had by 1840
largely moved out or been overwhelmed by later migrants. The
*Western Pennsylvania District* is focused on Pittsburgh.

In sociocultural terms the state of Pennsylvania dominates the
region. In spite of the southern inheritance of southern Delaware,

the dominance of Wilmington places the state of Delaware within the region. New Jersey is a divided state. In the region there is little sense of regional as opposed to state identification, although for most of the region Philadelphia plays a unifying role.

## Problems and Potential

Rural isolation continues to break down as a result of the opening of Interstate 80 across the north-central part of Pennsylvania and the expansion of tourism in certain areas. Renewed interest in coal resulting from higher petroleum prices in the 1970s may revive some areas. Yet new technologies use few men in mining. Most of rural and small-city Pennsylvania and southern New Jersey remain rather unattractive places, often with declining populations.

In the fifties and sixties, the civic leaders of Philadelphia and Pittsburgh have managed a considerable renaissance. Particularly dramatic has been the change in visible air pollution levels in Pittsburgh, which illustrates what concentrated wealth in private hands (Mellon) can do if it wishes. The Philadelphia area could have used the National Fair of 1976 as a lever to push further the start made with the rebuilding of the city's heart. But it failed to grasp the opportunity. Since their city was eclipsed by New York, Philadelphians have developed a tradition of talking themselves down, and they are not over it yet. The low morale of Pennsylvania State University students is ·illustrated by the fact that of students at four schools (California, Minnesota, Alabama, and Penn State), only the Pennsylvanians were unwilling to put their home area at the top as a place to live.[29]

But there are bright spots. Relations between the races are relatively good, and there are many excellent black leaders. What the Mellon family finally decided to do in this generation for Pittsburgh, the DuPont organization decided in a previous generation to do for the Wilmington area. Continued corporate involvement has resulted in Wilmington's enjoying some of the better social services in the nation and some of its highest wage levels.

MAP 30. The Subdivisions of the South

# *The South*

## Population

In 1970 there were about sixty-three million people in the South. The South covered a larger area geographically and had a larger population than any other region of the United States (see Map 30). At the same time the people of the South are the most "native" of any region. Whether white or black, nearly all Southerners trace their ancestry in this country back before 1850, and most of them before 1800. Foreign-born whites have settled since 1850 in significant numbers only on the fringes of the South, in Texas and Florida, Missouri, Kentucky, West Virginia, Maryland, and the District of Columbia. And many of those reported along the northern edge are in those portions of these states I have excluded from the South. In 1970 twelve million Southerners were black. While absolutely the Negro population in the South has continued to gain, percentagewise it has steadily fallen for the last generation: Negroes accounted for 24 percent of the Southern population in 1940, but only 19 percent in 1970. Aside from Georgia, recent population growth has been confined to the fringe states of Florida, Texas, Virginia, Maryland, and Delaware (especially in the Wilmington area outside the South). Movement off the land continues, with gains in large metropolitan areas accounting for considerable population shift. Negroes have moved out of rural areas faster than whites, and today such cities as Washington, D.C., and Atlanta are more than 50 percent black; however, this figure is partly illusory because of the growing importance of suburbs in metropolitan life. There is only a small, scattered Indian population outside of Oklahoma. As important are the Indian-Negro-white groups found in isolated areas in much of the region. The largest groups are the Lumbees of Robeson and surrounding counties in North Carolina and the Melungeons scattered through the mountains from Kentucky to Alabama.

Arguments as to the reality and boundaries of the South have been considered in foregoing chapters, while in this chapter they are considered in accompanying descriptions of regions surrounding the South. Clearly overlap and a process of gradual change can be discerned as one moves into the South from the North. To people in Philadelphia, Baltimore is thought of as more Southern than it seems to the people of Richmond. In regard to another border city, the *New York Times* recently wrote: "Many Louisvillians say 'you-all,' yet insist that the city is not Southern, since it was a Union stronghold in the Civil War. Yet what is it now? Certainly the people here seem warmer than in the Middle-West, quicker than in the Deep South and decidedly less likely to push you onto the subway tracks (if there were any here) than some New Yorkers are." [30]

## General Description

The physical geography of the South (see Map 2) begins with a coastal belt of low marshy areas such as are generally absent elsewhere in the country. Because of difficulty of access and use, much of this remains in a fairly primitive condition. Back of this strip are the lowlands. Although the land is generally good, in some places, especially in the Carolinas, large areas are pine barrens of low productivity. The classic home of the Southern plantation, the lowlands in recent years have been superseded economically by the Piedmont, a higher plateau extending south and west from central Virginia to the Mississippi River. Piedmont land is less regular, and small farms were traditional. It is also largely in this area that the industrialization of the eastern South has proceeded, developing cities such as Winston-Salem, Atlanta, and Birmingham.

The Piedmont shades into two parallel mountain ranges that run northeast-southwest. The first, the Blue Ridge, is a narrow range running from western Maryland into northern Georgia. West of the Blue Ridge is the Great Valley of the Appalachians. Called the Shenandoah Valley in Virginia, it widens out farther south to include the upper Tennessee River valley and the cities of Chattanooga and Knoxville. In the Great Valley, life is much like that in the Piedmont. Lying west of the Great Valley the Appalachian Mountains run from New York State to Alabama.

West of the mountains the situation to the east is repeated in its mirror image. South of the Appalachians the raised Piedmont plateau can be followed west into portions of northern Alabama and Mississippi, and then as it doubles back under other names to include central Tennessee, most of Kentucky, and portions of West Virginia. Most of this area is called by geographers the Cumberland or Appalachian Plateau, but together with the Piedmont and Great Valley we will refer to it as the Upland South. The lowlands extend up the Mississippi River to Illinois and west into Texas. In this part of the lowlands the flood plains of the Mississippi offer an extra bonus of productivity and danger. West of the lowlands the low Ozark and Ouachita mountains of Missouri, Arkansas, and Oklahoma repeat the pattern of the Appalachian and border highlands on a smaller scale.

Except for the higher reaches of the Appalachians, the South is characterized by a hot, humid climate. This characteristic climate sweeps in a great band from Maryland around to eastern Texas. Only near the coast in the far South and in Florida is the climate mild enough for truly subtropical conditions. Interior cities such as Nashville have a warmer version of the continental climate of the Midwest, while western Texas and Oklahoma have hot, dry plains conditions—with even hotter and drier conditions along the Rio Grande valley in southwest Texas.

# History

As pointed out in Chapter I, the history of the South differs from that of the rest of the United States in a number of ways. The force of historical precedent can be seen in the South since the first successful colony at Jamestown. Instead of being community- and religion-oriented, Jamestown was company-, individual-, and economics-oriented. Instead of being a "new start" in a new world, the elite of the seventeenth- and eighteenth-century South saw themselves as re-creating the old world, often as re-creating an old world that in fact had already ceased to exist. Class differences were extreme, with great landholders and many "servants" (indentured) and, later, slaves. The independent farmer or yeoman class developed from both indentured servants (freed after a period of servitude) and middle-class persons who came without indenture.

The South developed slowly, partially as a consequence of the land grabbing of the powerful. Holding the land for speculative and prestige purposes, the rich hoped to find lessors or buyers. However, few immigrants wanted to become tenants, and with land opening to the west, few were willing to pay the price asked for land in the lowlands. From these conditions there developed in some areas an authentic and more or less sophisticated aristocracy and an independent yeomanry. Each class had marked strengths and weaknesses. However, it is important to remember how few aristocrats there were in the South before the Revolutionary War. They were confined almost entirely to Virginia-Maryland and the Charleston area. For the first century Southern society had depended almost exclusively on England for trade. Roads were few and water transportation direct from plantation to England was frequent. Naturally, then, it was standard practice for the children to be educated in England. However, shortly before the revolution, Southern society had expanded west of the area of easy water access and roads were improving. In the mid-eighteenth century there developed at the College of William and Mary a class of young intellectuals of which Jefferson was the outstanding example. Men of Jefferson's type had a general, encyclopedic knowledge and took part in a wide variety of intellectual, political, and business ventures. In these circles the most enlightened thought of Europe was readily accepted. It was a period of deism and skepticism. Though holding slaves themselves, they generally felt slavery was an evil that must soon pass. Many forget that before 1827 most of the abolition societies were in the South.

However, as time passed and the South expanded to the west and south, the aristocrats were less often men of culture, and more often nouveaux riches of the worst sort. The increased isolation of the area farther west bred ignorance rather than originality. Instead of the steady evolution toward a society without slavery and dominated by independent farmers, the South grew in the early nineteenth century toward less and less liberality and more and more narrowness of vision. Perhaps indicative of this tendency was the waning of the liberal, rather careless anglicanism that originally dominated the South and the steadily growing influence of the less dignified Baptist movement, even among the upper classes. In 1831–32 the last great debate on slavery occurred in the South; significantly, it was in the Virginia legislature.

The independent farmers of the South came from diverse origins. Perhaps the majority were the descendants of indentured servants brought in from the British Isles, primarily England. In the Piedmont there were large numbers of Scotch-Irish, Germans, and others who entered the country through Maryland, New Jersey, and Pennsylvania and then moved south down the Piedmont and Great Valley, or later over the Appalachians into the West. Unlike those from the lowland South, many of those who came south from Pennsylvania were community-oriented (for example, Moravians), with considerable agricultural skill and interest in religious learning (especially Presbyterians).

Nevertheless, it was the Anglo-Saxon, lowlander South that eventually dominated the Piedmont and eroded the outlander traits of its transient Pennsylvanian settlers. The lowland Southerner had a passion for his own land, for being himself. He had little interest in education or abstractions, or generally in politics. Two factors are commonly used to explain the fact that as a group the yeomen were lazy and unskilled. Perhaps most important was that as the Negro became more and more important in the South, and as more and more whites came to consider the black man inferior, any form of hard work, whether in the fields or at the bellows, came to be seen as beneath the dignity of a white man. Even if he was willing to work in an activity at which Negroes also worked, the availability of slave labor depressed the wages that the white man was offered. A second reason was that without ease of transit, living far from others, the Southern yeoman tended to be a jack-of-all-trades. Southerners developed few skills in the depth that characterized the more interdependent European or New England communities.

In a recent study entitled *The Lazy South*, David Bertelson argues that the cause-and-effect relations suggested above should be turned around.[31] He points out that the accusation of indolence hurled at the earliest whites referred to two faults that soon became characteristic: physical laziness and unwillingness to work for social or long-range goods. While some poor Southerners might work hard for private gain, almost none worked for the public interest. This led to two results. First, it became a generally accepted fact that no one would work for others unless compelled to by force. Second, efforts were only expended to achieve short-term gain through cash crops. Building up subsistence farms or developing service and trade relationships were simply too slow for the Southern mentality.

Almost from the beginning the South became dependent on cash crops of tobacco, cotton, indigo, rice, and whiskey (from corn). Rich and poor alike emphasized specialty export crops to such an extent that at the time of the Civil War the overwhelmingly agricultural South was a food deficit area. The diversified family farm of New England or the Midwest was less common, and so were the values associated with it. Another result was the rapid exhaustion of the land. Although men such as Washington and Jefferson were scientific farmers, repeated crops of tobacco had worn out much of the land of Virginia before the Revolutionary War. With the arrival of cotton as the main crop, the plantation belt moved south. Before the Civil War the center of cotton production was in the black belt of central Mississippi and Alabama.

In many areas of the South, Indians disappeared rapidly after white settlement, in some cases because there were very few at the time of settlement. In the Lower Mississippi Delta the Natchez and neighboring groups rapidly disappeared, as did the tribes in most of Virginia, Kentucky, eastern Texas, and along the Atlantic coast—except for Seminole holdouts in the unwanted Florida swamps. But the Cherokee, Creek, Choctaw, and Chickasaw peoples inhabiting the area from North Carolina and Georgia to the Mississippi developed more staying power through native organization and the adoption of white ways. Finally, the combination of their possession of large areas of land desired by white Southern frontiersmen and the presence of a white Southern frontiersman in the White House led to their forcible and painful eviction to Oklahoma in the 1830s.

The interaction of the Indian and the invader was more intense and has left more of a cultural residue in the South than in any other eastern region of the country. As we have pointed out, in regions to the north colonialization proceeded on a solid front, but in the South it was more intermittent, with even "settled areas" having relatively low density. One result was widespread interbreeding of Indians with both whites and blacks. The extent of this mixing has often been overestimated by blacks, underestimated by Indians, and perhaps forgotten by whites. Another result was the enculturation of large numbers of Indians, particularly of Cherokee, Creeks, and Chickasaw to white, Southern patterns during the eighteenth and early nineteenth centuries, including the ownership of plantations and slaves, and the development of a written language (Cherokees). This probably made possible the persistence of a relatively well-off and successful segment of the Indian community in Oklahoma after removal of the Indians from east of the Mississippi. In addition, the persistence up to the 1830s of the Indian in the South and the long-continued poverty and ignorance of the Southern frontiersman meant a greater white borrowing of Indian culture than was common elsewhere. It was then a partially Indianized, and sometimes partially Indian, Southerner whose children went west or filled up bypassed valleys.

It is easy to forget that in the first half of the nineteenth century the South was still a fluid society. Although dominated by large plantation holders with their equally large holdings of Negroes, Southern society consisted mostly of poor white farmers. As a whole, the South was poor relative to the rest of the country, having much less manufacturing and urban development than the North. Because it was poor, the great immigration into the country of the nineteenth and early twentieth centuries largely passed the South by. There were few jobs for immigrant whites, and pay was poor for those jobs that were available. Moreover, there was little of the reality and practice of equality and freedom in the South that many immigrants craved.

In the immediate aftermath of the Civil War, the problems of the South were intensified. Its agriculture was ravaged, cities destroyed, and the enormous capital accumulation that slaves represented was confiscated. Confidence was broken, hatred engrained. Few Negroes had any experience or training preparing them for freedom, and most white Southerners tried to place them back in the role slavery had made seem so natural. However, in the 1870s the Negroes achieved a measure of freedom and political power in the South that they did not attain again until the 1960s. It was not until the 1890s and early 1900s that the Jim Crow laws disenfranchising the Negro and separating facilities became general. The causes of this reversion are complicated and unclear, but some reasons were Northern disinterest, job competition, fear, and backlash from the courting or buying of the Negro vote in the South by a new wealthy class. Whereas Negroes (both slave and free) had almost monopolized some trades before the war, now they were forced out of most. The Southern Negro had two choices: to do the most menial labor or to rise in a new, separate black hierarchy, isolated from the rest of society.

In the last decades of the nineteenth century many Southern businessmen, and some Northern capitalists, began to build a new South based upon industrialization. With a high birth rate and declining agriculture, Southern whites needed something to do and industry seemed the answer. At first heavily devoted to processing typically Southern products (especially cotton and tobacco), Southern industry developed in certain places along more traditional lines (for example, Birmingham iron and steel). Southern industrialization tended to be widely spread over the countryside, so that many small industrial centers were developed. This pattern is still a characteristic of Southern development, especially in the Carolinas.[32] Although these enterprises might initially be undertaken as much for the benefit of the people as for profit, conditions in the paternalistic factory towns were frequently miserable and wages were very low. Gradually, however, white Southerners learned patterns of work that were necessary for further progress.

In the twentieth century progress has been relatively rapid, particularly after World War II. In this century the first period of growth was accompanied by the rapid rise of the cotton and textile industry. This collapsed with overproduction in the 1920s. But out of the depression came (1) large development projects (such as TVA), (2) the distribution of federal wealth on a large scale (helping the South particularly because of the power of entrenched Southern congressmen), and (3) the general acceptance of soil conservation and soil-rebuilding crops such as the pine trees and legumes that now cover so much of the region. Since World War II the South has benefited in addition from the war footing that the nation has felt compelled to maintain. The Southerner's interest in the military is proverbial: the South is the only major area of the country where a choice of a military career has traditionally been socially esteemed. In addition, it is generally cheaper and more productive to maintain army camps and other military facilities (including production facilities) in the South. Moreover, from favored committee positions the South's congressmen work to obtain these facilities. Gains through government activity have been particularly pronounced in Texas, Florida, and around Washington, D.C. However, these states were, in fact, particularly well suited for the activities involved.

In the last two generations the exploitation of oil resources in Texas and Louisiana and the development of offshore sulphur resources have added a great deal to the economy. Largely confined to this century, the citrus industry added to the wealth of extreme southern Texas and central Florida. Florida has developed a tourist industry based on coast and climate that continues to make it one of the fastest growing states in the Union. To a lesser extent there has been growth in tourism along the entire Southern coast.

Socially the South also developed rapidly since the 1920s. Educational standards rose everywhere. For the whites, Southern birth rates fell to national rates some time ago, and black rates have been going down. Attitude polls show more and more acceptance of black equality in the South since 1940. There has been a long-term decline in lynchings and other racial violence going back at least to 1900. Nevertheless, although on the fringes of the South conditions had been equalized for some years, in many parts of the South integration and a Negro vote had to be forced on the whites from the outside. However, as equality of opportunity does come to the South, it seems likely to be more acceptable than in much of the North. After centuries together, Southerners, black and white, are more like one another than blacks are like most Northerners. In day-to-day life they have often had more contacts. Fear of Negro violence at and near school, which is the primary worry of Northern white parents, may be less intense in the South because the Southern white society and student body are inured to violence and are more than willing to use counterviolence. It is probable that the South also has more mature Negro leadership. Blacks moved into mayoralty offices in both Atlanta and Raleigh in 1973, in both cases with a substantial white backing (especially in Raleigh, where whites have an overwhelming majority). Thus, as bitterness and hatred grow in the North, they may decline in the South—although admittedly this evolution has a long way to go.

I have painted a picture of real change, yet it is wrong to imagine that all differences have been erased. The South remains poorer and less educated and more prejudiced than the North. It is only in recent years that the bitterness of black prejudice against whites, and especially white Southerners, has been understood.[33] Indicators such as those for education can be misleading, for twelve years of school in the South is on the average simply not what it is elsewhere. The differential in violence is decreasing, but it is still there. (For the evidence on education and violence, see

Chapter III.) Although Southerners are crowding into metropolitan areas, the South is still more rural than most regions, and its metropolitan people remain more rural in their attitudes.[34] The distinctively urban peoples of America—Irish, Poles, Italians, Jews—are mostly in the North.

## Nature and Achievements of Southern Culture

In this chapter and elsewhere I have frequently had occasion to describe the South in juxtaposition to the rest of the nation. So here I need only summarize those characteristics or features of Southern life that stand out with the most clarity. The Southerner is his own man, one who wants to be left alone, to be self-sufficient. He resists and resents government of any kind; yet while he often lacks self-discipline, he submits to discipline more readily than others. He does not trust himself, for there is less of an internalized puritan conscience. Individualism is also constrained by the Southern trait of violence, sometimes a passionate mob violence in the face of which the often weak law stands aside. The threat of violence forces conformity on white and black, but this should not be interpreted as more than a superficial outward conformity.

The Southerner loves show, the surface of things; he has always loved rhetoric, ability with words if not with ideas. Fun, violence, sex, alcohol—life for men was always to be lived to the fullest. Men and good women were put at extremes, symbols of two worlds that met only tangentially. In Southern mythology the woman is worshiped, but it is the man who rules. Yet there is also the curious attitude toward the use of liquor and other "sins" that may cause a man to act like a scared little boy in relation to his wife, to drink hard but support prohibition.[35] Lower-class Negro society could not have such women; indeed, their sex gave Negro women power unavailable to the men.

In spite of aristocratic pretensions, the South was fluid, men did rise rapidly on new wealth. The love of show and the absence of a very deep culture helped make this possible, as did the dislocations of the frontier, the rapid exhaustion of land, and the Civil

War. Traumatized by slavery and the later demands of segregation, and bitterly disappointed by defeat, the Southerner felt on
the defensive. This forced him to love and romanticize the good
side of the South far beyond what his reason told him. From the
first the Southerner lived by bursts of action followed by long
periods of idleness. Regular, orderly work did not suit the life of a
real man. However, with the passing of the agricultural world,
there has been a growth in the Southerner's acceptance of regular
work.

The South has long had the reputation as a savage, cruel,
sadistic society that quickly resorts to violence. The popular movie
image of the South has done much to reinforce this view and,
though greatly overdrawn, it does represent a portion of the
Southern reality. While brawling was common everywhere on the
frontier, the disfigurement of opponents, especially gouging out
the eyes and even castration, was in an earlier age particularly
associated with the South.[36] One reason often adduced was the
warped training in human relations afforded by slavery. The
slaves were kept in line by punishment in many cases, overseers
having little other function. A boy growing up in this world, and
with early access to power over others, both male and female,
easily developed an extreme idea of his own rights and a tendency
to treat others as objects. However, there is good evidence that
treatment of the slaves in the South was much more humane than
anywhere else in the Americas. The survival and rapid growth of
the slave population in the South was in marked contrast to that in
the Caribbean and even Brazil.[37]

With all this, more than most Northern regions, the South
developed a "way of life" in which people could take pride.
Southerners have always shown in ordinary social intercourse an
interest in manners unparalleled in the North. Southerners have
traditionally gone more out of their way for others. They are more
interested in people, whether white or black, good or evil, and it is
this drama of ordinary life played out by people of strong passion
that is the stuff of Southern existence. Action has always been an
integrator of Southern life; dogs, the hunt, fishing, the dance,
cockfights—all these have as their meaning not the technique, but
participation in a common enterprise.

To an extent unknown in the North, the South has lived under the influence of early nineteenth-century romanticism. Swept away by Scott and Byron, the Southerners came to conceive of themselves as "the chivalry." Medieval jousts were regularly held in the South (some still are) with all the paraphernalia of the medieval world. In New Orleans they actually used broadswords, with occasional fatal results. The duel was common and much praised, being especially highly developed as a social form in New Orleans and Charleston. Romanticism led eventually to dreams of a Southern nation, of a great slave nation replete with knights and ladies. And then the Civil War, the heroes of the lost cause, and the long awakening. The dream is over, but the attitudes and values in which it grew linger on.

Slavery, the Civil War, poverty, and romanticism forced Southerners together, to think of themselves as a separate society. No region in the country has produced so many people interested in it as a region. It is perhaps for this reason that it has long been the region that has improved its economic and social standing the fastest in the country. Out of adversity has come some of the depth that was lacking before. One likes to think that this progress will be more than an aping of Northern life, rather the creation and embellishment of something valuable for all of us.

In a number of arts, Southerners have made distinctive contributions. Discussion of Southern architecture may be found in a previous chapter. Whether white or black, the South has always been more musical than the North. While nearly all of the music of the Northern cultures rests on the contributions of recent American immigrants, that of the South is pre-1800 Anglo-Saxon or African. Most American music on the vernacular level is Southern—even "Western music" is the music of the Western South. Farther east we find the home of "bluegrass," mountain folk music, gospel music, and the current "country Western." Of course, Negro spirituals, jazz, and blues all have a Southern background (see also Chap. II).

Southern literature is a more mixed story. In the nineteenth century Southern writers generally produced little worth reading. Southerners were wedded to European and English styles and preoccupied with sentimentality, historical allusion, and the defense of the indefensible. It was in New England that serious American writing was found—and also, curiously, in California.

In the twentieth century emphasis has shifted toward the South, until the roll call of Southern writers makes the South perhaps the outstanding literary region. No other region has such a contemporary list as William Faulkner, Robert Penn Warren, Eudora Welty, Katherine Ann Porter, and Tennessee Williams. Even the Mountain South has produced a substantial literature, not limited to names such as Thomas Wolfe, James Agee, or Jesse Stuart.[38] Perhaps this Southern renascence is passing, as most on the list are now aged or dead; perhaps it was only on the edge of the old and the new that this literature could be built, for it is to a degree a literature expressing the tragedy of the death of the Southern past. The South has also witnessed most intensely the drama of great disparities of income and status and justice, the romance of hatred and violence and decay that may be an unfortunate precondition of great literature. Yet there remains in the South the interest in events, in people for their own sake, in people outside of the self, that literature requires.

There are, of course, many different kinds of Southerners, and to some degree class interests and distinctions cross-cut areal subdivisions. Samuel Lubell has made a useful division from the point of view of the political analyst. His first class is the elite, including both new and old elites. It is a strong-drinking, public-spirited group inclined increasingly to both vote Republican and support bond issues. The white masses, on the other hand, are religiously traditional, individualistic, against the use of alcohol (Wallace, Maddox, and Thurmond are all said to be teetotalers). They expect little of government, vote against bond issues, and for Wallace or other populist candidates (generally Democratic). The third group is that of the Negroes, who now vote solidly Democratic.[39]

Although a fifth of Southerners are Negroes, the discussion has subsumed Southern Negro culture as a version of Southern culture, varying much as white Southern culture does by area and class. Since most Southern Negroes are, and have been, lower-class and lowlanders, Lowland Southern lower-class traditions should be particularly decisive. This does not deny the fact that African or African–West Indian elements have been incorporated into black speech and culture in this country.[40] In addition, the partial separation of whites and blacks has allowed other dialectical usages to develop that are not found in Lowland Southern white speech. This includes the development of specialized argots and the general extension of the use of sexual symbolism in speech (recently widely adopted by the white avant-garde in the North). Perhaps because of West African patterns and the pressures and opportunities of Southern society before and after emancipation, the position of women in black society and the nature of the family were quite different than in lower-class white society. Closer to Southern patterns is the tradition of violence (see Chap. III), but intragroup black violence is perhaps more common than in corresponding white society. Black cooking is essentially that of the poor whites, yet there have developed distinctive black preferences.[41] As mentioned in Chapter II, the most creative difference has been the more varied development of music among poor Southern Negroes as compared with their white fellows, especially in Lowland areas. Discrimination and inequality have produced a variety of specifically black behavioral patterns. Aside from patterned role interactions, the different patterns of migration of white and black reflect differences in both social situation and culture, on occasion forcing the poor Negro to change and thus often to "progress" more rapidly than poor whites of Southern background.[42]

## The Eastern South

*Subregions, Districts, Special and Metropolitan Areas*

Since both culturally and socioculturally the Western South is regarded as a major subregion (see Map 30), it is treated separately at the end of this discussion. Culturally the rest of the South has been divided into three large districts, with several special districts within each. These might be considered subregions on a par with the Western South. However, the Western South has a more easily defined geographical area (Texas-Oklahoma), while the three districts of the remainder of the South overlap a wide range of political and other subdivisions. In addition, the eastern units have little possible justification as economic or social units. For example, while the Western South as a whole can develop in terms of a broad range of interdependencies, the "Mountain South" is a geographically divided area that is economically, educationally, and politically dependent on other districts. The cultural districts considered here are, then, Mountain South, Upland South (or "Upper South"), and Lowland South (or "Lower South").

The *Lowland South* is the classic South, the South originally based on slave labor, the South that insisted on the Civil War. Today it is the South in which Negroes, especially rural Negroes, are concentrated—and thus the South in which Negroes are now often taking over local governments through majority control.

In the first stage of colonialization, tobacco, indigo, and sugar cane were common crops, with cotton and rice being added later. Cotton, the crop most connected with the Lowland South in our thinking, was never very important in Virginia, the hearth of classic Southern life. After a long decline, it has now made a comeback in the Lowland South, especially in the Mississippi River valley.

By the time of the Civil War, Richmond, Charleston, and New Orleans were the great cities of the South, and all were lowland cities. Since Charleston and New Orleans were too cosmopolitan, too French or West Indian to be typical of the South, it was Richmond and lowland Virginia that the Southern elite looked on as their actual or spiritual homeland. Nevertheless, it was Charleston and South Carolina that led the movement for the Confederacy and the Civil War. Today much of the Lowland is in cattle or pine trees, while the modern or industrial centers of the Eastern South are in the Upland, especially in North Carolina, Georgia, and Tennessee.

In the Lowland district of the South four special areas should be distinguished. The first is a *Colonial Survival Area*. This includes most of the Delmarva Peninsula and a strip on the west bank of the Potomac, with offshoots farther south such as along the central North Carolina coast. This area participated very little in the Civil War cataclysm and its aftermath. The Delmarva Peninsula is the most heavily Methodist area in the country, while there is a strong old Catholic population in the west of the area.

The Colonial Survival Area adjoins the *Washington-Baltimore Metropolitan Area*. This metropolitan area has the most varied population of any area in the South, with middle- and upper-class

representation from every state in the nation. Baltimore has a less
varied population, but many more nineteenth- and twentieth-century immigrants than a typical Southern city. However, Northerners who visit both cities often feel that their physical climate
and cultural atmosphere remain Southern. The accent of the
common people is border Southern, and the effect is reinforced by
the numerical dominance of Southern Negroes in much of the
area.

*Southern Louisiana* was from the first a very special area. In
common with the Lowland South, it had an aristocratic tradition
based on Negro slave labor on large plantations. However, almost
everything else was different. Because of the population's Spanish-
French origin, Catholics have always been dominant. There has
always been a wide variety of peoples, of different languages and
races, in the city and throughout the marshlands. These are
French (including Cajuns originally from Nova Scotia), Spanish,
Canary Island Spanish (dark), various mulatto groups, Italians,
Irish, and Filipinos (locally including Chinese). Often these
arrived with a particular industry—for example, the Italians
developed the vegetable industry, the Dalmatians, the oyster, the
Filipinos, the shrimp. South of New Orleans, the definition of
Negro was traditionally different than in the rest of the South.
Here, as elsewhere outside of the United States, a variety of terms,
such as Quadroon, was used to refer to different degrees of black
or white inheritance. At least until the twentieth century, local
attitudes in the Delta might allow a person with obviously Negro
background to achieve a degree of social acceptance that was
impossible elsewhere in the South.

Nearly devoid of towns, the area south of New Orleans was a
refuge area in which pirates and later criminals could easily find
cover, and perhaps even help. During prohibition the antipathy of
the local peoples to restrictions on alcohol combined with a
chance for profit to convert the district into one of the most
uncontrolled in the nation. As in the Kentucky mountains, voting
irregularities and violence have been commonplace. Yet recently
there has been a growing influence of the rest of the South on local
customs. By mid-century the Baptists had become stronger,
English was becoming commonly used in areas where it had been
a foreign tongue, and the segregated patterns of the South were

replacing the Delta's mosaic. Today there is a last-ditch struggle to preserve what is left of Acadian French.[43]

The fourth special area is that of *Southern Florida*.[44] Growth in recent years in tourist, retirement, and space-age Florida has created a quite atypical Southern society. The exact boundaries of this new Florida are vague. If one drew a line from a point south of Daytona Beach southwest to a point north of Saint Petersburg, well over half of the people in the state would be in southern Florida. Manifestations of southern Florida culture are also found north along the Atlantic coast to Georgia. Clearly the focus of southern Florida lies in the southeast counties of Palm Beach, Broward, and Dade (Miami), which together contain a third of Florida's population. In size Florida grew from thirty-first in the nation in 1930 to ninth by 1965; in 1970 it was considerably larger than Georgia, often thought to be the "leading" Southern state. Most of this growth was in southern Florida, with northern and rural counties losing population in some years.

With this growth we must ask to what extent southern Florida remains Southern in culture. Some of the influx into Florida was from the rest of the South. Thus, while in 1970 about 35 percent of white Floridians had been born in the state, 60 percent had been born in the South.[45] However, it is likely that little more than 50 percent of the people of southern Florida are from the South. Already in 1952 the religious pattern of the South did not extend to southeast Florida, and today about one-third of the people of Miami are Jewish. In 1970 perhaps 22 percent of the people of Dade County were Cuban refugees, a population that has considerably altered the complexion of Miami in a very few years.

It would appear, however, that the influx of outlanders has not affected Florida as much as the figures would suggest. In 1969 the per capita income was still well below national averages, and a higher percentage of selective service draftees failed the mental test than the national average. It is significant that in spite of Florida's rapid urbanization and the national movement of Negroes to the cities at rates faster than those for whites, whites have continued to find Florida more attractive than Negroes do. The Negro share of the population of Florida dropped from 41 percent in 1910 to 15 percent in 1970. As emphasized before, the importance of interregional movement in altering regional characteristics is much reduced by the selectivity of migration—one moves to or stays where he feels at home—and by the ability of societies to mold newcomers to local patterns. The history of Senator George Smathers (retired 1968) is an example of both effects. Coming to Miami from New Jersey at the age of six, he graduated from the University of Florida and its law school. Not surprisingly, in politics Smathers often acted like a Southern conservative.

In 1972 the *New York Times* could still report that the power structures of the bigger towns, including Miami, were made up almost entirely of "crackers" originally from Georgia.[46] Neal Peirce suggested that the Florida primary would be a much better start for the election year than New Hampshire, for "it is more representative of the nation as a whole." [47] But the subsequent overwhelming Wallace primary victory in 1972 suggests that Florida is still more representative of the South than of America.

Although the plantation system was later to become quite important, the *Upland South* began as an area of small farms, supported by tobacco and general subsistence farming. Cotton became a leading crop after 1800, but recently has declined rapidly. The area was populated both from the Lowland South and from a stream of migrants south from Pennsylvania. The latter included large numbers of Scotch-Irish and Germans, as well as Swiss, Quakers, and others. Some of these came to establish close-knit communities and opposed slavery. With time, opposition to slavery faded, or its opponents relocated in the Midwest. But a sense of cultural distinction between Lowland and Upland has persisted. In general, the Upland in the twentieth century has been less rural and conservative, with more outsiders. Negroes have always been less numerous in the Upland, and yet they have always been a part of the way of life of the district. Their relatively small numbers meant that they were less feared as a danger to the white majority, and thus the white majority could turn to other issues. In this tradition, the first important black mayors in the South were elected in the Upland.

Although the Upland South is less cut up by heterogeneous special areas than the Lowland, several special areas may be mentioned. Aside from obvious transitional areas on the borders, Central North Carolina, Central Tennessee, and North Central

Fig. 9. "The dream is over, but the attitudes and values linger on. . . ." Greek revival as Southern Romantic: Greenwood, Thomasville, Ga. *Courtesy of the Library of Congress*

Fig. 10. Religion remains strongest in the South. Sunday morning at Daytona Beach, Fla., 1943. *Courtesy of the Library of Congress*

Fig. 11. The industrial South: U.S. Steel in Birmingham, Ala. *Courtesy of the Alabama Development Office*

Fig. 12. A dispersed rural settlement with an I-house on right, near Asheville, N.C., 1939. *Courtesy of the Library of Congress*

Fig. 13. A "hollow" in the Kentucky Mountain South, 1940. *Courtesy of the Library of Congress*

Fig. 14. The southern Great Plains in northwest Texas, 1937. *Courtesy of the Library of Congress*

Fig. 15. The new Texas: the Houston Civic Center. *Courtesy of the Texas Highway Department*

Kentucky have been designated, each with specific characteristics. They have in common a relatively greater interest in education, a more liberal view of the world, and perhaps more dedication to the development of what is best in Southern culture than is common in the rest of the South. The *Central North Carolina Area* is characterized by a number of small cities of roughly equal importance: Charlotte, Raleigh, Durham, Greensboro, and Winston-Salem. From the beginning the population here was more mixed than in the South as a whole; the religious census of the mid-fifties showed Lutherans, Presbyterians, and Methodists competing with Baptists for ascendancy. The area is one of the education foci of the South, with good colleges and universities such as the University of North Carolina, North Carolina State, Duke University, Davidson College, and Wake Forest. Perhaps no other area of the South boasts such a collection of institutions— and yet North Carolina is hardly a rich state.

*Central Tennessee* is focused on the city of Nashville, where the Methodism of the area has developed a relatively liberal tradition. Nashville is the home of Vanderbilt University, the base of the Southern agrarian literary movement, and is still a Southern leader in many ways. At the same time Nashville is a center of religious activity in the United States, especially in publishing, and the center of country Western popular music and of the music recording industry.

The third area, *North Central Kentucky*, includes the bluegrass country of bourbon and horse racing and its environs. While Nashville is Anglo-Saxon and Protestant, bluegrass Kentucky has a strong mixture of Catholics in both urban and rural areas. It is also an area of the western extension of the Virginia aristocracy, of plantations in the uplands, of emphasis on manners, food, and the good life. In addition to these areas, border areas included in the South, north of the Ohio, in Indiana and Illinois, as well as northern Missouri, are clearly transitional. The regional program of Southern Illinois University at Carbondale has been an attempt to carve out and develop both culturally and economically a transitional area along the border.

The area included in the *Mountain South District* includes populated valleys that are by no means primitive. Perhaps only half of the counties in the district have "folk populations" in the old sense. Yet the district is defined by its mountain folk. The homeland of the culture is a disconnected area above a certain height—in fact, nearly all of the mountain area of the South. Culturally the mountains are an extreme version of the Upland. Here there were few if any Negroes and no plantations. Although the original people were farmers, there were few of them and most lived at subsistence levels. In recent years specialty crops such as apples have become important, but with declining productivity and alternative sources of livelihood the bulk of the rural people have tended to abandon agriculture altogether (see fig. 13).

Although most of the people were of English or Scotch background, the mountains are a refuge area in which groups of people of unknown background, including those of mixed Negro and Indian genetic inheritance, are found. In West Virginia and parts of Kentucky and Tennessee, coal mining has long been a major activity. It has apparently done little to reduce the isolation of the people, but it may well have reduced their ability to grow food. As with American Indians, change to general American standards sometimes appears faster to contemporary observers than in retrospect; studies in 1900 and 1930 saw the same mountain cultural patterns rapidly disappearing that are reported by the latest observers (see, for example, Gazaway or Coles in the Bibliography). The lower Ozark Mountains are culturally Southern Appalachian, although the people are rather better educated and more apt to be active farmers. There was also perhaps less pro-Union feeling here than in the eastern mountains at the time of the Civil War. The grading of Upland South into Mountain South is more gradual west of the Mississippi than in some Appalachian areas, and Mountain Southern ways have even dominated parts of Texas.

Religiously West Virginia and western Virginia are Methodist, while the rest of the mountain area is largely Southern Baptist. Religious activity, however, often alternates between total inactivity and violent emotional release. As in poor areas in many Catholic nations, the Mountain South has often been too poor for religion. Ministry is often by lay preachers and frequently by unpaid outsiders.

Both cultural survivals and bizarre innovations have been associated with the Mountain South. Most remarked have been peculiarities of dialect and such excesses as snake handling or other demonstrations of spiritual power. More interesting is the preservation until recently of the old and new Christmas dates (25 December and 6 January), and the holding of funerals months after burial for convenience. "Survival" is often misapplied to aspects of the culture. Much of the classical, late-nineteenth-century Mountain culture of clans, blood feuds, use of bows and arrows for small game, dialectical development, and inertia was not part of the living culture of the ancestors of the mountain people when they arrived in the late eighteenth or early nineteenth centuries. Perhaps more a tradition was the depressed position of women, who were often handled very roughly. But these same women were the primary folk singers in the older Mountain society.

The survival of frontier traditions, distance from law officers or courts, legal corruption, and the popularity of the making of moonshine whiskey enhanced the tradition of violence and family feud. The tradition seems largely to have died out, but the danger that guns will be used to settle disputes continues to be a part of mountain life. With low educational levels, little community consciousness, and frequent layoffs from the mines or casual employment, the welfare programs of the last forty years have become an integral part of the mountain pattern—unfortunately re-enforcing many people's negative attitude toward work and responsibility. For many mountain people there may have been a steady decline in standards of living over generations.

Beyond the usual virtues of the rural poor, Southern mountaineers are more likely than poor elsewhere in the South to love the land, to show an almost religious appreciation of its beauty, and to be interested in the appearance of their surroundings.[48] But the love of the land is not the same as the peasant's attachment to farming. The mountain people are more likely to choose a life of episodic mining and frequent hunting. They are also among those modernizing people who are particularly interested in cars and trucks and make their lives revolve about them. The mountain white preserves a patriarchal family even with the weakness and joblessness of the male.

Historically, the mountain people identified least with the South as a region. Although their lives were generally dominated by those at lower elevations, they never saw their interests as the same. However, the fact that many mountaineers supported the Union in the Civil War does not remove the district from the orbit of Southern culture. They have disliked Negroes at least as much as slavery; mountain towns often let it be known that a Negro should not allow the sun to set on him within its confines.

Much of what we think of as Southern culture, especially the white music, has a southern mountain background. Yet detailed studies of isolated mountain areas have often shown no music at all, just as they may show no religion at all. This would appear to suggest that only at certain points along the frontiers of Upland and Mountain South, or where agriculture made sense, where religious enthusiasm flourished and there was a little surplus—this is where Southern mountain traditions have been best preserved. Aside from mountain music, quilts and whiskey are the liveliest folk arts in the hills.

*Sociocultural Subdivisions of the Eastern South*

Looking at the South from a sociocultural point of view, three border states are only in the South for certain purposes (see Map 5). The metropolitan centers of Missouri—Kansas City and Saint Louis—tie the state economically and socially to the Central Midwest society that surrounds the state on three sides. The opposite is the case of West Virginia, a rural state tied to metropolitan centers outside of the South on both the north and west. Maryland is in every way transitional: a rural Southern society partially submerged under the cosmopolitan influence of the Washington-Baltimore Metropolitan Area with its ties to the North.

In sociocultural terms the most important distinction within the Eastern South is between the Upper and Lower South (Map 5). The Upper South includes Virginia, North Carolina, Tennessee, and Kentucky, and for some purposes West Virginia, Maryland, and Missouri. All are today "border states." There are perhaps three reasons for the difference between Upper and Lower South. (1) Since the Civil War there has been more interchange of population and ideas with the North in the Upper South than in the Lower South. (2) Even before the Civil War, the Lower South had carried Virginian ideas to extremes less common in Virginia itself. (3) The Negroes have played a less central part in the Upper South.

Within the Upper South a further distinction may be made between the states east and west of the Appalachians. Those east have been more influenced by Pennsylvania, New York, New England, and Europe, while those west have been influenced by the Central Midwest. Arkansas is rural and so isolated from the influence of Northern cultures that it has been placed in the Lower South. However, this may be changing, as the success of politicians such as Winthrop Rockefeller, Senator Fulbright, and Senator Bumpers would suggest.

Within the Lower South, Southern Louisiana and Southern Florida are so distinct from the rest of the area that they have been distinguished in Map 5 as sociocultural districts in spite of an analytical reluctance to divide states in sociocultural analysis.

## Problems and Potentials of the Eastern South

The South probably has reason to be prouder of its recent progress than any other region of the country. Its main task has been to catch up in terms of mass education and living standards with the rest of the country. These are the advances that American society as a whole appears most able to promote; and as the South has been Americanized, it has progressively achieved these goals. The South has a ways to go to reach national standards, but it will clearly go at least most of the way. One reason for the South's relative improvement in a variety of indicators is that many of the people depressing Southern indicators in the past—poor whites and blacks—have gone to other parts of the country. While many parts of the South have imported educated people to man new facilities, it has often been able to export the less educated.[49] The fact that these people wanted to leave gives little credit to the South, but the fact they left may make it easier to handle the problems of the next generation.

Urban overdevelopment in the South has taken place in the Washington, D.C., and Houston areas and along a long strip of the eastern and southern coasts of Florida. As states, perhaps only Florida and Maryland are overpopulated. Both have the money to turn development from quantity to quality, but this shift seems most urgent for Florida. Florida bases its being and existence on amenities, and pollution and beaches shut off by development should have no part in that picture. A different kind of overdevelopment is the stripping of the Appalachians in the name of economic progress. In the process, TVA, the vision of the South's future, has become its nightmare.

Recent reports indicate that the South is integrating its schools faster than the North.[50] The reasons are that more pressure has been put on the South, and Southern Negroes have traditionally had their residences more among whites than have Northern Negroes (although this may be changing). However, it is also true, as suggested above, that there is less culture clash in the South than in the North between white and black.

Even when the South was industrializing in the late nineteenth century, its people continued to dream of re-creating the past, a golden vision of an age that could never be recalled. The more sophisticated Southern literature of this century has related the reader to the regional past, if not its glorification. Centered at Vanderbilt University, the literary "agrarian movement" of the twenties and thirties was explicitly a rejection of change, an attempt to re-establish the Jeffersonian vision. Paradoxically, as David Bertelson points out, they were trying to create a sense of community on the basis of the very individualistic and anarchic virtues that had made real community formation so difficult in the South. In the current ferment this would be more sympathetically received than it was then. Yet the evolution of the South and of agriculture has long since passed the agrarians by. What they wished to achieve was a more meaningful life and the preservation of the best of the past—but the mode of achieving this has not yet been found, for either the South or the nation.

The problems of the Eastern South are fourfold: (1) to maintain the material progress of the last generation while strengthening environmental control, especially of strip mining; (2) to improve the relation of the races until the South stands as a model for the nation; (3) to preserve the strengths of the South, those positive qualities that have always attracted the emulation or attention of the rest of the nation; and (4) to create new aspects of a positive culture, so that the future will have the creations of the South of the late twentieth century, as well as those of the early nineteenth century, to look back on.

## The Western South

Much of the general discussion of the South above applies equally well to the Western South. Yet, because it is also a new, dynamic amalgam of its own, far beyond the reach of Richmond, Atlanta, Nashville, or New Orleans, a short separate description is desirable.

In 1970 Texas and Oklahoma had a population of 13,700,000, although some of these persons were outside the Western South. The growth of the population of Texas was a little over, and that of Oklahoma a little under, the national average. The Western South of Texas and Oklahoma combines two very different states in one subregion; yet they are combined because the population base of both was the same. Unlike the Interior Southwest, neither aboriginal Indian nor Spanish-American culture plays a central role in the definition of the area. The people of Texas are mostly from the Lower, Upper, and Mountain South, and these Southerners easily outnumbered Spanish-speaking and Indian people even before the state joined the Union. Therefore, when we refer to a large Spanish-speaking population in Texas, we are speaking primarily of a relatively recent immigrant population quite different from that in the core area of the Interior Southwest. The Indian cultures of Texas were not highly developed, and the nineteenth-century Texans quickly wiped out or displaced nearly all of them. Oklahoma was settled first by displaced Indians under federal government protection and white squatters from neighboring states. When whites later poured in to take over most of the state, they were largely Southerners (as I have defined them) from neighboring states.

In both states there are today more non-Southern whites than in the rest of the South; in Oklahoma these are from the Central Midwest, and in Texas they are immigrants from the British Isles, Germany, or Mexico. However, consideration of religious affiliation in both states shows them thoroughly in the Southern Baptist world that I have taken as a principal marker of Southern culture (see Chap. II).

There are several arguments against categorizing Oklahoma with Texas. At first thought it would appear that the Indian origins of Oklahoma would place this state closer to the Interior Southwest than to Texas. Yet Indian influence is not culturally decisive. Most Oklahoma Indians were displaced, many highly acculturated even before they were forced to settle in the area. Strangely, Oklahomans have intermarried freely with Indians, although they have retained Southern anti-Negro prejudices. To be part Indian in Oklahoma is an honor; but this does not mean that Indian cultures are alive and well. Early integrated into the politics and society in the state, Indians were rapidly assimilated to the culture of the Western South. Already in 1950 only 2 percent of Oklahomans considered themselves to be Indian (6 percent in New Mexico, 9 percent in Arizona).

As a whole the Western South is the least "Southern" of Southern regions, and recent migrations to Texas have increased the mixture of Northerners with Southerners. Yet some quotations from a recent description of Houston suggest that it is easy to exaggerate the significance of recent changes on Southern patterns of thought and behavior:

For years Houston, New Orleans and Dallas have been handing back and forth the title "Murder Capital of the United States." The murder rate in these three cities is two, three or four times that of other metropolitan areas.

The one activity that most Americans associate with Houston— manned space flight—has no real connection with the city. The spacecraft center is 30 miles south of downtown Houston, and almost all of the astronauts, space technicians, and industry representatives live in small bedroom towns near Galveston Bay and come to the city only when forced to.[51]

Perhaps the best modern study of a cultural area in the country has been D. W. Meinig's *Imperial Texas*. Meinig distinguishes a *core area* of Texas culture found in a triangular area formed by San Antonio, Houston, and Dallas–Fort Worth, and a *primary domain* that covers most of the state, as well as a small strip of New Mexico along its eastern border. Meinig's *sphere* of Texas culture includes what I have called the Texan District in the Interior Southwest, and its *zone of penetration* covers all of New Mexico, most of Arizona and southern Colorado. However, Meinig's sphere covers only a portion of Oklahoma, and his zone of penetration no more. Meinig places Oklahoma largely outside of the Texas sphere for two reasons: it is not economically dependent on Texas, and the people came more from the "North" than the South.[52]

In the present analysis, economic relations are not as important as in Meinig's, and emphasis is placed on similarity in cultural background. The origin of the first effective settlement also seems to be more similar than Meinig imagines. An examination of the migration data suggests that the basic outlines of Texas were set in 1870 and of Oklahoma in 1910.[53] While the population of Texas by this test was almost entirely from the South, there were also about twice as many Southerners as Northerners in Oklahoma. (In this analysis those from Missouri are all counted as Southern. This is defensible because migrants of Southern background from elsewhere in the Central Midwest balance those of Northern background from Missouri, and the settlers in Oklahoma were largely rural people, and rural Missouri was and is largely Southern.) The analysis is also confirmed by an analysis of religious affiliation (see Chapter II, "Religion"). It is important to note that since 1910 Texas has been the largest single contributor to the population of Oklahoma, with Arkansas taking over Missouri's second-place standing. In its first settlement Oklahoma was distinctly different from Kansas. In both 1870 and 1910 more than twice as many in Kansas were from the North as from the South.

The rainfall of the Western South grades from an eastern fringe characteristic of most of the interior of the country to a dry, desertlike fringe toward the southwest. Average temperatures in winter rise toward the south and the Gulf. Although there are a few low hills, notably in eastern Oklahoma and the Big Bend area of Texas, and the rivers have cut deep canyons in much of the area, the Western South is notably flat and monotonous. The monotony is often more oppressive than that of equally flat stretches of Kansas, because drier conditions over much of the area force both agriculture and natural growth to be less intense.

With oil, cotton, cattle, sheep, and aerospace the greatness of the Western South is man-made. The whole area has been characterized by a relatively poor mass society in which a large number came into great wealth through chance (toughness and hard work played a part, but these surely did not guarantee success). The result has been a proliferation of some of the excesses of a thoroughly modernistic culture in which wealth and bigness and consumption for its own sake come to be worshiped.

There is perhaps no area in the nation in which economic development has been as effective in the last few years as in the Western South. Unemployment has remained low here while it spiraled elsewhere. While cattle, oil, and cotton fueled the process, these resources have been used to develop a complete, multisided economy that is relatively immune to all but the most general fluctuations of the economy. Texas does face severe problems of pollution in the Houston-Galveston area, but this can be solved by money. More serious is the depletion of oil and water stocks. Central and northern Plains agriculture that has been built on wells supplied by prehistoric water reserves may soon disappear. However, a base has now been laid in urban Texas that may be largely independent of these threatening resource calamities.

There are a number of ways in which to divide the Western South into districts as an alternative to Meinig's approach described above. The *Oklahoma District* is defined by the particular Indian heritage of the state, while portions of northern Oklahoma have been placed outside of the Western South on the basis of religious data. Although Tulsa is said to be dominated by people of Northern rather than Southern origins, they would be the elite, for the Southern Baptist denomination is dominant in that area as well.[54] Below Oklahoma the *North Texas District* extends from the cotton lands of east Texas northwestward into eastern New Mexico. Descended directly or indirectly from Upland and Mountain South origins, the people of this district are nearly all Southern Baptists and native white Americans.[55] (This is the "farmer Texas" tradition discussed under Interior Southwest.)

Above North Texas a small *Panhandle District* includes a mixture of North Texans with immigrants from the Central Midwest and the Oklahoma District. The *Rio Grande District* includes all of the southern border area, with a large Spanish-speaking population. Here there is little possibility of dry farming, and agriculture is irrigated. *Central Texas* runs from the Gulf coast through the old German area northwest of San Antonio. Compared to the rest of the Western South, this district has a cosmopolitan population with more post-1800 immigrants, especially Germans and English, and more colonial native Americans from outside the South. It is in both of the last two districts that I would place the home of a "Texas rancher" tradition that contrasts with the North Texas farmer society described by Vogt for his homestead culture in New Mexico. In this respect the Central and Rio Grande districts are in the Lowland South tradition (with Mexicans replacing blacks in the Rio Grande), while North Texas is in the Upland South tradition.

The Western South is a region of great cities (containing the sixth, eighth, and fifteenth largest in the nation), each with a distinctive characteristic of its own.[56] Let us consider them. By Texas standards, Dallas (844,000) is eastern and internationally oriented. Smaller than Houston, it is more often chosen for a headquarters city on account of its location. Less dependent on resources, it has based its economic development more on sophisticated and high technology industry. In spite of the Oswald affair, and domination by a moneyed elite, Dallas' leadership has been more liberal and more consensus-oriented than that of Houston, although its recent failure to support the Dallas Symphony is ominous. Despite its unlikely location, and the fact it is sinking below water level, Houston (1,232,000) is bigger and growing faster. Houston's astrodome set a style in America. In the midtown area there is now rapid growth, including an extensive new development, the Houston Center (fig. 15).[57] Next to Dallas, the old cow-town of Fort Worth (393,000) has emerged as a middle-class, largely white and WASP city of moderation—a city of smiles and unlocked cars, of little pollution and clean streets. Slightly smaller, Oklahoma City represents a similar WASP population. Most Spanish-American of the major cities in the Western South is San Antonio (654,000). The city represents historically and romantically perhaps the best synthesis of the Texas experience. Its city riverfront redevelopment is one of the most pleasant in the country. But aside from the HemisFair buildings, there has been little new building. A self-satisfied city, with a better climate than Dallas or Houston, San Antonio remains surprisingly moderate in its politics.

More than anywhere else in the nation, in the Western South a ruralistic people is in charge of a dynamic urban civilization. In spite of its violent traditions, it has probably had more success in recent years than the rest of the South in positively bringing its minority population into the mainstream. The Western South is wealthy enough to build its own world of beauty, man-made beauty, that can stand as more of an achievement than the preservation of nature. But to go ahead and build this it must become an original creative center that cares less about catching up, about the praise of others, and more about making its own unique contribution to civilization. Perhaps this is an area for pyramids; the world would be poorer without the pyramid building of the equally mad Egyptians.

Whatever the direction, it must be a direction appropriate to the people of the area. It is disappointing to find that in the *Goals for Dallas* literature there is little attention to the problem of regional relevance. Indeed, in the "Supplementary Reading" attached to their publication, *Goals for Dallas* offers essentially nothing on the character or potential of Texas or the Western South.[58] Similarly, a *New York Times* writer points out that Houston, "for all its wealth and burgeoning growth, still has lingering feelings of inferiority. . . . Houstonians, like most Texans, have not yet lost an almost child-like belief that anything foreign or anything from Hollywood is to be admired." [59]

# The Upper Midwest

## Population

In 1970 there were about twenty-four million people living in the Upper Midwest (see Map 31), half in the industrialized Michigan–northern Ohio area. During the 1960s the region was generally growing at less than national rates, with the Dakotas actually losing population. Foreign settlement was especially

MIDWEST CULTURAL REGIONS AND DISTRICTS

THE MIDWEST SOCIOCULTURAL REGION

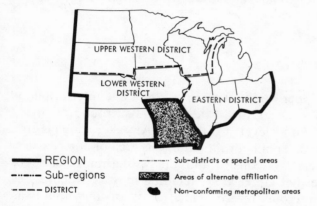

MAP 31. Midwest Cultural and Sociocultural Regions and Districts

heavy in the nineteenth century; countries of origin were primarily Scandinavian, German, and Canadian-British, with large numbers of Swiss and Dutch as well. With urbanization, the eastern cities of the area, as well as some western cities such as Milwaukee, received those peoples from Ireland, Eastern and Southern Europe who play a large part in most of urban America outside the South.

To the east, the first effective settlement was primarily from New England and its extensions, with a smaller stream from the Middle Atlantic region, and a heavy contingent from Northern Europe at or very near the beginning. There were a few Southern immigrants at the beginning (especially to the Wisconsin lead mining district), and more recently in the east. There are generally very few Negroes in the western part, but in the east they are heavily represented. Indians continue to play some part in the life of the western area, particularly the Dakotas. Movement within the region is not great, except rural to urban. White movement into the region is primarily from the Central Midwest, although the South has recently provided a steady source of population for the northern Ohio–Michigan subregion. More important has been the movement of blacks from Alabama and neighboring states into the industrial centers of this subregion. Since it is generally an area of out-migration, the Upper Midwest has tended to develop a relatively isolated regional population for an area outside of the East or South.

## General Description

Physically the Upper Midwest is part of the same interior plains region that includes the Central Midwest and surrounding areas. The area varies from level to rolling. An exception is the "Laurentian Upland," a hilly or mountainous area of northeastern Minnesota, northern Wisconsin, and the westernmost parts of Michigan. A somewhat larger area including most of Michigan is covered with coniferous forest, while most of the area was naturally either deciduous forest or grassland. Much of the conifer area remains forest (often poor second growth), with swamp and marshland in northern Minnesota. Most of Wisconsin and Michigan is dairyland today, as is a large part of Minnesota. Fruit and truck farming dominate the lake shores in western Michigan and northern Ohio, with only a small part of this region in the "typical" Midwestern feed grain and livestock pattern. Western Minnesota and the Dakotas are wheatlands shading off at the western extremity into grazing land.

On the west the drainage of the upper Mississippi and Missouri rivers dominates the landscape while to the east the Great Lakes are the unifying and determining factor. The western area is both colder and drier than the eastern. The entire region is, of course, cold, with the lakes somewhat moderating the climate in Wisconsin, Michigan, and northern Ohio.

## History

The Upper Midwest was known for its fur-bearing animals for a century or two before there was any more substantial white settlement. Aside from the Western Reserve area of Ohio settled after the Revolutionary War, agricultural settlement came late. In 1820 there were only 8,096 people in Michigan, with only 400 people coming to the old city of Detroit during the first twenty years of United States occupation. Movement into northern Illinois and Wisconsin was retarded by distance and difficulty of access. In particular, the swampland of northwest Ohio interrupted the western flow. As a result, the first census that reported any considerable population in these two areas was that of 1840. Later settlement is partially responsible for the immigrant domination of the Upper Midwest; native Americans had filled up much of the Central Midwest before the strongest tides of foreign immigration began to flow in the nineteenth century. After 1840 the agriculturally usable lands were rapidly settled by a tide moving first north and then west. The surge played out shortly after 1900 in North Dakota.

In the Great Lakes area lumber brought in another population as it boomed at mid-century, finally reaching its peak in the 1890s. The lumbermen were of many sorts. Originally dominated by French Canadians from Maine, the industry became primarily Scandinavian. However, like most things in the area, it was Yankee owned and directed. By 1920 the last of the large-scale lumbering in northern Minnesota was over, with the virgin forest largely consumed. Unlike areas to the south, this forest did not give way to agriculture; once cut, decline generally followed. Mining also drew people into the area as it did not farther south. The lead mines of Wisconsin attracted adventurers even before general settlement. More important were the iron mines around the edge of Lake Superior that brought Cornishmen, Welsh, Irish, and Slavs. The rapid industrialization of the region was and is facilitated by exceptional communications, especially through the Great Lakes, its central location in North America, the presence of extensive iron reserves, a New England entrepreneurial elite, and a relatively well-educated and industrious mass population.

## Regional Definition

The Midwest does not offer very convincing support for the hypothesis advanced in Chapter I that regional cultures defined in terms of differences in the cultures of the people of first effective settlement will significantly influence later behavior differentials or be useful in creating foci for regional loyalty. And the Midwest offers some evidence for the alternative hypothesis that a similar environment and economy will tend to homogenize people of originally dissimilar origins. Nevertheless, even in the Midwest, in order to understand regional behavior, environmental determinism must be supplemented by the hypothesis of cultural continuity.

Deciding on the regional definition of the Midwest and its subdivisions is one of the most difficult jobs in the regionalization of the country. This should suggest that the result is most open to question. There are four problems: (1) Is there more than one Midwest? (2) Do Michigan and northern Ohio belong to the Upper or Central Midwest? (3) Should there be an east-west division between "old" and "new" Midwests? (4) Should the Great Plains be considered a separate region? Since the Great Plains are considered in a later discussion of the Rocky Mountain Region, we need consider only the first three questions here.

The first argument for making the Midwest one region is that much literary, historical, and geographical discussion has assumed that economically, culturally, and physiographically it is a unit. The people of the area have been taught to think of it as one region, or as one and a half regions.[60] A second argument is that all of the Midwest is tied to Chicago.

Yet in terms of our hypothesis that emphasizes original cultural heritage, there are two cultural regions in the Midwest. The Upper Midwest is characterized by settlement either directly or indirectly from the New England cultural region, with almost no Southern heritage. Immigrants into the area have been primarily German, Scandinavian, Canadian, and British, and in all of these areas except Michigan–northern Ohio, the nineteenth-century immigrants clearly overwhelmed the native Americans—at least numerically. Many of the newcomers, especially the Michigan Dutch, had a culture reminiscent of that of early New England. On the other hand, the Central Midwest has less New England influence, more Southern, Middle Atlantic, Jewish, Italian, and East European population. Except in some of the largest cities, pre-1800 native Americans have remained dominant.

Part of the evidence for differences in migration patterns is provided by Map 1, but Table 12, showing population origins, may also be helpful.

TABLE 12
POPULATION ORIGINS (1850)

| State of Residence | Native of | | | | | |
|---|---|---|---|---|---|---|
| | Own State | North-west | New England | Middle Atlantic | South | Europe |
| Ohio | 1,284,000 | . . . | 66,000 | 300,000 | 150,000 | 200,000 |
| Indiana | 500,000 | 130,000 | 11,000 | 76,000 | 175,000 | 55,000 |
| Illinois | 344,000 | 110,000 | 37,000 | 112,000 | 128,000 | 110,000 |
| Michigan | 140,000 | 18,000 | 31,000 | 150,000 | 4,000 | 55,000 |
| Wisconsin | 63,000 | 23,000 | 27,000 | 80,000 | 5,000 | 107,000 |

SOURCE: From Ray Billington, *Westward Expansion* (New York: Macmillan, 1950), p. 308. Coming from upstate New York, most of those of New England background will appear in the table as Middle Atlantic.

It will be noted that the greatest difference is in the general absence of Southerners in the Upper Midwest in the formative period. If we could exclude the Upper Midwest portions of Illinois and Ohio we would also notice the tendency of the Upper Midwest to have a much higher percentage of European immigrants.

Settlement in the Michigan–northern Ohio area began like that in the rest of the Upper Midwest, but its history has deviated since. It remained more native American. The immigrants were of a somewhat different mixture, for more Irish, Italian, and East European peoples immigrated to this area than to the rest of the Upper Midwest. In recent years there has been a large movement of Southerners, particularly Negroes, into the largest cities in the Michigan–northern Ohio subregion. Also, there is relatively little population exchange between this area and the rest of the Upper Midwest. I placed it, nevertheless, with the Upper Midwest because of its early settlement and because recent studies of political behavior, such as those of Phillips and Elazar (see Chap. II) place this area closer to the New England traditions than to the Central Midwest.

In a recent study of Midwest politics, Michigan, Wisconsin, and Minnesota are described as issue-oriented as contrasted with "job-oriented" Ohio, Indiana, and Illinois.[61] Elazar's similar distinction between moralistic and individualistic political cultures (Chap. II) is supported by recent qualitative discussions of state politics, such as Neal Peirce's discussion of Illinois, Ohio, and Michigan.[62] Although the record to the north is often faulty, the political tone in Cleveland, Toledo, and the cities and states of Michigan and Wisconsin is different than that in Columbus, Chicago, or the states of Ohio and Illinois. Cleveland and Michigan are less boss-dominated, the blacks have achieved more, and education, especially higher education, has been much more fully supported and successful.

Like most analysts, John Fraser Hart discusses the Middle West as one region. However, on two points at least he suggests a continuing distinction based on the different regional heritage.[63] In discussing the tendency of Republican voters to adhere to the party over time, he contrasts a "volatility belt" from northern Ohio through Minnesota to a region of "reliability" in the Central Midwest. This accords well with the political education and attitudes of the people in the two regions suggested by such authors as Elazar. Hart also points to the fact that dairy farming is concentrated in the Upper Midwest and may be related to the greater willingness of the people to work regularly. This suggests that the "values" Hart ascribes to the Middle West family farm ideology vary considerably from north to south. For example, hard work is regarded more moralistically to the north, while the belief that the best governed are the least governed has historically been weak there. Negative attitudes toward Washington notwithstanding, the northern Midwest has been an area remarkable in the United States for the extent of its social experimentation at voter request.

Finally, there is something to be said for dividing the Midwest into a portion that is really "western" and another that is clearly eastern. There is a gradation of life styles, population densities, and so on from east to west, but distinct lines are hard to find. The requirements of life at very low densities in the Dakotas and western Nebraska are discussed in a special section on the Great Plains below. In terms of indicators of cultural heritage such as state of origin and religious affiliation, the distinctions are more remarkable as we move north to south rather than east to west.

There are relatively few institutions or images that refer to the region we have defined as Upper Midwest. It is approximately the upper Great Lakes plus the Dakotas. Minneapolis–Saint Paul-based regions such as that defined by the Upper Midwest Research and Development Council or the Ninth Federal Reserve District extend farther west into Montana and exclude lower Michigan and Wisconsin. It may be significant that the state systems of higher education in Minnesota and Wisconsin have developed a reciprocal system for the admission of students that has been described as an educational common market.[64]

## Regional Characteristics

Because of literary tendencies to lump the Midwestern peoples together, it is difficult to find descriptions that differentiate the Upper Midwest peoples from those of the Central Midwest in terms of general characteristics. Nevertheless, a few points can be made.

With its elite dominance by Yankees, the Upper Midwest generally has a tradition of home-owned industry that separates the region from areas to the south and west. In parts of Wisconsin, the New England town meeting still exists.[65] Although the region is beyond the "Bible belt" of the South and Central Midwest, religious belief is perhaps stronger and families more stable than in the Bible belt areas. The western areas have had high fertility that is correlated more with stability and rural virtues than with poverty, as it often is elsewhere. There is also a strong liberal tendency in the region. This is based on a relative absence of Southern culture and the pressure of liberal elements in the cultures of the peoples who immigrated to the region. Until the recent movements of Southern peoples, white and black, into the northern Ohio–Michigan area, there was a long tradition of relatively good intrasocietal relations, making it an area in which the "melting pot" was healthiest and most effective. Specifically liberal movements have included La Follette progressivism in Wisconsin, the Farmer-Labor party in Minnesota, and the Non-partisan League in North Dakota. The cooperative movement has been strong throughout the area. From the first, New England influence on education at all levels has been greater and more continuous in the Upper Midwest than in the Central Midwest.[66]

This area is relatively advanced at all levels of education. It is not surprising, therefore, that the Universities of Michigan and Wisconsin are the outstanding public institutions in the center of the country, while Macalester College in Saint Paul is chosen by more merit scholars than any other private college between Princeton and Stanford.[67]

Merle Curti's study of the settling of Trempealeau County in western Wisconsin illustrates the kind of regional imprinting that characterized much of the area.[68] The county was rural, a part of the Norwegian area, and yet it was much more than that. The first settlers were that combination of Upland Southerners, French Canadians, and Indians that was characteristic of so much of the West. But the first people to come in numbers were from New England and New York State. They promoted and developed. Along with promoting their own interests, they promoted education and civilization of a remarkably high level for a frontier rural area. They quickly developed newspapers and "colleges," and much of the output of these enterprises was highly creditable. In fact, although the bulk of the population was rural, the quality of town-based elite leadership made Trempealeau perhaps less "rural" in 1880 than it is today.

It was into this framework that there then came a population of Norwegians and other northern Europeans. Elazar's study of Rockford, Illinois, a more urban area within the same Upper

Midwest world, makes much the same point. The region's later cultural evolution has been the story of the interaction of the New England elite (including some English) with an immigrant mass rising fairly rapidly in status. But this "progress" must be understood in the context of a declining ability of rural areas (or the Upper Midwest in general) to offer challenge to the best of their younger people. Comparison of nineteenth-century beginnings with the present suggests the eroding effect of Midwestern "isolation" on the generations that followed the era of the founders.

Geographically removed from the rest of the world, the Upper Midwest has also been accused of political isolationism. A better way to consider the issue is to note a simple difference in interests. The region is far from coasts and international conflicts. But the special population is also important. It must be remembered that three of the strongest ethnic groups in the region—Swedish, Finnish, and German—were naturally ambivalent about both world wars. And the people most concerned with World War II, the Jewish, were poorly represented in the region. From their ethnic perspective, the people of the area have tended to view the foreign excursions of the country as foolish. From their viewpoint, our interactions may easily come to look like an internationalist-Communist plot. It is in this ethnic perspective rather than in that of a fundamental conservatism that the rise of both McCarthys in the Upper Midwest should be seen.

## Subregions and Districts

The Upper Midwest can be divided down the middle of Lake Michigan into *Eastern* and *Western* subregions. The Eastern Subregion is more native, more Italian and Irish, and now more Southern Negro and Southern white. Except for the latter, it might be included in an alternate regional classification with upstate New York. Although the Eastern Subregion contains slightly more than half of the population of the region, and Detroit and Cleveland are its earliest major population centers, it is not the regional core. In a sense, the regional core of the Upper Midwest is still in New England and Northern Europe.

Within the Eastern Subregion it is difficult to define districts. Population was greatly mixed from the first, and in recent years industry has been able to draw people in from outside the region to an extent uncommon elsewhere. The biggest differentiations are between rural (New England, German, Dutch) and industrial (more heterogeneous). The nonconforming areas of Detroit and Cleveland have populations now overwhelmingly Southern and East European. Rural areas are divided between general farming, fruit and truck farming, and sparse wooded areas used primarily for recreation. Fruit and truck farming is found primarily in a strip along the southeast shore of Lake Michigan (many Dutch) and the southern shore and islands of Lake Erie (including some Italians). The interior of Michigan forms the general farming and the better dairying areas, while the northern part of the lower peninsula of Michigan is sparsely populated.

The Western Subregion has the largest nineteenth-century immigrant population and influence of any large nonmetropolitan area in the nation. In spite of several important cities, rural populations and rural ways of thinking have retained their importance. The districts of the area should likewise be defined in ethnic terms. The *German-Swiss District* has as its cultural core Milwaukee–Madison and includes a broad stretch of eastern and southern Wisconsin, the northern edge of Illinois, most of northern Iowa, southeastern Minnesota, and northeastern Nebraska, as well as the southeastern corner of South Dakota. There is a mixture of many other peoples here, particularly along the more industrialized eastern edge. Most important are the Poles, Italians, and Irish, while Racine is a center of Danish culture in America. The *Scandinavian District* includes western Wisconsin, most of Minnesota, and the eastern part of the Dakotas.

The *Wilderness District* covers the essentially nonagricultural lands of northern Minnesota, Wisconsin, and Michigan's Upper Peninsula. The sparse population here contains many Finns, Slavs, Irish, French Canadians, and old stock Americans engaged in specialized pursuits. Indians are locally important. As in other areas of raw material extraction, the economy of this district has been characterized by boom and bust; but lately this area has been doing better than many agricultural areas, particularly in the Plains. In the western Dakotas and into Montana the *Plains*

*District* of low population contains many Germans and Scandinavians, as well as a substantial Indian group (primarily Sioux). It is differentiated by the necessity of dealing with the specialized climate and extremely sparse population (see discussion of the Plains under Rocky Mountain Region).[69]

## Problems and Potential

The primary problem of the Western Subregion is to reduce or transform the rural decline of the Dakotas and portions of the other states. Most believe that the rural people in this area are by and large happier where they are than they would be in a city, but as agricultural productivity per man continues to rise, there is less and less to do in rural areas. In the Wilderness District there are new exploitative activities arising to take the place of declining mine employment, but these opportunities tend to be short-lived. However, sustained-yield timber and fish production and tourism might be able to support the light population in the district.

In southeastern Wisconsin, northern Illinois, and the southern half of the Eastern Subregion the problems are the more familiar ones of the submergence of the environment under the pressure of human growth and productivity. The recreational and aesthetic properties of Lake Erie and Lake Saint Clair have already been seriously eroded by growth and carelessness. A program to restore the quality of these waters is urgently needed, even though the effects will take years to mature.

But perhaps a more critical problem of the Eastern Subregion is that of integrating the diverse groups of people that now make up the population, particularly the very large black population in the central cities. Since Detroit and Cleveland may well have black majorities in the near future and the states as a whole will continue to be predominantly white, the old city-state conflict is emerging in a more acute form than ever. The problem is to develop an ability for all groups to live together cooperatively, while not demanding the elimination of group interests and characteristics. In regional focus the problem is to accommodate and include these people within the tradition of the area. One suspects that historically Negroes chose Cleveland over more southerly Ohio cities because there were New England vibrations in day-to-day encounters that seemed more likely to give blacks a chance. One hopes that the clash of interests and direct confrontations of peoples, as well as the immigration of white Southerners, will not destroy what is still viable in this foundation.

# The Central Midwest

## Population

In 1970 there were about twenty-seven million people in the Central Midwest (see Map 31), with the entire area growing at a rate well below both the average Upper Midwest and national growth rates. In much of the region first effective settlement was from the Upper South. It is a more native region than the Upper Midwest, although many of its cities have heavy ethnic populations. German influence is predominant among foreign stocks both urban and rural and includes elite influence in Saint Louis and Cincinnati. A wide variety of immigrant peoples settled the western half of the region, yet they were generally small minorities in the now heavily populated areas.[70] Irish, Italian, and Slavic peoples are important in the cities. Native people came from New England, Middle Atlantic, and Southern states. Taken together, they represent a cross section of pre-1800 "old stock" Americans. But the Central Midwest does not simply have a mixed culture; it is the outstanding citadel in which the typical American sects— Methodist, Presbyterian, and Northern Baptist—are dominant. The black population of the cities is very large; in the river cities this is an old population, and in Chicago mostly second generation. Here the origin of the black population is Mississippi and surrounding states. Southern Mountain whites are also important regional immigrants, especially in Ohio. The Central Midwest is not a region with a great deal of movement; and the population exchange that does occur has generally taken place among neighboring states.

## General Description

Physically the Central Midwest is low and flat, although there are rolling hills in a few areas. Since there is no large area that is not agriculturally usable, there is considerable sameness to the landscape. The bulk of the land is in feed grain and livestock, although there is "general farming" along the southern fringe, and wheat and grazing are the predominant agricultural activities along the western edge. Originally the region was deciduous forest (eastern) and grassland (mostly western), the rainfall becoming less as one moves west. The area is dominated physically by the Mississippi, Ohio, and Missouri rivers and their tributaries. The climate is warmer both winter and summer than in the Upper Great Lakes area. An area of hot, humid summers and cold, overcast winters, the Central Midwest has relatively little to offer of either good climate or natural beauty, although its well-cared-for farmland is quite attractive.

## History

The wedge of western settlement that had already crossed the mountains by the time of the Revolutionary War was then extended directly west through Kentucky and Tennessee and Missouri. While there was repeated trouble on the frontier, the Indians fell back rapidly before the white advance. There were a few settlements in eastern and southern Ohio in 1800, but most of the rest of the Central Midwest is considerably younger. By 1820 the wedge of settlement included a swath from central Ohio to central Missouri. It was 1840 before Indiana and Illinois were generally settled, while the states beyond were occupied in the next few decades—much of the plains area only after the Homestead Act and the coming of the railroads. Thus, settlement in Iowa was less than ten years previous to that in Oregon, while settlement in Nebraska and Kansas followed that in Oregon. During its first period the Central Midwest was Southern-oriented: most of the settlers coming through Kentucky were of Southern origin, and the Ohio-Mississippi drainage system was the main means for the movement of goods and production. In addition, as a thoroughly agricultural and frontier society, it had sectional interests that aligned it with the South. Rapidly, however, the New England and Pennsylvanian peoples and German and other foreign settlers arrived. Since they were more aggressive in agriculture, business, and industry, after the Civil War these were the people that dominated the area, even if Southern attitudes have remained strong in most of the region.

## Regional Characteristics[71]

Illinois, Indiana, Ohio, and Iowa are characterized by a large number of rather similar middle- and small-sized cities, mostly laid out on the level and with little more geographical context than a small river. Ohio is perhaps the most "balanced" state in the nation: Cleveland, in the Upper Midwest, faces the lakes and reflects New England culture. In the middle Columbus represents typical American life and is the leading city in what might be considered an Ohio core area for the Central Midwest. Cincinnati, on the Ohio River, is a relatively sophisticated city of Southern and German as well as Midwest background. There are also many other important cities such as Youngstown, Akron, Dayton, and Toledo. There is even a Little Appalachia in southeast Ohio. Exceptional Upper Midwest–style communities are scattered throughout the region, such as Galesburg, Illinois, and the Antioch College community in Yellow Springs, Ohio.

The Central Midwest is what most commentators mean when they speak of the Middle West. Sinclair Lewis' *Main Street* was in Minnesota, but Sherwood Anderson's Winesburg was in Ohio, Middletown (Muncie) in Indiana, and Warner's Jonesville (Morris) in Illinois. Significantly, a recent attempt to compare the quality of life in a small American city to that in an equivalent English city chooses the city of "Midwest" somewhere in Kansas.[72] In terms of more popular images, Kokomo is in Indiana and Peoria in Illinois. It is the area of the large, prosperous, family-run farm with little outside labor. It is also the area where business and business success are most openly extolled as a proper purpose in life. Openness and friendliness are characteristic, everyone talks to his neighbor, and community interest is strong. Almost as strong is the region's inferiority complex.[73] It has produced numerous men of note, but many others have left, evidently feeling that the real action of life was outside the region. It is true, however, that skyscrapers were first promoted in Midwestern cities, and the frame house now generally used nationally was developed to meet the wood shortage of the area west from Chicago.

Lincoln was a product of the Central Midwest in its age of confidence. In the afterglow of this age, writers such as Edgar Lee Masters and Vachel Lindsay, Carl Sandburg, Sherwood Anderson, Theodore Dreiser, Willa Cather, and William Allen White produced a Midwest literature of substance and significance both to the region and beyond. But it was the subtradition of romanticized and border southern Hoosier literature from Edward Eggleston, James Whitcomb Riley, Lew Wallace, Booth Tarkington, and Ross Lockridge, Jr., that has shown the most continuity. Today we hear little from the region.

Much of what the world thinks of as "American" is Midwestern and especially Central Midwestern. It is a commercially minded area because of its New England heritage, yet ruggedly individualistic as a heritage from the Upper South. It is here that the rationalism of nineteenth-century Yankees fused with the familism and folk beliefs of central Pennsylvania and the Upper South to produce a new industrial folk ideology.[74] The American cult of the average, which in fact gives the average man a good deal, owes much to the Middle West. In this region reform has generally been a middle-class rather than upper- or lower-class concern. This naturally follows, for the middle class rules. The idea that all men are equal is felt strongly, and only at the southern fringe, in Saint Louis or Cincinnati, do observers find the strong class lines that produce both a leisure and a pauper class.

Elsewhere the material directness of discourse allows for little irony or wit. It is a most unsophisticated area no matter how many Ph.D.'s are produced by its universities. In the social sciences it is often remarked that Midwestern scholars tend to be thorough and dull, to emphasize quantitative methods to the exclusion of meaning. Like the Upper Midwest, the Central Midwest is isolationist, anti-British, and anti-Northeast. In the

Eastern District it is less liberal and pacifist than the Upper Midwest, although liberal individuals such as Eugene Debs emerged from the region. Most Central Midwesterners take what they like to think of as a no-nonsense attitude toward the world. Typical Midwestern statements might be: "If we are going to fight a war, fight it"; "If a policy doesn't work, drop it"; "It is foolish to continue to help other people who don't do much to help themselves." The result is a kind of black and white, outside-of-the-game attitude toward international relations that can lead to rapid changes in foreign policy support.

John Fraser Hart sums up his analysis by listing a group of traits that he believes characterize the Middle West, but seem to me more distinctively Central Middle West. They are:

| | |
|---|---|
| pecuniaristic | measure man by his income |
| materialistic | conspicuous consumption |
| self-assured | economy succeeds and this is the measure |
| functionalist | does it work? |
| technologic | almost unbroken prosperity gives faith in technology |
| competent | understand technology of work |
| simplistic | answers easily satisfy |
| present-oriented | latest thing, ignores past and origins |
| xenophobic | distrusts outsiders, government, difference.[75] |

# Districts, Nonconforming Metropolitan Areas, and Sociocultural Subdivisions

The Central Midwest can be divided into two districts, east and west, with differences not great enough to call the areas "subregions," as in the Upper Midwest. The line of division is at the Mississippi River, except for a small westward salient in the Saint Louis area. Differentiation is based on the difference between a relatively old and a relatively new area, a relatively more and a relatively less industrialized area. The moralistic, rural-virtues attitude common to the western portion of the Upper Midwest is also commonly found in the Western District of the Central

Midwest, even in the cities. Within this district a Plains subdistrict should also be distinguished. The Great Plains are discussed more fully in an annex to the Rocky Mountain section below.

As a border state, Missouri presents particularly severe problems of regional differentiation. On the basis of the religious censuses, and analysis of the origin of settlers by county, it is possible to distinguish those areas settled largely from the Eastern Midwest from those settled from the South or Germany.[76] Although there is a great deal of interpenetration, northwest Missouri and the immediate Kansas City area is by and large Midwestern-Southern, while the Saint Louis area and a narrow stretch west is German-Midwestern-Southern. The bulk of Missouri, however, should be classified as belonging to one or another variety of Southern culture. The southwest is Mountain Southern, the extreme southeast and some of upper central is Lowland Southern, the remainder is Upland Southern.

There are three nonconforming metropolitan areas in or on the borders of the Central Midwest. Both Kansas City and Saint Louis reflect the border position of Missouri. Kansas City (Jackson County) is heavily influenced by the South; counties immediately to the north and south are dominated by Southern Baptists. Nevertheless, Kansas City, Missouri, is as much a part of Kansas as of Missouri. A portion of its metropolitan area is in definitely non-Southern Kansas, and the city has historically faced west.

Saint Louis and a small area west into Missouri and east and north into Illinois present more of an anomaly within the eastern district of the Central Midwest than Kansas City does in the western district. In every direction the hinterland of the city of Saint Louis is under stronger Southern influence than is true of that west of Kansas City. Saint Louis also has an old Negro population more similar to that of a Southern city. Yet I have placed it in the Midwest because it is different from truly Southern cities such as Memphis. Historically, Saint Louis was the gateway to the West, the channel through which Americans moved from old regions. Its dominant German population imparted an interest in education and international culture unusual in the South, and outstanding even in the Middle West. Yet Saint Louis is so much a Southern city, and so similar to Southern border towns such as Louisville, Kentucky, that it needs to be separated by some designation from the rest of the Central Midwest.

The nonconforming Chicago Metropolitan Area serves as the sociocultural core of the Central Midwest and to some extent of the Upper Midwest as well. Its people have always been a mixture of a wide variety of ethnic variations, containing perhaps a more varied group of people than even New York. In addition, as one writer points out, "Chicago has always had strong Southern ties. . . . It has employed Southern workers, supplied Southern factories with machines, money and engineers, and in my view it has some of the ease of Southern cities today." [77] To contrast New York and Chicago is in a way to contrast the Central Midwest and the Northeast, in spite of Chicago's nonconforming regional character. There is, of course, a great deal of difference between the recent political systems, but this may be due to the personalities and organizations of Daley and Lindsay (New York has had effective machines in the past). It may, however, be significant that these days even the Mafia seems to run more smoothly in Chicago. Beyond politics, Chicago businessmen have the local booster spirit of the Midwest while the New Yorker does not. Chicago is still primarily a city of low buildings, one- and two-family houses, where half of the families own their own houses. The people are more relaxed and disciplined. Ethnically, Chicago is dominated by conservative Irish, Polish, and Middle Europeans while New York has a greater admixture of liberal Jews and New Englanders, as well as people of all types attracted by the liberal professions. One result is that while New York may have better schools, hospitals, and museums, Chicago has cleaner streets, better lighting, better suburban train service, and the telephones work. As noted above, there is Southern influence in Chicago, brought by Southern whites and blacks from the interior South.

Stretching out in all directions Chicago's suburbs are relatively self-contained; each seems to have more of a sense of community than those around New York. Those to the north are wealthier, more Upper Midwest, those to the west and south are more "Middle American." Chicago's universities are as distinguished as those of New York and constitute a center of conservative thought, particularly in economics. However, in spite of the academics, the intellectual and cultural elite of the Chicago area is quite small for a city of its size. This may account for more segregation in Chicago, a greater difference between the educational and employment levels of whites and blacks, and perhaps a greater tendency to resort to violence. But New York and Newark are insolvent, while Chicago is not.[78]

Socioculturally the Midwest should be considered one region, with Missouri and West Virginia transitional to it. Two recent studies reported that the official respondents (primarily postmasters) in the Upper and Central Midwest and Missouri identify their region as "Midwest," [79] although "Great Lakes" was preferred by many in Wisconsin and Michigan. Significantly, the Midwest was a preferred designation in nearly all of the Great Plains, even in western Oklahoma. In one study respondents in a small portion of southern Ohio and Indiana preferred other designations. Within the Midwest sociocultural region, district boundaries have been drawn (Map 31) in such a way as to permit several variations. There is clearly a distinctively more industrialized *Eastern District* composed of Illinois, Indiana, Ohio, and most of Michigan. Here the clash of peoples and high industrial activity make the image very much like that in parts of the New York Metropolitan Region. The western districts are still much more influenced by their agricultural background. They are divided into *Upper Western* and *Lower Western* districts because of differences in cultural background leading to different natural allegiances and socioeconomic policies.

## Problems and Potential

The Central Midwest dominated the story of nineteenth-century growth. In four generations Chicago grew from nothing to a great city. The region could confidently look forward to being the economic and cultural leader of the nation. Yet, it never happened: relative to California, New York, and New England (culturally), the region has slipped back. Like Philadelphia, it must overcome or live with this fact.

The Central Midwest has a tradition of community involvement and family-centered activity that has been continually threatened by progress over the last sixty years. Much of it was eroded long ago: Robert and Helen Lynd's *Middletown* suggests that the rural paradise of 1895 had already lost a great deal by 1925. But there are still many towns and portions of small cities that reflect the kind of stability and commitment John Martin describes for Winamac, Indiana, in the 1940s.[80] For some people this way of life will always be rewarding and for them the nation should try to make it possible. Alf Landon has recently evoked this sense of mission by writing of "the desire . . . to change from the tensions and insecurity of life in the big cities to the pleasure and comfort that come from the security of living in smaller towns. In the Middle West, it has increasingly taken the form of people remaining in the smaller cities and giving them new life and intelligence." [81]

But for many Central Midwesterners, recently arrived from the South or from the nineteenth-century urban ethnic blocks, the problem is one of community formation and, beyond that, of achieving a way of life that is more distinguished than that found today in most of the area. To the outsider, drabness and sameness are pervading ills, and the land around Chicago and throughout Ohio seems in danger of becoming a vast suburb. If other values are there, or being created, let the people explain them to the world—and thus ultimately to themselves.

There are exceptions, places that have done a great job of either preserving old values or creating new ones. One example is Columbus, Indiana, which "probably has the finest architecture per capita of any city in the United States." [82] Here a local businessman set up a foundation that pays the cost of having major new buildings designed by international architects as well as that of redesigning more modest buildings (see fig. 17). Perhaps the result is too eclectic, too superficial, but one man made something of his community, and the Central Midwest would be a much richer area if other individuals or groups would do equally well by their communities.

# The Rocky Mountain Region

## Population

In the Rocky Mountain Region (see Map 32) there were approximately three million people in 1970, two-thirds of them in Colorado. While Colorado grew at a rate well above the national average in the 1960s, Wyoming and Montana stagnated. Now more than a third of the population of the region is concentrated in the Denver metropolitan area. There is little intraregional

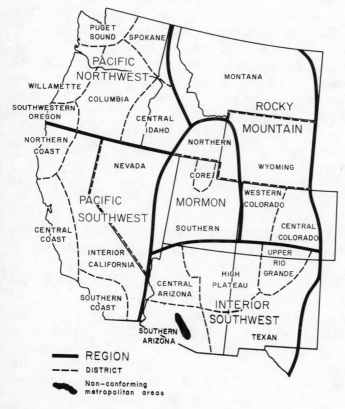

MAP 32. Western Cultural Regions and Districts

movement, and a great deal of movement in and out, especially in Wyoming and Montana. These two states also had a large foreign-born population in early years. Today the region as a whole is largely white Anglo-Saxon Protestant; there is heavy Catholic population in parts of Montana and Colorado, although the latter is primarily in the portion of the state we have placed in the Interior Southwest. There have been small Spanish American, American Indian, and Negro (in Colorado) populations since the early days of settlement.

## General Description and Regional Borders

The Rocky Mountains are a tangle of mountain ranges, with the central mass generally less than two hundred miles wide. They stretch from the Canadian border through western Montana, crossing from northwest Wyoming through east central Wyoming and central Colorado into New Mexico. It is a high and dry region, with forests only at very high elevations and along streams, except in Montana. Although there is a short growing season and it is very cold, the year-round sunshine and dry air makes this region relatively pleasant except on the most exposed plains. The region is the source of great river systems (Missouri, Columbia, Colorado, Arkansas), but there is almost no navigable water.

I have allowed climate and physiography to determine borders for the Rocky Mountain Region more than for any other, as the region is defined by the fact that it includes the top of the Rockies and their eastern slope. In Colorado and Wyoming, the regional border has been extended to the edge of the High Plains, while in Montana the border extends farther onto the Plains (for the Plains, see below). The southern boundary is determined by the limits of dominant Spanish-American settlement and associated Indian cultures radiating from Santa Fe. In the southern two-thirds of the region, the western border is defined as the border of the Mormon domain, although there are a few Mormon colonies within the region. The problems of definition are along the northwest boundary—parts or all of Montana are often included in the Pacific Northwest—and the demarcation of the region from the Upper and Central Midwest. In cultural terms, a portion of western Montana, including Missoula, could be incorporated in the Pacific Northwest Region; alternatively, the Rocky Mountain Region could stretch west to include all northern Idaho and Spokane, Washington. In our cultural analysis, compromise was struck near the "wheat frontier" in the Idaho Panhandle, with the thought that the strictly mining areas partake more of the culture of Missoula than of Spokane (which would probably be news to many in Spokane).

The influence of Minneapolis might lead us to include Montana in the Upper Midwest socioculturally. However, two recent studies of the Upper Midwest show a clear separation. A map of population flow within the Upper Midwest, 1955–60, shows significant movements within Montana and within the rest of the Upper Midwest, but essentially none between Montana districts and those to the east (except for the extreme northeast corner of Montana).[83] A map of metropolitan trade and service areas shows most of Montana connected to the Northwest, south-central Montana to Denver, and eastern Montana to Minneapolis-Saint Paul.[84]

Compared to the Midwest regions, the Rocky Mountain people are less homogeneous in regard to occupations and ethnic backgrounds. The Upper Midwest's characteristic domination by Scandinavian and German groups does not extend to Montana and Wyoming. The Rocky Mountain Region has been dominated by ranching, mining, and irrigated oasis agriculture; the Midwests by more traditional agriculture and then industry. Present patterns of rapid growth in central Colorado suggest that the Central Colorado District, at least, is likely to diverge more and more from areas farther east. Some suggestion of the reality of a three-state Rocky Mountain Region is provided by the academic geographers contacted by Ruth Hale in these states. They were apparently the only ones identifying their national region as "the West." In the larger vernacular study, only Wyoming firmly saw itself as in a "Rocky Mountain Region," although the term was accepted by large percentages in Colorado (majority), Utah, Montana, and Idaho.[85] Nevertheless, the Rocky Mountain Region is the most poorly defined of our regions and might well be divided among surrounding regions, especially the Pacific Northwest and the two Midwests.

## History and Regional Characteristics

Passed over by the westward movement until the late 1850s, the Rocky Mountain Region was the last frontier in the continental United States. At the time of the first penetration of the region by Lewis and Clark, the Indians were bison-hunting, horse-riding nomads with little settled agriculture. Because their land was least valuable, they were the last to be subdued. With the loss of their extensive way of life based on warfare and bison, they suffered more than most by the confinement of reservation life. Today the region differs from the Interior Southwest in that Indian and Spanish culture is much less important, and both the California and Western Southern cultures have less influence there.

The first wave of white settlers in the region consisted of trappers who settled down as traders in the 1840s and 1850s. The next waves resulted in the almost simultaneous development of ranching (sometimes by the trapper-traders) and mining. Trading with migrants to California and then to closer gold fields developed the requirement for the first livestock. Mining is still important in Colorado and Montana, and many of the people of the region in other occupations are descended from stranded miners. However, mining has historically been less important than transit in Wyoming. The state developed initially along the Oregon Trail, the route later followed by the Union Pacific, Highway 30, and Interstate 80.

Once the Indian threat was controlled, ranches of great size developed; they were frequently owned by wealthy easterners and foreigners (especially English). Ranchers had to struggle for their rights to public land almost immediately with sheep raisers and as early as the 1890s with homesteaders (who were often former cowboys). Nonirrigated agriculture was impossible before dry farming techniques were perfected and has remained erratic because of the wide fluctuation in precipitation. Although most of the homesteaders eventually failed this far west on the Plains or in intermontane valleys, some dry farming continues on very large acreages. Irrigation, necessary for any substantial agriculture in most areas, was used as the basis of agriculture in Colorado in the nineteenth century and has been developed extensively through government projects since then. In much of the region the growing season is too short for agriculture other than grazing.

The despoliation of the relatively slow-growing forests of the area began with the mining fever of the 1860s and 1870s. Large areas were destroyed for fuel and construction for both living and smelting. Later, with the decline in the forest reserves of the old Northwest and the access provided by the railroads, the timber gained national importance and was cut with abandon on public land, much as the ranchmen consumed freely the open range. The result was the gradual imposition of direct federal control over a large portion of the entire region under national forest and other public land regulation. Since then the struggle of the exploiters and the preservationists has revolved around the establishment of national parks, wilderness areas, reclamation dams, and the meaning of "multiple use" in much of the national forest.

Although mining has remained important to the economy of the area, the number of workers needed to extract or process the ore has greatly declined. The importance of gold and silver is long gone, but molybdenum, uranium, the perennial copper, and other minerals have taken their place. In recent years, oil and gas have become increasingly important to Wyoming, while the future economic base of the state, as well as of southeast Montana, seems now to lie in the extraction of the enormous quantities of coal that underlie the area. In addition, the possible extraction of oil from shale may play a large role in the regional future.

Until the sudden importance of these energy sources, the area's future seemed to be based on the development of tourism. The history of Colorado has been influenced since 1860 by the state's reputation as a healthful area for invalids, and many of the invalids who survived decided to stay. The old-fashioned resort industry founded on this faith at places such as Colorado Springs, along with the dude ranch industry, was replaced by the auto tourist, hunter, angler, and most recently the skiing enthusiasts, who have produced a proliferation of resorts based on the Aspen and Sun Valley (Idaho) models. To the north, Yellowstone and Glacier national parks have developed into primary attractions.

Development in the fifties and sixties was also due to the establishment of military bases and facilities (for example, the Air

Force Academy at Colorado Springs) and the importance of Denver as a distribution and governmental center. There is relatively little heavy industry outside of Pueblo, Colorado. Aside from missile sites and air bases, Montana and Wyoming participated less in recent development, and before 1970 were in a long-term decline relatively and even absolutely.

Politically and socially, the region experienced the full flavor of the frontier tradition of violence connected with ranching and mining and the conflicts of Indians and whites. In many areas the tough independence and careless indifference of the Texan and frontiersman remain. However, from the beginning, there was an infusion of upper-class New York and foreign adventurers who have continued to play a part, or to pass in and out of the scene. Compared to areas to the west and east, local elites have probably less intense interest in local affairs and more in national affairs. In spite of Western camaraderie, Rocky Mountain society is less middle-class than that of Iowa and the Pacific Northwest, resembling more the highly stratified societies of the Northeast and the South. This difference has been reinforced by the ability of Boulder, Aspen, Colorado Springs, and Denver to attract wealthy Easterners in recent years. Today the Central Colorado District is a Western outpost of eastern civilization and sophistication. But among the less educated and wealthy there is a populist hatred of bigness, of the wealthy corporation, although not of the self-made man.

Ownership of land and industry by outsiders (including the federal government) has been a continuing part of the regional experience, as has reliance on federal funds for relief, reclamation, price support, transportation, and so on. The result has been an acerbic relation with "the outside," a love of individual freedom, and a hatred of the government and the outside investment upon which the area is so dependent. For this reason, the area's history of exploitation, often by locals, supports a fierce desire to maintain old ways against encroachment, finding in the process a ground swell of support for ecologists.

# Districts and Sociocultural Subdivisions

The region's cultural and sociocultural borders are defined primarily in terms of political divisions. Montana and Wyoming both form sociocultural and cultural districts of rather similar dimensions. Socioculturally, Colorado stretches farther east and south than the Rocky Mountain cultural region. Culturally, eastern Colorado is an extension of the Central Midwest, and southern Colorado of the Interior Southwest.

The most important cultural district in the region is *Central Colorado,* including the state's central Rockies' tourist areas, Denver and Colorado Springs. In this district are most of the region's higher education facilities, as well as at least half of its population. It has most of the region's newcomers and nearly all of its urban problems. At the southern edge of the district, Pueblo, Colorado, is an atypical industrial city with a high percentage of Irish, Slavs, and Spanish-Americans. Pueblo is transitional to the Interior Southwest, although its cultural pattern is also more Central Midwestern and Western Southern than that of the rest of the district.

In recent years a heavy movement of population into Central Colorado has brought new life, but also the threat of change. This movement has included people from California, the Midwest, and the Northeast. But it is the Western South or Texan invasion that has been more worrisome, both numerically and qualitatively. Fear of Western Southerners was heightened recently by apprehensions that the corrupt Denver police force of a few years back was dominated by Western Southerners, and that the trade of southeast Colorado was being attracted to Amarillo. At times, the construction of great buildings in Denver by Dallas millionaires has been actively discouraged.

*Western Colorado* is a mixed mining, oasis, and ranching area, resembling Wyoming or Utah without the Mormons; where penetrated from the Western South, it is perhaps more like New Mexico. Except when a mine is active, population is sparse.

The district of *Wyoming* to the north includes all of that state outside of a Mormon fringe in the southwest. The capital, Cheyenne, with little more than forty thousand people, is in the shadow of Denver, and local centers elsewhere in the state are often nearly as important. More centrally located, Caspar has had the largest newspaper circulation of a Wyoming newspaper (14,353).[86] Many Wyomingites read Denver, Salt Lake, or Billings (Montana) papers and listen to out-of-state radio and television stations. Economically, possession of the best route through the central Rockies, stock ranching, and other agricultural interests continue to be dominant influences. In northwest Wyoming tourism is of special importance; to the east, oil and gas; and in the south, transport. Perhaps Wyoming is after all an artificial district. In one recent study of the future of the Rocky Mountain area, the region is shown divided among a Northern Plains complex and a Front Range complex (central Colorado), with Wyoming included in the fringes of both or as a buffer zone.[87]

The *Montana District* was historically an area of greater conflict and violence—probably because of its mining interests. The laborers of the world were brought to Montana, and nationality groups such as the Irish are still said to dominate Butte. For years the Anaconda Copper Company ruled the state, even owning half its newspapers. While mining remains important, ranching (cattle, sheep, and wheat) have in recent years been more important economically. Farther from anything than Wyoming, with fewer tourists and with periods when greatness seemed close at hand, Montana displays more of a sense of statehood than Wyoming. There have been repeated efforts to vitalize the state both culturally and economically, with modest but significant results. Montana has no central city, but a collection of small cities, with the capital one of the smaller. However, because of isolation from larger cities, places such as Billings or Great Falls are much more like cities than towns of similar size (fifty to sixty thousand) in more developed regions.

## Problems and Potential

The Rocky Mountain Region needs solutions to two very different problems. For Central Colorado, the problem is that of many boom areas elsewhere, particularly those with natural beauty such as the California coast or the Interior Southwest. It must preserve the natural environment in the midst of both population growth and even more rapid increase in utilization. Because there is little industry in Colorado, many problems of development have so far been avoided; yet industrial and power demands will grow as a more diversified base develops. Elsewhere in the region, the problem has been one of developing new economic opportunities in areas of steadily declining population. People are encouraged to leave by recurrent droughts, the fragility of one-industry towns, and the shortness of residence of so many fellow citizens.[88]

Because the economy of the Rocky Mountains is based on tourism and the exploitation of natural resources, because it is the playground of the wealthy and the homeland of rugged individualists who believe it is *their* land, *their* fauna and flora to do with as they wish, ecological and conservation disputes are often sharper here than elsewhere. On the other hand, the sparse population also leads the nation to think that local interests can more easily be ignored in favor of national interests in this region than in most others. Again, a more balanced economy, aided perhaps by changes in freight rate systems and the erosion of overly narrow interest groups, would greatly lessen the bitterness of the dispute.

From the standpoint of 1970 the region needed little more than stabilization, for the economic base in districts such as Wyoming was fairly good for the low population being supported. Opposition in Montana to new mining ventures, and even to the kind of recreation facility promoted by Chet Huntley, suggested that the area might opt for a very low density future. If the people did not want to go beyond present population levels, they could preserve a relatively unspoiled area for future generations, although "unspoiled" would be in local terms rather than those of naturalists.

However, extrapolated national energy demands and the place of the region's coal and possibly oil shale in meeting them means that there will be no escape from some widespread ecological and probably cultural dislocation. The people of the region may try to hold back this development or take full immediate advantage of it. They can strive to emphasize (1) local use of power for industrialization, or (2) the development of only power plants at the source and thus an extensive development of new transmission lines, or (3) the shipment of coal and other raw materials out of the region.

The latter choice will change the region least, but under what assumptions can the people of the region, particularly in eastern Wyoming and Montana, decide that this is the use they wish to make of their resource? Whatever the decision, many individuals in the areas immediately affected will give up their way of life. As always in this region, development will be limited by available water, an important factor for the thirsty thermal electric plants and any associated industry that may develop.

## The Great Plains

In the United States, the Great Plains (see Map 2) comprise a largely flat, treeless area stretching from Canada through Montana and the Dakotas into western Texas. Toward the Rio Grande their defining characteristics are lost as rocky hills and brush replace short grass and flat vistas. The Great Plains were the land of the buffalo herds and of the Plains Indians who, with the mobility provided by the horse, developed many common cultural traits over the entire area. The limitation of the Plains for human habitation was prescribed by its low precipitation (ten to thirty inches, but varying widely year to year), heavy snows in the north, and strong winds (drying in the summer, chilling in the winter), as well as periodic minor calamities such as hail, prairie fires, grasshopper plagues, and (later) dust storms. As a result, population generally falls off rapidly as one moves west from the Central Lowlands (Map 2) at the eastern edge of the Dakotas, Nebraska, Kansas, and Oklahoma toward the heart of the area. The "plains" vary from the most "typical" flat lands of Kansas to much rougher and even mountainous areas in the north, particularly the Sand Hills of Nebraska and the Badlands and Black Hills (which actually become forested mountains) in South Dakota. On the west the Plains merge into a trough or piedmont area. High, very dry and cold, this approach to the Rockies affords very little nonirrigated cropland.

In the nineteenth century, the Plains were commonly called the "Great American Desert." Some called the area a desert simply because it was uninhabited, while others believed it would never support more than range cattle or sheep. Ranchmen had a vested interest in the image of an arid waste, and, in terms of the technology of the times, facts were on their side. Yet the settlers came. Congress did not want the homesteading frontier to be cut short by lack of rain; the railroads had a great financial stake, both direct and indirect, in development; and the future of a number of new and potential states seemed to rest on proving the inhospitality of the desert to be a myth. The boomers lied, many suffered years before they finally gave up their homesteads. Yet the Plains states did offer opportunity to hundreds of thousands. In the end, the care of range cattle, extensive, low-density dry-farming, and intensive irrigated farming in small areas proved to be all the western part of the Plains could support even with new agricultural methods; yet faith, hope, and self-interest had won a partial victory.

The Great Plains, then, cut a swath from Canada to Mexico through the center of the United States, crossing five of the cultural regions of this analysis. In a physiographic sense, they lie almost entirely east of the Rocky Mountain Region. Nevertheless, the Plains are included as an annex to this region because to analysts such as Carl Kraenzel the key characteristics to which the Plains people and those who would plan for them have never adjusted are aridity and low population density.[89] Today, these are perhaps more critical for the Rocky Mountain states, especially Wyoming and Montana, than for any other states. Kraenzel points out, for example, that while school consolidation may make sense elsewhere, it does not in the Plains. On the other hand, a township level of government is unnecessary in North Dakota where a low population may make even counties superfluous. To Walter Prescott Webb and Kraenzel the tragedy of the Plains has been caused by an attempt to apply solutions based on experience in more humid conditions. One of the first examples was the difficulty of getting away from the 160-acre homestead when it was clearly too small for the area. Another has been the taxing of income and property on the basis of stable income when, in fact, income to ranchers and farmers in this area fluctuates wildly and unpredictably.

Kraenzel makes an interesting class analysis of the area under the strange heading of "minorities." One class (or minority) is that of the ranchmen (subdivided into sheep and cattle in some areas). Kraenzel relates the ranchman's conservatism to his ties to buyers and the outside interests they represent. However, his history, origin, and current experience may be as important. The dry farmers are in the majority and represent radical, local, anti-estab-lishment views; many today live in cities and commute out to their farms.[90] (The strength of this group is outside the Rocky Moun-tain Region in the Midwestern fringe.) In the middle are the irrigated farmers, a group gaining power in the 1950s. Labor is a fractionated minority, while most business managers are outsiders educationally or by origin and are passing through to better positions. The professionals are likewise outsiders; even if of local origin, they hold foreign views and interests. Businessmen operate on a very small scale and are bitterly opposed to the dry farmers and their cooperatives. Now, of course, we would have to add for certain parts of the Plains parallel and conflicting class hierarchies based on coal mining and oil drilling, and on the military base structures.

For the issues that interest Kraenzel or Webb, it is a mistake to chop up the Plains as we have, but the point of the present work is that there are different people in the Plains from north to south. The continuity that does exist on the Plains in spite of original cultural differences is less noticeable in the southern plains of the Western South and the Interior Southwest. Urbanization and population levels are much higher in the Western South plains.[91] In the Western South, there is more of a gap between the classes of peoples, more discrimination, fewer post-1800 European immi-grants, and more individualistic attitudes than in the Upper Midwest plains. Nevertheless, in the Rocky Mountain Region, the Texas cowboy pattern plays a determining role in general culture that is not true of that part of the Plains farther to the east.

# The Mormon Region

## Population

In 1970 there were perhaps 1,250,000 people in the Mormon Region (see Map 32), with 900,000 of these concentrated in a small metropolitan strip of northern Utah. Utah was growing at somewhat more than national rates on account of a long and continuing record of high fertility. Although the original Mormon community was of upstate New York–New England background, most immigrants to Utah in the second half of the nineteenth century were foreign born. In fact, the 1870 figure of 35 percent foreign-born in Utah suggests that over half the population has foreign (post-1800 immigrant) rather than old native origin.[92] Foreign origin is largely English, but also represents many people from Scandinavia, Germany, and Switzerland. The rapid and quite thorough assimilation of this group under the elite dominance of the native American Mormon church is unexampled elsewhere. It should be noted that since 1950 Idaho was the main outside source of Utahans, indicating a close intraregional tie.

## Regional Borders and General Description

I have designated the Mormon Region as approximately that of the Mormon "domain" of D. W. Meinig, based on the areas of overwhelming Mormon population (see Map 9).[93] This includes Utah, southeastern Idaho, and small strips of Nevada, Wyoming, and Arizona. Culturally this is the best-defined region in the nation. The area penetrates on the north and east into the valleys of the Rockies, on the north into the upper reaches of the Columbia Basin (Snake River), and on the west and south into areas of desert and canyon. The area is dry, cold in winter and often hot in summer. At its best it can be an extremely pleasant and exhilarating country. But only in a few, favored irrigated valleys is farming possible. Most of the area is, and will probably remain, unoccupied.

## History and Regional Characteristics

The Mormon movement was a popular response to religious agitation in upstate New York among displaced New Englanders in the 1820s and 1830s. Although Mormon prophecies were new, the beliefs they contain, and the practices that supplement the beliefs, represent no more than a special version of developments in New England and American popular life that were common at the time. In the Church of the Latter Day Saints God came to be seen as a superman who had *achieved* much that He was. Men could through individual and collective effort come closer and closer to being gods themselves. The purposes of life were seen in fulfilling the possibilities of men to strive, to achieve happiness in this life and hereafter. The body's health should be preserved, physical exercise encouraged, and all harmful substances avoided. Children were to be produced for the happiness of their own souls and because they were an eternal blessing to their parents, just as all men were to God.

Lowry Nelson suggests that in addition to the doctrine of perfectibility, there were three other essential integrative values in the Morman movement. First was the doctrine of the superiority of the common man. All males could become priests, and the concept of a special paid minister was rejected for most communities. Second was the sense of exclusiveness and mystery surrounding the origin of the movement and some of its rituals. The initiated came to possess secrets the outside world could never know. Finally, there was a universalist outreach. All "truths" were held to be incorporable in Mormonism, and both liberal and conservative Christians were welcomed.[94]

The period of Mormonism's birth was a period of social experiment, and directly and indirectly an experimental attitude was incorporated into the movement. Like New England, Utah was a theocracy, and even today Boston and Salt Lake City are the only major cities with churches at the center.[95] The degree to which Mormon life was dominated until 1900 by the interpenetration of church and state is suggested by Joseph Spencer when he writes:

A large share of county taxes was paid in labor and the balance often in produce. The tithes, so important a part of the Church operations, were likewise originally paid in labor or kind. Prices lower than retail rates were set for these products and a considerable amount of bartering by all concerned effected a distribution of articles locally needed, and a concentration of the surplus and of export commodities. These were then shipped out by the Church, the county, individuals, or traders, and sold or exchanged as the case might be. The million-dollar valuation of the St. George Temple is primarily on the basis of tithes contributed in labor for construction purposes over the decades. The tabernacle (the ordinary Sunday-service church), the schools, the roads, the courthouse, and the irrigation ditches were all financed in the same way.[96]

The settlement of Utah was a product of a desire to get far away, to be isolated enough to create an entirely new life. Although many aspects of the rural American collectivist communities of the first half of the nineteenth century were rejected, many of their principles of mutual aid and sharing under a theological directorate were carried over into Mormonism and the development of Utah. There were cooperative herds, cooperative stores, and cooperative ditching projects. These principles continue to affect the attitudes of Mormons today. Although the movement's founders were not highly educated, the Mormons from the first were very interested in education, the University of Utah being the first university established in the West. Education also prospered by the very fact of tight community organization and community-wide budgeting. In education, as in most things, what the Mormons wanted to do they generally did.

Mormon settlement in Utah succeeded where it had failed in the Midwest because they chose an area that was largely unpopulated by Indians and unwanted by other white settlers. The Mormons began to shift to Utah in 1847, and organized parties continued to be brought in from the Midwest for the next decade. However, as pointed out above, between 1855 and 1890 the majority of immigrants were from England and northern Europe. There have been relatively few new immigrants since. The settlements in Utah were established in regular order and settlers ordered to them as needed. The result was a proliferation of distinctive rural communities of broad streets, with large lots for farmers who were to live in town rather than on their farms. The Mormons were the first to irrigate on a large scale in the West, and even today the main streets may be lined with irrigation ditches. Their monumental buildings include the Tabernacle built in the 1860s and the great Temple built between 1853 and 1893. The specialties of the Mormon culture have become their buildings, their music, and their economic, social, and religious success.

After they came to Utah, the Latter Day Saints struggled to maintain their separateness. For a time this meant a deliberate attempt to keep non-Mormons out. During the first fifty years in Utah, outside control threatened both economically through the establishment of gentile business and mining property and socially through the establishment of United States civil government and Washington's attempt to suppress polygamy. Polygamy was a secondary addition to the basic body of Mormon belief. Originally the Book of Mormon had condemned the practice, but in the early 1840s it was secretly introduced, becoming public after removal of the community to Utah. Although polygamy had a strengthening function as a symbol of difference, many Mormons were glad to give it up in the 1890s. The symbols of separateness for the dedicated Mormon are now abstention from coffee, tea, liquor, and tobacco.

Mormonism succeeded economically, and the economy of the Mormon church and of Mormon areas is generally strong. The original ideals of the movement were agrarian, yet their structuring of even agrarian lives in towns meant that Mormon areas were from the outset more agricultural than rural. The key to Mormon economy has always been balance, self-sufficiency, and stability. At first this meant the avoidance of mining in favor of agriculture, but as agriculture became a small part of the national economy it has meant a rapid shift out of agriculture into modern industrial and service occupations supplemented by the extraction of copper, uranium, and fossil fuels.

Politically the region has a balanced two-party system. Yet the church hierarchy has always been conservative and generally Republican. In the late sixties there was hardly a Democratic paper available in the region, even among the smaller weeklies. Although there is a vocal far-right movement, associated with the Benson family, both Republicans and Democrats are generally moderate and do not appear to be elected with an eye to Washington's favor, as is often alleged for other mountain states such as Montana.

The continued vitality of the Mormon church in regional life bears additional examination. The ability of an extremely aged, partially hereditary hierachy to maintain control of a growing church bespeaks an unusual kind of strength. Politically the church lost its dominance of the state after 1900, and after that many non-Mormons have been elected to office. Since World War II, however, while the church hierachy continues to have little weight, the influence of Mormons in the region's political life has increased. In this same period the number of Mormons in the world has more than doubled as the result of high fertility, a great outpouring of missionary effort, and a remarkable ability to preserve membership. Brigham Young University expanded rapidly and is today the largest institution in the region at a time when church-supported institutions in other regions have generally faded. Yet it is hard to be a Mormon: tithes are sizable, and social pressures and demands on the individual's time are heavy.

The church keeps its vitality largely through the material success of its members both within and outside the region. Also, regional life continues to be infused with a theological strain that persists even in those who have fallen away from the church to the right (polygamist and other underground movements) or the left (liberals). It succeeds because through involving members in constant church-related activity, a pattern of intense church-related life is developed that would make life empty on the outside. Vitality is maintained through the strict attention of the many layers of officials to any wavering among persons in their care. Every attempt is made to keep an individual from slipping into wrong belief or practice, and to isolate faithful Mormons from the society of those who have placed themselves outside the pale.

As we have pointed out several times in preceding sections, Utah is a state with superior social statistics. Its educational superiority has long been noted. Although birth rates are high, mortality (including infant mortality) ranks with the lowest in the nation. However, superiority in education and health care is accomplished with relatively little expense (lower than national averages in hospital beds or hospital admissions, physicians per 100,000, dietitians). Utah has a very low rate of illegitimate births, of suicides and homicides, while a very high percentage of the population votes. This is a participant and stable society.[97]

## Districts and Sociocultural Divisions

Socioculturally Utah is the basic unit, with southeastern Idaho tied to it by economics and culture in spite of the political boundary at the Idaho border. The main cultural district of the Mormon Region is, of course, the *Mormon Core District*, a narrow strip of five counties running from Provo, Utah, to the Idaho border. This is the area of original settlement and now comprises the ecclesiastical, educational, and distribution centers. Three-fourths of the population of the region live here. Although there are many non-Mormons, the district remains clearly a majority Mormon area. Beyond this, Meinig's analysis in terms of concentric subregions is probably as good as any. However, following the format of our study, I distinguish a *Northern District* including those parts of the region in Idaho and Wyoming and a *Southern District* including those areas falling outside of the core in Utah (and a small portion of Arizona and Nevada). Both of these districts contain some intensely irrigated agricultural areas similar to the core district, but they are generally remote and often have non-Mormon special-purpose populations. In some ways these areas can preserve more of the original agrarian way of life of the Mormons than is possible in the heavily populated core. Although locally dominant, the Mormons in the Northern District have to react to the somewhat different experiences of living in states they do not dominate, while the people in the Southern District do not have this problem except for those few in Nevada and Arizona.

## Problems and Potential

The problems of the Mormon community are not so much creative as preservative. Will a highly educated population, with ever-increasing intercourse with the outside society, be able to preserve its élan, faith, or community spirit for future generations? Inevitably, outside influences flow in with improvement in transportation and communication. And with less outside pressure and less necessity to depend on one's fellows in the community, the pressure on religion as the integrative value cannot help but become stronger. Only liberalization will keep many of the better educated in, and yet a really liberal spirit may cause the whole to fall apart into a declining and pale Protestantism. A compromise might be to liberalize the Mormon position on Negroes, which some believe is theologically weak in any case. Although it is an outside possibility, the future might see a tacit acceptance of polygamist sects as family and sexual deviations become more acceptable nationally. This greater social flexibility would broaden the Mormon appeal to both the left and the right, but would do little to decrease the difficulty of the central tenets of the faith for many brought up as Mormons.

Relative to the nation, regional growth will be slow. Although many Mormons leave the state, they often bring money back to enrich the society. Tourism based on the resorts to the east of Salt Lake ( if the problem of the lake's rise is solved) and the national parks will grow, as will income from the extraction of minerals and fuels. As the Mormon elite becomes increasingly prosperous in and outside of the Mormon region, there is little threat of financial takeover by non-Mormons. Mormon fertility, and the absence of the amenities of California, Arizona, or Nevada, makes it unlikely that an influx of non-Mormons will overwhelm the region.[98] Yet with change the Mormons may want to develop new bases of regional identity that may replace those social and material adjustments of early Utah that gave the area its decisive stamp.

# The Interior Southwest

## Population and Regional Characteristics

In 1970 there were about 3,200,000 people in the Interior Southwest (see Map 32), with more than half of them in Arizona.

Arizona had grown faster in the decade of the 1960s than California, while New Mexico and El Paso were growing at rates well below the national average.

Nowhere in the country are so many distinct cultures persisting side by side, with positive contributions to the lives of all of us. In other western areas such as California or the Pacific Northwest, many peoples tend to be fused into the regional life. Yet the Southwest is a kind of rural New York City in which the melting pot also does not melt. Because of distance, low population density, and the character of the original peoples, the area has added on new versions of life without destroying the old, and attempts to preserve the old alongside the new seem less strained here than they do elsewhere. There are at least seven major cultural groupings in the Interior Southwest: (1) Spanish-American, (2) Pueblo Indian, (3) non-Pueblo Indian, (4) Texan, (5) Central Midwestern, (6) Northeastern American and European, and (7) Californian. Each of these should, of course, be subdivided. For example, among non-Pueblo Indians, Pima and Mescalero Apache are very different peoples; the old Spanish community of Santa Fe may seem quite foreign to the recent immigrant from Mexico; the Mormon and the New Yorker are both from Europe and the Northeast. In spite of years of co-existence, relatively little regional homogenization has occurred. Northeastern American and European try to learn from and unite the whole, while Indian and Spanish American are slowly enculturated in Midwestern, Texan, and Californian patterns.

The seven cultural groups of the Interior Southwest are highly intermixed geographically, yet the districts of the Southwestern region are much less the result of physical geography and much more the result of the dominance of particular cultural groups than is true of many other regions. Cultural mixture is naturally most common in the region's metropolitan areas, with the Midwestern, Californian, and Northeastern group concentrated in these areas. The Texans (or Western Southerners) are most evident in rural areas and dominate eastern and southern New Mexico, El Paso, and rural southern Arizona.[99]

# History, Regional Borders, and Regional Characteristics

The Spanish entered the Southwest in the sixteenth century, establishing small communities primarily along the Rio Grande. As in Texas and California, the Spanish presence was always weak; in fact, the Pueblo Indians drove the Spaniards out for an extended period. Although there must have been racial mixture, the Spanish Americans of northern New Mexico retained a surprisingly pure Spanish culture, while the Indians preserved their own culture in nearby villages. However, Navaho culture was greatly altered by contact with both Spanish and Pueblo Indians. The "Anglos" came into the region relatively late, and development was slow. Because of the slow rate of Anglo development, New Mexico and Arizona were the last of the forty-eight continental states to be admitted to the Union (1912). Nineteenth-century growth in Arizona was mostly through immigration of Mexicans, while in New Mexico growth was largely confined to the expansion of the Spanish in the north. Ranchers from all over, but mainly from Texas and California, were beginning to press in, as well as a sprinkling of farmers, especially Mormons, in favored locales. The range and Indian wars and the hostility of the peoples involved are still close to the present.

In the twentieth century southern Arizona was radically altered by the development of a new urban population recruited from the whole nation. In addition, a new population of farmers, primarily from the Upland and Western South, moved into portions of southern Arizona, eastern and southern New Mexico in the fifty years after statehood. In World War II and the subsequent era, the urban centers of Albuquerque, El Paso, Phoenix, and Tucson have grown rapidly as both light manufacturing and retirement centers, with a population of diverse origins.

The continuous history of the pre-Anglo peoples of the Southwest is more apparent and alive today than that of any other region. The centers of Indian culture in the region were in northern and north-central New Mexico and in southern Arizona; however, the latter had largely declined by the time of the advent of the Spanish. The Spanish population center was in northern New Mexico, and this remained the most populated area for years. Since 1900 the regional population center has shifted to El Paso and southern Arizona, yet the core of what is distinctively the culture of the Interior Southwest is in north-central New Mexico. Without this core area, it would be necessary to parcel out the region among the Pacific Southwest, Rocky Mountain, and Southern regions. The Interior or Desert Southwest has often been included in a "Southwest" that is dominated by the larger population of Texas. There is surely overlap, yet it seems to me that there are quantitative and qualitative differences in the cultures of Texas and New Mexico that cannot be ignored.

Cultural heterogeneity and the historical importance of Roman Catholicism in the Interior Southwest result in a considerable spiritual difference from the more homogeneous Western South. This is illustrated most dramatically in a dialogue in the fifties between J. B. Priestley and Jacquetta Hawkes on Texas and northern New Mexico.[100] The Texas visited was an exaggerated version of the ills and splendors of the American civilization: wealth, expansiveness, furious "enjoyment," noise, the worship of bigness and efficiency for their own sake, and finally boredom, a prevailing sense of unease. In contrast, the northern New Mexico scene was one of quiet beauty, varying cultures, and people who cherished these things. While the authors deliberately selected their experiences to sharpen the contrast, my own experience suggests a valid contrast. Another contrast is provided by Ross Calvin's comparison of Clovis to Silver City, New Mexico.[101] Although both are under heavy Texan influence, Clovis lies in the Western South and Silver City in the Interior Southwest. Clovis is under farmer Texan influence, heavily religious and business-orientated. Silver City is under rancher-Texan influence, with few church-goers and many imported men of leisure.

Today the borders of the region can be defined by a series of contact zones. To the south the Mexican border separates the dominance of two distinct ways of life. On the west the lower Colorado River irrigated areas represent a contact zone between California and the southwest. The zone has two Indian reservations, a large Mexican-American population, is rural-agricultural (including cotton), and is in the oasis-style of all the Interior Southwest borderlands. Discontinuities of desert and canyon cut this world off from the rest of California and Las Vegas. To the Northwest the contact between the outliers of Mormon culture and the Navaho and Ute reservations is determinative. On the east the edge of continuous plain farming separates the Western South from the Interior Southwest. The hardest borders to define are to the northeast and east of El Paso in Texas. In southern Colorado, the limits of the solid expansion of the Spanish Americans of northern New Mexico form the approximate line, while in Texas the cultural influence of El Paso dies rapidly to the east. The movement of Texan influence has always been east to west, while Spanish Americans and Mexicans soon cease to play other than a laboring role in society as one goes east of El Paso.

Meinig has developed an excellent regional analysis that visualizes the Southwest at various periods in its history.[102] His treatment is cultural, yet departs from his approach in the Mormon and Texan studies referred to previously. He tends to follow the standard geographer's emphasis on physical geographical determination or such things as the growth of railroads, as opposed to the movements of particular peoples. Secondly, since the area did not have any simple expansion from a core of one dominant culture, Meinig's treatment reads much more like the treatment we have had by necessity to use for most regions. In any event, Meinig's "Southwest" is defined with margins similar to my own, although more of eastern New Mexico, the lower Colorado River, and southern Colorado seem to be excluded. Coming after his analyses of both Mormon and Texas regions, Meinig's boundaries, which were developed independently, give me a considerable sense of assurance.

The growth of the Interior Southwest beyond its pre-Anglo pattern has been quite recent, so the pattern of much of the life of the area reflects different conditions than those found in areas that grew significantly at an earlier stage. Education is a good example. Higher education has been well developed in the area through public funds, but the private colleges that sprang up almost everywhere along the advancing frontier were almost entirely absent in this region until the 1960s. Recently the character of the region has been threatened by the reduction in the non-Anglo (Spanish and Indian) representation in the population. However, the Indian and (outside of New Mexico) the Spanish American have gained in visibility and at least short-term power through recent trends.

Harvard University's "Comparative Study of Five Cultures" produced a wealth of studies of the rural peoples juxtaposed in one small area of western New Mexico.[103] The peoples were the Zuni, Navaho, Spanish Americans, Texans, and Mormons. Mormons lived in a highly organized community able to unite to provide good irrigation services, schools, and church. The Mormon worked steadily and took his responsibilities very seriously. Texans were more individualistic, more hostile to other peoples, and less able to cooperate among themselves on community undertakings. This disorganization was reflected in factional quarrels and a pattern that alternated periods of idleness with periods of intense activity. Yet compared to the other groups, Mormons and Texans had much in common: both placed considerable stress on education for their children, both rejected a fatalistic view of life and looked toward the future for their rewards. The other three groups were much more concerned with the present, with man as part of nature. Although some were more active than others, they were much less change-oriented than either of the "Anglo" groups. Yet these peoples persist, grow in numbers, and adapt to Anglo culture without losing their distinctive cultural identities.

Navahos are representative of a group of less settled Indian peoples including Apaches, Utes, Walapais, Papagos, and others who live scattered in single dwellings or small clusters. In the five cultures area they seemed everywhere and nowhere; they were the only group that mingled regularly with the others. The old Spanish-American culture in the Southwest was generally characterized by small irrigated fields, but this was not true in the very arid country of the study. In any case, Spanish-American villages are very small, probably averaging smaller than the Indian pueblos. Perhaps the Pueblo Indians needed larger communities to survive, since they had no general system of government offering them security. For whatever reason, the Pueblos developed a remarkably complex social and religious structure, a structure that has been able to resist outside influences more successfully than those of other Indian groups. There are Roman

Catholic elements in the life of most Pueblos (except Hopi), but most have avoided all but a superficial acceptance of this outside religion (see fig. 22).

Although old Spanish-American and Pueblo Indian villages appear superficially to have much in common, and the Spanish Americans are in fact largely Indian biologically, the two do not simply grade into one another. These Spanish Americans came as colonists centuries ago from Mexico and are not, as one might suppose, largely the more acculturated remnants of local Indian populations.[104] In some areas the Spanish American accepts much more the idea of personal leadership both in the paternalistic *patron* sense of obligation and service between classes and in the tyrannical sense of domination by political bosses in politics, or the father and elder brother in the home. In spite of this heritage, the Spanish American in many areas of New Mexico has become active politically and has attained leadership in both parties. Most Spanish Americans in the Southwest, especially in El Paso and southern Arizona, are Mexicans (Chicanos) who are recent immigrants to the area. They have traditionally participated little in Anglo social and political life.

Erma Fergusson has particularly detailed the continuing presence of Texans in New Mexico and what she considers to be the deleterious effects of their influx.[105] In the far eastern fringe of the state (for example, Hobbs County), there is little Interior Southwestern influence at all. Here she found the typical Texan pattern of oil, cattle, and segregated schools to be dominant, and I have placed this small strip outside the region. On the other hand, in the district I call "Texan," Fergusson found a mixture of cultures. In this division El Paso falls into the latter area more than the former, for it is more bicultural than the rest of west Texas and more closely related to the life of New Mexico.[106] (San Antonio and the far south of Texas have other truly bicultural areas, but they are cut off from New Mexico by a wide strip of Western South cattle, sheep, and goat country.)

## Districts and Sociocultural Division

Because of its mild winters, *Southern Arizona* is the most heavily populated district in the region, and the only one characterized by the extreme heat and aridity of the classic southwestern desert. The district has attracted the region's largest industrial and retirement population to live in or near its irrigated areas. This has made it possible for it to add a majority of Midwesterners, Californians, and elite Northern foreigners to the earlier population base. To the east the landscape is varied and includes an interesting desert flora and fauna, but the Lower Colorado Subdistrict which overlaps with the Pacific Southwest region is hotter and drier and barren unless irrigated. It is heavily Californian, with large numbers of immigrants from the Western South and Mexico.

The *High Plateau* of northern Arizona and northeastern New Mexico and southwestern Colorado is Navaho country, with Utes in the northeastern fringe, and the pueblos of Hopi, Zuni, Acoma, and Laguna on the south. It is dry, cold in winter, moderately hot in summer, largely treeless, but often beautiful. In recent years there has developed a complex of irrigated agriculture, coal mining, oil, gas, and uranium in the Four Corners area of the plateau that has brought a new population, especially of Texans, into the district.

A *Central Arizona District* lying between Southern Arizona and the High Plateau stretches from the Grand Canyon southeastward to the Apache reservations. Its colder winters, mountains, and the beautiful Ponderosa pine offer a combination that can reach surpassing beauty, and its people are less likely to be retirees or Midwesterners than in southern Arizona.

The core area of the Interior Southwest is the *Upper Rio Grande District.* Here the relation of Santa Fe to Albuquerque reflects that of Tucson to Phoenix, although in New Mexico the university is in the larger, more Midwestern Albuquerque and the capital is in the older, more Spanish Santa Fe. Unlike Southern Arizona, the district is spiritually dominated by the smaller Santa Fe (and Taos), symbolic of the old Spanish American, Pueblo, and other Indian cultures. This is also the district most often settled by those Northeastern and European elites that support artistic colonies and the "ambitious and adventuresome" Santa Fe Opera.[107] From Santa Fe north the area offers the dramatic scenery of the Rockies; to the south the district does not extend far from the narrow Rio Grande Valley and its plateau desert environs. The district reaches north into south-central Colorado almost to the city of Pueblo, but the Colorado area is marginal on account of lack of Indian, Northeastern, and recent immigrant cultures.

To the east and south of the core there is the large *Texan District*, extending from southeastern Colorado into West Texas, including El Paso, and then westward into eastern Arizona.[108] Here a Western Southern population dominates, but Spanish-speaking people of both the old and new immigration are often important, particularly in the Rio Grande Valley and along the Mexican border.

Meinig's regionalization is in terms of fewer units and does not include all of the area he defines as Southwest. His units are "Northern New Mexico" (essentially identical with our Upper Rio Grande, although Meinig would not carry it as far into Colorado), "Central Arizona" (essentially Phoenix and environs), the "Southern Borderlands" (including El Paso and Tucson), and the "Northern Corridor and Navaholands" (essentially our High Plateau). Meinig emphasizes the differences between Phoenix and Tucson, pointing to the more essential Spanish character of the latter. However, in other ways Phoenix and Tucson are similar in history and development, and both much less under the influence of the rougher Texan culture than El Paso. The fact that Tucson has preserved and strengthened Spanish culture suggests that the aggressive West Texan influence is weakened there. On the other hand, I feel that in the east and southeast a large, Texan-dominated area within the region should be distinguished from the Little Texas area of Plains agriculture and oil wells outside. There is a break in continuity of Texas influence west of Clovis and another about Wilcox, Arizona. Compared to Little Texas, the people of the Texan District are more likely to be rancher-Texans, and there is a larger mixture of people from the East, Midwest, and the rest of the Interior Southwest.

## Problems and Potential

The distinctive resources of the Southwest are climate, scenery, cultural diversity, and minerals. A primary problem has always been, and remains, water. To the danger that the Southwest will run out of water must be added the threat of pollution, a particularly severe threat in a dry country. The power requirements of surrounding areas and increasing reliance on air conditioning within the area intensify the pressure. On land surfaces with little growth and moisture, trash accumulates in vast middens. The fact that the marks of man's mechanical tracks are slow to heal in this country exacerbates the dangers of increased human activity. Unfortunately, the combination of easily stripped coal and low population density has led to a rapid and continuing build-up of stripping and thermal power development on the high plateau. Lack of other economic resources has led the Indian leaders to seize these opportunities as white leaders have in similar circumstances. But the results may bring second thoughts and a curtailment of this exploitation. This problem is critical for the whole region because scenery and the purity of the air are two of the main reasons for living in the Southwest.

On the human side, another issue is whether the accommodation of different races can be preserved in at least the northern part of the region in the face of the influx of outsiders.[109] Put in other terms, can the distinctive cultural mixture of the Interior Southwest outlast the twentieth century? There are two reasons for hope. First, Santa Fe and Tucson and many smaller cities have both preserved and enhanced aspects of the distinctive regional culture in an urban environment. This generation of Arizonans, including Barry Goldwater, seems more conscious of the vitality of the non-Anglo cultures. Second, the non-Anglo peoples now have more political power and more education, and are more able to use this power for the benefit of their peoples, and thus ultimately for all the people of the region.

# The Pacific Southwest

## Population

In 1970 there were about 20,500,000 people in the Pacific Southwest (see Map 32), with the majority of these in southern

California. It was at the same time the fastest growing and most urban region in the United States. The first population influx in California was dominated by the Northeast, the next by the Midwest, the third by the Western South. The foreign-born white has been and remains more important in California than in any other Western state. Many of the foreign-born were from the big cities of the East or represented populations characteristic of those cities—especially Italians and Irish. There has recently been a considerable increase in the percentage of Californians who are black or of other nonwhite races (Chinese, Japanese, Filipino, and American Indian). Blacks in California are largely from the Gulf States and Arkansas.

It is commonly said that the people of California are a more or less even mixture of people from other regions of the United States. Insofar as this is the case, it may be because the state is so economically and culturally diverse that it has a wide variety of attractions and opportunities. However, it should be noted that some parts of the country figured little in the settling of California. In terms of numbers, the Southeast and New England have played the smallest role, especially after the Gold Rush days, while the Middle West regions and Western South Subregion have played the largest.[110]

## General Description

The Pacific Southwest is dominated by its climate and geography. From its northwestern redwood fringe, precipitation generally declines as one moves south or east, but rises with elevation. Rain is concentrated in the winters. Proximity to the ocean leads to lower summer temperatures and moderate winter temperatures along the coast, while desert areas of extreme heat and dryness reach from the southeast to within one hundred miles of the coast. The result is that at lower elevations California has essentially no winter. Except along the wet northern coast this makes for a different life, with lighter clothes, lighter furniture, and flatter roofs. In nature it makes for some of the most varied vegetation in the world.

A relatively low (about as high as anything east of the

Mississippi) Coast Range sweeps down from Oregon to Santa Barbara and connects to another "coast range" continuing into Mexico (see Map 2). The much higher Sierra Nevada runs south and southeast from northeastern to south-central California just west of the Nevada border. The northern end of California is a maze of mountains, and the state is again crossed by the east-west transverse ranges and the Tehachapi Mountains north of Los Angeles. Between these, and west of the Sierra Nevada, lies the Central Valley, one of the world's most productive agricultural regions. Because of differences of physiography and climate, the Central Valley plays the social role in California that the area east of the Cascades plays in the Northwest. Although physiographically similar to the Central Valley, the Northwest's Puget Sound and Willamette Valley are incorporated in the "coastal areas" of the Northwest because major ports and most of the population are located in this interior trough rather than on the open ocean. It is only east of the Sierra Nevada in the state of Nevada that a physiographic analogy to the east-west dichotomy of the Pacific Northwest occurs. Because of the poverty of Nevada's natural resources, its very low rainfall, and to most eyes dull scenery, Nevada has tended to be a dependent addition to the Pacific Southwest.

## History and Regional Characteristics[III]

The Pacific Southwest is California, and the history of California has always run counter to that of the rest of the nation. From pre-Spanish days it has been seen as an island, and even today most Californians remain relatively self-sufficient and *sui generis*. While most of the country imports European trees, much of California is dominated by the Australian eucalyptus, South American pepper trees, or Middle Eastern palms and citrus.

While most of the West spent years in a dependent, territorial status, almost immediately after the United States took possession of it, California became a state, a state thoroughly dominated by Americans. By the 1830s the Mission Indians had largely been destroyed by disease, and in the rest of the state Indians lived in small groups unprepared for organized resistance. The few

Spaniards and Mexican Indians in California were already coming under American and English influence before the war with Mexico. Then suddenly in the late 1840s and early 1850s the Gold Rush brought hundreds of thousands of Americans. Most of these came to be independent miners, and many turned out to be urbanites of considerable sophistication. Although there have been occasional halts, the pace of growth in California from the Gold Rush to 1970 has been surprisingly rapid and persistent.

With time, mining was replaced by oil extraction, and ranching was replaced by large-scale irrigated agriculture. Never a rural society, California rapidly developed cities and its agriculture became large-scale and industrialized, with the proprietors viewing agriculture as merely another form of business. California has the most specialized and varied agriculture in the country. Its chief products are not the more romantic wines and oranges, but meat, milk, hay, tomatoes, and cotton. Industry developed slowly, but, like everything else in California, is highly diversified. Aerospace and military industry developed partially because of the climate, but also because of the state's highly developed technical and educational base. Gradually, population and income have reached a point where industry siting in California for local needs, and agricultural production for local use, have become the most important bases for growth.

Because of its rapid growth and its attraction for the better educated and wealthier, California was almost from its inception at or near the top on a wide variety of American social indices. Part of the explanation was the bulge in the middle of California's population curve, so that a higher percentage of the population was in the middle productive years rather than the dependent ages (very old or very young). This bulge has persisted in spite of the state's long record of attraction to the retired. Its exceptional population and industrialized farming structure (especially in the interior) and the tendencies of those with Southern backgrounds to settle in rural areas led to the anomaly of a non-Southern state having a Democratic rural population surrounding Republican cities. This was also related to the fact that immigrant groups that elsewhere moved almost exclusively to cities were important in rural California—for example, the Italians in wine grapes or Japanese in truck farming.

Its special history also meant that California was not a wild frontier that gradually became civilized, but an almost instantly civilized frontier. Unfortunately it has been forced more and more into the general mold of Middle America as relatively poorer classes of people found it possible to move to the area. One thinks of exclusive suburbs elsewhere in the country that better transportation and too much publicity have transformed into more "balanced" but less "desirable" cities.

California has always been a center of growth, change, and alienation—alienation perhaps because it appears to offer more than it really does. It has been the center of countless religious movements and experimental communities, and continues to be today. The people who came West were dissatisfied, and dissatisfied people generally remain dissatisfied. Today they move to Australia or Canada. Pleasures, sports, and avocations have become more important to Californians than economic roles, perhaps because of the lower value that Californians place on function, or because pleasure-seeking becomes another disguise for dissatisfaction. For a hundred years, California has been alternately described as a human and cultural paradise or as a disaster area. Good or bad, the state's way of life has generally been seen as the wave of the future. It is a standard by which others became conservative or liberal to protect or attain their vision. Perhaps this is why life in California is given to extremes.

## Problems and Potential

In one of the most significant regional studies of intellectual history in recent years, Kevin Starr has brought out the complexity and depth of the California experience.[112] The dream, destroyed by our war with Mexico, of a western paradise of peace and development was succeeded in the frenetic fifties by hope of the re-creation of the old New England dream in the West. Ministers from New England such as Samuel Willey and the Unitarian Thomas Starr King had a great influence on education and the ministry, even politics; but their efforts were in the end lost in a swirl of other movements. Historical writing had one of its greatest explosions in history, when San Francisco's Hubert H.

Fig. 16. The Chicago River today: Chicago, Ill. *Courtesy of the Chicago Convention and Tourism Bureau*

Fig. 17. Baptist church at Columbus, Ind. *By permission of Harr, Hedrich-Blessing*

Fig. 18. A dispersed settlement in the Midwest: Monona County, Iowa, 1940.
*Courtesy of the Library of Congress*

Fig. 19. The northern Great Plains: a modified I-house near Havre, Mont., 1940.
*Courtesy of the Library of Congress*

Fig. 20. Spanish-American village, with surrounding fields, near Taos, N.M., 1939. *Courtesy of the Library of Congress*

Fig. 21. Taos Pueblo, Taos, N.M. *Courtesy of the New Mexico Department of Development*

Fig. 22. Keresan Pueblo Indian settlement, with Catholic church, in western New Mexico, 1943. *Courtesy of the Library of Congress*

Fig. 23. Navaho hogans near Manuelito, N.M., 1943. *Courtesy of the Library of Congress*

Fig. 24. The ultimate development: Los Angeles, Calif. *Photo by William Garnett*

Fig. 25. A Wrightian mission-style courthouse, Marin County, Calif. *Photo* © *Dandelet*

Fig. 26. "From old Spain, new Spain, California missions . . . dominated by the Australian eucalyptus." *Photo by Palmer Sabin, Architect*

Fig. 27. The end of the Oregon Trail: Willamette Valley, Ore., 1941. *Courtesy of the Library of Congress*

Fig. 28. The rolling hills of Nez Perce County, Ida., 1941. *Courtesy of the Library of Congress*

Fig. 29. The mining frontier: Reid Inlet, Glacier Bay, Alaska, 1969. *Photo by Dave Bohn*

Fig. 30. Eskimo hunter in northern Alaska. *Photo by Frank Whaley, used by permission of Wien Air Alaska*

Bancroft formed large teams to write and sell the many volumes of his history of western America. (That he made profits with what were essentially large volumes of collected documents must be a challenge to the scribblers of all ages.) The California of the promoters, or of writers such as Bret Harte or Mark Twain, was juxtaposed to that of the more serious intellectuals such as Josiah Royce, Henry George, and Frank Norris who wrote of both promise and missed opportunity, of violence, social injustice, and crass materialism. For many Californian writers, the state came to be felt as a burden about which they could be creative only in exile. Nevertheless, the literary achievements of the 1860s, in a state so new, remain remarkable and can be faulted only in contrast with the height of the ambitions of the men involved.

It is fair to say that in no other place in America with so few people has there been anything like it. Even the next wave of creation, around the turn of the century, with writers such as John Muir, Frank Norris, Jack London, Mary Austin, Gertrude Atherton, Helen Hunt Jackson, and Charles Loomis reflected a remarkably vital culture. The creative work of the critic Ambrose Bierce, Joaquin Miller, and the poet Charles Stoddard spanned both periods. And they were surrounded by creative and supportive amateurs. These were the years in which the University of California reached considerable stature, in which Leland Stanford poured twenty million dollars into his attempt to create with private money a free institution for practical education that would at the same time match the best private college in the country. Luther Burbank produced an ideal of the creative garden at the same time that the Sierra Club eloquently supported the ideal of the creative wilderness.

Models for life and architecture were taken from Greece (Isadora Duncan), old Spain, new Spain, California missions, the American Indians, perhaps even India, and were objectified in the San Francisco and San Diego expositions, numerous mission-style houses (from the houses of the wealthy to the tract homes of the poor), the California bungalow, and the Bay Region style; and yet so much seemed to be only on the surface. The masses gradually converted much of the state to the intellectual condition of a wealthier Missouri, with the intellectuals an uncomfortable froth on the surface. Today, however, Californians in many fields, if not the arts, are more confident than they were, less likely to see their lives as wasted on the frontier, and to struggle in a paroxysm of overaffirmation. The Pacific Southwest is one of the three self-sufficient regions in the country.

## Districts and Sociocultural Subdivisions

It has often been proposed that northern and southern California are really two separate regions, and attempts to separate California into two states have been made. Most recently Meinig has proposed that distinctions between the two parts of the state were as important historically as those between either northern or southern California and other Western regions such as Mormon Utah or the Pacific Northwest.[113] However, it seems to me that this distinction has been overdrawn by local enthusiasts (much as that between Portland and Seattle in the Northwest). At the beginning, San Francisco was dominant in every way, and southern California was merely a backwater. Later the San Francisco area maintained financial and collegiate dominance while the popular culture and popular architecture of southern California came to dominate the state and much of the world.

More recently, the financial and commercial dominance has slipped to the south, along with a good deal of intellectual strength, while the quirky, radicalist counterculture that extends influence beyond California has again centered in the Bay Area. The ability of California to be the hope and magnet of millions, and to spark ideas and to carry them to extremes whatever they are, is as common to the southern part of the state as the Bay Area. The very different "northern California" of those who make the north-south distinction is confined to a narrow coastal strip from Big Sur to Santa Rosa. The Central Valley and the California far north, and cities such as San Jose, Oakland, and Sacramento, have about as much in common with southern California as they do with San Francisco.

There is no difference between the cultural and the sociocultural divisions in the region. The two main districts of the Pacific Southwest are the *Central Coast* (San Francisco) and the *Southern Coast* (Los Angeles, San Diego). The small city of Santa Barbara lies on the cultural boundary of the two areas, although its physical geography assigns it to the Southern Coast. The Central Coast is persistently a coastal or Bay region. It runs from about ninety miles north of San Francisco to Santa Barbara, including the cities of Santa Rosa, Napa, Berkeley, Livermore, and Palo Alto. It never goes beyond the Coast Range and is never more than sixty miles from the ocean. The Southern Coast, on the other hand, includes the San Bernardino complex, a hot, dry area quite removed from thoughts of coast and ocean. San Francisco and its historical predecessor as capital of the Central Coast, Monterey, were and are ports, with population traditionally coming by way of the ocean. In contrast, Los Angeles started as an inland city, and more of its people have come from the American midlands.

In the middle of the nineteenth century, the *Central Coast* was the California to which the people of the world were attracted. Gateway to the gold fields, it had little of that arid heat of southern California to which easterners and the foreign immigrants of the day were unaccustomed. San Francisco grew as the cultural and intellectual capital of the West. Many of the best-known writers of the era, as well as reformers such as Henry George, were from this area. The University of California and Stanford University were both established here, and both quickly became national centers of learning. The Central Coast is old California: for years, the dominant social clubs were the local branches of the "Native Sons," while in southern California the "State Clubs" for recent immigrants from the Midwest were dominant.

Today, San Francisco is one of the most beautiful and vital cities in the nation. In addition to some attractive suburbs, the restoration and beautification of thousands of old houses gives the city a living charm that even the best areas of New York or Washington, D.C., do not approach. The beauty of thousands of individual decisions that this represents is reinforced by the area's willingness to establish a mass transit system that will further promote its Old World urbanity.

It was not until after 1920 that the *Southern Coast* emerged as the largest district in California. In the first few years of statehood, southern California was considered the cow country, the backwoods of the state. For a time, the Mexicans and Indians of the area continued to play an important part in its political and social life. Then land promotions brought in retirees, people looking for a dream, or the ill, often to establish themselves upon small "ranchos" to grow oranges. Much of what we associate with southern California did not exist before 1910, while many aspects are post-World War II. These include the aerospace industry, "Cal Tech," Rand, and the rest of the "knowledge industry," as well as the movie and entertainment industry.

The Southern Coast was the district of promotion, the displaced "Iowa," the district of dreams, tinsel, and money. It was the land of longings and loneliness, the land of unusual religious movements and sun worshipers. It was also a completely artificial environment. Los Angeles had to incorporate a narrow strip twenty miles long to a possible port area and then construct a harbor where there was none. Already at the beginning of the century Los Angeles had to reach hundreds of miles for sufficient fresh water; later the thirsty area turned to the Colorado River, and most recently to the far north of California. Of course, the effort and ingenuity required to transform the district has made for an inventive people that is likely to be well able to meet the demands of the future. Yet, with all the new sophistication that money, power, and the attractions of climate are able to bring, there is a feeling of Texas about the Southern Coast. It is along this coast that harsh political and social conservatism is strongest. In comparison, the Central Coast reminds us of the Northeast, both in the composition of its population and its ideals.

While to many Los Angeles is a symptom of all that is wrong with the country, it is possible by changing perspective to take a very different approach. An architect, Reynar Banham, has recently described Los Angeles in terms of the interactions of four "ecologies": the beach, the foothills, the plain, and the freeways.[114] Actually, of course, this means three ways of life, with the freeways connecting and interweaving the whole. Crowned by the freeway system, the structure of the area has done away with any possibility or need for a central, downtown focus. Within this maze, many are able to live a superficial, external, but exciting fantasy life—if they can clear away the smog, why should we hope for more? Civilization is found in beautiful fragments such as the Los Angeles County Museum or the immaculate grounds of the

Huntington Library. Banham confirms for Los Angeles Elazar's claim that Americans have striven mightily to escape the narrow frame of the European city; in these terms Los Angeles is the great American success (fig. 24; cf. figs. 6, 15, 16).[115]

Around Los Angeles was created in the early days a unique blending of rural and urban life, based on the ideal of the garden and the orange or avocado grove. In this area were developed the garden apartment and the suburban town that in their national development were to be so disparaged by a later generation. Here idealists developed communities of a human size such as Pasadena, San Bernardino, and Anaheim that now often bring images to the mind that would sorely disappoint their founders.

The *Northern Coast* district is that area of mountains, woods, and rain beyond the effective reach of San Francisco. Here in a lightly populated area economically based on the extraction or harvest of raw materials, life is little different from that in southwestern Oregon or the Rocky Mountain area. Its redwood and Douglas fir have been heavily cut, but fortunately also grow rapidly, so that economically there is an extractive future for the area as long as population remains low. Perhaps even brighter is the tourist future offered by the trees, the coast, and, farther inland, Mounts Shasta and Lassen. However, some counties in this area were the only ones to decline in population in 1960–70.

The *Interior California District* includes the Central Valley and extensions north and east, as well as the desert and irrigated field agriculture of the eastern southern California desert. This is an area of farming and ranching people with most of the land in the hands of large proprietors, often companies. The Spanish period bequeathed to American California a large landholding pattern quite different from the traditional Midwestern patterns (hence Henry George preached against large landholdings in California at a time when men were still settling on homesteads in the Midwest). Interior California also preserves the Spanish colonial pattern of few owners and many field hands. In successive periods laborers were Indians, then Mexicans, then Chinese (or Japanese and Filipino); most recently Negroes, poor whites from the Western South, and Mexicans have divided up the work. Today "Mexicans" again seem the dominant source of field hands. Great disparities in wealth have been an important aspect of the situation, reminiscent of the South (especially in the cotton fields of California's Fresno and Kern counties).

Although culturally thin, this is not a wasteland. Fresno, the hometown of William Saroyan, has one of the most delightful pedestrian center malls in the country. Much of the area is extremely hot in summer; with the coming of air conditioning, the difference between classes has widened still further. On the other hand, mechanization spurred by labor organization in the fields may rapidly eliminate most of the workers and dramatically raise the standard of living for those who remain. Farther east a Sierra recreational subarea includes the dramatic attractions of Yosemite, Kings Canyon, and Sequoia national parks as well as Mount Whitney and Lake Tahoe. Economic activity other than tourist and vacation business is very slight.

The *Nevada District* is highly dependent on California, both for its population and as a destination when population leaves. Reno and Tahoe are the playgrounds of the Central Coast and Las Vegas of the Southern Coast, with Las Vegas now much the wealthier and larger. Like Los Angeles, Las Vegas is a highly artificial locale in which there are few natural beauties. Of course, Lake Mead is about fifteen miles away, but for most this is not the drawing card of Las Vegas. It is a super-modern spot without the distractions of the Riviera or the Bahamas. Outside of Reno and Las Vegas, population is extremely sparse, the economy dependent on mining, large ranches, and transit.

Although the stable population of Nevada is very small, there is a surprising continuity and stability in its history. Indian population was also sparse, and native cultural development minimal as a consequence. After 1848, Nevada lived on the leavings of the Gold Rush to California. With the Comstock boom, there were a few years of the kind of regal extravagance that accompanied major finds of mineral ore elsewhere in the West. However, San Franciscans earned more from Nevada's Comstock Lode than Nevadans. In the course of the 1850s, the Mormons both planted colonies in western Nevada and withdrew them (as a part of a general withdrawal for defense purposes). In the twentieth century, Mormons have taken up irrigated agriculture again in a few small colonies and more or less prospered, but more commonly the state has served as a refuge for Mormon renegades. Sheepmen, including Basque herders, cattle ranchers, a few oasis farmers, and miners make up the rural population. Many Nevadans remain part-time prospectors.

Nevada is and always has been a comic strip version of a masculine world in which the towns are largely made up of gambling dens, saloons, and prostitutes. In part, Reno and Las Vegas developed into sin cities because of the taste of the local population. Outsiders built on a firm basis; gambling and prostitution, if not divorce, are popular far beyond the usual tourist stops. It is a fair guess that Nevadans are the loneliest people in the nation.

In the Pacific Southwest the problem of the key centers of the central and southern coast is that they have built their life on superior climate, beauty, and the beach. This environment is threatened by numbers, wealth, and the multiple problems of pollution that accompany them. Highly desirable areas are limited and some of the best have been seriously damaged in quality by overdevelopment. Perhaps the dream is ending. In 1971 more people seemed to be leaving California than entering, with air pollution cited as a leading negative factor. Yet a short-term economic slump, current fads, and technological lags may be playing a part in what is only a temporary decline.[116]

It is easy to lose perspective on crowding in California as its population grows. The state is larger than England or West Germany. Japan has five times its population in a smaller area and with less "usable" land. There is as much "wilderness" area left in San Diego County in densely populated southern California as in any part of New England outside of Maine. The coastal ranges between San Francisco and Los Angeles are much wilder, with at least a seventy-five-mile stretch of the coastal highway almost untouched by development. The east and the north of the state have even larger and wilder areas such as Europe lost centuries ago and the eastern part of the United States before 1900. Although it has the largest population and a small cropland, California is still our most productive agricultural state. This is not to say California should maintain a pattern of rapid growth, but to suggest that the state can preserve and enhance its attractiveness at population levels considerably higher than those in 1970.

The elemental struggles for land and water remain to embitter the region as they no longer do in most of the country. Part of the problem can be attributed to the growing and changing values of land and water, and part to the pressure of the development mentality. Too often special privilege undermines the efforts of those with more general goals. Often it is the highly developed concern of Californians that magnifies regional problems that would be ignored elsewhere in the country. California remains a leader and grows in leadership. In spite of riots and budget cutting, the University of California at Berkeley is still a national leader in graduate education quality, while in recent years other great schools such as the San Diego (La Jolla) branch of the University have been added to the state system. While pollution in many urban areas is frightening, the clean-up of San Diego Bay is one of the outstanding national achievements, and California has been a leader in air pollution control. It is California's Sierra Club that leads the effort to save the nation's wilderness areas. It is California's Chavez who organizes the field workers.

As the national birth rate declines and California becomes more conservative in its attitude toward environment, growth may fall off rapidly. This will mean that the demographic "bulge in the middle" will be gone, and with it many of the advantages for education and other services that have traditionally given California much of its distinction. Perhaps this will be a blessing, for only as growth slows down can California develop a pattern of life in terms of which a new culture can be built that is more than the plaything of passing emotions. Yet today most people see only the struggles over welfare and higher education that the transition necessarily entails.[117]

# The Pacific Northwest

## Population

In 1970 there were about six million people in the Pacific Northwest (see Map 32), with over half of them in the state of Washington. Washington and Oregon grew in the fifties at somewhat higher rates than the nation (though well below those of California, Arizona, and Colorado), while Idaho grew at rates well below national averages. Always characterized by a mobile population, in 1970 the region was only slightly more native than other, non-Mormon western regions. The people of the Northwest represent a fair cross-section of the country, with the Eastern Southern and Northeast regions underrepresented. The foreign stock has been primarily English, Canadian, Scandinavian, and German, sometimes after a generation's sojourn in the Upper Midwest. Nevertheless, the foreign stock has always been relatively thin here. The main sources of population have been the Midwest and Missouri, especially non-Catholic, rural, or recently rural areas. California has been an important source of population in recent years.

## General Description

More than many other regions, the Pacific Northwest is an expression and result of physical geography, and its districts are similarly delimited. Aside from the Canadian boundary, only at the border of the Northwest and the Mormon area in the southeast of the region is there a strictly cultural boundary. The Northwest as we have defined it is very close to being the American portion of the Columbia River drainage basin, to which Puget Sound and small areas on the coast and in southern Oregon have been added. The Columbia binds the area together just as the Cascades divide it. The Rockies cut off the Northwest from the plains of the Dakotas, while the intricate mountain systems of southern Oregon and northern California form a considerable barrier to easy north-south commerce.

Geographically, the Pacific Northwest is divided by climate into two zones. The Pacific zone runs from the ocean to the top of the Cascades and is characterized by frequent rainfall, especially in winter, and the absence of climatic extremes. The interior has a modified interior Western climate, characterized by low rainfall, more evenly distributed in the year, and more extreme temperatures. Heat and aridity increase as one moves down from higher elevations and toward the south.

# History

The modern history of the Pacific Northwest began with the settlement of the lower Willamette Valley, south of the present city of Portland, in the 1840s. Although there had been trappers and ships concerned with exploration or the fur trade in the area for decades, the few thousands who came to establish farms in the 1840s quickly outnumbered all other non-Indians, and by 1850 outnumbered the Indians as well. In the Willamette Valley the Indians had been destroyed by disease on the trapping frontier even before settlement. Elsewhere they held back settlement briefly and endangered movement from the east and California. The majority of the migrants of this first period came overland in families to farm. Their background was similar to that of those who also came overland in families to farm in California, yet this element formed a minority of the California population in 1850. Many of the people who made the journey to the Northwest had run out of cheap, "inhabitable" land in Missouri. The next area with good land seemed to them to be in the Pacific coast valleys. The majority of those in this movement were from the Upland South, many of whom had moved more than once already.[118]

The leaders in the early colony represented Northeastern cultural backgrounds and interests. At first the leaders of the Hudson's Bay Company at Fort Vancouver were dominant. To these were added missionaries who later merged into the religious and business leadership of the community. The clash between New Englanders and Northeasterners on the one hand and Upland Southerners and Midwesterners on the other has often been remarked. As the leading chronicle of the area says of the early period:

> There is a marked difference between the people who came to the Pacific Coast by sea and those who crossed the continent, that is not accounted for by the fact that one class came from the Atlantic seaboard, and the other from the western frontier; because the origin of both classes was the same. These western men came in larger numbers, and Americanized Oregon, stamping upon its institutions, social and political, their virtues and their failings. There was an almost pathetic patience and unlimited hospitality, born of their peculiar experiences rather than of any greater largeness of heart or breadth of views.
>
> It will be observed that those who came by sea were New Englanders.

As the Missionaries were all from New England and New York, they received these traders and sea-going people with a welcome warmer than that they extended to the western settlers. Their impression on the country was distinct. One class bought and sold, built mills, and speculated in any kind of property. The other, and now the larger class, cultivated the ground, opened roads, exercised an unbounded hospitality, and carried the world of politics on their shoulders.[119]

It was a diversified population, then, that set out to settle the Northwest. The first major offshoot from the Willamette Valley was formed by communities on Puget Sound that came eventually to focus on Seattle. From the first, farming was less important here, the exploitation of the forests and the Alaska trade more important. Cut off from easy trade routes to the interior, Seattle had to work harder, and eventually it rather than Portland became the chief city of the Northwest. Yet the isolation of Puget Sound from the rest of the Northwest has never been overcome. The culture of the Willamette also spread to the east over a vast area, centering on Spokane, Washington, in the north, and to a lesser extent on Pendleton, Oregon, and Boise, Idaho, to the south. This ranching, mining, and wheat farming area is now supplemented by potatoes, irrigated agriculture, and new industry.

The original agriculture and trapping base of the Northwest was soon augmented by lumber, fishing, and mining. More recently certain industries have chanced to be developed in the Northwest, such as Tektronics at Portland and Boeing and Pacific Car and Foundry at Seattle, and have stayed in the area. The combination of water, space, and low-cost power brought the processing of atomic materials and aluminum refining to the area. Nevertheless, the particular contributions of the region remain agriculture, which continues to be developed, and lumber.

# Regional Characteristics[120]

The average Seattleite has more in common with a native of Columbus, Ohio, than either does with the citizens of Boston, New York, Atlanta, or San Francisco. Yet the Northwesterner has both gained and lost something of the culture of central Iowa or Ohio. He is probably somewhat more likely to have what passes for a general education, less likely to attend church, more likely to spend his time in outside, participant sports or camping, less likely to be a spectator. His politics are more likely to be those of the Upper Midwest and New England. Washington's and Oregon's movement from Republican to Democratic ranks in recent years has been the obverse of the movement of the South and border states, and the Republicans elected for top state and national offices are remarkably liberal. All in all, politics are moderate and relatively nonprofessional.

The climate of the Northwest is in many respects ideal. Almost nowhere in the population strip from Eugene, Oregon, to the Canadian border is air conditioning needed except to reduce noise. As most Americans move into the air conditioning age, such an area may seem more than ever desirable. Yet for many, the long, wet winters of continual light rain are depressing. Outdoor activities are possible most of the year; it seldom snows in Seattle and Portland, but there are even cold June days that remind one of the British Isles.

The Northwest coast is one of the most beautiful in the nation, yet the possession of its coastline fails to attract people to the Northwest the way it does in the rest of the nation. One reason is that the population centers are located far from the open ocean. Beaches are nearly a two hours' drive from Portland, and are considerably farther from Seattle. Another reason is that the water is simply too cold to make swimming a pleasure. Thus, while a recreation culture dominates life in the Northwest, it is not a California or Hawaii beach culture.

Natural beauty is a prized possession of the Northwest, yet it is a quiet beauty, and not what Northwesterners fondly imagine. The forests are seldom more than monotonous, with little of the splendor of an eastern deciduous forest or of the redwoods that touch the southern edge of the region. Where there are no trees east of the Cascades, the land is barren, with a beauty that will not appeal to many. Outside of the national parks, exceptional beauty is to be found in the settings of Washington's San Juan Islands and the gorge of the lower Columbia near Portland. The cities are often magnificently located. The people of Seattle are surrounded by beautiful views of mountains and water, and pollution control has made nearly all of the water usable.

Culturally the area seems anemic, the cities abandoned to a grid pattern of streets and the general American taste this implies. Restaurants and lodgings tend to be standardized and dull. Yet the region has been surprisingly creative in certain areas, such as painting, and Seattle has a creditable symphony, opera, and repertory theater. Higher education boasts national institutions in the University of Washington and Reed College, and private colleges are relatively more important than in the rest of the West.

## Districts and Sociocultural Subdivisions

Culturally and economically, we can define five districts in the Pacific Northwest. The *Willamette District* includes extreme southwestern Washington and northwestern Oregon. This is an area under the direct influence of Portland, although in the Willamette Valley there are a number of other important regional cities. The cities of small industry and commerce are surrounded by lumber and agriculture. Below the Willamette is *Southwestern Oregon.* With no large city, the area focuses on Medford, a center of small industry and agriculture. The *Puget Sound District,* containing perhaps 50 percent of the people in the region, is the most heterogeneous, cosmopolitan, and rapidly growing area in the Northwest. Historically a center of socialist activism, with the decline of the wood products industry and the satisfaction of union demands, the people of the area remain self-satisfied even in depression. Here the influence of Scandinavians, Catholics, and industry is greatest, and there is less of the tendency to look to the past that so characterizes Oregon.

Most of eastern Oregon and south-central Washington form a *Columbia District,* based on a variety of small cities such as the "Tri-Cities," Yakima, Walla Walla, Bend, and Pendleton. This is an area of great distances, largely agricultural except for the industries that have grown around the Atomic Works at Hanford. Although there are beautiful forested areas on the margins, most of the district is desert or near desert unless irrigated. Northeastern Washington and a part of the panhandle of Idaho form the *Spokane District.* This is a cooler, wetter area, with dry farming (wheat especially) important to the south and mining the key factor to the east. The mining area brought in a very different population to mix with the largely northern background people of eastern Washington. The *Central Idaho District* focusing on Boise has a greater mixture of recent arrivals from the Upper South and of Mormons from Utah than do the other interior districts. The economy has been based traditionally on the development of large-scale irrigated agriculture, but Boise is now the headquarters of several national corporations with a variety of engineering and resource development interests.

A case could be made for separating the Central Idaho and Spokane districts from the rest of the Pacific Northwest. These are areas of considerably later development, and areas with much more cultural similarity than the rest of the west with the people of both the Rocky Mountain and Mormon regions. It is partially with these considerations that socioculturally (Map 5) Idaho is considered a region of alternate or multiple affiliations. The affiliations are with the three bordering regions. The original settlers were from Oregon and Washington. Today Spokane, Portland, and Salt Lake compete with the growing importance of Boise as an independent center of economic activity. Religiously, Idaho is split between the Mormon southeast and the remainder of the state with a complexion similar to that of Wyoming and Montana. In terms of common interests and style of life, most of Idaho is closest to the Rocky Mountain Region.

## Problems and Potential

The problems of California are those of arresting or channeling growth, while those of the Northwest are more complex. The Northwest has yet to establish the diversified productive base that a region so isolated from American society must build if it is to bring stability to the life of its people. Although a beautiful area, it needs more than just tourism; even Switzerland has had to go far (perhaps much too far) beyond tourism into finance and industry. Traditionally, many of the capitalists of the Northwest have been content to rely on a few industries, yet this has led to recurrent cycles of boom and bust, and the devastation of such cycles in the lives of those affected. Perhaps the necessities of an earlier age devoted to the dynamics of the exploitation of fur, timber, and mineral resources have contributed to the pattern.

Continuing to deplete the region are the hostilities between its subdivisions. These are particularly those between Tacoma and Seattle, Portland and Seattle, or Spokane and the smaller urbanized areas in its realm.[121] Or one can speak of the opposition of Oregon and Washington, cross-cut by the east-west division produced by the Cascades. The pronounced hostility of Oregon Democrats to the presidential candidacy of Washington's Senator Henry Jackson in 1972 is a recent example of Oregon-Washington relations. Thus, the individualism and atomism of Northwest society is mirrored on the political and economic level, with results that are to no one's advantage. It is hoped that common concern with the physical environment, and particularly the Columbia River valley, will gradually help to improve regional cooperation.

Even if we confine ourselves to beauty, the Northwest has less to offer than it should. Decay is rapid, discard is rapid, and pride in appearance not too common outside of the larger cities. Many smaller towns and cities such as Forest Grove, Oregon, or Cashmere, Washington, seem built on a New England ideal and preserve some beauty, often because of a local college. But even then the edges are apt to be ragged. As a native friend of the region, Dorothy Johansen, says: "[Oregon] shares with Washington a surprising monotonous shabbiness in the appearance and morale of its many small towns. . . . Approaches are made through dumps, junk yards, and run-down buildings or shacks." [122] For years, the people of the Olympic Peninsula fought the national park; these people came as exploiters rather than nature lovers. Now, perhaps, it is changing for the park, but how much the mentality that disputed the land and ignored beauty can, will, or even should change is in question.

The people of the Northwest interact within their narrow circles and with nature. Focused on New York City and the Northeast, the elite is cosmopolitan, especially fond of outdoor living and vacation homes. Yet it is also quite uninterested in the mass of Northwesterners, and there is little identification on either side. Preserving its own interests on most public issues, the elite stands aside, passively letting others take the rewards and risk the dangers of participation. Part of the "mass" below is a many-layered middle class that is highly mobile economically and geographically. Members of the class are frequently newcomers to the area. Participating in a national job market, they often believe that an extended stay in the Northwest means they are second-rate. In self-defense most of those who stay must shift their goals from career to sports and pleasures. The longer they stay, the more parochial and isolated members of this class become. They cannot afford to be a part of world civilization, for that is a long way off. The lower classes are relatively well educated, live fairly well, and their children can rise into the middle classes with relative ease. Either a more regionally oriented elite or a more stable and self-confident middle class could help to build an authentic Northwestern society. The former is easier to achieve, and more likely to sustain growth in the vitality of the middle class than vice versa.

Yet the picture is by no means all dark. Blessed with enlightened political leaders and a populist mass culture, the Pacific Northwest has a long tradition of social innovation and leadership which it continues today. Oregon was a leading state in the reform of the senate electoral system and in promoting the initiative and referendum early in this century. Today it is pioneering in a number of areas such as billboard control, seashore control, pollution control, and taxing policy. Oregon is doing perhaps more to clean up and open up the Willamette River than is being done for any other river in the country.[123] Seattle's ability to purify Lake Washington through municipal effort is probably the outstanding national example of pollution control for an urban lake. Although major cities such as Portland and Seattle have gone through cycles of boom and bust characteristic of the region's frontier past, these cycles are now much dampened. In addition, many smaller population centers such as those in the central Willamette Valley or Boise, Idaho, have long histories of slow growth and stability. Thus, the basis may have been laid in the Pacific Northwest upon which a valid, dynamic regional society can evolve.

# *Alaska*

## Population

In 1970 there were 302,000 people in Alaska (see Map 33), while there were only 73,000 in 1940. It was one of the fastest-growing states in the country in the 1960s, its rate of growth (33.6 percent) almost equaling those of Arizona and Florida. In 1970 about 17 percent of Alaskans were nonwhite native, divided among the interior and southeastern Indians, Eskimos, and a few thousand Aleuts, while 76 percent were native American whites. Yet the influence of Eskimos and Indians is considerable because of their staying power. For example, since 34 percent of Alaskans in 1970 were born in Alaska, but only 21 percent of the whites were Alaska natives, calculation suggests that a slight majority of the native-born were Eskimo and Indian.[124] The white Alaskan

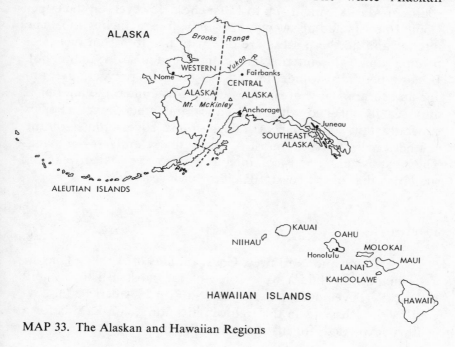

MAP 33. The Alaskan and Hawaiian Regions

population represents a cross section of the old forty-eight states. As the birthplace of 11 percent of Alaska's population in 1970, the Pacific Northwest was overrepresented, while the Northeast was underrepresented. It has recently been suggested that oil booms and military retirement have brought a large Southern population into central Alaska. The percentage from the South actually shows little increase over 1960, with Texas the origin of 5 percent of the population in 1970, but Southern Baptists are now the second most important religious group.

## General Description

Alaska covers an area twice the size of Texas, has a coastline longer than those of the forty-eight states combined, and contains the highest mountain in the nation. The rugged mountains in south and southeast Alaska divide relatively temperate southern Alaska from the extreme cold of the interior and northern portions. Except in rain-shaded valleys, rainfall is very high in southern Alaska, ranging up to 150 inches. However, on the upper Cook Inlet, including Anchorage, only fifteen inches fall. The interior and northern areas are dry, with five to fifteen inches of precipitation. The interior in summer can also be quite hot. Because permafrost underlies most of the area, preventing drainage and turning large areas into swamp in summer, the interior is also heavily infested with mosquitoes and other insects. Soil is generally thin and poor. Although forest covers much of the southern half of Alaska, most of this is sparse and slow-growing. The most useful forest is confined to a narrow coastal strip and is similar to that of the coastal Pacific Northwest.

## History

The Eskimos and Northwest Coast Indians of Alaska (Tlingits, Tsimshian, and Haida) were some of the most artistically and technically developed native groups in North America. Discovered by the Russians in the eighteenth century, Alaska was for a century exploited for its furs and other products of its sea mammals. Although few Russians stayed after the colony was sold to the United States in 1867, the Russian Orthodox church continued as a force in the state, supporting schools and churches until 1917, and there are still thousands of Russian Orthodox, mostly natives. Under United States administration, the territory did not thrive. It was largely ignored until the gold rush of the 1890s, and did not become an organized territory with limited legislative powers until 1912. In the 1890s and for a short time thereafter, several gold rushes in the Alaskan and Yukon interior brought rapid increases in population; but the gold soon played out, and the population of Alaska declined for several decades.

Alaskan development was held back by three factors: (1) distance and disinterest, (2) conservationists, and (3) monopoly exploiters. A consequence of all three was the fact that it was almost impossible to acquire clear land titles until well into the twentieth century, and then only in a small part of the state. Alaskans bitterly resented the near destruction of their fur seals on the Pribilof Islands and of their salmon by outsiders. The right to hunt the seals was sold for years to a monopoly, while the salmon were endangered by overuse of fish traps often controlled by outside canneries. Monopoly shipping interests deepened local distrust of Washington, D.C., and its regulators. An economy of boom and bust, resulting from the real difficulties of the land, combined with outside discrimination to develop in Alaskans a petulant local patriotism.

In the twenties the first railroad was completed between the coast and the interior. In the 1930s the Matanuska agricultural colonies and homesteading opportunities increased popular interest. With World War II the state was opened up by the necessities of the war. A road was pushed through Canada to Fairbanks (although most of it remains gravel). Airports were completed, and many servicemen came to know the area. With the cold war and its attendant development of defense facilities, federal involvement continued. The 1950s saw a reversal in the decline in the salmon runs and a final enthusiastic push toward statehood. Adopting a constitution and electing senators and representatives before statehood, the people of the state finally overcame in 1958–59 most of the human obstacles that had barred their way.

Mining has been a mainstay of Alaska since the last century, but its fortunes have varied. It has often been destructive—placer operations are hardly ecology-minded—and the oil explorations and findings of the 1950s and 1960s opened new dangers as well as opportunities. As the state was also deciding which federal lands it would take for itself in the 1960s, the native peoples organized themselves to make the most massive land claims in history. In December 1971, President Nixon signed a land claims bill giving the native nonwhites forty million acres and nearly one billion dollars. Among reasons for the size of the grant are the lack of previous reservation delimitation beyond townsites, the lack of significant private ownership, and the low value of the land except for minerals and petroleum. Another reason was the anxious desire of the state and the petroleum companies to get production of the North Slope oil underway. Both native claims and environmentalist forces (government and private) stood in the way, but by early 1974 the pipeline was underway. At the same time the progress of new native regional corporations created to handle the new money and land was encouraging.[125]

## Characteristics and Regional Definition

Religiously, the people of Alaska cover the full spectrum, with the Russian Orthodox a distinctive minority group.[126] Missionary activity has divided up much of the native countryside by faith. In the state as a whole the largest denomination is Catholic, closely followed by the Southern Baptists (the highest percentage outside of the South and Interior Southwest). Other significant groups are Mormons, Presbyterians, Methodists, Episcopalians, and Lutherans.

Alaska is still a frontier area, with native nonwhites remaining an important part of the population. As on other frontiers, although stable, bourgeois, nine-to-five citizens constitute the majority, exploiters, loners, and civilizational misfits form a relatively large part of the population.

As a sparse, frontier people, Alaskans have a sense of community sharing that has been lost in most of the country. Many have a sense of inferiority, of being "out of it," far away, isolated; even those who come to get away may feel deprived by isolation. Thus climate is not the only reason a large percentage of the people leave every winter and retire to the south after sixty. Alaskans take pride in existing in a difficult environment, although the particular problems of survival in each part of the state are different. The earthquake of 1964 did a good deal to strengthen this sense of struggle. Since they see themselves oppressed by both man and nature, many white Alaskans bitterly resent the desire of many Americans to tie up Alaska as a wilderness for all time, or to give most areas to the nonwhites. Yet at the same time that they attack the land with the most modern machinery, these frontiersmen take pride in Alaska as an endless, trackless wilderness.

Although Alaska is a center of extreme individualism, of both aggressive and retiring varieties, it is supported to a remarkable extent by the activities of the federal government. The military, the native population, perhaps the distances officials of all kinds must cover have drawn special consideration. As a result, in 1970 government services constituted a larger proportion (36 percent) of the gross national product of Alaska than of the Washington metropolitan area.[127] The state's road system is nevertheless poorly developed, with exceptional dependence on airplanes since the 1920s. Cars are still a necessity, though, and even the Eskimos use snowmobiles and outboard motors.

Alaskans have generally lived in communities rather than in the dispersed Midwestern pattern. Although some are suburbs of Anchorage, most of these communities are so small that they appear as rural in the census. Forty percent of Alaskans live in the Anchorage area. Anchorage dominates the economic life of the state, yet it is of such recent growth that it contains neither the state university, near Fairbanks, nor the state government, until now in Juneau. Whether large or small, Alaskan towns and cities have a continuing reputation of ugliness, of scattered shacks combined with "motel-modern" business construction where population is booming. The settings of communities, however, are often beautiful, and the older fishing villages in the south and southeast are certainly picturesque.

If Alaska were not considered a separate region, it would be included in the Pacific Northwest. It has much in common with Washington, Oregon, and Idaho. Its southern coastal zone has similar climate and flora, and the interior at Fairbanks is a

northern replica of much of the interior Northwest. The weather is
more extreme in both cases, but analogous. Yet the northern third
of Alaska, with only a thin layer of soil over the permafrost, and
the barren, foggy west have no correspondence with the Pacific
Northwest. Historically, the relations between Alaska and the
Northwest have always been close. Often these have been colored
by hatred and envy aroused in Alaskans by monopolies based in
Seattle and Portland, but lately there has seemed to be more
community of interest. The same kind of nineteenth-century
foreign immigrants came to Alaska and to the Northwest,
especially from northern Europe—Britain, Germany, and Scandinavia.

However, there are also important differences. Dorothy Johansen contrasted those who came to Oregon to be farmers, to raise
families, or organize missions with those who went to California
for a quick fortune. Comparatively, Oregon and Washington have
remained stable, farming states.[128] Alaska has not had this
background historically, and the current North Slope oil boom is
unlikely to remake its image.

## Districts and Subcultures

George Rogers has divided Alaska into three areas, which for
our purposes may be considered cultural districts.[129] The panhandle, or *Southeast Alaska,* is cut off from the rest of the state by an
impassable coastal strip. The southeast is a region of high rainfall,
dramatic vertical scenery, forests, glaciers, and snow-capped
peaks. This was a land of the Northwest Coast Indians, and their
descendants still make up a substantial part of the population. In
an area almost deprived of land transportation, the people
overwhelmingly live in small island cities. Salmon, tourism (along
the Inland Passage from Seattle), and forest products are primary
industries. Both the old and current state capitals are here, and
history hangs heavy. Unlike Central Alaska, the area has grown
very slowly in all periods, but steadily and with more continuity.

*Central Alaska* was defined by Rogers as stretching from the
Katmai National Park east along the central coast to Mount Saint
Elias, and north to include the interior Yukon drainage. With the

development of North Slope oil, this area should be extended to the Arctic Ocean east of Point Barrow. Climatically the region has most of the variation of Alaska: the wet commercial forests of the coast, the drier south-central valleys, the peaks of the Alaska Range such as McKinley, the extreme cold, hot, and dry interior Yukon River valley, the dry cold of the Brooks Range and the high Arctic coast. The district, is, however, bound together by road and railroad, and many areas share a history of boom and bust. This is where the placers were largely found, and where oil and gas are today. Here in Fairbanks and Anchorage are the centers of recent growth. The population of Central Alaska is much greater than the other two districts combined. The district includes most of the agriculture and agricultural potential, particularly in the Matanuska Valley and the Kenai Peninsula. The central district has had a shifting population, and today it is a new population, with native nonwhites making up an insignificant fraction.

*Western Alaska* includes the Aleutian Islands, the islands of the Bering Sea, and the western and northwestern coastal zones. It is a virtually treeless area, depending largely on ocean mammals and fish. Although beach placers led to population growth at Nome at the turn of the century, and there has been periodic military activity, the great majority of the people are nonwhite natives, mostly Eskimos. Transportation is by air or water, and isolation is perhaps the most enduring impression for the outsider. As one moves south to north through this area, precipitation decreases and cold increases, until on the northern coast no more than seventeen days may separate killing frosts and there is no more than five inches of precipitation. The land is covered with tundra, a carpet of slow-growing, dwarf vegetation only inches thick. Just as in some desert areas in the western United States, minor environmental damage and discarded junk are visible for generations (a problem, of course, for the northern part of the central district as well).

## Problems and Potential

Alaska faces the familiar problems of economy and environment, but from a highly favored position. It has three great problems of preservation: (1) the preservation of distinctive ways of life, especially that of the Eskimo; (2) the preservation of vast areas of scenery and wild beauty in stateside terms; and (3) the preservation of areas of true wilderness such as no longer exist in the other forty-nine states. On the other hand, the state is poor in everything but raw materials such as oil and lumber, coal and iron. The processes of extracting, transporting, and refining these resources may well preclude careful preservation.

One of the mythologies of Alaska has always been its agricultural potential. Its boosters have claimed that this potential has been blocked by land regulations established in Washington, D.C., that hindered acquisition, or by exorbitant transportation charges. This is just part of the story. Land rights were often in dispute on the western frontier and transportation was expensive; but settlement proceeded anyway. Even with the reduction of these barriers, Alaskan agriculture remains limited; a large percentage of the homesteads that have been established have gone out of production. Except for a few favored spots, the combination of poor soil, permafrost, and extreme climate makes it hard for local products to compete even on the local market, and only a small percentage of Alaskan food is produced locally. The land is too poor and the climate too severe.

Tourism is a better answer to the economic problem of the state, but it is unlikely to fill up the slack in Alaskan economy caused by failure to exploit a major natural resource. Alaska is remote, and distances are great within the state. As air transportation improves, Anchorage becomes little more than an emergency stop on the way to the Orient. Siberia is an unlikely tourist goal. At no season of the year does Alaska have the climatic attractiveness of Hawaii, southern California, or Florida. It is a long way for Americans to go for skiing, and hunting is apt to decline in importance for future generations. However, as long as Siberia is closed, Alaska may become an important travel area for Japanese.

A Resources for the Future study in the early 1960s saw the primary hope for Alaska's staggering economy to be in the exploitation of its forest, mineral, and hydroelectric potential. This development would require expensive, destructive operations (iron, copper, and coal were prime hopes), and would be located in the south and southeast for the most part. Compared to this grim prognosis, the exploitation of North Slope oil seems less destructive. North Slope petroleum will be exploited, moved in large volume through a pipeline cutting the Brooks Range wilderness in two, and exported by tanker from Valdez. Every part of this process has ecological hazards, and there will be losses, particularly to North Slope tundra, to the Brooks wilderness, and to Prince William Sound at the southern terminus.

If the income from petroleum is carefully husbanded, however, Alaska will be rewarded with sufficient additional income to make feasible reduction in the scale of exploitation of its coastal timber, the temporary tying up of the development of many areas, and increase in the size of the permanent wilderness. In the flush of new income and before population has grown to take up the slack, most of the Brooks Range west and east of the pipeline and its accompanying road could be set aside, as well as other large sections of the state, including thousands of miles of coastline.

In late 1973 the secretary of the interior recommended setting aside 23 percent of Alaska for additions to our national park and wildlife refuge systems.[130] Further measures may be desirable. For example, in some wilderness areas, access for any purpose could be forbidden beyond an outer ring or buffer zone for tourists. In addition, in large areas new exploitation projects could be made very difficult to initiate, while the recovery of abandoned areas previously exploited could be hastened. The cut for pulp might particularly be restricted for the time being. Most will agree that the most valuable and usable natural beauty in Alaska is in the southeastern and south-central areas, where the most tourism, economic activity, and population growth are now found. Two of the proposed national parks are to be in this area. Although not "needed" by Alaskans today, they would provide national and international insurance against the day when world-wide growth makes such areas more desirable than ever.

After initial destruction by Russian fur traders, the native people of Alaska declined to half of their precontact number, in large part because of disease. They are fast recovering in number and now, with large cash and land settlements, they have a chance to develop a base upon which they can defend the best of their old cultures. Land controversy and new social currents have led to a renaissance of native interest in their past. Revival of the old cultures would be a gain for Alaskans, but unfortunately this may all be short-lived and superficial. Succeeding native generations may prefer simply to blend into a composite Alaskan society.

# The Hawaiian Islands

## Population

In 1970 there were 770,000 people in Hawaii (see Map 33), with over 80 percent of them in the Honolulu area on the island of Oahu. Growth was above the United States average in the 1960s, but not as fast as in mainland states such as California, Florida, or Colorado. The people of Hawaii are an amalgam of different races or ethnic groups. In 1970 39 percent were native white. However, because of the transient military presence, the portion white and Negro is greatly overstated by the census. In 1970 a state statistician listed the nonmilitary population as: Japanese, 34.3 percent; Hawaiian and part-Hawaiian, 21.1 percent; Caucasian, 19.0 percent; Filipino, 8.8 percent; Chinese, 6.2 percent; other races and mixtures, 10.6 percent.[131] Although because of transients the effect of the growth in the 1960s on the population balance is hard to determine, the long-term stability of the population is remarkable. The 1970 census showed Hawaii to have a higher percentage of its population born in the state than any other western state.[132] The origins of the population from the mainland that is now resident in Hawaii reflect primarily the differences in the size of mainland regions. Although in 1970 California stood out as a state of origin, the South and North Central states had contributed almost as much as the West.

## General Description

The Hawaiian Islands consist of five major islands, three minor islands, and, to the west, a number of very small islands or atolls. The islands are thousands of miles from any other major islands or mainland. As a result, the native plant and animal life has developed unique characteristics in relative isolation. The Hawaiian Islands are a chain of volcanic islands, with the largest, Hawaii, still in active formation. Topography is rugged, with much of the land area very steep. The climate is even and tropical. Summer temperatures never get over ninety degrees and winter temperatures never below fifty degrees in most localities, although there is some snow at the highest elevations. Rainfall is highly variable, with most islands ranging from areas with less than twenty inches to areas with more than three hundred inches. There are several desert coasts receiving less than ten inches.

## History and Characteristics

Occupying the land for more than one thousand years, the native Hawaiians had a Polynesian culture similar to that found thousands of miles away in Samoa or New Zealand. It was a feudal society with highly developed caste distinctions, idol worship, strict taboos, human sacrifice, and periodic warfare. The people lived primarily on the coast, subsisting easily by fishing, gathering seafood, raising taro and bananas in small irrigated plots, and caring for pigs and dogs.

When the first white people came in 1778, rule of the islands was fragmented. But by the nineteenth century, a chief of the island of Hawaii had extended his rule to all the islands. The wars of consolidation were destructive, while growing contact with the outside brought a spread of white man's diseases and a collapse of the religious system at the top. Shortly after the death of Hawaii's first great king, his widow persuaded his successor to abandon the old taboos and with them much of the belief structure of the people.

When the missionaries arrived the next year, they found a people numerically in decline and searching for new beliefs. The missionaries were New England Puritans who brought along with their beliefs education and training in a wide variety of skills. The natives were faced on the one hand with visiting colonies of sailors and on the other with dedicated Puritans. The religion and education took well and rapidly with the Hawaiians, but the

Puritan attitudes toward sex and work did not. The decline of the
native Hawaiians continued, from disease, alcoholism, sterility,
and probably infanticide.[133] Since the decline affected both nobles
and commoners, the continuation of the kingdom was biologically
endangered by the time of the American take-over in the 1890s.
Interbreeding began very early, so that when the Hawaiian people
began to make a biological comeback, after 1910, it was increasingly as part-Hawaiian.

Whaling and the sandalwood trade brought the first whites after
the explorers. When sugar cane became an important crop, in the
mid-nineteenth century, there were not many Hawaiians willing or
able to work in the fields, and their subsistence economy gave
them little reason to go to the fields. As a result, other labor had to
be imported. At first, this was largely Chinese, then Japanese,
Portuguese, and other Europeans, and finally Filipino. Many from
each of these groups stayed, and as soon as they could get out of
their labor contracts, they drifted away to other occupations. The
missionaries had early developed a good educational system, and
partly as a result each group was able to rise economically and
socially with comparative rapidity.

The missionary period of Hawaii was largely over by the 1850s.
But the missionaries had created an educated population, especially at the top, and a government modeled on that of Great
Britain. Land and other investments, largely in sugar, cattle, and
shipping, were controlled by a small white aristocracy dominated
by New Englanders, largely the children of the missionaries.
During the last half of the century, the native Hawaiian population declined, the size of the investments increased, and the
democratic Hawaiian legislature and king reportedly threatened
to take white property away by egalitarian, but also irresponsible,
taxation and corruption. After many rounds of backing and
filling, the kingdom was finally overthrown by the American elite
in the 1890s. At first Washington refused to annex the islands, but
with the coming of the Spanish-American War, Hawaii became an
American territory.

The political evolution of Hawaii in the nineteenth and
twentieth centuries has been the story of a gradual but inevitable
extension of democracy. Civil rights were highly developed even
under the Christian kingdom and were seldom abrogated. Thus,

advocates and opponents of joining the United States could operate quite openly before and after the Americans took over. However, on the plantations, labor agitation was suppressed. Political rights grew much more slowly. Under the kingdom, voting rights varied, but generally native Hawaiians outnumbered whites and could control elections. With the coming of American rule, the whites and native Hawaiians (including part-Hawaiians) united to hold on to political power long after they were greatly outnumbered by Orientals. It was not until after World War II that the Japanese were able to achieve the power that their numbers should give them. It was the rise of the nonwhite immigrant groups that destroyed the remaining advantage of the native Hawaiians—their political power.

In order to secure their estates, the whites convinced the kings to abolish the feudal structure in which the chiefs theoretically owned all land. Although this gave the Hawaiian commoner a chance to own land, gradually both rich and poor natives lost most of the land. To arrest loss of land by the natives, there have been several rather unsuccessful schemes to develop Hawaiian family farms. But most native homesteads are now leased to large companies. Later, Chinese and other immigrants through thrift and enterprise established their right in business and the professions to develop urban fortunes alongside the whites.

## Regional Characteristics

Though they made many mistakes, New England missionaries in Hawaii played a positive role in creating present conditions. Only a tiny group, their emphasis on work, education, democratic principles, and altruism continually leavened what could easily have been just another story of economic exploitation. Their descendants created an elite class that could pursue these higher objectives because a dominant white middle class such as existed in much of the rest of the country did not exist in Hawaii until very recently. Emphasis on education and a relatively open policy led to a proliferation of private and public educational institutions in a variety of languages and religions that produced a most capable and multihued people. Even the native Hawaiian nobility became infused with these ideals, supporting a range of schools and other charities, most notably on the basis of the Bishop family estate. The educational systems' inculcation of democratic ideals led to the ultimate democratizing of the islands.

Whether the day-to-day behavior of ordinary people was affected by the Puritan tradition is more doubtful. On the political level the hard-driving Japanese combine with perhaps half of the Caucasians (from northern United States and European backgrounds) and other smaller groups to form an activist, liberal majority. As a result, the state government opened its first decade (the 1960s) as one of the most progressive in the country—a well-equipped legislature, the first state ombudsman, an effective master plan. Government is highly centralized and acts with authority, as befits its military and missionary heritage. The island of Oahu and the city of Honolulu are administered as one unit, and there is only one school district for the whole state. The northern Caucasians and Orientals are balanced by the other peoples of the islands that have been more noted for their *joie de vivre*. But the reputation and selectivity of the islands over the years would seem to work in the favor of the latter forming the eventual island culture. The recreation-orientation of tourist centers fits much better the life-value of the Southerner, the Polynesian, and the Filipino.

Today tourism is the fastest growing industry, although national defense remains more important. There is a great deal that is coarse and unreal in the tourist promotion of Hawaii. Tourist Hawaiian culture is 50 percent promoter-created. Yet even at its most crowded, Waikiki displays a degree of authenticity in local color and mass that is missing in similar creations such as Miami or Atlantic City or Las Vegas. The invasion of the outer islands is well begun, but most of the area is still unspoiled. After tourism come the older stand-bys in the economy of sugar, pineapples, and cattle, including the second-largest cattle ranch in the country on the island of Hawaii.

The characteristic of the islands that is most remarkable in terms of general American experience is the established standard and degree of interracial marriage. There has been a steady increase in the percentage of interracial marriage between 1910 and 1965. Between 1960 and 1964, 38 percent of marriages were mixed. The lowest percentages of interracial marriages (Caucasian, 21 percent, and Japanese, 25 percent) were in the largest groups, and so represent only in part special prejudice in these groups.[134] There is, of course, prejudice. In elections people of each racial or ethnic group tend to vote for candidates of their own background, everything else being equal. But there is little doubt that the spirit of "aloha" ("love," and now particularly, "interracial amity") does have more reality here than in most of the country. At the same time, there is a re-emergence of interest in varying cultural backgrounds, as the non-Caucasians become more confident of their Americanism.

It is important to reiterate that the economic relationship among the races and ethnic groups is not what one might suppose. In 1959 and 1964–66, the median incomes of Chinese and Japanese were well above those of Caucasians, while the Filipinos and Hawaiians were below. The income gap between Chinese and Caucasian was greater than that between Caucasian and Hawaiian.[135]

The Hawaiian and part-Hawaiians are open, personally free, but family-centered. Representing the community myth of the islands, they are least likely to be socially rejected by other ethnic groups;[136] on the other hand, Hawaiian families show high crime rates and much family disorganization.

## Districts and Subcultural Divisions

The Hawaiian Islands do not have the divisions common elsewhere in the country. As in the case of the Mormon Region the core-periphery distinction of Meinig is preferable for the purpose of further subdivision (see Chap. I). Although the native and missionary roots of the region are not confined to Oahu, today the outer islands have low populations and thorough agricultural development. Lanai, for example, is nearly entirely devoted to pineapples. Tourism is important on Maui, Hawaii, and Kauai, and is growing rapidly. In a few pockets of the outer islands aboriginal native beliefs are more alive than on Oahu—notably on the protected island of Niihau.

## Problems and Potential

In 1970 Hawaii had a somewhat denser population, and smaller land area, than New Hampshire. Although the land is very rugged, most of the usable areas have long since been exploited—except for housing and tourism. However, what remains is a beautiful tourist landscape of mountains, waterfalls, jungle, and beach. If the agriculture recedes, and the future is in tourism, the dangers of destruction through sprawl are considerable. Fortunately, in some areas sprawl development is hard to accomplish because the physical geography provides a degree of natural protection. Even the island of Oahu has retained much of its natural beauty. The beach-to-population ratio should be good for a very long time.

Hawaii has a good chance to add positive variation to our national civilization. It is isolated by distance, climate, and national origins. It looks more than the mainland to the rest of the world, especially the Polynesian and Pacific worlds, for its future trade and cultural relationships. However, the development of a distinctive Hawaiian way of life is under two threats. The first is that before they can become acculturated to local ways, new immigrants and new wealth from the United States and Japan will overwhelm local traditions. The second is that culturally the islands will succumb completely to the pallid, recreation-oriented version of general American culture that has already developed such a strong hold on island life. Sadly, a recent conference to discuss Hawaiian futures was dominated more by currently popular Euro-American intellectual fashions than by anything Hawaiian.[137]

Beyond the beaches, romance, and moonlight, many Hawaiians have shown that hard work and accomplishment are possible in the environment of the state. Perhaps with the Hawaii 2000 project and a newly structured creative elite, a center of civilizational growth can be fashioned with higher standards and more stability than the islands have been blessed with in the past. The cultures of the islands would then not be merely the playthings of tourist agents and antiquarians, but the living pieces of a more distinguished synthesis for which tourism would provide the income but not the purposes.

## CHAPTER V

# Conclusion

## *The Present and Future of Regional Cultural Variations*

TRADITIONALLY, and at the higher levels of culture, New England and New York have dominated the nation except during the early years of the republic. For example, Wilbur Zelinsky uses a minor cultural trait as a basis for serious generalization as follows:

The historical geography of classical town names reinforces the notion of the primacy of "New England Extended," in the cultural, social, and economic evolution of the nation, despite the paucity of classical terms in nuclear New England. It also strengthens the suspicion that this region may have been the source of most of the characteristics that make the United States peculiarly American. A practice originating and flourishing along the growing edge of the culture area that was clearly the intellectual pacemaker of the young Republic spread vigorously outward to the farther reaches of the expanding region. Eventually, like many another idea and innovation of similar nativity, only a few of which have been studied, it diffused throughout the country and became continental in scope.[1]

This dominance has often been bitterly resented by those who feel unfairly "left out." For example, Katherine Ann Porter writes:

. . . There is a crowd with headquarters in New York that is gulping down the wretched stuff spilled by William Burroughs and Norman Mailer and John Hawkes—the sort of revolting upchuck that makes the old or Paris-days Henry Miller's work look like plain, rather tepid, but clean and well-boiled tripe. There is a stylish sort of mob promoting these writers, a clique apparently determined to have an Establishment such as their colleagues run in London. It's perfect nonsense, but it can be sinister nonsense, too. . . .
Also it is very hostile to the West and, above all, to the South. They read us out of the party ever so often; they never tire of trying to prove that we don't really exist, but they haven't been able to make it stick, so far. . . . Truly, the South and the West and other faraway places have made and are making American literature. We are in the direct, legitimate line; we are people based in English as our mother tongue, and we do not abuse it or misuse it, and when we speak a word, we know what it means. These others have fallen into a curious kind of argot, more or less originating in New York, a deadly mixture of academic, guttersnipe, gangster, fake-Yiddish, and dull old wornout dirty words— an appalling bankruptcy in language, as if they hate English and are trying to destroy it along with all other living things they touch.[2]

Miss Porter *might* be glad to know that in many ways the Southern heritage has been growing in importance. A recent study of the national culture concludes that vernacular American culture is *neo-Southern.* The aristocratic South remains regional, but the "distinct way of life [of] the poorest and most obscure of Southern blacks and whites . . . has emerged to lend a new style to our speech, our dress, our music, our sports, our ways of enjoying ourselves and of coming together."[3] The violence, the motorcycle gangs, the revivalist religiosity and anti-intellectualism and populism, the smile and friendly concern for people, the first-name basis, and the elimination of any formal first name at all have the flavor of the South.

Since it was a more rural area, until recently Southern birth rates have been higher than national averages. For this reason, in share of the national population the South has managed to maintain itself over the past eighty years better than either the Northeast or the Middle West, even though these areas received most of the immigration of the period. In this century the

Southern cultural area has exported many more people, both white and black, to the Northeast and Middle West than it has received. Although recently the South has been diluted by an invasion of Northerners, outside of enclaves in a few cities Northerners tend to adapt to the local culture. It is also significant that in 1972 the Southern Baptist church was the largest Protestant church, the first to go over one billion dollars in yearly contributions, and the only major Protestant church to gain members.[4]

If Northerners fear this Southern expansion, they should remember that a good portion of what seems negative in Southern culture is a product of lack of education and interest in education, particularly since education in America tends to express Northern values. General access to education, certainly Northern-style education, has come much more recently to the South than to the rest of the country, and when Southerners move they come into a different educational climate. The abysmal poverty and isolation that characterized so much of the South is fast decreasing; we should hope that the upswing of violence in certain areas of the North accompanying the recent influx of large numbers of Southerners will be temporary.

It is commonly believed that regional differences are no longer of importance. Patterns are changing, television is having an impact, and of course people are moving around a great deal. Lillian Hellman writes, for example, that "the divisions of America—North, South, East, West—have long been blurred. We have moved too much, intermarried with too many other split levels, cars and freezers to leave behind anything more than pockets of the past."[5] It should be noted, however, that most movement is short-distance or, if long-distance, it is often to areas containing people similar to the migrant. Most metropolitan areas collect the people of their hinterland. Over 80 percent of the congressmen in most states were born in the region they now represent.[6] We should also remember that people listen to radio or television or read the paper in terms of their own interests.

If a national economy were able to eliminate regional differences, more thorough homogenizing should have occurred before now. One reason it has not is that there are tendencies in the development of the country that go the other way. Not so many years ago most states were very limited in educational and economic opportunities, being often dependent on one or two products. Just as in colonial times, when Americans had to go to Europe for many pursuits, until recently they have had to go to New York or one or two other isolated spots on the cultural map for more diversified opportunity. In many fields this is no longer so. Isolated states are staffing new technical facilities with ex-native specialists who may now return to their native regions and make a living. A basis is therefore being laid for regional differentiation on elite levels that was not possible before.

In addition, easier movement makes it possible for ideological attraction to resegregate the population. In the past, differences of North and South, or East and West, were accentuated by the movement of individuals from less congenial to more congenial regions in terms of their personal values. In the future such movement will be easier than in the past, and the variety of different life patterns with self-selective potential is increasing. Zelinsky points out explicitly that "the traditional spatial and social allocation of individuals through the lottery of birth is being replaced gradually by a process of relative self-selection of life style, goals, social niche and place of residence." [7] The power of self-selection is suggested by a recent poll of university students at four schools. The Northerners and Westerners rejected the South and vice versa, except for California, which was ranked high by all as a place to live.[8] Whether future differentiation should or will occur in the face of obvious counterpressures is, of course, open to question.

One study directly examining the hypothesis that regional cultural differences are diminishing has concluded that they are more likely unchanging or increasing.[9] The authors examined the difference between the opinions of the old and young as reported in a wide variety of polls since World War II. Although only a breakdown of the country into the four basic census regions was possible, they found that there was more difference between regions among those under forty or forty-five than among those over this age. Only on attitudes toward work and some religious and discipline issues was there less regional difference among the young. On moral, political, racial, occupational, and some other issues there was a greater spread among the young. On most issues the young were more "liberal," and the South was generally most conservative. However, on several issues the North Central region was the most conservative. Because of the phenomenon of message rejection, the authors suggest that the mass media may actually strengthen opinion differences. The study seems to be confirmed by what trend data are available.

## Policy Implications

Increasingly public policy is determined by the examination of social indicators of performance or "output." It is often suggested that we adopt new policies because a current policy is "failing" in our locality, state, or nation. Often the suggested new policy is copied from another locality or nation where there seems to be more "success." In either case, imputing success or failure to programs and policies is often based on a lack of understanding of the cultural differences among the populations compared, differences that are likely to persist for decades in spite of the implementation of excellent policies. For example, it is wrong to relate the suicide rate in Sweden to its socialistic policies or its decaying Protestantism, for Sweden is part of a European suicide belt that includes capitalist Switzerland and Catholic Austria. Apparently Swedish rates have been higher than those of nearby countries such as Norway or Holland for a very long time.[10] On the other hand, the United States has a history of a relatively severe problem of criminal violence that may be due primarily neither to our general "system" of government nor to our criminal laws and their enforcement. Using Swedish solutions in our context is unlikely to produce Swedish results, and vice versa.

With refinement, however, the comparative approach over time and space is a good way, perhaps the only way, to see how well we are doing and to develop by analogy improved policies or programs. If we are to set out to study the ways in which one might improve police protection in the United States, we would want to look at the achievements of particular police departments in terms of what one would expect could be achieved because of the population mix with which they had to deal. Populations would have to be compared, at least in terms of status, education, and regional culture. For example, we should develop expected violent crime rates for cities in terms of both cultural and sociological variables, then evaluate the success or failure of the police and social services in relation to those expected rates. If Fort Worth's homicide rate is three times Boston's, the difference might be traceable to differences in the training and other practices of the police department. It might be due to the fact that the percentage of blacks in Fort Worth is a little higher. But probably the primary reason is that the regional cultures are different. Homicide is only an example—a good one, because the rates are more comparable place to place—but this analysis could eventually be done for those crimes that police action is more apt to influence.

Education is another area in which this type of study could be beneficial. In the late 1960s there was great concern over the declining achievement of New York City pupils, and in an unthinking way many people blamed the New York City school system for this decline. The proposed study of cultural variations within our society would show how much of this decline could properly be traced to a change in the composition of the student body of the New York City schools. It could well be that just when a school system is improving its actual performance in terms of the proposed analysis, it will be receiving its severest criticism because of its lack of achievement in terms of unrealistic comparisons with the achievements of school systems at other times and places.

In his recent study of "territorial social indicators" in the United States, David Smith has again raised the old claim of regional injustice advanced by Howard Odum in his regionalization in the 1930s.[11] Simply put, the suggestion is that if social indicators of well-being vary by region, then the government should expend particular effort to bring up the level of those regions that continue to "lag." Smith sees laying the groundwork for such equalization as a major purpose of regional social study. But I feel that Smith's approach presents several problems from either a socioeconomic or regionalist point of view. First, it may be to the advantage of all of us for migration flows to move toward areas of greater economic activity, even if areas of outflow are going to be depressed. Second, we are pleading for people of the several regions or proto-regions of the country to take a greater interest in their regions, to try to improve and contribute to their regional way of life. If they make this effort—and they will to some extent—then we would expect people in one area to make a greater effort or be more effective in their effort than those in another. We certainly cannot expect much effort anywhere if national policy is to flatten out differences. Moreover, we expect that the people of different regions will have different goals. Some will want to attract more population and industry, some to retard growth. Some will emphasize high per capita income as a goal, while other regions may not. Some will emphasize hard work and inequality, others perhaps less work and economic equality.

Understanding regional variations qualitatively may eventually be more important in public policy than improving our understanding of statistical indicators. However, precise knowledge of qualitative implications will come only from study of particular regional cultures and concrete policy questions. An example of qualitative policy implications may be found if we examine the relative success of the metropolitan consolidation movement in the North and South. A recent study pointed out that up to that time the only Northern success in the United States had been Indianapolis, while several consolidations had taken place in the South and more were projected for the near future. These had generally been based on the county government. Two of the primary reasons for Southern success were that the county has always been relatively strong in the South and that in several cases there had been relatively few municipalities within the counties consolidated.[12] The county was the basic unit of organization in the South, while towns and cities were few and weak in the eighteenth century. In this period towns and cities were the basic units in the North. Significantly, Indianapolis is considered by many to be heavily influenced by Southern culture. Recent experiments with contracted public services from the county have come from California and Missouri—strong county states.[13]

Understanding regional traditions would have helped in predict-
ing both the relative success and the likely forms of success of
consolidation in different parts of the country. This should have
led to different regional strategies to achieve the objectives of
consolidation (for example, city accretion or the use of state
agencies may fit the Northern pattern more effectively).

Ultimately the regional approach would be concerned primarily
with much more finely tuned concepts than "North" and "South."
This is particularly true when we consider aid to the poor. Rena
Gazaway suggests this approach in discussing the failure of the
governmental programs to reach the people of the Kentucky area
she has studied: "I would not refer to the deprived in a single
frame of reference applicable alike to the urban poor, the poor in
the deep South, and the poor in the hollows. The problems and
the solutions are different. . . . The factory-made approach
emanating from Washington would be abolished." [14]

Unfortunately, the use that Gazaway would make of her
knowledge of the people of the hollows also suggests the dangers
of misapplying cultural knowledge. Gazaway knows that charity
and good intentions have had little impact, but her solutions are
more frightening. Although she says that the values of the people
of the hollows "would come first," she outlines a plan meant to
compel them to change rapidly, with provisions such as four years
of militarylike training for the young. If we understand some
groups of impoverished people well, and sincerely want their
children to have the opportunities of middle-class children,
compulsion may be the only answer. Yet perhaps a more
respectful view would be that the people of the hollows do not
have a right to our charity, but neither do we have a right to force
them to be different than they are. Working out a compromise
between our desires and theirs, establishing reciprocal responsibilities, will require particular knowledge of their culture as well as a
certain amount of controlled "benign neglect." The relation of the
larger society to the hollows is in many respects an extreme
example of the relationships that exist among many cultural
groups in this country, and how we handle these relations remains
a critical part of a future in which demands that we achieve
equality may easily result in coerced conformity to the latest
accepted version of the good life.

# Cultural Regions and the Future of Our Society

In a recent edition of *The Public Interest*, Irving Kristol notes that the issues of the time have changed from those of economics to those of philosophy, from means to ends, from "reordering our priorities" to "choosing our goals." [15] Perhaps this is because everyone now wants to be a prophet and is no longer willing to be a technician, or maybe the public actually demands a more explicit ordering of goals. More likely this change is another phase in the developing "crisis of our age" that Pitirim Sorokin and others have been warning us about for a long time. The fact is that we simply do not know what all of our effort in life is about, and the more leisure this effort produces through economic advance, and the more education is generalized in the population, the more time there is to worry about the purposelessness of our existence.

It is quite possible that loss of meaning is the problem of our time. But if so, what do we do about it? What kind of resources do we have to reduce its intensity? No one knows. But it may help to mention several aspects of our current situation that seem to be related to the problem, and then go on to show the role that emphasis on regional culture might play in contributing to a national and personal revival.

First, on both elite and mass levels few leading Americans have a sense of mission. The people who established this country were confident and hard-working. They did not all believe strongly in revealed religion, but most of them believed strongly in the purpose of their lives. They might be narrow and selfish, but there was always room for a great deal of faith, a faith that gave their lives personal meaning and distinction, and made it possible for them to inspire, drive, or coerce others to supportive efforts.

The pattern of colonial life was always strongest in New England. Ideals of capability, superiority, and mission were established in that society that have influenced us ever since. In the South a different elitist tradition was created that produced outstanding colonial leaders and some of the outstanding science, architecture, and literature in the nation. The experience of the Civil War produced a sense of unity and regional identification that continues to distinguish both liberals and conservatives from the South, to influence poor and wealthy, the prosaic and the intellectuals. While less united internally, the myriad peoples that established themselves in the Middle colonies were equally convinced of their worth and mission. For 170 years these colonial peoples built a new world along a narrow fringe of the Atlantic.

After 1770, however, there began a new movement west that rapidly spread the Atlantic people over the whole country. To this movement was joined a great migration of new immigrants. Each area in the west received a distinctive stamp from the cultures that were dominant in its settling. Each new area, each new state produced by this explosive movement into the West went through a period, or several periods, of hope and achievement. By 1900 the Middle West and its offshoots farther west were putting their stamp on American culture. But seventy years later there is a widespread feeling that something went wrong, the expectations were not fulfilled. There is a sense of loss, of technology grinding on to little purpose, of bigness for its own sake, of the ineffectual person lost in the mass. This is a world in which diversion has become the end rather than the accompaniment of life for the vast majority.

With all their faults and narrowness, colonial leaders saw themselves as part of a community, and their purpose in life was to build, serve, or lead that community. It is true that religion played a large part, but men like Ethan Allen and Thomas Jefferson had slight belief in traditional religion. What they did have was faith in their mission and role. Many of those who went west in the first half of the nineteenth century carried this faith with them, but change and opportunity and the character of frontier society made their mission ever more material, more individual and fragmented. Their descendants' interests became personal, cut off from the community, a carryover of the exploitative, "get in and get out" attitude of the Westerners de Tocqueville found in the 1830s.

The Westerner was brash and superior, but also materialistic and superficial. Perhaps the dream of an ever-expanding future made it difficult for man to accept the challenges of sin and failure, of struggle and loss. Concerned with current problems, too many of us forget that the message of the 1920s was already one of failure, a message that was forgotten when depression and war and a sense of international mission brought confidence back with a rush (a rush that in its time naturally resulted in the baby boom). The sixties went a long way toward undermining this frail self-confidence born of adversity and the international role it thrust upon us. For many, young and old, the last decade has quite thoroughly eroded any sense of personal mission.

A second approach to the problem of meaning in America is to measure the scope of the humanities, of the arts in American life. In most communities there is unfortunately a very low level of general knowledge and of taste. This opinion is not simply a reflection of civilized disdain for the rustic and simple arts of the people. Rather, it is a realization that most of what we find in our lives is what J. B. Priestley has characterized as "hashadmass" or the standardized, consumer world of convenience, comfort, and commercialism that surrounds so much of our life with franchise chicken and celluloid sex.[16] In the end this packaged existence detracts from the meaning of life and flattens the taste of what should be its greatest pleasures.

But along with this chilling uniformity in the nation, it is also paradoxically true that the American "masses," which most intellectuals are inclined to cut into arbitrary sociological categories by sex or age or income, are in fact quite differentiated in common experience. While there is in some generalized sense an American "way of life," in their day-to-day life most Americans follow a particular pattern that is confined to their region, locality, occupation, status, religious or ethnic community. Although regional variations in culture are often remarked and noted in detail for certain groups, for many social analysts most of the people remain a vast mass, conventionally thought to make up something called middle class or WASP society. There have been competent studies of the country in terms of economic and agricultural regions, and some good work in the areas of religious and political culture, or of particulars such as language. The greatest amount of relevant work on the origins and movement of cultures in this country has been done by historians, and it is perhaps for this reason so few generalizing efforts to spell out the cultural map of the nation have ever been undertaken.

There is also a pervading inability in this country for social and intellectual elites to understand the quality of life of the people they pretend to lead. The result is an underevaluation of the distinctiveness of the people with whom they deal and a general lack of understanding of the strengths and weaknesses of their communities. Similarly, the mass generally fails to understand the elites that guide them. If different than their own, they are almost sure not to understand the historical traditions and affiliations of the elites that affect so much of what they say and do. The situation is similar to that in India where the Brahmans are frequently unable to distinguish among the lower orders of Hindus, while the untouchables in turn tend to lump the several types of Brahmans together. It may be a general fact that unless we have a differentiated view of a people, it is very difficult to communicate with them.

At the same time society is faced with a wide variety of new social movements. A popular technical concern with the dissemination of poisons in the environment or with the pollution of air and water has been combined with a largely elite concern for the preservation of rural or wild areas in their pristine form. These legitimate concerns have been grasped by many of those searching for meaning. They have been taken to heart in a mystic search for the unity of man and nature, thereby affiliating the thought of much of the college generation to a very old, pantheistic, generally passive tradition (now often dressed up in scientific jargon). Alongside passive pantheism and equally a part of the youth tradition is the desire to right the wrongs, the injustices of life, to achieve an authentic rule of law in a mixed society. Unlike many movements of the past of this kind, the emphasis of the most skilled and intelligent of those involved in this movement is often on local action and local change. This "youth movement" interacts with the demand of the American Negro for a better place in society, a demand echoed by many smaller minorities. This has in turn increased the assertiveness of a variety of white ethnic groups long thought to have entered the mainstream of American life.

Emphasizing the history and variety of American life can be approached in several different ways. Many believe that the best way is to approach the problem directly, developing consciousness of the variety of ethnic, religious, class, and occupational groups. This would strengthen at the same time the consciousness of the groups described, for they will become progressively more concerned with their own past and future. Unfortunately, class, ethnic, and professional consciousness is also community-splitting, for most Americans live in areas where these groups are highly mixed, and they are likely to be more rather than less mixed in the future.

I believe that it would be preferable to understand the variety of America within the framework of a spatial (or local and regional) analysis of cultural variations. In these terms, earlier patterns of variation are considered through their influence in particular localities and areas and the role they play in contemporary life. This description may form the basis for a new synthesis, or at least a new *modus vivendi*. It will suggest the process of continual change of traditions under the influence of changing physical and human environments. Variety then becomes a community-forming and innovative force as much as a divisive force; and as the old loyalties are rebuilt to strengthen personalities and groups, they may at the same time be attached to larger local loyalties that affect communities that exist or are coming into being.

These observations suggest some of the reasons why it would be useful to society to develop an understanding of the nation in terms of its spatial cultural variations, whether these be local, state, or regional. It may be possible on this basis to interrelate the concerns of Americans in such a way that the quality of our life is improved and the meaning of life deepened. For the more a person sees the natural and human past of the environment that immediately surrounds him, the more he is able to relate his life to the present and future of that same environment. It is almost impossible for an individual not to leave some trace on the situation in which he lives; the more he realizes this, the more he will be interested in the size and character of this trace. The improvement of regional life has a chance, it seems to me, to become a theme in terms of which the widest variety of people can agree. For some the emphasis will be on ecology, for others schools, for others architecture; some will think in terms of the high cultural traditions of western civilization as they persist in the region, others in terms of the little traditions of particular ethnic groups. To some the area of concern will be only the neighborhood or town, to others the concern will cover several states. Regardless of residence, some will experience the region with which they identify only occasionally, while others will want to live actively in the environment of which they feel a part. Happily if a man decides to improve his world, no matter how small, he will be creating an image of universal value, and if a man creates a new invention or new philosophy or a new painting for all men, he will be equally contributing to the quality of civilization of that place in which he works.

Some have suggested the development of a new humanities of environmental appreciation, of understanding the infinite number of patterned variations in our surroundings, most of which are residue of the interaction of man and nature.[17] On this basis it may be possible to relate ourselves spiritually to the land of a region even though few of us any longer have the role of farmer. In such bonds there is implicit the development of a cooperative community spirit, and yet there is the freedom that an individual gains from realizing that his relationship is to much more than the opinions and pressures of those people who currently may be playing leading roles in the history of the land. Each contributes to the future as he sees it, each member of the family contributes in his own way, the way of life the family creates contributes in turn to the set of models by which subsequent generations will live. Many of us move often, particularly at the most literate, upper-middle-class level, and so seem cut off from this possibility. Yet it takes little time to identify with one or more regions. Very often the most valuable regional contributions have been made by dedicated newcomers or expatriates who did or did not return.

It is significant that in Robert Coles's extensive studies of forms of Southern poverty, it is the migratory worker's life that seems most destructive of human potentiality. Migratory workers have the least pride and are most looked down upon by those around them. Life goes out of the children so fast that they often seem hollowed out well before age ten. Although Coles is opposed to generalization and ascribing causality prematurely, he suggests the difference is in lack of place, in the numbness that comes from having so little to relate to that can be counted on.[18] Is it possible to draw an analogy with a certain hollowness in the lives of many at a higher level?

Vance Packard, in *A Nation of Strangers*, has most recently elaborated this theme by suggesting that there are at least forty million uprooted in the country at any time, and many more strangers in the communities in which they reside.[19] He documents the emotional waste that such mobility entails, the privatization, superficiality, and uniformity it develops. Packard's solution is to emphasize community life on the neighborhood basis, and quasi-rootedness where real roots are impossible. This is, it seems to me, part of the solution, but only part. For it is after all the possibility of creating special communities on order that has ended by imposing the same "variety" of community possibilities almost anywhere. The individual must be interested in the larger life around him at a level between the national and neighborhood scale. At this level of identity considerable mobility is possible without becoming a stranger, for one remains a contributor to the regional life.

The answer to the problems that Packard raises would seem, then, to be well expressed by the following words of Rene Dubos:

Modern societies will have to find some way to reverse the trend toward larger and larger agglomerations and to recreate units compatible with the limits of man's comprehension—in other words, small enough that they can develop a social identity and spirit of place. By cultivating regionalism, the United States could derive from its rich geographical diversity cultural values and also forms of economic wealth far more valuable because more humanly meaningful than those measured by the artificial criteria of a money economy.[20]

However, regional pride is rare. For in the competitive American life most regional people feel they have lost before they start. Regionally, the South has the greatest sense of distinctiveness, but a sense that includes love and hate, pride, bitterness, and self-contempt. A more relaxed self-confidence is found in the New England, New York Metropolitan, Mormon, and Pacific Southwest regions (at least until the 1970s), while the Midwest, Alaskan, Hawaiian, and Pacific Northwest regions are characterized by a general feeling of inferiority behind a veil of assertion (with

exceptions perhaps in Kansas and Oregon), and most Pennsylvanians may lack even the assertion.

One reason for a pervading sense of inferiority outside of
California and the Northeast is that the people of other regions
have been taught to think in terms of *comparison* rather than
*contribution.* In many professions and businesses, especially in
national corporations, employees think in terms of success
through moving to a job in the centers of success (usually the New
York area). If they never make this move, they remain adrift,
defeated before their time in "the boondocks." One often notices
how small a constructive role academics play in the regions in
which they reside. One reason is that most of them are eternally
"passing through," on their way somewhere else. When it becomes
apparent they have stopped moving, in their own minds they retire
to live out their lives as best they can. This attitude can never be
totally avoided, yet if the academic came to know more of the
richness of the area in which he finds himself—to concern himself
with its future as well as his own, his contribution and feeling of
personal worth would be enhanced.

One of the most homogenizing and discouraging aspects of
current life is the flow of news that reaches the public through
radio, newspapers, magazines, and television. The inflow of news
magnifies trouble and worry and excitation at a spectator level;
the reality is one the average person can neither relate to nor
affect. If a regional emphasis were taken to heart, it might be
possible to develop guidelines that would improve the relevance
and significance of journalism. For example, each station or paper
should be encouraged to select a locality, state, or region of
interest as its communications sphere. Human interest reports
(including crime, tragedy, marital troubles) should be largely
confined to this sphere. Beyond the selected communications
sphere, news should be confined to events of real national or
international importance (in spite of disagreement, an area of
agreement as to what is "important" can be found). While not yet
threatening seriously common journalistic beliefs in what it takes
to sell a paper or television program, this approach should help to
develop a sense of community within limits more psychologically
meaningful than we find today.

It cannot be denied that there is danger that the regional

approach could break down national unity and thereby destroy the capacity of the nation to play a positive political, cultural, and economic role in the world. However, there is no reason why different cultural regions cannot form a strong nation. Cultural borders of the Swiss regions are much sharper than those in the United States, and the country is perhaps stronger and more viable as a result. Moreover, the danger to the United States today is not the sectionalism that led to the Civil War, but that we will find ourselves in desperation beginning a cycle of oppression, anarchy, repression, and totalitarianism such as struck Germany and Russia in the recent past. It is possible that if most Americans cannot be taught to have loyalties closer to home, they may end up with no loyalties at all. Real allegiances for most people are to a hierarchy of levels from family and friends to the human race. Experience at the lower levels is likely to be a prerequisite for self-sacrifice on higher levels.

In conclusion, there is a crisis of meaning in our lives. It may be that most men in most places are forever condemned to lead lives of quiet desperation, or that only the discipline of totalitarian religious or political movements can give meaning to most lives. If this is the either-or of the future, then we must strive to build a free and just society that gives man more of a responsible part. We do not know how to do this or even how to approach the problem. But as Alf Landon recently wrote: "Possibly one reason we have so much difficulty in resolving our problems of a complex society is that we have tended to lose not only a sense of national identity, but a sense of pride in and strong feeling for the special qualities of our local area. What Americans must find is a way to square their diversification, and the freedom upon which it is based with the older sense of identity and stability." [21] Or as Daniel Elazar suggests: "In an era of collapsing society-wide values it may well be that men will once again have to gather together in communities of their choice to work out common ways of life on a more restricted scale—as a prelude to renewal of public conscience for our larger civilization." [22]

Although any single action may do little to create this world of deeper meaning, there is a great deal of intellectual and social action that might help. Both academics and the general public need to know what regional patterns have been, why they came to be, and how and why they are evolving under the pressure of mobility, more general education, and technical change. Historians, cultural geographers, and many others must contribute to the enterprise. Our scattered information on linguistic evidence, the distribution of religious affiliations, migration patterns, social indices, voting behavior, as well as evaluations of common qualitative judgments of regional difference should be brought together. At the same time communities, states, and regions should be encouraged to study their own backgrounds, examining the nature and possibilities, weaknesses and strengths, of their local human capital.

While the results will not initially be what everyone might like, the approach should increase the significance of individual lives by sharpening consciousness of the relation of the individual's influence on those around him to the processes of history. In policy terms, improving understanding of the texture of our society should improve our ability to predict program effectiveness in different regions, to tailor programs to different people, and to help each community build a more satisfying pattern of life for all classes and groups.

# Notes

## CHAPTER I

1. The work most often cited is Robin Williams, Jr., *American Society*, 2nd ed. (New York: Knopf, 1960).

2. A standard work is Max Lerner's ambitious *America as a Civilization* (New York: Simon & Schuster, 1957). Lerner does have a useful regional discussion, but in general the book is devoted to one society and one culture.

3. Warner's system is described in his *Social Class in America* (New York: Harper & Bros., 1949).

4. Especially, Nathan Glazer and Daniel Moynihan, *Beyond the Melting Pot*, 2nd ed. (Cambridge, Mass.: M.I.T. Press, 1970); Milton Gordon, *Assimilation in American Life* (New York: Oxford University Press, 1964).

5. Evon Vogt, "American Subcultural Continua as Exemplified by Mormons and Texans," *American Anthropologist* 57 (1955): 1163–73.

6. Charles O. Lerche, Jr., *The Uncertain South: Its Changing Patterns of Politics in Foreign Policy* (Chicago: Quadrangle Books, 1964), p. 255.

7. Samuel Lubell, *The Hidden Crisis in American Politics* (New York: Norton, 1970). This was before the 1972 primaries in which Wallace showed surprising Northern strength.

8. The following discussion is based on a number of different sources: a good summary of part of the story is Ray Billington's *Westward Expansion* (New York: Macmillan, 1950). On the background to this see

Marcus L. Hansen, *The Atlantic Migration, 1607–1860* (Cambridge, Mass.: Harvard University Press; New York: Harper & Row, 1961).

9. For a classification of the immigrant groups in terms of the original three cultural patterns, see the discussion of Elazar's work under "Political Variation" in Chap. II.

10. Daniel Elazar, *Cities of the Prairie: The Metropolitan Frontier and American Politics* (New York: Basic Books, 1970), pp. 44–63, 326, 432.

11. For movement to the cities in poorer countries, much the same point has been documented by Joan Nelson, *Migrants, Urban Poverty, and Instability in Developing Countries* (Cambridge, Mass.: Center for International Affairs, Harvard University, 1969), pp. 15–20.

12. For detailed tables see R. D. Gastil, "Internal Origins of State Populations" (Seattle, Wash.: Battelle Seattle Research Center, 1975). This may be obtained by request from the research center, 4000 Northeast 41st Street, Seattle, Washington 98105.

13. Carl F. Kraenzel, *The Great Plains in Transition* (Norman: University of Oklahoma Press, 1955).

14. Morris Garnsey, *America's New Frontier: The Mountain West* (New York: Knopf, 1950).

15. The basic reference is Donald J. Bogue and Calvin L. Beale, *Economic Areas of the United States* (Glencoe, Ill.: The Free Press, 1960). See also Harvey Perloff, *Regions, Resources and Economic Growth* (Baltimore, Md.: Johns Hopkins Press, 1960).

16. For example, see the definition of the Midwestern regions in John H. Garland, ed., *The North American Midwest: A Regional Geography* (New York: John Wiley, 1955), esp. p. 15. In this approach, Kentucky and southern Missouri are in the Midwest rather than in the South as in Bogue and Beale.

17. Wilbur Zelinsky, *The Cultural Geography of the United States* (Englewood Cliffs, N.J.: Prentice-Hall, 1973), p. 23 and *passim.*

18. Conrad Arensberg, "American Communities," *American Anthropologist* 57 (1955): 1142–61; Vogt, "American Subcultural Continua."

19. *The Case for Regional Planning* (New Haven, Conn.: Yale University Press, 1947).

20. See Chap. III below.

21. Howard Odum and Harry Moore, *American Regionalism: A Cultural-Historical Approach to National Integration* (New York: Henry Holt, 1938), pp. 28ff., 423ff. See also Odum, *Southern Regions of the United States* (Chapel Hill: University of North Carolina Press, 1936), esp. pp. 4–11; Odum, *The Way of the South* (New York: Macmillan, 1947); and Gerald Johnson, *The Wasted Land* (Chapel Hill: University of North Carolina Press, 1938).

22. Odum and Moore, *American Regionalism*, p. 539; also pp. 526, 630, 534, 423–467. Odum, *Southern Regions of the United States.*

23. Robert Coles, *The South Goes North*, Children of Crisis, vol. 3 (Boston, Mass.: Little, Brown, 1971), p. 3.

24. Odum, *Southern Regions of the United States*, p. 110. A Carnegie Report in 1971 shows about the same distribution of Negro institutions, but there were no longer Negro institutions in West Virginia or Missouri. *New York Times*, 18 February 1971.

25. G. Etzel Pearcy, *Thirty-Eight States U.S.A.* (Fullerton, Calif.: Plycon Press, 1973). See also Rexford Tugwell, "Constitution for a United States of America," *The Center Magazine* 3, no. 5 (1970): 24–49.

26. Daniel Elazar, *American Federalism: A View from the States* (New York: Thomas Y. Crowell, 1966); Elazar, *Cities of the Prairie*.

27. Elazar, *American Federalism*, p. 112. In a note to another discussion of the spheres and sections (*Cities of the Prairie*, p. 145), Elazar claims to give much more attention to purely cultural factors (especially religion) than appears to be the case.

28. Ruth F. Hale, "A Map of Vernacular Regions in America" (Ph.D. diss., University of Minnesota, 1971), esp. pp. 15, 74.

29. Zelinsky, *Cultural Geography of the United States*, esp. pp. 109–39 (quotation on p. 118).

30. Ibid., pp. 112–13.

31. A. L. Kroeber, *Cultural and Natural Areas of Native North America*, University of California Publications in American Archaeology and Ethnology, 39 (1939).

32. Examples of such studies are Wilbur Zelinsky, "Where the South Begins," *Social Forces* 30 (1951): 172–78; and Hans Kurath, *A Word Geography of the Eastern United States* (Ann Arbor: University of Michigan Press, 1949).

33. R. I. McDavid, "Outline of the Principal Speech Areas of the United States," *Orbis* 5 (1956): 358–71. See also Chap. V below.

34. Carle C. Zimmerman and R. E. DuWors, *Graphic Regional Sociology* (Cambridge, Mass.: Phillips Book Store, 1952), p. 1.

35. See Albert Baugh, "The American Dialects," in *Aspects of American English*, ed. E. Kerr and R. Aderman, pp. 104–11 (New York: Harcourt & Brace, 1963); and Jean Malmstrom and Annabel Ashley, *Dialects-USA* (Champaign, Ill.: National Council of Teachers of English, 1963), esp. the map on p. 43. For further discussion, see Chap. II below.

36. *New York Times*, 5 October 1971.

37. D. W. Meinig, "American Wests: Preface to a Geographical Introduction," *Annals of the Association of American Geographers* 62, no. 2 (June 1972): 159–84. See also the pieces by James Vance, Jr., and John R. Borchert, in the same edition of the *Annals*.

38. See Brian Berry and Duane Marble, eds., *Spatial Analysis* (Englewood Cliffs, N.J.: Prentice-Hall, 1968), esp. pp. 387–430. Also, see the discussion of David Smith's work at the beginning of Chap. III.

39. See discussion in Rupert Vance, "The Regional Concept as a Tool of Social Research," in *Regionalism in America*, ed. Merrill Jensen, pp. 119–40 (Madison: University of Wisconsin Press, 1951).

40. For migration data, see Gastil, "Internal Origins of State Populations."

41. See, for example, George H. T. Kimble, "The Inadequacy of the Regional Concept," in *London Essays in Geography*, ed. L. D. Stamp and S. W. Wooldridge, pp. 151–74 (London and New York: Longmans, Green, 1951); and Louis Wirth, "The Limitations of Regionalism," in *Regionalism in America*, ed. Jensen, pp. 381–93.

42. For the reasoning behind rejecting the dichotomy between culture and social structure, as well as the nondifferentiating definition of culture, see R. D. Gastil, "The Determinants of Human Behavior," *American Anthropologist* 63 (1961): 1281–91.

43. Zelinsky, *Cultural Geography of the United States*, pp. 72–74.

44. Based on material in Andrew G. Caranfil, *Student Movements: A Five-Country Comparison*, The Future of Youth, Background Paper, vol. 3, Hudson Institute Report HI-1461-RR, July 1971.

45. These terms are based on D. W. Meinig, "The Mormon Culture Region: Strategies and Patterns in the Geography of the American West, 1847–1964," *Annals of the Association of American Geographers* 55, no. 2 (June 1965): 191–220; and his *Imperial Texas: An Interpretive Essay in Cultural Geography* (Austin: University of Texas Press, 1969), esp. p. 116. I have used "periphery" as a shorthand term covering the meaning of both "sphere" and "zone of penetration." The term "zone of penetration" is too vague, while "sphere" is too strong a word to cover areas Meinig elsewhere places in other domains.

46. See, for example, Robert Redfield, *Peasant Society and Culture: An Anthropological Approach to Civilization* (Chicago: University of Chicago Press, 1956), chap. 3.


## CHAPTER II

1. Based on a comparison of Illinois affiliation maps in National Council of Churches of Christ in the U.S.A., *Churches and Church Membership in the United States*, Series C, 1956–58; and U.S. Census Office, *Statistical Atlas of the United States* (Washington, D.C., 1898), pl. 34 (based upon the results of the eleventh census).

2. Wilbur Zelinsky, "An Approach to the Religious Geography of the United States," *Annals of the Association of American Geographers* 51, no. 2 (June 1961): 139–93. Another less categorical attempt at regionalization is that of David Sopher, *Geography of Religions* (Englewood Cliffs, N.J.: Prentice-Hall, 1967), pp. 84–85. In addition to Zelinsky and Sopher, general understanding of denominational differences and the relation of these differences to behavior and current affairs may be found in Frank S. Mead, *Handbook of Denominations in the United States*, 4th ed. (Nashville, Tenn.: Abingdon Press, 1965); Leo Rosten, ed., *Religions in America* (New York: Simon & Schuster, 1963); and Edwin Gaustad,

*Historical Atlas of Religion in America* (New York: Harper & Row, 1962). After Zelinsky's analysis the National Council published another census: Douglas W. Johnson, Paul R. Picard, and Bernard Quinn, *Churches and Church Membership in the United States* (Washington, D.C.: Glenmary Research Center, 1974).

3. See especially John S. Reed, *The Enduring South* (Lexington, Mass.: D. C. Heath, 1972), pp. 57–82.

4. See National Council of Churches of Christ in the U.S.A., *Churches and Church Membership in the United States*, 1956–58 (esp. Series C). Also Gaustad, *Historical Atlas of Religion*, esp. map included in jacket, and Johnson et al., *Churches and Church Membership in the United States* (map included). Modifications were based on a careful evaluation of the data from several states. Using Zelinsky's qualification of Catholic data and the National Council of Churches figures, I calculated religious dominance, major denominations, and percentage churched by county for Washington, Oregon, California, Nevada, Utah, Idaho, Illinois, Missouri, and upper New England. In several of those states I also recorded the degree of presence of marker denominations (Southern Baptist, Episcopalian, Congregational, Unitarian). In examining the maps of Gaustad and Johnson et al. the reader should remember: (1) Zelinsky (pp. 155 and 168) proposed reducing the Catholic percentages in the 1952 census by one-half relative to most Protestant figures; (2) "Baptist" on the maps generally represents Southern Baptists; and (3) for the 1971 census, Mormons outside of Utah were often reported only on a state basis, thereby invalidating part of the map (e.g., although Idaho is more than 50 percent Mormon on page 12 in Johnson et al., Johnson's map shows no Mormon strength). In the 1971 study there was a correction of Catholic figures, but it seems to have been quite insufficient.

5. Will Herbert, *Protestant-Catholic-Jew* (New York: Doubleday, 1955), pp. 118–46.

6. See Mead, *Handbook of Denominations*, pp. 215–16.

7. Lois Kimball Mathews, *The Expansion of New England: The Spread of New England Settlement and Institutions to the Mississippi River, 1620–1865* (1909; reprint ed., New York: Russell & Russell, 1962), pp. 163–64, 187, 234. It must be remembered that "Presbyterian" and "Congregational" refer to methods of organization and/or sectarian beliefs. Frontier churches in need of support sometimes chose to rely on the more organized Presbyterian administration.

8. See Whitney Cross, *The Burned-Over District* (Ithaca, N.Y.: Cornell University Press, 1950).

9. Analysis based on M. Barone, G. Ujifusa, and D. Matthews, *The Almanac of American Politics* (Boston: Gambit, 1972).

10. See especially V. O. Key's *Southern Politics in State and Nation* (New York: Knopf, 1949); William C. Havard, ed., *The Changing Politics of the South* (Baton Rouge: Louisiana State University Press, 1972); John

Fenton, *Politics in the Border States: A Study of the Patterns of Political Organization, and Political Change, Common to the Border States* (New Orleans, La.: Hauser Press, 1957); Frank J. Jones, ed., *Western Politics* (Salt Lake City: University of Utah Press, 1961); and Alfred de Grazia, *The Western Public, 1952 and Beyond* (Stanford, Calif.: Stanford University Press, 1954).

11. Daniel Elazar, *American Federalism: A View from the States*, 2nd ed. (New York: Thomas Y. Crowell, 1972), and *Cities of the Prairie: The Metropolitan Frontier and American Politics* (New York: Basic Books, 1970). Kevin P. Phillips, *The Emerging Republican Majority* (New Rochelle, N.Y.: Arlington House, 1969). A much less developed, but perhaps more open approach may be found in Samuel C. Patterson, "The Political Cultures of the American States," Laboratory for Political Research, Report no. 4 (Iowa City: University of Iowa, 1966).

12. See Elazar, *Cities of the Prairie*, p. 195.

13. Ira Sharkansky, "The Utility of Elazar's Political Culture," *Polity* 2 (1969): 66–83. Sharkansky's work suffers from two defects, however. First, state totals are taken as averages of the notations in Map 10, although the notations refer to very different numbers of people in the parts of the states marked; second, the numbers attached to the notations are linearly arranged although in fact they cannot be so arranged (if $M = 1$, $I = 5$, and $T = 9$, then MT cannot be given a correct number). Sharkansky's study is based on maps in the first edition of Elazar's *American Federalism* (1966), which differs somewhat from Map 10.

14. Fenton, *Midwest Politics* (New York: Holt, Rinehart & Winston, 1966), pp. 3–7 and *passim*.

15. Elazar found echoes of this in recent changes in the politics of Yankee Rockford, Ill. (*Cities of the Prairie*, p. 313). For an opinion base for this shift, see Lloyd Free and Hadley Cantril, *The Political Beliefs of Americans* (New Brunswick, N.J.: Rutgers University Press, 1967), esp. p. 35.

16. See, for example, Robert Coles, *Migrants, Sharecroppers, Mountaineers* (Boston: Little, Brown, 1972).

17. Elazar, *American Federalism* (1966), pp. 186–88.

18. Charles O. Lerche, Jr., *The Uncertain South: Its Changing Patterns of Politics in Foreign Policy* (Chicago: Quadrangle Books, 1964). For consideration of a very different regional tradition in foreign policy see Barbara Stuhler, *Ten Men of Minnesota and American Foreign Policy: 1898–1968* (St. Paul: Minnesota Historical Society, 1973).

19. Alfred O. Hero, Jr., *The Southerner and World Affairs* (Baton Rouge: Louisiana State University Press, 1965), esp. pp. 60–61, 346.

20. Phillips, *Emerging Republican Majority*, p. 243.

21. The following discussion is based on Key, *Southern Politics*; Havard, ed., *Changing Politics of the South*; as well as Joseph Schlesinger, "The Politics of the Executive," in *Politics of the American States*, ed.

Herbert Jacob and Kenneth Vine, pp. 207–38 (Boston: Little, Brown, 1965).

22. Richard Scammon, *America at the Polls* (Pittsburgh, Pa.: University of Pittsburgh Press, 1965), pp. 62, 375.

23. For example, deGrazia, *The Western Public*.

24. Richard Scammon and Ben Wattenberg, *The Real Majority* (New York: Coward-McCann, 1970).

25. DeGrazia, *The Western Public*, pp. 119, 123.

26. Dennis D. Riley and Jack L. Walker, "Communications," *American Political Science Review* 63 (1969): 900–3.

27. See Charles Adrian, "Regional Analysis in Political Science," *Social Science Quarterly* 49 (1968): 27–32.

28. Ira Sharkansky, *Regionalism in American Politics* (Indianapolis, Ind.: Bobbs-Merrill, 1970).

29. Ibid., pp. 116–22. Marvin Hoffman and James Prather found a predominant effect of region on welfare and educational expenditures, but only the South (or Southeast) was an important determinant with the variables they used for multiple correlation. Hoffman and Prather, "The Independent Effect of Region on State Governmental Expenditures," *Social Science Quarterly* 52 (1972): 52–65.

30. Sharkansky, *Regionalism in American Politics*, pp. 67–71.

31. Ibid., pp. 153–60.

32. Ibid., pp. 126–44.

33. Ibid., pp. 176–78.

34. Ibid., pp. 9–16.

35. Fred Kniffen, "Folk Housing: Key to Diffusion," *Annals of the Association of American Geographers* 55 (1965): 549–77. See also Rexford Newcomb, "A Brief History of Rural Architecture in the United States," in *The President's Conference on Home Building and House Ownership*, vol. 7: *Farm and Village Housing* (Washington, D.C., 1932), pp. 36–56.

36. Sidney Hyman et al., *With Heritage So Rich* (New York: Random House, 1966), pp. 8–9.

37. Richard Francanviglia, "Mormon Central Hall Houses," *Annals of the Association of American Geographers* 61, no. 1 (March 1971): 65–71.

38. Marcus Whiffen, *American Architecture since 1780: A Guide to Styles* (Cambridge, Mass.: M.I.T. Press, 1969), pp. 12–15, and Newcomb, "Brief History of Rural Architecture."

39. Henry Glassie, *Pattern in the Material Folk Culture of the Eastern United States* (Philadelphia: University of Pennsylvania Press, 1968), pp. 118–21. However, other double front door, "double-pen" houses were also common elsewhere in the Lowland South (see pp. 101–4). See also Eric Sloane, *American Barns and Covered Bridges* (New York: Wilfred Funk, 1954).

40. Glassie, *Pattern in Material Folk Culture*, esp. pp. 33–39.

41. The following discussion is based on Whiffen, *American Architecture since 1780*, and Newcomb, "Brief History of Rural Architecture."

Thomas Jefferson Wertenbaker, *The Old South: The Founding of American Civilization* (New York: Charles Scribner's Sons, 1949), is also much concerned with Southern architecture.

42. For quotation and other material on Bay Region style, see Kevin Starr, *Americans and the California Dream, 1850–1915* (New York: Oxford University Press, 1973), pp. 409–10.

43. In addition to Whiffen, the following discussion is based largely on Trent E. Sanford, *The Architecture of the Southwest: Indian, Spanish, American* (New York: Norton, 1950); Rexford Newcomb, *Spanish Colonial Architecture in the United States* (New York: J. J. Augustin, 1937) and *Mediterranean Domestic Architecture* (Cleveland, Ohio: J. H. Jansen, 1928); and E. E. Bangs, *Portals West* (Menlo Park, Calif.: California Historical Society, 1960).

44. On Texas-California interchange, see Sanford, *Architecture of the Southwest*, pp. 245, 250. See also John E. Rickert, "House Façades of the Northeastern United States," *Annals of the Association of American Geographers* 57 (1967): 211–38.

45. See especially Harold Kirker, *California's Architectural Frontier* (San Marino, Calif.: The Huntington Library, 1960), pp. 125–29.

46. Robert Finley and E. M. Scott, "A Great Lakes to Gulf Profile of Dispersed-Dwelling Types," *Geographical Review* 30 (1940): 412–19.

47. See Rickert, "House Façades of the Northeastern United States."

48. On the Los Angeles area, see Reyner Banham, *Los Angeles: The Architecture of Four Ecologies* (New York: Harper & Row, 1971).

49. See especially M. D. Ross, *A Century of Architecture in Oregon* (Portland: Oregon Chapter of A.I.A., June 1959); and Joe Stubblebine, ed., *The Northwest Architecture of Pietro Belluschi* (New York: The Dodge Corp., 1953). To some extent this may reflect an earlier tradition of unpainted farmhouses and barns. See Glenn T. Trewartha, "Some Regional Characteristics of American Farmsteads," *Annals of the Association of American Geographers* 48, no. 3 (1948): 169–225 (esp. 204–10).

50. This is apparently a trend heartily endorsed by most architects. See, for example, Edward Waugh and Elizabeth Waugh, *The South Builds: New Architecture in the Old South* (Chapel Hill: University of North Carolina Press, 1960). While endorsing the regional originality of the Old South, they seem to condemn any tendency of the sort today.

51. Glenn T. Trewartha, "Types of Rural Settlement in Colonial America," *Geographical Review* 36 (1946): 568–96.

52. See Sumner Chilton Powell, *Puritan Village: The Formation of a New England Town* (Middletown, Conn.: Wesleyan University Press, 1963).

53. Ray Billington, *Westward Expansion* (New York: Macmillan, 1950), pp. 71, 541.

54. See Stewart H. Holbrook, *The Yankee Exodus: An Account of Migration from New England* (1950; reprint ed., Seattle: University of

Washington Press, 1968); Lois Kimball Mathews, *The Expansion of New England: The Spread of New England Settlement and Institutions to the Mississippi River, 1620–1865* (1909; reprint ed., New York: Russell & Russell, 1962); and Page Smith, *As a City upon a Hill: The Town in American History* (New York: Knopf, 1966). Note also the Marietta colony of the Ohio Co., in Billington, *Westward Expansion*, p. 218.

55. Leonard J. Arrington, *Great Basin Kingdom: An Economic History of the Latter-Day Saints, 1830–1900* (Cambridge, Mass.: Harvard University Press, 1958), pp. 24–25 (quotation is on p. 10); and Lowry Nelson, *The Mormon Village: A Pattern and Technique of Land Settlement* (Salt Lake City: University of Utah Press, 1952), esp. pp. 1–53.

56. For a description of the patterns in the Ramah area of New Mexico and its contrast with Southern tradition, see Florence Kluckhohn and Fred Strodtbeck, *Variations in Value Orientations* (Evanston, Ill.: Row, Peterson, 1961), pp. 61–65, 259–84.

57. Alexis de Tocqueville, *Democracy in America* (New York: Knopf, 1945), pp. 305–8 *passim.*

58. Semple, *American History and Its Geographic Conditions* (Boston: Houghton Mifflin, 1933), pp. 162–63.

59. Pillsbury, "The Urban Street Pattern as a Culture Indicator: Pennsylvania, 1682–1815," *Annals of the Association of American Geographers* 60 (1970): 428–46. See also the "Commentary" and discussion in the *Annals* 61 (March 1971): 204–13.

60. Edward T. Price, "The Central Courthouse Square in the American County Seat," *Geographical Review* 57, no. 1 (1968): 30–60.

61. Albert Baugh, "The American Dialects," in *Aspects of American English*, ed. Elizabeth Kerr and Ralph Aderman, pp. 104–11 (New York: Harcourt & Brace, 1963).

62. I have simplified these from such sources as Hans Kurath, *A Word Geography of the Eastern United States* (Ann Arbor: University of Michigan Press, 1949); Hans Kurath and Raven I. McDavid, Jr., *The Pronunciation of English in the Atlantic States* (Ann Arbor: University of Michigan Press, 1961). I have particularly taken into account the revision of the North-South distinction in Gordon R. Wood, *Vocabulary Change: A Study of Variation in Regional Words in Eight of the Southern States* (Carbondale: Southern Illinois University Press, 1970), esp. the map on p. 358.

63. This was the basis of criticism by Glenna Pickford, "American Linguistic Geography: A Sociological Appraisal," *Word* 12 (1956): 211–33.

64. William Labov, *The Social Stratification of English in New York City* (Washington, D.C.: Center for Applied Linguistics, 1966).

65. Baugh, "The American Dialects."

66. Cf. Labov, *Social Stratification of English.*

67. One of the best examples of the working out of the details of a boundary may be found in Roger Shuy, "The Northern-Midland Dialect

Boundary in Illinois," *Publication of the American Dialect Society*, 38 (November 1962).

68. For New York City see, in addition to the Labov study, Lee Pederson, "The Pronunciation of English in Metropolitan Chicago," *Publication of the American Dialect Society*, 44 (November 1965).

69. In addition to Carroll Reed, *The Dialects of American English* (Cleveland, Ohio: World, 1967), see D. W. Reed, "Eastern Dialect Words in California," *Publication of the American Dialect Society* 21 (1954): 3–15; and Frederick Brengelman, "Native American English Spoken in the Puget Sound Area" (Ph.D. diss., University of Washington, 1956).

70. On this type of influence, see R. I. McDavid, Jr., "The Dialects of American English," in *The Structure of American English*, ed. W. Nelson Francis, pp. 480–543, esp. pp. 527–34 (New York: Ronald Press, 1958).

71. See Raven I. McDavid, Jr., "The Relationship of the Speech of American Negroes to the Speech of Whites," *American Speech* 26 (February 1951): 3–17; Oma Stanley, "Negro Speech of East Texas," *American Speech* 16 (1941): 3–16; Lorenzo D. Turner, *Africanisms in the Gullah Dialect* (New York: Arno, 1969); Robert Hall, *Pidgin and Creole Languages* (Ithaca, N.Y.: Cornell University Press, 1966); William A. Stewart, "Continuity and Change in American Negro Dialects," *The Florida FL Reporter* 6, no. 1 (Spring 1968): 3–4, 14–16, 18.

72. On the West, see especially Reed, *Dialects of American English*, and the references cited there. I have not attempted here to cite the many special studies of particular linguistic issues. See, for example, *Publications of the American Dialect Society*, 1959–61, and other years.

73. In addition to other sources, see E. E. Hale, "Geographical Terms in the Far West," *Dialect Notes* 6, pt. 4 (1932): 221–33.

74. Wilbur Zelinsky, "Cultural Variations in Personal Name Patterns in the Eastern United States," *Annals of the Association of American Geographers* 60, no. 4 (1970): 743–69.

75. Meredith Burrill, "Topographic Generics," *Names* 4, no. 3 (1956): 129–37; 4, no. 4 (1956): 226–40.

76. Alan Lomax, *The Folk Songs of North America in the English Language* (London: Cassell, 1960).

77. Ibid., p. 153.

78. J. Anthony Lucas, "As American as a McDonald's Hamburger on the Fourth of July," *New York Times Magazine*, 4 July 1971 (esp. p. 25). On variations in folk-food styles, see also Glassie, *Pattern in Material Folk Culture*, pp. 25 (footnote), 73–74, 115.

79. Dale Brown, *American Cooking: The Northwest* (New York: Time-Life Books, 1970).

80. Sam Hilliard, "Hog Meal and Cornpone: Food Habits in the Antebellum South," *Proceedings of the American Philosophical Society* 113 (1969): 1–13.

81. Cf. Wilbur Zelinsky, *The Cultural Geography of the United States* (Englewood Cliffs, N.J.: Prentice-Hall, 1973), p. 106.

82. Ibid.

83. Wilbur Zelinsky, "Selfward Bound? Personal Preference Patterns and the Changing Map of American Society," *Economic Geography* 50 (April 1974): 145–79. See also Chapter III for a brief criticism of his factorial groupings.

84. Fred Kniffen, "The American Agricultural Fair," *Annals of the Association of American Geographers* 41, no. 1 (1951): 42–57.

85. Ray L. Birdwhistell, *Kinesics and Context* (Philadelphia: University of Pennsylvania Press, 1970), pp. 30–31.

## CHAPTER III

1. John P. Cole and Cuchlaine A. M. King, *Qualitative Geography: Techniques and Theories in Geography* (London: John Wiley & Sons, 1968), pp. 294–305. My discussion is based on the authors' factors I and II, which they emphasize. Factor III apparently taps data similar to those considered in Smith's analysis (below).

2. Wilbur Zelinsky, "Selfward Bound? Personal Preference Patterns and the Changing Map of American Society," *Economic Geography* 50 (April 1974): 144–79.

3. Ibid. Cf. especially map on page 172 with the preceding figures 4–10.

4. David Smith, *The Geography of Social Well-Being* (New York: McGraw-Hill, 1973), p. 101.

5. Ibid., p. 100.

6. Ibid., p. 16.

7. For a more extended critique, see R. D. Gastil, "Social Indicators and Quality of Life," *Public Administration Review* 30 (1970): 596–601. For a good example of what not to do, see Ben-Chieh Liu, *The Quality of Life in the United States, 1970* (Kansas City, Mo.: Midwest Research Institute, 1973), esp. pp. 21–23.

8. The following section is modified from R. D. Gastil, "Homicide and a Regional Culture of Violence," *American Sociological Reivew* 36 (1971): 412–27.

9. Marvin Wolfgang and Franco Ferracuti, *The Subculture of Violence* (London: Tavistock Publications, 1967).

10. Marvin Wolfgang, *Patterns in Criminal Homicide* (Philadelphia: University of Pennsylvania Press, 1958).

11. Ibid., pp. 37–38.

12. Frederick Hoffman, *The Homicide Problem* (Newark, N.J.: The Prudential Press, 1925); H. C. Brearley, *Homicide in the United States* (Chapel Hill: University of North Carolina Press, 1932); Stuart Lottier, "Criminal Offenses in Sectional Regions," *Journal of Criminal Law and*

*Criminology* 29 (1938): 329–44; Austin Porterfield, "Indices of Suicide and Homicide by States and Cities: Some Southern–Non-Southern Contrasts," *American Sociological Review* 14 (1949): 481–90; Lyle Shannon, "The Spatial Distribution of Criminal Offenses by States," *Journal of Criminal Law and Criminology* 45 (1954): 264–73.

13. Sheldon Hackney, "Southern Violence," in *Violence in America*, ed. H. D. Graham and T. R. Gurr, pp. 479–500 (New York: Signet Books, 1969).

14. John Shelton Reed, "To Live and Die in Dixie: A Contribution to the Study of Southern Violence," *Political Science Quarterly* 76 (1971): 429–45.

15. Monica Blumenthal et al., *Justifying Violence: Attitudes of American Men* (Ann Arbor: Institute for Social Research, University of Michigan, 1972), esp. pp. 213–27, 189–91.

16. Andrew Henry and James Short, *Suicide and Homicide* (Glencoe, Ill.: The Free Press, 1954).

17. Donald R. Cressey, "Epidemiology and Individual Conduct," in *Delinquency, Crime and Social Process*, ed. D. R. Cressey and D. A. Ward, pp. 557–78 (New York: Harper & Row, 1969); Edwin M. Sutherland and Donald M. Cressey, *Principles of Criminology*, 7th ed. (Philadelphia: Lippincott, 1966).

18. R. D. Gastil, "The Determinants of Human Behavior," *American Anthropologist* 63 (1961): 1281–91.

19. Cressey, "Epidemiology and Individual Conduct."

20. See Wolfgang and Ferracuti, *Subculture of Violence*, and references cited there.

21. Wolfgang, *Patterns in Criminal Homicide*, p. 175.

22. For recent statistics, see *Crime in the United States* (Washington, D.C.: U.S. Department of Justice, 1969).

23. Graham and Gurr, eds., *Violence in America*, pp. 93–233.

24. Calvin Schmid, "Urban Crime Areas," *American Sociological Review* 25 (1960): 527–47, 655–78.

25. Wolfgang and Ferracuti, *Subculture of Violence*, p. 97 and *passim.*

26. John Hope Franklin, *The Militant South: 1800–1861* (Cambridge, Mass.: Harvard University Press, 1956).

27. H. V. Redfield, *Homicide, North and South* (Philadelphia: Lippincott, 1880).

28. Richard Brown, "The American Vigilante Tradition," in *Violence in America*, ed. Graham and Gurr, pp. 184–218.

29. Henry and Short, *Suicide and Homicide*, pp. 90–92.

30. Wolfgang, *Patterns in Criminal Homicide*, pp. 116–18.

31. Cf. the discussion of the regions below (Chap. IV); also R. D. Gastil, "Internal Origins of State Populations" (Seattle, Wash.: Battelle Seattle Research Center, 1975) (obtainable by request from the research center, 4000 Northeast 41st Street, Seattle, Washington 98105).

32. Recently Colin Loftin and Robert Hill ("Regional Subculture and Homicide: An Examination of the Gastil-Hackney Thesis," *American Sociological Review* 39, no. 5 [October 1974]) have correlated data similar to ours with an index that combines together infant mortality rates, percentages of those illiterate or with very little education, percentage of families with very low incomes, armed forces mental test failures, and the percent of children living with one parent. The authors find that the resulting "structural poverty index" is more explanatory of homicide rates than any other variables, including the Southernness index. The result seems to be determined by the fact that while black homicide rates are three to more than ten times white rates, the authors have constructed an index that correlates much more closely with percent black than does the Southernness index (an index with variables weighted by their contribution to the dependent variable is also going to have a considerable advantage over one not so constructed). But their work does make the valuable point that it may not be averages, but percentages in the extremes of a distribution that should be correlated with homicide. Their study also reinforces my view that the clearer case for the significance of the correlations considered here is for the white homicides taken separately (see below).

33. Thomas Pettigrew and Rosaline Spier, "The Ecological Structure of Negro Homicide," *The American Journal of Sociology* 67 (1962): 621–29.

34. Brearley, *Homicide in the United States; Vital Statistics of the United States, 1964*, vol. 2, pt. B (Washington, D.C.: U.S. Public Health Service, 1966), pp. 7–197. Wolfgang, *Patterns in Criminal Homicide*, p. 331.

35. Rates for Puerto Rico are found in United Nations, *Demographic Yearbook* (New York: International Publications Service, 1953).

36. The following section is modified from R. D. Gastil, "The Relationship of Regional Cultures to Educational Performance," *Sociology of Education* 45 (1972): 408–25.

37. Abbott L. Ferriss, *Indicators of Trends in American Education* (New York: Russell Sage Foundation, 1969). Cf. also Eleanor Sheldon and Wilbert Moore, eds., *Indicators of Social Change* (New York: Russell Sage Foundation, 1968).

38. Alexander Astin, "Undergraduate Achievement and Institutional Excellence," *Science* 161 (1968): 661–68; Olive Banks, *The Sociology of Education* (New York: Schocken Books, 1968); James S. Coleman, *Equality of Educational Opportunity* (Washington, D.C.: Office of Education, 1966); Richard Raymond, "Determinants of the Quality of Primary and Secondary Education in West Virginia," *Journal of Human Resources* 3 (1968): 452–70.

39. John K. Folger and Charles B. Nam, *Education of the American Population* (Washington, D.C.: Bureau of the Census, 1967), pp. 118–19.

40. Ibid., pp. 154, 158, 161.

41. "How Good Are Our Schools?" *American Education* 2 (October 1966): 1–9.

42. Stuart Altman, "Earnings, Unemployment and the Supply of Enlisted Volunteers," *Journal of Human Resources* 4 (1969): 33.

43. Cf. John O. Wilson, "Quality of Life in the United States" (Kansas City, Mo.: Midwest Research Institute, 1969).

44. Herschel T. Manual, *Spanish-speaking Children of the Southwest* (Austin: University of Texas, 1965); and Folger and Nam, *Education of the American Population*, p. 151.

45. "How Good Are Our Schools?" p. 6.

46. Notes for 1969 are in *Statistical Abstract of the United States, 1970* (Washington, D.C.: Bureau of the Census, 1970), p. 264.

47. Coleman, *Equality of Educational Opportunity*.

48. Albert Bowker, "Quality and Quantity of Higher Education," *Journal of the American Statistical Association* 60 (1965): 1–15.

49. Coleman, *Equality of Educational Opportunity*, pp. 274–75.

50. Altman, "Earnings, Unemployment and the Supply of Enlisted Volunteers."

51. National Academy of Sciences/National Research Council, *Doctorate Production in United States Universities 1920–1962*, Publication 1142 (Washington, D.C., 1963), pp. 28–29, 198.

52. Ibid., pp. 16–17, 28–29.

53. Florence Kluckhohn and Fred Strodtbeck, *Variations in Value Orientations* (Evanston, Ill.: Row, Peterson, 1961).

54. Sam Shapiro, Edward Schlesinger, and Robert Nesbitt, Jr., *Infant, Perinatal, Maternal, and Childhood Mortality in the United States* (Cambridge, Mass.: Harvard University Press, 1968), pp. 3ff., 114–32.

55. *Statistical Abstract of the United States, 1969*, p. 112; *Vital Statistics, 1960*, "Mortality A," pp. 3–8.

56. *Infant Mortality Trends: United States and Each State 1930–1964* (Washington, D.C.: U.S. Public Health Service, National Center for Health Statistics, 1965), series 20, no. 1.

57. Derived from data in Children's Bureau, Department of Health, Education and Welfare, and Maternal and Infant Health Computer Project, *Infant and Perinatal Mortality Rates by Age and Color: United States Each State and County, 1951–55 and 1956–60* (Washington, D.C.: George Washington University, 1967).

58. In a recent study it was found that the population more than 15 miles from a doctor was 0.8 percent in Minnesota, 9.8 percent in North Dakota, 6.0 percent in South Dakota, and 11.2 percent in Montana. In an area of similar culture, this is reflected approximately in infant mortality rates (Map 28). Ivan Fahs and Osler Peterson, "Towns without Physicians. . . ," *American Journal of Public Health* 58 (1968): 1200–13.

59. Barkev S. Sanders, "Measuring Community Health Levels," *American Journal of Public Health* 54 (1964): 1063–70.

60. Edwin Scott Gaustad, *Historical Atlas of Religion in America* (New York: Harper & Row, 1962), jacket map.

61. *Statistical Abstract, 1969*, p. 49; *United States Census of 1880*, vol. 2, p. 710; *Vital Statistics of the United States, 1950*, vol. 1 (Washington, D.C.: U.S. Public Health Service 1953), p. 133; *Infant Mortality Trends, 1930–1964*, pp. 1–37ff.

62. *Statistical Abstract, 1970*, pp. 37, 56, 59.

63. Shapiro, Schlesinger, and Nesbitt, *Infant, Perinatal, Maternal, and Childhood Mortality in the United States*, pp. 34–35.

64. Ibid., pp. 274–75, 34–35, 200–1, 182–83, and *passim*.

65. Ibid., pp. 66–67.

66. *Statistical Abstract, 1969*, pp. 57, 809; Shapiro, Schlesinger, and Nesbitt, *Infant, Perinatal, Maternal, and Childhood Mortality in the United States*, pp. 24–25.

67. Richard Auster, Irving Leveson, and Deborah Saracheck, "The Production of Health: An Exploratory Study," *Journal of Human Resources* 4 (1969): 411–36.

## CHAPTER IV

1. For a compilation of data on state of residence by state of birth at different periods see R. D. Gastil, "Internal Origins of State Populations" (Seattle, Wash.: Battelle Seattle Research Center, 1975) (obtainable by request from the research center, 4000 Northeast 41st Street, Seattle, Washington 98105).

2. Neil Morgan, *Westward Tilt: The American West Today* (New York: Random House, 1963), p. 215.

3. New York State had 185,000 people in 1775, or less than Connecticut; New England as a whole had almost one million. While New England had grown hardly at all by 1790, New York nearly doubled, a growth rate that continued for the next several decades. Most of New York's new population upstate came from New England. See John H. Thompson, ed., *Geography of New York State* (Syracuse, N.Y.: Syracuse University Press, 1966), pp. 137, 143–44; and *Historical Statistics of the United States* (Washington, D.C.: Bureau of the Census, 1960), p. 13.

4. Thomas Jefferson Wertenbaker, *The Puritan Oligarchy: The Founding of American Civilization* (New York: Charles Scribner's Sons, 1947), pp. 64–65.

5. Sumner Chilton Powell, *Puritan Village: The Formation of a New England Town* (Middletown, Conn.: Wesleyan University Press, 1963), p. 83. See also Kenneth A. Lockridge, *A New England Town: The First Hundred Years, Dedham, Massachusetts, 1636–1736* (New York: Norton, 1970).

6. Samuel E. Morison, *The Maritime History of Massachusetts, 1783–1860* (Boston: Houghton Mifflin, 1921), p. 22.

7. Paraphrased from George W. Pierson, "The Obstinate Concept of New England: A Study in Denudation," *The New England Quarterly* 28 (March 1955): 3–17.

8. The reader is advised to compare the *Maine Manifest* ($.10) cited in the Regional Bibliographies under Barringer et al. with the similarly produced and motivated *The California Tomorrow Plan* ($1.00) (San Francisco: California Tomorrow, 1971). The latter is bombastic, argumentative, opinionated; the former is careful, constructive, and modest.

9. Lura Beam, *A Maine Hamlet* (New York: Wilfred Funk, 1957), p. 186.

10. In this regard the role of Elliott Richardson in Nixon's administration may be regarded as a continuation of the attitude in difficult surroundings. See Juan Cameron, "A Boston Brahmin in Heartbreak House," *Fortune*, October 1971, pp. 88ff. This was before Watergate.

11. Henry Adams, *The Education of Henry Adams* (New York: Modern Library, 1931).

12. Van Wyck Brooks, *The Flowering of New England* (New York: Dutton, 1937), p. 528.

13. Cf. Neal R. Peirce, *The Megastates of America: People, Politics, and Power in the Ten Great States* (New York: Norton, 1972), p. 131 and *passim.*

14. Cf. *Ripon Forum* 8 (February 1972): 32. Also George K. Lewis, "Population Change in Northern New England," *Annals of the Association of American Geographers* 62, no. 2 (June 1972): 307–22.

15. Barrows Mussey, ed., *We Were New England: Yankee Life by Those Who Lived It* (New York: Stackpole, 1937).

16. Douglas W. Johnson, Paul P. Picard, and Bernard Quinn, *Churches and Church Membership in the United States* (Washington, D.C.: Glenmary Research Center, 1974), p. 3.

17. Peter R. Gould, "On Mental Maps," in *Man, Space and Environment*, ed. P. W. English and R. C. Mayfield, pp. 260–82 (New York: Oxford University Press, 1972).

18. Wilbur Zelinsky, *The Cultural Geography of the United States* (Englewood Cliffs, N.J.: Prentice-Hall, 1973), pp. 84, 121. Zelinsky includes upstate New York with Pennsylvania and New York City in the Midlands, yet he refers to upstate New York as "New England extended."

19. Edmund Wilson, *Upstate: Records and Recollections of Northern New York* (New York: Farrar, Straus & Giroux, 1971), p. 131.

20. Ada Louise Huxtable, *Will They Ever Finish Bruckner Boulevard?* (New York: Macmillan, 1963), pp. 111–15.

21. Thomas Griffith, *The Waist-High Culture* (New York: Harper & Bros., 1959), pp. 61–62.

22. See Eric F. Goldman, "Middle States Regionalism and American

Historiography," in *Historiography and Urbanization: Essays in American History in Honor of W. Stull Holt*, ed. Eric F. Goldman, pp. 211–20 (Baltimore: Johns Hopkins Press, 1941).

23. Richard L. Merritt, *Symbols of American Community, 1735–1775* (New Haven, Conn.: Yale University Press, 1966), pp. 55–111.

24. *New York Times*, 21 October 1973, pp. 1, 71, and 14 January 1974, pp. 1, 18. The latter is the first of a series of eight articles on a recent survey of opinions of New Yorkers.

25. E. Digby Baltzell, *Philadelphia Gentlemen* (Glencoe, Ill.: The Free Press, 1958), p. 245.

26. Adams, *Education of Henry Adams*, pp. 333–34.

27. Baltzell, *Philadelphia Gentlemen*, p. 31.

28. Zelinsky, *Cultural Geography of the United States*, pp. 84, 128.

29. Richard Shryock, "Historical Traditions in Philadelphia and in the Middle Atlantic Area," *The Pennsylvania Magazine of History and Biography* 118 (April 1943): 115–41; and Gould, "On Mental Maps."

30. *New York Times*, 8 February 1971.

31. Bertelson, *The Lazy South* (New York: Oxford University Press, 1967).

32. See especially Richard Lonsdale and Clyde Browning, "Rural-Urban Locational Preferences of Southern Manufacturers," *Annals of the Association of American Geographers* 61, no. 2 (June 1971): 255–68.

33. See especially Donald R. Matthews and James W. Prothro, *Negroes and the New South* (New York: Harcourt, Brace & World, 1966), especially pp. 332–33.

34. In fact, one recent study shows almost no relative change in the South's position in the nation for many of these indicators. See R. I. Hofferbert, "Socioeconomic Dimensions of the American States," *Midwest Journal of Political Science* 12 (1968): 401–18. For a summary of the evidence see John S. Reed, *The Enduring South* (Lexington, Mass.: D. C. Heath, 1972).

35. See Evan Vogt, *Modern Homesteaders* (Cambridge, Mass.: Harvard University Press, 1955), for a displaced Western South version, and H. C. Nixon, *Lower Piedmont Country* (New York: Duell, Sloan & Pearce, 1946), p. 128, for its more easterly origin. See also Reed, *The Enduring South*, pp. 69–81.

36. J. C. Furnas, *The Americans* (New York: G. P. Putnam's Sons, 1969), pp. 182, 215–16.

37. One of the earliest to comment on the effect of slavery on white character was Thomas Jefferson, *Notes on the State of Virginia*, ed. William Peden (Chapel Hill: University of North Carolina Press, 1955), pp. 162–63. On the demographic results, see C. Vann Woodward, *American Counterpoint: Slavery and Racism in the North-South Dialogue* (Boston: Little, Brown, 1971), pp. 47–106.

38. See especially the discussion in Thomas R. Ford, ed., *The Southern*

*Appalachian Region: A Survey* (Lexington: University of Kentucky Press, 1962), pp. 259–70.

39. Samuel Lubell, *The Hidden Crisis in American Politics* (New York: Norton, 1970), p. 151 and *passim.*

40. On language, see discussion in Chap. II; on some other aspects of culture, see Melville J. Herskovits, *Myth of the Negro Past* (Boston: Beacon Press, 1941).

41. There is a large body of literature on the black family made famous by Daniel Moynihan's Department of Labor study and going back to Frazier's classic study. Recent studies of great value are Robert Coles's, cited in the "Specific Regional Sources: General" for the South; David A. Schulz, *Coming Up Black: Patterns of Ghetto Socialization* (Englewood Cliffs, N.J.: Prentice-Hall, 1969); and Elliot Liebow, *Tally's Corner: A Study of Negro Streetcorner Men* (Boston: Little, Brown, 1967). On cooking see Henry Glassie, *Pattern in the Material Folk Culture of the Eastern United States* (Philadelphia: University of Pennsylvania Press, 1968), p. 115, and Lewis Killian, *White Southerners* (New York: Random House, 1970), p. 116.

42. For Mississippi, see Mark Lowry II, "Population and Race in Mississippi, 1940–1960," *Annals of the Association of American Geographers* 61, no. 3 (September 1971): 576–88.

43. *New York Times*, 7 May 1972.

44. The discussion is based on Charlton W. Tebeau, *A History of Florida* (Coral Gables, Fla.: University of Miami Press, 1971), esp. pp. 431–52, as well as *Statistical Abstract of the United States*, 1970, and the other standard sources of this study. See also *New York Times*, 12 March 1972, p. 46; *New York Times Magazine*, 12 March 1972, pp. 31ff.; and Peirce, *Megastates of America*, pp. 450–94.

45. See Gastil, "Internal Origins of State Populations."

46. *New York Times*, 12 March 1972.

47. Peirce, *Megastates of America*, p. 474.

48. These remarks may seem strange in view of much of the literature. Yet the comparative study of the Southern poor by Robert Coles, *Migrants, Sharecroppers, Mountaineers* (cited under "Specific Regional Sources"), allows us to see the mountaineer in a quite different light.

49. This has been especially true of the whites. See Niles M. Hansen, *Rural Poverty and the Urban Crisis: A Strategy for Regional Development* (Bloomington: Indiana University Press, 1970), pp. 49–52.

50. For example, *New York Times*, 5 September 1971, sect. 4, p. 1, or 16 January 1972. See also Willie Morris, *Yazoo: Integration in a Deep-Southern Town* (New York: Harper's Magazine Press, 1971).

51. *New York Times*, 4 June 1971, p. 31.

52. D. W. Meinig, *Imperial Texas: An Interpretive Essay in Cultural Geography* (Austin: University of Texas Press, 1969), pp. 76, 113.

53. Data are in Gastil, "Internal Origins of State Populations."

54. On Northerners in Tulsa see William Eugene Hollon, *The Southwest: Old and New* (New York: Knopf, 1961), p. 449.

55. See map in Meinig, *Imperial Texas*, p. 93, and accompanying discussion. See also Terry Jordan's discussions of the origin of Texan populations in two volumes of *Annals of the Association of American Geographers*: "The Imprint of Upper and Lower South on Mid-nineteenth Century Texas" (57, no. 4 [1967]: 667–90), and "The Texas Appalachia" (60, no. 3 [1970]: 409–27).

56. Texas cities have a larger size relative to their metropolitan areas than is true elsewhere in the country.

57. The combination of violence, hospitality, pretentiousness, disorganization, and civilization in modern Houston is well sketched by Vance Packard in *A Nation of Strangers* (New York: David McKay, 1972), pp. 38–45.

58. *Goals for Dallas* (Dallas, Texas, 1966), p. 310.

59. *New York Times*, 4 June 1971.

60. Thus in Ruth Hale, "A Map of Vernacular Regions in America" (Ph.D. diss., University of Minnesota, 1971), pp. 61–64, we find that the majority of respondents in the Central and Upper Midwest states considered their state to be "Midwest"; but for the Dakotas, Iowa, Minnesota, and Wisconsin an undetermined number added "Upper."

61. John H. Fenton, *Midwest Politics* (New York: Holt, Rinehart & Winston, 1966).

62. Peirce, *Megastates of America*, pp. 299–449.

63. John Fraser Hart, "The Middle West," *Annals of the Association of American Geographers* 62, no. 2 (June 1972): 258–82 (esp. pp. 266, 279–80).

64. *New York Times*, 16 September 1973.

65. See Ira Sharkansky, *Regionalism in American Politics* (Indianapolis, Ind.: Bobbs-Merrill, 1970), p. 137.

66. For the early period, see Avery Craven, "The Advance of Civilization into the Middle West in the Period of Settlement," in *Sources of Culture in the Middle West: Background vs. Frontier*, ed. D. R. Fox, pp. 39–73 (esp. pp. 56–60) (New York: Appleton-Century, 1934).

67. National Merit Scholarship Corporation, *Annual Report*, 1970, pp. 22–27. Recently per capita state spending for higher education in Minnesota, Wisconsin, and Michigan has been higher than in Illinois, Indiana, and Ohio. *The Chronicle of Higher Education* 6, no. 13 (3 January 1972).

68. Merle Curti, *The Making of an American Community: A Case Study of Democracy in a Frontier County* (Stanford, Calif.: Stanford University Press, 1959).

69. The Midwest as a sociocultural region is briefly discussed in the section on the Central Midwest.

70. For an example of the pattern of this dispersion see J. Neale

Carman, *Foreign Language Units of Kansas* (Lawrence: University of Kansas Press, 1967), esp. pp. 33–34.

71. For the full argument on separating the Upper and Central Midwest, see the foregoing section on the Upper Midwest.

72. See Roger Barker and Phil Schoggen, *Qualities of Community Life* (San Francisco, Calif.: Jossey-Bass, 1973).

73. This point is made most clearly by Randall Stewart in contrasting Midwestern and Southern literature in "Outlook for Southern Writing," *Virginia Quarterly Review* 31, no. 2 (Spring 1955): 252–63. Apologetics is also the approach of most of the authors in Thomas T. McAvoy, ed., *The Midwest: Myth or Reality?* (Notre Dame, Ind.: University of Notre Dame Press, 1961).

74. See the interpretation of Frank R. Kramer, *Voices in the Valley: Mythmaking and Folk Belief in the Shaping of the Middle West* (Madison: University of Wisconsin Press, 1964).

75. Hart, "The Middle West," pp. 258–82 (esp. p. 280).

76. For political patterns, reference was made especially to Daniel Elazar, *American Federalism: A View from the States* (New York: Thomas Y. Crowell, 1966), p. 97; and John Fenton, "The Border States: Population and Politics," in *Democracy in the Fifty States*, ed. Charles Press and Oliver Williams, pp. 109–19 (Chicago: Rand McNally, 1966).

77. Richard Stern, quoted in Harold M. Mayer and Richard C. Wade, *Chicago: Growth of a Metropolis* (Chicago: University of Chicago Press, 1969), p. 466.

78. This discussion is based in large part on a comparison in the *New York Times*, 16 May 1971, p. 50. See also Neal R. Peirce's discussion in *The Megastates of America*, pp. 349–84.

79. See Joseph Brownell, "The Cultural Midwest," *Journal of Geography* 59, no. 2 (February 1960): 81–85; and Hale, "Map of Vernacular Regions in America." Unfortunately the methodologies of both allowed some respondents to think more in terms of direction-location and official terminology than was desirable.

80. John Bartlow Martin, *Indiana: An Interpretation* (New York: Knopf, 1947), pp. 217–34.

81. *New York Times*, 1 February 1971, C-31.

82. Ibid., 17 May 1971, p. M-31.

83. Russell B. Adams, *Population Mobility in the Upper Midwest*, Upper Midwest Economic Study, Urban Report no. 6 (Minneapolis, Minn.: Upper Midwest Research and Development Council, 1964), p. 30.

84. John R. Borchert and Russell B. Adams, *Trade Centers and Trade Areas of the Upper Midwest*, Upper Midwest Economic Study, Urban Report no. 3 (Minneapolis, Minn.: Upper Midwest Research and Development Council, 1963), p. 25.

85. Hale, "Map of Vernacular Regions in America," pp. 61–69.

86. Frank H. Jonas, ed., *Western Politics* (Salt Lake City: University of Utah, 1961), p. 341.

87. Civic Design Study, *A Statement on the Mountain-Plains Area of the United States* (Colorado Springs: Colorado College, 1962).

88. See John Borchert, "The Dust Bowl in the 1970's," *Annals of the Association of American Geographers* 61, no. 1 (March 1971): 1–22.

89. Carl F. Kraenzel, *The Great Plains in Transition* (Norman: University of Oklahoma Press, 1955).

90. See the mapping of distinctions between rural (resident), sidewalk (commuter), and suitcase (absentee) farmers in South Dakota in Samuel Dicken and Forrest Pitts, *Introduction to Cultural Geography* (Waltham, Mass.: Ginn & Co., 1970), p. 253.

91. Kraenzel, *The Great Plains in Transition*, pp. 214–15, 230.

92. See the Utah data in Gastil, "Internal Origins of State Populations."

93. See D. W. Meinig, "The Mormon Culture Region: Strategies and Patterns in the Geography of the American West, 1847–1964," *Annals of the Association of American Geographers* 55, no. 2 (June 1965): 191–220.

94. Lowry Nelson, *The Mormon Village: A Pattern and Technique of Land Settlement* (Salt Lake City: University of Utah Press, 1952), pp. 48–50.

95. Noted by Wilbur Zelinsky, *Cultural Geography of the United States*, p. 95, note.

96. Joseph E. Spencer, "The Development of Agricultural Villages in Southern Utah," *Agricultural History* 40 (1970): 181–89 (quotation is on p. 186). This is reminiscent of the mixed religiopolitical systems of early Mesopotamia.

97. See Chaps. II and III. Also Merlin B. Brinkerhoff and Phillip R. Kunz, *Utah in Numbers: Comparisons, Trends, and Descriptions* (Provo, Utah: Brigham Young University Press, 1969), pp. 107, 156–65, 175–77, 312.

98. For example, in a recent study (Gould, "On Mental Maps") of the preferences of college students of places to reside, Utah generally ranked lower than surrounding states as a place to live.

99. There is, of course, an extensive literature on the Indians, and to a lesser extent the Spanish Americans, of the Interior Southwest. Although somewhat outdated, the *Southwest Issue* of the *American Anthropologist* (56, no. 9 [August 1954]) is a good place to start. There are also three valuable pieces on Southwest Indian acculturation in Edward Spicer, ed., *Perspectives in American Indian Culture Change* (Chicago: University of Chicago Press, 1961). See also the specific regional sources for the Interior Southwest listed in the Bibliography.

100. J. B. Priestley and Jacquetta Hawkes, *Journey down a Rainbow* (London: Heinemann-Cresset, 1955). See also J. B. Priestley, *Midnight on the Desert* (London: Harper & Bros., 1937).

101. Ross Calvin, *Sky Determines: An Interpretation of the Southwest*, rev. and enl. ed. (Albuquerque: University of New Mexico Press, 1965), pp. 342–44.

102. D. W. Meinig, *Southwest: Three Peoples in Geographical Change* (New York: Oxford University Press, 1971).

103. See especially Florence Kluckhohn and Fred Strodtbeck, *Variations in Value Orientations* (Evanston, Ill.: Row, Peterson, 1961).

104. Meinig, however, sees the Mestizo population as developing in place from the Indian-Spanish contact. This is directly contradicted by Winfield Scott, "Chimayo, New Mexico," in *A Vanishing America*, ed. Thomas Wheeler (New York: Holt, Rinehart & Winston, 1964), pp. 122–35 (see esp. p. 127). In any case, the evidences of peasant Spanish and Mexican culture, little related to local forms, suggest that the dominating cultural elements were from Mexico.

105. Erna Fergusson, *New Mexico: A Pageant of Three Peoples*, 2nd ed. (New York: Knopf, 1964), pp. 264–80.

106. Hollon, *The Southwest*, pp. 460–62; Fergusson, *New Mexico*, p. 377 (on Tom Lea); D. W. Meinig, *Southwest*, p. 102. On the special culture of El Paso, see also Duncan Aikman, "El Paso," in *Rocky Mountain Cities*, ed. Ray West, Jr. (New York: Norton, 1949).

107. *New York Times*, 14 August 1971.

108. The Texan District is the "Texas Sphere" distinguished by D. W. Meinig in his analysis of the Texas culture area. See his *Imperial Texas*, p. 116.

109. On the Albuquerque riots, see *New York Times*, 20 June 1971, p. A-44. For another type of acculturation see Elliott McIntire, "Changing Patterns of Hopi Indian Settlement," *Annals of the Association of American Geographers* 61 (September 1971): 510–21. Other problems of change in the special circumstances of the Interior Southwest are analyzed in Calvin Trillin, "U.S. Journal: Gallup, New Mexico," *The New Yorker*, 25 September 1971, pp. 108ff., and "U.S. Journal: Tesuque, New Mexico," *The New Yorker*, 18 December 1971, pp. 93–97.

110. For further details see Gastil, "Internal Origins of State Populations."

111. Regional borders are established in descriptions of surrounding regions.

112. Kevin Starr, *Americans and the California Dream, 1850–1915* (New York: Oxford University Press, 1973).

113. D. W. Meinig, "American Wests: Preface to a Geographical Introduction," *Annals of the Association of American Geographers* 62, no. 2 (June 1972): 159–84.

114. Reynar Banham, *Los Angeles: The Architecture of Four Ecologies* (New York: Harper & Row, 1971).

115. See Daniel Elazar, *Cities of the Prairie: The Metropolitan Frontier and American Politics* (New York: Basic Books, 1970), pp. 44–64 *passim*.

116. *New York Times*, 12 September 1971, A-1.

117. Ibid., 26 June 1971, A-12.

118. See Jesse Douglas, "Origins of the Population of Oregon in 1850,"

*Pacific Northwest Quarterly* 41 (1950): 95–112. However, Douglas overestimates the number of families from the Northeast.

119. H. H. Bancroft, *History of the Pacific States of North America*, vol. 24: *Oregon*, vol. 1: *1834–1848* (San Francisco: The History Co., 1886), pp. 524, 424.

120. For a further discussion of population characteristics see R. D. Gastil, "The Pacific Northwest as a Cultural Region," *Pacific Northwest Quarterly* 64 (1973): 147–56.

121. This was one of the main concerns of the National Resources Committee in 1936 (*Regional Planning*, pt. 1: *Pacific Northwest* [Washington, D.C., 1936], pp. 130–31), and it is still a central issue.

122. Dorothy Johansen, "Libraries and the Intellectual Environment of the Pacific Northwest," in *Libraries and Librarians of the Pacific Northwest*, ed. Morton Kroll, pp. 3–50 (see p. 44) (Seattle: University of Washington Press, 1960).

123. *Sunset Magazine* (Pacific Northwest edition), July 1972, pp. 54ff., 176; also Ethyl Starbird, "A River Restored: Oregon's Willamette," *National Geographic* 141, no. 6 (June 1972): 816–35.

124. See Gastil, "Internal Origins of State Populations."

125. *Seattle Times*, 16 December 1973, D-8. This was part of a series in the *Times* by Stanton Patty on the Alaskan natives and the settlement of the claims case.

126. See E. S. Gaustad, *Historical Atlas of Religion in America* (New York: Harper & Row, 1962), pp. 152–55.

127. *New York Times Almanac*, 1971, pp. 195, 274.

128. See Dorothy Johansen, "A Working Hypothesis for the Study of Migrations," *Pacific Historical Review* 36 (February 1967): 1–12. If we take Mary McCarthy's *Portrait of a Catholic Girlhood* (spent largely in Seattle) as a model, Alaska contrasts with the Northwest as Montana contrasted with the Northwest in her narrative. Writers have loved to picture Seattle as a wild city of boom and bust, but in fact McCarthy's picture is more just. Even the recent Boeing bust caused hardly a ripple in its complacency.

129. George Rogers, *The Future of Alaska: Economic Consequences of Statehood* (Baltimore, Md.: for Resources for the Future by Johns Hopkins Press, 1962), pp. 119–21.

130. *Seattle Times*, 18 December 1973.

131. See Neal R. Peirce, *The Pacific States of America: People, Politics, and Power in the Five Pacific Basin States* (New York: Norton, 1972), pp. 331, 334.

132. For the census data on nativity and state of origin, see Gastil, "Internal Origins of State Populations."

133. Native peoples often declined on contact for these reasons. In Hawaii, there is little evidence that natives were directly killed off by the whites or through unaccustomed work on the plantations. Sterility seems to have been a major problem because of venereal diseases or other

reasons. The royal family was very unproductive in the nineteenth century, while the island census at mid-century shows remarkably few children (median age 32.2). Robert C. Schmitt, *Demographic Statistics of Hawaii, 1778–1965* (Honolulu: University of Hawaii Press, 1968), p. 43.

Infanticide and abortion probably played an unusual part in the decline. The closely related Marquesans were said to have a declining population at contact for this reason (Ralph Linton, *The Study of Man* [New York: Appleton-Century, 1936], p. 297), and the Hawaiians were unusual among Polynesians for allowing infanticide at any age, and with surprising generality. See J. C. Furnas, *Anatomy of Paradise: Hawaii and the Islands of the South Seas* (New York: William Sloane Associates, 1948), p. 100, and Laura Judd's remarks on her experiences, excerpted in Gerrit P. Judd, ed., *A Hawaiian Anthology* (New York: Macmillan, 1967), pp. 34–35.

Nevertheless, the decline was probably less precipitous than is generally reported. The figure of 300,000 accepted by Schmitt and others for precontact Hawaii was probably too high. The detailed evidence we have for this period on an island basis (Schmitt, *Demographic Statistics of Hawaii*, p. 22) leads to lower estimates and should be taken more seriously than it has been.

134. Andrew W. Lind, *Hawaii's People*, 3rd ed. (Honolulu: University of Hawaii Press, 1967).

135. Andrew W. Lind, *Hawaii: The Last of the Magic Isles* (London and New York: for the Institute of Race Relations by Oxford University Press, 1969), pp. 64–65.

136. Graham Kinloch and Jeffrey Borders, "Racial Stereotypes and Social Distance among Elementary School Children in Hawaii," *Sociology and Social Research* 56, no. 3 (April 1972): 368–77. Also Lind, *Hawaii*, pp. 82–86.

137. George Chaplin and Glenn D. Paige, eds., *Hawaii 2000: Continuing Experiment in Anticipatory Democracy* (Honolulu: University Press of Hawaii for the Governor's Conference on the Year 2000, 1973).

## CHAPTER V

1. Wilbur Zelinsky, "Classical Town Names in the United States: The Historical Geography of an American Idea," *Geographical Review* 57, no. 4 (1967): 463–95 (see p. 466).

2. Katherine Ann Porter, "A Country and Some People I Love," *Harper's Magazine* 231 (1965): 58–68 (see p. 68).

3. John B. Jackson, *American Space* (New York: Norton, 1972), pp. 165–66.

4. *New York Times*, 7 October 1973.

5. Lillian Hellman, review of Eli Evans, *The Provincials*, in *New York Times Book Review*, 11 November 1973, pp. 4–5.

6. Based on an analysis of data in M. Barone, G. Ujifusa, and D. Matthews, *The Almanac of American Politics* (Boston: Gambit, 1972).

7. Wilbur Zelinsky, *The Cultural Geography of the United States* (Englewood Cliffs, N.J.: Prentice-Hall, 1973), p. 111.

8. Peter R. Gould, "On Mental Maps," in *Man, Space and Environment*, ed. P. W. English and R. C. Mayfield, pp. 260–82 (New York: Oxford University Press, 1972).

9. Norval Glenn and J. L. Simons, "Are Regional Cultural Differences Diminishing?" *Public Opinion Quarterly* 31 (1967): 176–91. See also Norval Glenn, "Massification Versus Differentiation: Some Trend Data from National Surveys," *Social Forces* 46 (1967): 172–80.

10. Herbert Hendin, *Suicide and Scandinavia* (New York: Grune & Stratton, 1964); Veli Verkko, *Homicides and Suicides in Finland and Their Dependence on National Character*, Scandinavian Studies in Sociology, 3 (Copenhagen: G. E. C. Gads, 1952); *World Health Statistics Annual, 1965*, vol. 1 (Geneva: World Health Organization, 1968).

11. David Smith, *The Geography of Social Well-being in the United States* (New York: McGraw-Hill, 1973). Howard Odum, *Southern Regions of the United States* (Chapel Hill: University of North Carolina Press, 1936), and other writings.

12. Joseph Zimmerman, "Metropolitan Reform in the United States: An Overview," *Public Administration Review* 5 (1970): 531–43.

13. Conrad M. Arensberg, "American Communities," *American Anthropologist* 57 (1955): 1143–61. Robert Bish and Robert Warren, "Scale and Monopoly Problems in Urban Government Services," 1971 (unpublished).

14. Rena Gazaway, *The Longest Mile* (Garden City, N.Y.: Doubleday, 1969), pp. 328ff.

15. Irving Kristol, opening remarks in *The Public Interest* 24 (1971): 3.

16. J. B. Priestley and Jacquetta Hawkes, *Journey down a Rainbow* (London: Heinemann-Cresset, 1955).

17. See D. W. Meinig, "Environmental Appreciation," *Western Humanities Review* 35 (1971): 1–11; David Lowenthal and Hugh Prince, "The English Landscape," *Geographical Review* 54 (1964): 309–46; David Lowenthal and Hugh Prince, "English Landscape Tastes," *Geographical Review* 55 (1965): 186–222; and David Lowenthal, "The American Scene," *Geographical Review* 58 (1968): 61–88.

18. See especially Robert Coles, *Migrants, Sharecroppers, Mountaineers* (Boston: Little, Brown, 1972).

19. Vance Packard, *A Nation of Strangers* (New York: McKay, 1972), esp. p. 2.

20. Rene Dubos, *A God Within* (New York: Scribners, 1972), p. 286.

21. *New York Times*, 1 February 1971, C-31.

22. Daniel Elazar, *Cities of the Prairie: The Metropolitan Frontier and American Politics* (New York: Basic Books, 1970), p. 442.

# Regional Bibliographies

## FOR CHAPTER IV

## *Selected References*
## *for Several or All Regions*

Arrington, Leonard. *The Changing Economic Structure of the Mountain West, 1850–1950.* Utah State University Monograph Series, vol. 10, no. 3. Logan: Utah State University Press, 1963.

Dorson, Richard M. *American Folklore.* Chicago: University of Chicago Press, 1959 (especially pp. 74–134 on regional folk cultures).

Furnas, J. C. *The Americans: A Social History of the United States, 1587–1914.* New York: G. P. Putnam's Sons, 1969.

Green, Constance M. *American Cities in the Growth of the Nation.* New York: Harper and Row, 1957.

Gunther, John. *Inside U.S.A.* New York: Harper and Row, 1947.

Jackson, John Brinckerhoff. *American Space: The Centennial Years, 1865–1876.* New York: Norton, 1972.

Lerner, Max. *America As a Civilization: Life and Thought in the United States Today.* New York: Simon and Schuster, 1957 (especially pp. 182–206).

Marriott, Alice, and Carol K. Rachlin. *American Epic: The Story of the American Indian.* New York: G. P. Putnam's Sons, 1969.

Morgan, Neil. *Westward Tilt: The American West Today.* New York: Random House, 1961.

Morris, James. *As I Saw the U.S.A.* New York: Pantheon, 1956.

*National Atlas of the United States of America.* Washington, D.C.: United States Department of the Interior, Geological Survey, 1972.

Owings, Nathaniel Alexander. *The American Aesthetic.* New York: Harper and Row, 1969 (for its photographs by William Garnett, especially of California and the Interior Southwest).

Paterson, J. H. *North America: A Geography of Canada and the United States.* 3rd ed. London: Oxford University Press, 1965.

Paullin, Charles O. *Atlas of the Historical Geography of the United States.* Edited by John K. Wright. Washington, D.C.: Carnegie Institution; New York: American Geographical Society, 1932.

Smith, Page. *As a City upon a Hill: The Town in American History.* New York: Alfred A. Knopf, 1966.

Spencer, Robert F., Jesse D. Jennings, et al. *The Native Americans: Prehistory and Ethnology of the North American Indians.* New York: Harper and Row, 1965.

Trillin, Calvin. *U.S. Journal.* New York: E. P. Dutton, 1971 (as well as the other articles in Trillin's continuing series in *The New Yorker* under this title).

Underhill, Ruth. *Red Man's America: A History of Indians in the United States.* Chicago: University of Chicago Press, 1953.

Ward, David. *Cities and Immigrants: A Geography of Change in Nineteenth-Century America.* New York: Oxford University Press, 1971.

Wheeler, Thomas C., ed. *A Vanishing America: The Life and Times of the Small Town.* New York: Holt, Rinehart and Winston, 1964.

# *Specific Regional Sources*
## New England

Adams, Henry. *The Education of Henry Adams.* New York: Modern Library, 1931.

Bailey, Anthony. *In the Village.* New York: Alfred A. Knopf, 1971.

Barringer, Richard, et al. *A Maine Manifest.* Portland, Me.: The Allagash Group, 1971.

Beam, Lura. *A Maine Hamlet.* New York: Wilfred Funk, 1957.

Black, John Donald. *The Rural Economy of New England: A Regional Study.* Cambridge, Mass.: Harvard University Press, 1950.

Brooks, Van Wyck. *The Flowering of New England.* New York: E. P. Dutton, 1937.

Carmer, Carl, ed. *The Tavern Lamps Are Burning: Literary Journeys through Six Regions and Four Centuries of New York State.* New York: David McKay, 1964.

*The Case for Regional Planning, with Special References to New England.* New Haven: The Directive Committee on Regional Planning, Yale University, Yale University Press, 1947.

Cobb, Elijah. *Elijah Cobb, 1768–1848: A Cape Cod Skipper.* New Haven, Conn.: Yale University Press, 1925.

Conover, Jewel Helen. *Nineteenth-Century Houses in Western New York.* Albany: State University of New York, 1966.

Cross, Whitney. *The Burned-Over District: The Social and Intellectual History of Enthusiastic Religion in Western New York, 1800–1850.* Ithaca, N.Y.: Cornell University Press, 1950.

Enzer, Selwyn, and Raul deBrigard. *Issues and Opportunities in the State of Connecticut, 1970–2000.* Middletown, Conn.: Institute for the Future, March 1970.

Estall, R. C. *New England: A Study in Industrial Adjustment.* New York: Frederick A. Praeger, 1966.

Gould, R. E. *Yankee Boyhood.* New York: W. W. Norton, 1950.

Hicks, Granville. *Small Town.* New York: Macmillan, 1946.

Holbrook, Stuart. *The Yankee Exodus: An Account of Migration from New England.* 1950. Reprint. Seattle: University of Washington Press, 1968.

Kozol, Jonathan. *Death at an Early Age: The Destruction of the Hearts and Minds of Negro Children in the Boston Public Schools.* Boston: Houghton Mifflin, 1967.

Lane, Roger. *Policing the City: Boston 1822–1885.* Cambridge, Mass.: Harvard University Press, 1967.

Lewis, George K. "Population Change in Northern New England." *Annals of the Association of American Geographers* 62, no. 2 (June 1972): 307–22.

Lockridge, Kenneth A. *A New England Town: The First Hundred Years, Dedham, Massachusetts, 1636–1736.* New York: W. W. Norton, 1970.

Mathews, Lois Kimball. *The Expansion of New England: The Spread of New England Settlement and Institutions to the Mississippi River, 1620–1865.* 1909. Reprint. New York: Russell and Russell, 1962.

Mayer, Kurt B., and Sidney Goldstein. *Migration and Economic Development in Rhode Island.* Providence, R.I.: Brown University Press, 1958.

Miller, Perry. *The New England Mind: From Colony to Province.* Cambridge, Mass.: Harvard University Press, 1953.

Miller, William L. *The Fifteenth Ward and the Great Society: An Encounter with a Modern City.* Boston: Houghton Mifflin, 1966.

Morison, Samuel E. *The Maritime History of Massachusetts, 1783–1860.* Boston: Houghton Mifflin, 1921.

Mussey, Barrows, ed. *We Were New England: Yankee Life by Those Who Lived It.* New York: Stackpole Sons, 1937.

Peirce, Neal R. *The Megastates of America: People, Politics, and Power in the Ten Great States.* New York: W. W. Norton, 1972 (especially pp. 13–79, 130–80).

Pierson, George W. "The Obstinate Concept of New England: A Study in Denudation." *The New England Quarterly* 28 (March 1955):3–17.

Powell, Sumner Chilton. *Puritan Village: The Formation of a New England Town.* Middletown, Conn.: Wesleyan University Press, 1963.

Thompson, John H., ed. *Geography of New York State.* Syracuse, N.Y.: Syracuse University Press, 1966 (especially chaps. 7–9 by D. W. Meinig).

Vidich, Arthur J., and Joseph Bensman. *Small Town in Mass Society: Class, Power, and Religion in a Rural Community.* New York: Anchor Books, 1960.

Warner, W. Lloyd, ed. *Yankee City.* New Haven, Conn.: Yale University Press, 1945.

Wertenbaker, Thomas Jefferson. *The Puritan Oligarchy: The Founding of American Civilization.* New York: Charles Scribner's Sons, 1947.

Weygandt, Cornelius. *The Heart of New Hampshire.* New York: G. P. Putnam's Sons, 1944.

Whyte, William F. *Street Corner Society: The Social Structure of an Italian Slum.* Enl. ed. Chicago: University of Chicago Press, 1955.

Wilson, Edmund. *Upstate: Records and Recollections of Northern New York.* New York: Farrar, Straus and Giroux, 1971.

# New York Metropolitan Region

Carmer, Carl, ed. *The Tavern Lamps Are Burning: Literary Journeys through Six Regions and Four Centuries of New York State.* New York: David McKay, 1964.

Cordasco, Francis, ed. *Jacob Riis Revisited: Poverty and the Slum in Another Era.* New York: Anchor Books, 1968.

Cunningham, John T. *This Is New Jersey.* Rev. ed. New Brunswick, N.J.: Rutgers University Press, 1968.

Ellis, David M. "New York and Middle Atlantic Regionalism." *New York History* 25, no. 1 (January 1954):3–13.

First National City Bank, Economics Department. *Profile of a City.* New York: McGraw-Hill, 1972.

Glazer, Nathan, and Daniel Patrick Moynihan. *Beyond the Melting Pot: The Negroes, Puerto Ricans, Jews, Italians, and Irish of New York City.* 2nd ed. Cambridge, Mass.: M.I.T. Press, 1970.

Goldman, Eric F. "Middle States Regionalism and American Historiography: A Suggestion." In *Historiography and Urbanization: Essays in American History in Honor of W. Stull Holt,* ed. Eric F. Goldman, pp. 211–20. Baltimore: Johns Hopkins Press, 1941.

Gordon, Milton. *Assimilation in American Life: The Role of Race, Religion, and National Origins.* New York: Oxford University Press, 1964.

Gottmann, Jean. *Megalopolis: The Urbanized Northeastern Seaboard of the United States.* New York: Twentieth Century Fund, 1961.

Hoover, Edgar M., and Raymond Vernon. *Anatomy of a Metropolis: The Changing Distribution of People and Jobs within the New York Metropolitan Region.* Cambridge, Mass.: Harvard University Press, 1959.

Howe, Irving. "The New York Intellectuals." In *Decline of the New,* pp. 211–68. New York: Harcourt, Brace and World, 1963.

Huxtable, Ada L. *Will They Ever Finish Bruckner Boulevard?* New York: Macmillan, 1963.

Jacobs, Jane. *The Death and Life of Great American Cities.* New York: Random House, 1961.

Osofsky, Gilbert. *Harlem: The Making of a Ghetto.* New York: Harper and Row, 1966.

Peirce, Neal R. *The Megastates of America: People, Politics, and Power in the Ten Great States.* New York: W. W. Norton, 1972 (especially pp. 13–129, 181–226).

*Plan for New York City: 1969, A Proposal, I, Critical Issues.* New York: New York City Planning Commission, 1969.

Pomerantz, Sidney I. *New York, an American City, 1783–1803: A Study of Urban Life.* New York: Columbia University Press, 1938.

Thompson, D. G. *Gateway to a Nation: The Middle Atlantic States and Their Influence on the Development of the Nation.* Peterborough, N.H.: William Bauhan, 1956.

Thompson, John H., ed. *Geography of New York State.* Syracuse, N.Y.: Syracuse University Press, 1966.

Vecoli, Rudolph. *The People of New Jersey.* New Brunswick, N.J.: Rutgers University Press, 1965.

Vernon, Raymond. *Metropolis 1985: An Interpretation of the Findings of the New York Metropolitan Region Study.* Cambridge, Mass.: Harvard University Press, 1960.

Wacker, Peter O. *The Musconetcong Valley of New Jersey: A Historical Geography.* New Brunswick, N.J.: Rutgers University Press, 1968.

Wertenbaker, Thomas Jefferson. *The Founding of American Civilization: The Middle Colonies.* New York: Charles Scribner's Sons, 1938.

Whalen, Richard J. *A City Destroying Itself: An Angry View of New York.* New York: William Morrow, 1965.

# The Pennsylvanian Region

Baltzell, E. Digby. *Philadelphia Gentlemen: The Making of a National Upper Class.* Glencoe, Ill.: The Free Press, 1958.

Bowen, Ezra. *The Middle Atlantic States: Delaware, Maryland, Pennsylvania.* New York: Time-Life Books, 1968.

Buck, Solon J., and Elizabeth Hawthorn Buck. *The Planting of Civilization in Western Pennsylvania.* Pittsburgh, Pa.: University of Pittsburgh Press, 1939.

Cunningham, John T. *This Is New Jersey.* Rev. ed. New Brunswick, N.J.: Rutgers University Press, 1968.

Fletcher, Stevenson W. *Pennsylvania Agriculture and Country Life, vol. 1: 1640–1840.* Harrisburg: Pennsylvania Historical and Museum Commission, 1950.

Garber, John. *The Valley of the Delaware.* Port Washington, N.Y.: Ira Friedman, 1934.

Goldman, Eric F. "Middle States Regionalism and American Historiography: A Suggestion." In *Historiography and Urbanization: Essays in American History in Honor of W. Stull Holt*, ed. Eric F. Goldman, pp. 211–20. Baltimore: Johns Hopkins Press, 1941.

Gottmann, Jean. *Megalopolis: The Urbanized Northeastern Seaboard of the United States.* New York: Twentieth Century Fund, 1961.

Hostetler, John A. *Amish Society.* Baltimore: Johns Hopkins Press, 1963.

Lemon, James T. "The Agricultural Patterns of National Groups in 18th Century Southeast Pennsylvania." *Geographical Review* 56, no. 4 (1944):467–96.

Lewis, Peirce F. "Small Town in Pennsylvania." *Annals of the Association of American Geographers* 62, no. 2 (June 1972):323–51.

Peirce, Neal R. *The Megastates of America: People, Politics, and Power in the Ten Great States.* New York: W. W. Norton, 1972, pp. 181–298.

Pillsbury, Richard. "The Urban Street Pattern as a Culture Indicator: Pennsylvania 1682–1815." *Annals of the Association of American Geographers* 60, no. 3 (September 1970):428–46 (see also "Commentary" by Michael Conzen, and Pillsbury's reply, in the March 1971 issue, pp. 204–13).

Shryock, Richard. "Historical Traditions in Philadelphia and in the Middle Atlantic Area." *The Pennsylvania Magazine of History and Biography*, April 1943, pp. 115–41.

Thompson, D. G. *Gateway to a Nation: The Middle Atlantic States and Their Influence on the Development of the Nation.* Peterborough, N.H.: William Bauhan, 1956.

Vecoli, Rudolph. *The People of New Jersey.* New Brunswick, N.J.: Rutgers University Press, 1965.

Wertenbaker, Thomas Jefferson. *The Founding of American Civilization: The Middle Colonies.* New York: Charles Scribner's Sons, 1938.

# The South

There is a continual flow of literature on the South. For recent bibliography beyond what I have consulted, see especially the entries for Havard (pp. 3–36, 731–40), Hero, and Woodward (1968, 1971).

## GENERAL

Beale, Calvin. "American Triracial Isolates." *Eugenics Quarterly* 4, no. 4

(December 1957):187–92. See also a collection of articles on "The American Isolates" in *American Anthropologist* 74, no. 3 (June 1972):693–733.

Bertelson, David. *The Lazy South.* New York: Oxford University Press, 1967.

Cash, W. J. *The Mind of the South.* New York: Alfred A. Knopf, 1941.

Coles, Robert. *Migrants, Sharecroppers, Mountaineers.* Children of Crisis, vol. 2. Boston: Little, Brown, 1971.

———. *The South Goes North.* Children of Crisis, vol. 3. Boston: Little, Brown, 1971.

Foster, M. I. "Is the South Still a Backward Region and Why?" *American Economic Review* 62 (May 1972):195–203.

Franklin, John Hope. *The Militant South, 1800–1861.* Cambridge, Mass.: Harvard University Press, 1956.

Gottmann, Jean. *Virginia in Our Century.* Charlottesville: University Press of Virginia, 1969.

Hansen, Niles M. *Rural Poverty and the Urban Crisis: A Strategy for Regional Development.* Bloomington: Indiana University Press, 1970.

Hart, John Fraser. *The Southeastern United States.* Princeton, N.J.: D. Van Nostrand, 1967.

Hartshorne, Truman. "The Spatial Structure of Socioeconomic Development in the Southeast, 1950–1960." *Geographical Review* 61 (April 1971):265–93.

Havard, William C., ed. *The Changing Politics of the South.* Baton Rouge: Louisiana State University Press, 1972.

Hero, Alfred O., Jr. *The Southerner and World Affairs.* Baton Rouge: Louisiana State University Press, 1965.

*I'll Take My Stand: The South and the Agrarian Tradition.* By Twelve Southerners. 1930. Reprint. New York: Peter Smith, 1951.

Jefferson, Thomas. *Notes on the State of Virginia.* Edited by William Peden. Chapel Hill: University of North Carolina Press, 1954.

Killian, Lewis M. *White Southerners.* New York: Random House, 1970.

Levy, Babette M. "Early Puritanism in the Southern and Island Colonies." *Proceedings of the American Antiquarian Society*, Worcester, Mass., 1960, pp. 69–345.

Lonsdale, Richard, and Clyde Browning. "Rural-Urban Locational Preferences of Southern Manufacturers." *Annals of the Association of American Geographers* 61, no. 2 (June 1971):255–68.

Marshall, F. Ray. "Some Rural Economic Development Problems in the South." *American Economic Review* 62 (May 1972):204–11.

Matthews, Donald R., and James W. Prothro. *Negroes and the New Southern Politics.* New York: Harcourt, Brace and World, 1966.

Merrens, Harry Roy. *Colonial North Carolina in the Eighteenth Century: A Study in Historical Geography.* Chapel Hill: University of North Carolina Press, 1964.

Morland, J. Kenneth, ed. *The Not So Solid South: Anthropological Studies in a Regional Subculture.* Southern Anthropological Society, *Proceedings,* no. 4. Athens: University of Georgia Press, 1971.

Morris, Willie. *Yazoo: Integration in a Deep-Southern Town.* New York: Harper's Magazine Press, 1971.

Myrdal, Gunnar. *An American Dilemma.* New York: Harper and Row, 1944.

Olmsted, Frederick Law. *The Cotton Kingdom: A Traveller's Observations on Cotton and Slavery in the American Slave States.* Originally published in the 1850s. Reprint. New York: Alfred A. Knopf, 1953.

Reed, John Shelton. *The Enduring South: Subcultural Persistence in Mass Society.* Lexington, Mass.: D. C. Heath, 1972.

————. "To Live—and Die—in Dixie: A Contribution to the Study of Southern Violence." *Political Science Quarterly* 86, no. 3 (September 1971):429–43.

Rubin, Louis D., Jr., and Robert D. Jacobs, eds. *Southern Renascence: The Literature of the Modern South.* Baltimore: Johns Hopkins Press, 1953.

Taylor, William R. *Cavalier and Yankee: The Old South and American National Character.* New York: George Braziller, 1957.

Thorp, Willard, ed. *A Southern Reader.* New York: Alfred A. Knopf, 1955.

Vance, Rupert. *Human Geography of the South: A Study in Regional Resources and Human Adequacy.* Chapel Hill: University of North Carolina Press, 1932.

*Virginia Quarterly Review* 31, no. 2 (Spring 1955) (Anniversary Issue on change in the South).

Watters, Pat. *The South and the Nation.* New York: Pantheon Books, 1969.

Waugh, Edward, and Elizabeth Waugh. *The South Builds: New Architecture in the Old South.* Chapel Hill: University of North Carolina Press, 1960.

Wertenbaker, Thomas Jefferson. *The Old South: The Founding of American Civilization.* New York: Charles Scribner's Sons, 1942.

Woodward, C. Vann. *American Counterpoint: Slavery and Racism in the North-South Dialogue.* Boston: Little, Brown, 1971.

————. *The Burden of Southern History.* Rev. ed. Baton Rouge: Louisiana State University Press, 1968.

————. *Origins of the New South, 1877–1913.* Baton Rouge: Louisiana State University Press, 1951.

————. *Tom Watson, Agrarian Rebel.* New York: Macmillan, 1938.

Zinn, Howard. *The Southern Mystique.* New York: Alfred A. Knopf, 1964.


## LOWLAND (OR LOWER) SOUTH

Bodine, A. Aubrey. *Chesapeake Bay and Tidewater.* Baltimore: Hastings House, 1954.

Davis, Allison, Burleigh B. Gardner, and Mary R. Gardner. *Deep South: A Social Anthropological Study of Caste and Class.* Chicago: University of Chicago Press, 1941.

Dollard, John. *Caste and Class in a Southern Town.* New Haven, Conn.: Yale University Press, 1937.

Frazier, E. Franklin. *The Negro Family in the United States.* Chicago: University of Chicago Press, 1939.

Herskovits, Melville J. *Myth of the Negro Past.* Boston: Beacon Press, 1941.

Kane, Harnett T. *Deep Delta Country.* New York: Duell, Sloan and Pearce, 1944.

Liebow, Elliot. *Tally's Corner: A Study of Negro Streetcorner Men.* Boston: Little, Brown, 1967.

Lowry, Mark, II. "Population and Race in Mississippi, 1940–1960." *Annals of the Association of American Geographers* 61, no. 3 (September 1971):576–88.

Schulz, David A. *Coming Up Black: Patterns of Ghetto Socialization.* Englewood Cliffs, N.J.: Prentice-Hall, 1969.

Tebeau, Charlton W. *A History of Florida.* Coral Gables, Fla.: University of Miami Press, 1971.

(See also the works of Robert Coles cited under "General" above.)


## UPLAND (OR UPPER) SOUTH

Allen, John W. *Legends and Lore of Southern Illinois.* Carbondale: Area Services Division, Southern Illinois University, 1963.

Colby, Charles. *Pilot Study of Southern Illinois.* Carbondale, Ill.: Southern Illinois University Press, 1956.

Crockett, David. *A Narrative of the Life of David Crockett, of the State of Tennessee.* Philadelphia, Pa.: Carey and Hart, 1834.

Fenton, John. *Politics in the Border States: A Study of the Patterns of Political Organization, and Political Change Common to the Border States.* New Orleans, La.: Hauser Press, 1957.

Hunter, Floyd. *Community Power Structure: A Study of Decision Makers.* Chapel Hill: University of North Carolina Press, 1953.

McKeeken, Clark. *Old Kentucky Country.* New York: Duell, Sloan and Pearce, 1957.

Mayo, Bernard. "Lexington: Frontier Metropolis." In *Historiography and Urbanization: Essays in American History in Honor of W. Stull Holt,* ed. Eric F. Goldman, pp. 21–42. Baltimore: Johns Hopkins Press, 1941.

Mott, Frank Luther, ed. *Missouri Reader.* Columbia: University of Missouri Press, 1964.

Nixon, H. C. *Lower Piedmont Country.* New York: Duell, Sloan and Pearce, 1946.

Prunty, M. C., and C. S. Aiken. "The Demise of the Piedmont Cotton Region." *Annals of the Association of American Geographers* 62, no. 2 (June 1972):283–306.

Ramsey, Robert W. *Carolina Cradle: Settlement of the Northwest Carolina Frontier, 1747–1762.* Chapel Hill: University of North Carolina Press, 1964.

(See also W. J. Cash, *The Mind of the South,* cited under "General.")

## MOUNTAIN SOUTH

Arnow, Harriette Louisa. *Hunter's Horn.* New York: Macmillan, 1949.

Bell, Richard. "A Poverty Case: The Analgesic Subculture of the Southern Appalachians." In *Community Organization,* edited by I. A. Spergel, pp. 71–86. Beverly Hills, Calif.: Sage Publications, 1972.

Caudill, Harry. *My Land Is Dying.* New York: E. P. Dutton, 1971.

———. *Night Comes to the Cumberlands: A Biography of a Depressed Area.* Boston: Little, Brown and Atlantic Monthly Press, 1963.

Cressey, Paul. "Social Organization and Reorganization in Harlan County, Kentucky." *American Sociological Review* 14 (June 1949):389–94.

Davis, Will. "Study of the Succession of Human Activities in the Kentucky Mountains." *Journal of Geography* 29 (1930):85–100.

Ford, Thomas R., ed. *The Southern Appalachian Region: A Survey.* Lexington: University of Kentucky Press, 1962.

Gazaway, Rena. *The Longest Mile.* Garden City, N.Y.: Doubleday, 1969.

Miller, E. Joan Wilson. "The Ozark Culture Region as Revealed by Traditional Materials." *Annals of the Association of American Geographers* 58, no. 1 (1968):51–77.

Pearsall, Marion. *Little Smoky Ridge: The Natural History of a Southern Appalachian Neighborhood.* Birmingham: University of Alabama Press, 1959.

Peterson, Bill. *Coaltown Revisited: An Appalachian Notebook.* Chicago: Henry Regnery, 1972.

Plunkett, H. Dudley, and Mary Jean Bowman. *Elites and Change in the Kentucky Mountains.* Lexington: University Press of Kentucky, 1973.

Semple, Ellen C. "The Anglo-Saxons of the Kentucky Mountains." *Geographic Journal* 17 (1901):588–723.

Thomas, Jean. *Blue Ridge Country.* New York: Duell, Sloan and Pearce, 1942.

Weller, Jack E. *Yesterday's People: Life in Contemporary Appalachia.* Lexington: University of Kentucky Press, 1965.

Wigginton, Eliot, ed. *The Foxfire Book.* Garden City, N.Y.: Doubleday, 1972.

Wilson, Charles M. *The Bodacious Ozarks.* New York: Hastings House, 1959.

Zimmerman, Carle C., and Merle Frampton. *Family and Society: A Study of the Sociology of Reconstruction.* New York: D. Van Nostrand, 1935, especially pp. 153–336.

(See also the works of Robert Coles cited under "General" above.)

## WESTERN SOUTH

*Goals for Dallas.* Dallas, Texas: Graduate Research Center of the Southwest, 1966 (also later publications of the Research Center).

Hollon, William Eugene. *The Southwest: Old and New.* New York: Alfred A. Knopf, 1961.

Jordan, Terry. *German Seed in Texas Soil: Immigrant Farmers in Nineteenth-Century Texas.* Austin: University of Texas Press, 1966.

———. "The Imprint of Upper and Lower South on Mid-Nineteenth Century Texas." *Annals of the Association of American Geographers* 57, no. 4 (1967):667–90.

———. "Population Origin Groups in Rural Texas." *Annals of the Association of American Geographers* 60, no. 2 (1970) (Map Supplement no. 13).

———. "The Texas Appalachia." *Annals of the Association of American Geographers* 60, no. 3 (1970):409–27.

Meinig, D. W. *Imperial Texas: An Interpretive Essay in Cultural Geography.* Austin: University of Texas Press, 1969.

Peirce, Neal R. *The Megastates of America: People, Politics, and Power in the Ten Great States.* New York: W. W. Norton, 1972 (especially pp. 495–563).

Priestley, J. B., and Jacquetta Hawkes. *Journey down a Rainbow.* London: Heinemann-Cresset, 1955.

Richardson, R. N., and C. C. Rister. *The Greater Southwest.* Glendale, Calif.: Arthur Clark, 1934.

## Upper Midwest

Adams, Russell B. *Population Mobility in the Upper Midwest.* Upper Midwest Economic Study, Urban Report no. 6. Minneapolis, Minn.: Upper Midwest Research and Development Council, 1964.

Bjorklund, Elaine. "Ideology and Culture Exemplified in Southwestern Michigan." *Annals of the Association of American Geographers* 54, no. 2 (1964):227–41.

Blegen, Theodore C. *Minnesota: A History of the State.* Minneapolis: University of Minnesota Press, 1963.

———, ed. *Readings in Early Minnesota History.* Minneapolis: University of Minnesota, 1938.

Borchert, John R. *Minnesota's Changing Geography.* Minneapolis: University of Minnesota Press, 1959.

———, and Russell B. Adams. *Trade Centers and Trade Areas of the Upper Midwest.* Upper Midwest Economic Study, Urban Report no. 3. Minneapolis, Minn.: Upper Midwest Research and Development Council, 1963.

Buley, Roscoe Carlyle. *The Old Northwest Pioneer Period, 1815–1840.* 2 vols. Indianapolis: Indiana Historical Society, 1950.

Curti, Merle. *The Making of an American Community: A Case Study of Democracy in a Frontier County.* Stanford, Calif.: Stanford University Press, 1959.

Derleth, August. *The Wisconsin, River of a Thousand Isles.* The Rivers of America, ed. B. V. Benét and Carl Carmer. New York: Farrar and Rinehart, 1942.

Elazar, Daniel J. *Cities of the Prairie: The Metropolitan Frontier and American Politics.* New York: Basic Books, 1970.

Engler, Richard E., Jr. *The Challenge of Diversity.* New York: Harper and Row, 1964. Pp. 149–66, 185–214.

Flanagan, John T., ed. *America Is West: An Anthology of Middle-Western Life and Literature.* Minneapolis: University of Minnesota Press, 1945.

Garland, John H., ed. *The North American Midwest: A Regional Geography.* New York: John Wiley, 1955.

Hart, John Fraser. "The Middle West." *Annals of the Association of American Geographers* 62, no. 2 (June 1972):258–82.

Hatcher, Harlan. *The Great Lakes.* New York: Oxford University Press, 1944.

————. *Lake Erie.* Indianapolis, Ind.: Bobbs-Merrill Company, 1945.

Havighurst, Walter. *Upper Mississippi: A Wilderness Saga.* The Rivers of America, ed. Constance Lindsay Skinner. New York: Farrar and Rinehart, 1944.

Holmes, Fred L. *Old World Wisconsin.* Eau Claire, Wis.: E. M. Hale, 1944.

Jakle, John, and James L. Wheeler. "The Changing Residential Structure of the Dutch Population in Kalamazoo, Michigan." *Annals of the Association of American Geographers* 59, no. 3 (September 1969):441–60.

Jones, Evan. *The Minnesota: Forgotten River.* The Rivers of America. New York: Holt, Rinehart and Winston, 1962.

Mathews, Lois Kimball. *The Spread of New England Settlement and Institutions to the Mississippi River, 1620–1865.* New York: Russell and Russell, 1962.

Peirce, Neal R. *The Megastates of America: People, Politics, and Power in the Ten Great States.* New York: W. W. Norton, 1972 (especially pp. 299–310, 403–49).

# Central Midwest

Bell, Robert G. "James C. Mallin and the Grasslands of North America." *Agricultural History* 56, no. 3 (1972):414–24.

Buley, Roscoe Carlyle. *The Old Northwest Pioneer Period, 1815–1840.* 2 vols. Indianapolis: Indiana Historical Society, 1950.

Calkins, Earnest Elmo. *They Broke the Prairie.* New York: Charles Scribner's Sons, 1937.

Carman, Justice Neale. *Foreign-Language Units of Kansas.* Vol. 1: *Historical Atlas and Statistics.* Lawrence: University of Kansas Press, 1962.

Elazar, Daniel J. *Cities of the Prairie: The Metropolitan Frontier and American Politics.* New York: Basic Books, 1970.

Flanagan, John T., ed. *America Is West: An Anthology of Middle-Western Life and Literature.* Minneapolis: University of Minnesota Press, 1945.

Garland, John H., ed. *The North American Midwest: A Regional Geography.* New York: John Wiley, 1955.

Hart, John Fraser. "The Middle West." *Annals of the Association of American Geographers* 62, no. 2 (June 1972):258–82.

Havighurst, Walter. *The Heartland: Ohio, Indiana, Illinois.* The Regions of America. New York: Harper and Row, 1956.

————. *Upper Mississippi: A Wilderness Saga.* The Rivers of America, ed. Constance Lindsay Skinner. New York: Farrar and Rinehart, 1944.

Hostetler, John A. *Amish Society.* Baltimore: Johns Hopkins Press, 1963.

Hutton, David Graham. *Midwest at Noon.* Chicago: University of Chicago Press, 1946.

*Iowa: A Guide to the Hawkeye State.* Federal Writer's Project. New York: Hastings House, 1949.

Kramer, Frank R. *Voices in the Valley: Mythmaking and Folk Belief in the Shaping of the Middle West.* Madison: University of Wisconsin Press, 1964.

Lynd, Robert S., and Helen Merrell Lynd. *Middletown: A Study in Contemporary American Culture.* New York: Harcourt, Brace, 1929.

————. *Middletown in Transition: A Study in Cultural Conflicts.* New York: Harcourt, Brace, 1937.

McAvoy, Thomas T., ed. *The Midwest: Myth or Reality?* Notre Dame, Ind.: University of Notre Dame Press, 1961.

Mallin, James C. *Grasslands of North America: Prolegomena to Its History.* Lawrence, Kans.: by the author, 1947.

Martin, John Bartlow. *Indiana: An Interpretation.* New York: Alfred A. Knopf, 1947.

Mathews, Lois Kimball. *The Expansion of New England: The Spread of New England Settlement and Institutions to the Mississippi River, 1620–1865.* 1909. Reprint. New York: Russell and Russell, 1962.

Mayer, Harold M., and Richard C. Wade. *Chicago: Growth of a Metropolis.* Chicago: University of Chicago Press, 1969.

Mott, Frank Luther, ed. *Missouri Reader.* Columbia: University of Missouri Press, 1964.

Peirce, Neal R. *The Megastates of America: People, Politics, and Power in the Ten Great States.* New York: W. W. Norton, 1972 (especially pp. 299–402).

## Rocky Mountain Region

Arrington, Leonard. *The Changing Economic Structure of the Mountain West, 1850–1950.* Utah State University Monograph Series, vol. 10, no. 3. Logan: Utah State University, 1963.

Atwood, Wallace W. *The Rocky Mountains.* American Mountain Series, vol. 3. New York: Vanguard Press, 1945.

Civic Design Study. *A Statement on the Mountain-Plains Area of the United States.* Colorado Springs: Colorado College, 1962.

Elazar, Daniel J. *Cities of the Prairie: The Metropolitan Frontier and American Politics.* New York: Basic Books, 1970 (for Colorado, especially pp. 338–52).

Garnsey, Morris E. *America's New Frontier: The Mountain West.* New York: Alfred A. Knopf, 1950.

Gomez, Rudolph. "Colorado: The Colorful State." In *Politics in the American West,* edited by Frank H. Jonas, pp. 125–52. Salt Lake City: University of Utah Press, 1958.

Gould, Lewis L. *Wyoming: A Political History, 1868–1896.* New Haven, Conn.: Yale University Press, 1968.

Howard, Joseph Kinsey. *Montana: High, Wide, and Handsome.* New illus. ed. New Haven, Conn.: Yale University Press, 1959 (originally published 1943).

Josephy, Alvin M., Jr. "Agony of the Northern Plains." *Audubon Magazine,* July 1973, pp. 71–101.

Lavender, David. *The Rockies*. The Regions of America. New York: Harper and Row, 1968.

Lee, W. Storrs, ed. *Colorado: A Literary Chronicle*. New York: Funk and Wagnalls, 1970.

Payne, Thomas. "Montana: Politics under the Copper Dome." In *Politics in the American West,* edited by Frank H. Jonas, pp. 203–32. Salt Lake City: University of Utah Press, 1968.

Peirce, Neal R. *The Mountain States of America: People, Politics, and Power in the Eight Rocky Mountain States*. New York: W. W. Norton, 1972 (especially pp. 29–119).

Perkin, Robert L. *The First Hundred Years: An Informal History of Denver and the Rocky Mountain News*. Garden City, N.Y.: Doubleday and Co., 1959.

Poston, Richard Waverly. *Small Town Renaissance: A Story of the Montana Study*. New York: Harper and Brothers, 1950.

Thane, Eric. *High Border Country*. New York: Duell, Sloan and Pearce, 1942.

Toole, K. Ross. *Montana: An Uncommon Land*. Norman: University of Oklahoma Press, 1959.

————. *Twentieth-century Montana: A State of Extremes*. Norman: University of Oklahoma Press, 1972.

Wade, Ralph M. "Wyoming: The Frontier State." In *Politics in the American West,* edited by Frank H. Jonas, pp. 417–42. Salt Lake City: University of Utah Press, 1968.

West, Ray Benedict. *Rocky Mountain Cities*. New York: W. W. Norton, 1949.

## The Great Plains

Emmons, David M. *Garden in the Grasslands: Boomer Literature of the Central Great Plains*. Lincoln: University of Nebraska Press, 1971.

Haines, Francis. *The Buffalo*. New York: Thomas Y. Crowell, 1970.

Kraenzel, Carl F. *The Great Plains in Transition*. Norman: University of Oklahoma Press, 1955.

Mather, Cotton E. "The American Great Plains." *Annals of the Association of American Geographers* 62 (June 1972):237–57.

Stewart, Edgar I., ed. *Penny-an-Acre Empire in the West*. Norman: University of Oklahoma Press, 1968.

Vestal, Stanley. *Short Grass Country.* American Folkways, ed. Erskine Caldwell. New York: Duell, Sloan and Pearce, 1941.

Webb, Walter Prescott. *The Great Plains.* Boston, Mass.: Ginn and Company, 1931.

## The Mormon Region

Arrington, Leonard J. *Great Basin Kingdom: An Economic History of the Latter-Day Saints, 1830–1900.* Cambridge, Mass.: Harvard University Press, 1958.

Brinkerhoff, Merlin B., and Phillip R. Kunz. *Utah in Numbers: Comparisons, Trends, and Descriptions.* Provo, Utah: Brigham Young University Press, 1969.

Francanviglia, Richard V. "The Mormon Landscape: Definition of an Image in the American West." Association of American Geographers, *Proceedings* 2 (1970):59–61.

Jonas, Frank H. "Utah: The Different State." In *Politics in the American West,* edited by Frank H. Jonas, pp. 327–80. Salt Lake City: University of Utah Press, 1969.

Martin, Boyd A. "Idaho: The Sectional State." In *Politics in the American West,* edited by Frank H. Jonas, pp. 181–201. Salt Lake City: University of Utah Press, 1969.

Meinig, D. W. "The Mormon Culture Region: Strategies and Patterns in the Geography of the American West, 1847–1964." *Annals of the Association of American Geographers* 55, no. 2 (June 1965):191–220.

Nelson, Lowry. *The Mormon Village: A Pattern and Technique of Land Settlement.* Salt Lake City: University of Utah Press, 1952.

O'Dea, Thomas F. *The Mormons.* Chicago: University of Chicago Press, 1957.

———. "The Sociology of Mormonism: Four Studies." Massachusetts Institute of Technology *Publications in the Humanities,* vol. 14 (1955).

Peirce, Neal R. *The Mountain States of America: People, Politics, and Power in the Eight Rocky Mountain States.* New York: W. W. Norton, 1972 (especially pp. 183–213).

Sellers, Charles L. "Early Mormon Community Planning." *Journal of the American Institute of Planners* 28 (1962):24–30.

Spencer, Joseph E. "The Development of Agricultural Villages in Southern Utah." *Agricultural History* 14 (1940):181–89.

————. "House Types of Southern Utah." *Geographical Review* 75 (1945):444–57.

Turner, Wallace. *The Mormon Establishment.* Boston: Houghton Mifflin, 1966.


# Interior Southwest

Calvin, Ross. *Sky Determines: An Interpretation of the Southwest.* Rev. and enl. ed. Albuquerque: University of New Mexico Press, 1965.

Cushing, Frank Hamilton. *Zuñi Breadstuff.* Indian Notes and Monographs, vol. 8. New York: Museum of the American Indian, 1920.

Durrenberger, Robert. "The Colorado Plateau." *Annals of the Association of American Geographers* 62, no. 2 (June 1972):211–36.

Fergusson, Erna. *New Mexico: A Pageant of Three Peoples.* 2nd ed. New York: Alfred A. Knopf, 1964.

Forrest, Earle R. *Arizona's Dark and Bloody Ground.* Caldwell, Ida.: Caxton Printers, 1950.

Hollon, William Eugene. *The Southwest: Old and New.* New York: Alfred A. Knopf, 1961.

Holmes, Jack E. *Politics in New Mexico.* Albuquerque: University of New Mexico Press, 1967.

Josephy, Alvin M., Jr. "The Murder of the Southwest." *Audubon Magazine*, July 1971, pp. 54–67.

Kluckhohn, Clyde, and Dorothea Leighton. *The Navaho.* Cambridge, Mass.: Harvard University Press, 1946.

Meinig, D. W. *Southwest: Three Peoples in Geographical Change.* New York: Oxford University Press, 1971.

Nostrand, Richard L. "The Hispanic-American Borderland: Delimitation of an American Region." *Annals of the Association of American Geographers* 60, no. 4 (1970):638–61.

Peirce, Neal R. *The Mountain States of America: People, Politics, and Power in the Eight Rocky Mountain States.* New York: W. W. Norton, 1972 (pp. 214–92).

Richardson, R. N., and C. C. Rister. *The Greater Southwest.* Glendale, Calif.: Arthur Clark, 1934.

Sanford, Trent E. *The Architecture of the Southwest: Indian, Spanish, American.* New York: W. W. Norton, 1950.

Saunders, Lyle. *Cultural Difference and Medical Care: The Case of the*

*Spanish-speaking People of the Southwest.* New York: Russell Sage Foundation, 1954.

Spicer, Edward H. *Cycles of Conquest: The Impact of Spain, Mexico, and the United States on the Indians of the Southwest, 1533–1960.* Tucson: University of Arizona Press, 1962.

————, and Raymond H. Thompson, eds. *Plural Society in the Southwest.* New York: Interbook, 1972.

Vogt, Evon. "American Subcultural Continua as Exemplified by Mormons and Texans." *American Anthropologist* 57 (1955):1163–73.

————. *Modern Homesteaders: The Life of a Twentieth-century Frontier Community.* Cambridge, Mass.: Harvard University Press, 1955.

————, and Ethel M. Albert, eds. *People of Rimrock: A Study of Values in Five Cultures.* Cambridge, Mass.: Harvard University Press, 1966.

Wormington, H. M. *Prehistoric Indians of the Southwest.* Denver, Colo.: Colorado Museum of Natural History, 1959.


## Pacific Southwest

Bright, Elizabeth S. *A Word Geography of California and Nevada.* Berkeley: University of California Press, 1971.

Burma, John H. *Spanish-speaking Groups in the United States.* Durham, N.C.: Duke University Press, 1954.

*California: People, Problems, Potential.* San Francisco: Bank of America, 1971.

*The California Tomorrow Plan.* San Francisco: California Tomorrow, 1971.

Caughey, John. *California.* 2nd ed. New York: Prentice-Hall, 1953.

————, and LaRee Caughey. *California Heritage: An Anthology of History and Literature.* Los Angeles: Ward Ritchie Press, 1962.

Cleland, Robert Glass. *California in Our Time (1900–1940).* New York: Alfred A. Knopf, 1947.

Durrenberger, Robert W., ed. *California: Its People, Its Problems, Its Prospects.* Palo Alto, Calif.: National Press Books, 1971.

Fellmeth, Robert C., ed. *Power and Land in California.* Washington, D.C: Center for Study of Responsive Law, 1971.

Gentry, Curt. *The Last Days of the Late, Great State of California.* New York: Ballantine Books, 1968.

Goldschmidt, Walter. *As You Sow.* New York: Harcourt, Brace, 1947.

Kroeber, A. L. *Handbook of the Indians of California.* 1925. Reprint. Berkeley, Calif.: California Book Company, 1953.

Lamott, Kenneth. *Anti-California: Report from Our First Parafascist State.* Boston: Little, Brown, 1971.

McWilliams, Carey. *California, The Great Exception.* New York: Current Books, 1949.

————. *Southern California Country: An Island on the Land.* New York: Duell, Sloan and Pearce, 1946.

————, ed. *The California Revolution.* New York: Grossman Publishers, 1968.

Meinig, D. W. "American Wests: Preface to a Geographical Introduction." *Annals of the Association of American Geographers* 62, no. 2 (June 1972):159–84.

Morgan, Dale. *The Humboldt: Highroad of the West.* The Rivers of America, ed. S. V. Benét and Constance L. Skinner. New York: Farrar and Rinehart, 1943.

Ostrander, Gilman M. *Nevada: The Great Rotten Borough, 1859–1964.* New York: Alfred A. Knopf, 1966.

Peirce, Neal R. *The Megastates of America: People, Politics, and Power in the Ten Great States.* New York: W. W. Norton, 1972 (pp. 564–694).

————. *The Mountain States of America: People, Politics, and Power in the Eight Rocky Mountain States.* New York: W. W. Norton, 1972 (pp. 154–82).

————. *The Pacific States of America: People, Politics, and Power in the Five Pacific Basin States.* New York: W. W. Norton, 1972.

Powers, Alfred. *Redwood Country: The Lava Region and the Redwoods.* New York: Duell, Sloan and Pearce, 1949.

Rogin, Michael Paul, and John L. Shover. *Political Change in California: Critical Elections and Social Movements, 1890–1966.* Westport, Conn.: Greenwood, 1970.

Royce, Josiah. *California: From the Conquest in 1846 to the Second Vigilance Committee in San Francisco: A Study of American Character.* Boston: Houghton Mifflin, 1886.

Starr, Kevin. *Americans and the California Dream, 1850–1915.* New York: Oxford University Press, 1973.

Thomas, William L., Jr., ed. "Man, Time and Space in Southern California." *Annals of the Association of American Geographers* 49, no. 3, pt. 2, Supplement (September 1959).

Thompson, Warren S. *Growth and Changes in California's Population.* Los Angeles: Haynes Foundation, 1955.

Vance, James E., Jr. "California and the Search for the Ideal." *Annals of the Association of American Geographers* 62, no. 2 (June 1972):185–210.

Wolfinger, R., and F. Greenstein. "Comparing Political Regions: The Case of California." *American Political Science Review* 63, no. 1 (1969):74–85.

Wilson, James Q. "A Guide to Reagan Country: The Political Culture of Southern California." *Commentary* 43, no. 5 (May 1967):37–45.

## Pacific Northwest

Bancroft, Hubert Howe. *History of the Pacific States of North America*, vol. 24, *Oregon, 1834–1848*. San Francisco: The History Company, 1886.

Binns, John. "Northwest Region—Fact or Fiction?" *Pacific Northwest Quarterly* 43, no. 3 (July 1957):65–75.

Bone, Hugh A. "Washington State: Free Style Politics." In *Politics in the American West,* edited by Frank H. Jonas, pp. 381–416. Salt Lake City: University of Utah Press, 1969.

Chittick, Victor L. O., ed. *Northwest Harvest, a Regional Stocktaking.* New York: Macmillan, 1948.

Clark, Norman. *The Dry Years: Prohibition and Social Change in Washington.* Seattle: University of Washington Press, 1965.

———. *Mill Town: A Social History of Everett, Washington,* . . . Seattle: University of Washington Press, 1970.

Cohn, Edwin J. *Industry in the Pacific Northwest and the Location Theory.* New York: King's Crown Press, 1954.

Douglas, Jesse. "Origins of the Population of Oregon in 1850." *Pacific Northwest Quarterly* 41 (1950):95–112.

Engler, Richard E., Jr. *The Challenge of Diversity.* New York: Harper and Row, 1964 (especially pp. 167–84, 215–46).

Freeman, Otis W., and Howard H. Martin, eds. *The Pacific Northwest: An Overall Appreciation.* 2nd ed. New York: John Wiley, 1954.

Highsmith, Richard. *Atlas of the Pacific Northwest: Resources and Development.* 4th ed. Corvallis: Oregon State University Press, 1968.

Holbrook, Stewart. *Far Corner: A Personal View of the Pacific Northwest.* New York: Macmillan, 1952.

———, ed. *Promised Land, A Collection of Northwest Writing.* New York: McGraw-Hill, 1945.

Hult, Ruby El. *The Untamed Olympics: The Story of a Peninsula.* Portland, Ore.: Binfords and Mort, 1954.

Johannessen, Carl, et al. "The Vegetation of the Willamette Valley." *The Annals of the Association of American Geographers* 61, no. 2 (1971):286–302.

Johansen, Dorothy O. "A Working Hypothesis for the Study of Migrations." *Pacific Historical Review* 36 (1967):1–12.

———, and Charles M. Gates. *Empire of the Columbia: A History of the Pacific Northwest.* 2nd ed. New York: Harper and Row, 1967.

Lucia, Ellis, ed. *This Land around Us: A Treasury of Pacific Northwest Writing.* Garden City, N.Y: Doubleday, 1969.

Meinig, Donald W. *The Great Columbia Plain: A Historical Geography, 1805–1910.* Seattle: University of Washington Press, 1968.

Miller, Delbert C. *International Community Power Structures: Comparative Studies of Four World Cities.* Bloomington: Indiana University Press, 1970 (see material on Seattle).

National Resources Committee. *Regional Planning, Part 1: Pacific Northwest.* Washington, D.C: National Resources Committee, 1936.

Peirce, Neal R. *The Pacific States of America: People, Politics, and Power in the Five Pacific Basin States.* New York: W. W. Norton, 1972.

Pollard, Lancaster. "The Pacific Northwest." In *Regionalism in America,* edited by Merrill Jensen, pp. 187–212. Madison: University of Wisconsin Press, 1951.

Pomeroy, Earl. *The Pacific Slope.* New York: Alfred A. Knopf, 1965.

Stern, Theodore. *The Klamath Tribe: A People and Their Reservation.* Seattle: University of Washington Press, 1965.

Stevens, James, and J. L. Davis. *Status Rerum: A Manifesto on the Present Condition of Northwest Literature.* The Dalles, Ore., n.d.

Swartout, John M., and Kenneth R. Gervais. "Oregon: Political Experiment Station." In *Politics in the American West,* edited by Frank H. Jonas, pp. 297–326. Salt Lake City: University of Utah Press, 1969.

Warren, Sidney. *Farthest Frontier: The Pacific Northwest.* New York: Macmillan, 1949.

# Alaska

Bohn, Dave. *Glacier Bay, the Land and the Silence.* New York: Ballantine Books, 1967.

Brown, Tom. *Oil on Ice: Alaskan Wilderness at the Crossroads*. San Francisco: Sierra Club, 1971.

Chasen, Daniel J. *Klondike '70: The Alaskan Oil Boom*. New York: Praeger, 1971.

Colby, Merle. *A Guide to Alaska, Last American Frontier*. Federal Writers Project. New York: Macmillan, 1945.

Cooley, Richard A. *Alaska: A Challenge in Conservation*. Madison: University of Wisconsin Press, 1966.

Federal Field Committee for Development Planning in Alaska. *Alaska Natives and the Land*. Anchorage, Alaska, October 1968.

Gruening, Ernest, ed. *An Alaskan Reader, 1867–1967*. New York: Meredith Press, 1966.

————. *The State of Alaska*. Rev. ed. New York: Random House, 1968 (political history).

Hrdlicka, Ales. "Anthropological Survey in Alaska." In American Bureau of Ethnology, Forty-sixth Annual Report, 1928–1929, pp. 19–374. Washington, D.C.: U.S. Government Printing Office, 1930.

Hughes, Charles Campbell. *An Eskimo Village in the Modern World*. Ithaca, N.Y.: Cornell University Press, 1960.

Mathews, Richard. *The Yukon*. The Rivers of America. New York: Holt, Rinehart and Winston, 1968.

Patty, Ernest N. *North Country Challenge*. New York: David McKay, 1969.

Peirce, Neal R. *The Pacific States of America: People, Politics, and Power in the Five Pacific Basin States*. New York: W. W. Norton, 1972 (pp. 264–313).

Reynolds, Robert. *Alaska*. Portland, Ore.: Charles Belding, 1971 (art photography).

Rogers, George. *Alaska in Transition: The Southeast Region*. Baltimore, Md.: for Resources for the Future by Johns Hopkins Press, 1960.

————. *The Future of Alaska: Economic Consequences of Statehood*. Baltimore, Md.: for Resources for the Future by Johns Hopkins Press, 1962.

————, ed. *Change in Alaska: People, Petroleum, and Politics*. College: University of Alaska Press; Seattle: University of Washington Press, 1970.

# Hawaiian Islands

Carlquist, Sherwin. *Hawaii: A Natural History.* Garden City, N.Y.: for the American Museum of Natural History by the Natural History Press, 1970.

Chaplin, George, and Glenn D. Paige, eds. *Hawaii 2000: Continuing Experiment in Anticipatory Democracy.* Honolulu: University Press of Hawaii for the Governor's Conference on the year 2000, 1973.

Daws, Gavan. *Shoal of Time: A History of the Hawaiian Islands.* New York: Macmillan, 1968.

duPlessix Gray, Francine. "The Sugar-Coated Fortress, I (and II)." *The New Yorker,* 4 March 1972, pp. 41ff. (and 11 March 1972, pp. 39ff.).

Fuchs, Lawrence H. *Hawaii Pono: A Social History.* New York: Harcourt, Brace and World, 1961.

Furnas, J. C. *Anatomy of Paradise: Hawaii and the Islands of the South Seas.* New York: W. Sloane Associates, 1948.

Goodman, Robert B., et al. *The Hawaiians.* Sydney, Australia: Island Heritage, 1970.

Hunter, Louise H. *Buddhism in Hawaii: Its Impact on a Yankee Community.* Honolulu: University of Hawaii Press, 1971.

Judd, Gerrit P., ed. *A Hawaiian Anthology.* New York: Macmillan, 1967.

Krauss, Bob. *Bob Krauss' Travel Guide to the Hawaiian Islands.* New York: Coward-McCann, 1965–66.

———. *High-Rise Hawaii.* New York: Coward-McCann, 1969.

Lind, Andrew W. *Hawaii: The Last of the Magic Isles.* London and New York: for the Institute of Race Relations by Oxford University Press, 1969.

———. *Hawaii's People.* 3rd ed. Honolulu: University of Hawaii Press, 1967.

Michener, James A. *Hawaii.* New York: Random House, 1959.

Peirce, Neal R. *The Pacific States of America: People, Politics, and Power in the Five Pacific Basin States.* New York: W. W. Norton, 1972 (pp. 314–59).

Porteus, Stanley D. *A Century of Social Thinking in Hawaii.* Palo Alto, Calif.: Pacific Books, 1962.

Schmitt, Robert C. *Demographic Statistics of Hawaii, 1778–1965.* Honolulu: University of Hawaii Press, 1968.

Tate, Merze. *The United States and the Hawaiian Kingdom: A Political History.* New Haven, Conn.: Yale University Press, 1965.

# Index

*Italicized page references indicate discussions of particular importance.*